Weapons of Mass Destruction

WEAPONS OF MASS DESTRUCTION SERIES

Series Editors: Joseph M. Siracusa and Aiden Warren

The series focuses on weapons of mass destruction (WMDs), discussing all issues surrounding nuclear, chemical, radiological, and biological weapons. The volumes aim to present varying historical, contemporary, state, non-state, traditional, and non-traditional approaches from emerging scholars, established academics, and those involved in the foreign and security policy domains. In the context of the nuclear section of the WMD series, it is evident that despite there being fewer nuclear weapons today than during the Cold War era, the threat remains paramount. More states in more unstable regions have attained such weapons, terrorists may pursue them, and the command and control systems in even the most sophisticated nuclear-armed states remain susceptible not only to system and human error but, increasingly, to cyberattacks. The failure of armed states to disarm, the inability to prevent new states and non-state actors from gaining access to WMDs, and the expansion of nuclear energy plants present a real security danger today. As such, the series is timely and necessary.

Joseph M. Siracusa is professor of human security and international diplomacy at the Royal Melbourne Institute of Technology (RMIT) University, Australia, and president of Australia's Council for Humanities, Arts and Social Sciences.
Aiden Warren is senior lecturer in the School of Global, Urban and Social Studies at the Royal Melbourne Institute of Technology University in Melbourne, Australia.

Titles in the Series

For a full list of titles in the series, visit https://rowman.com/Action/SERIES/RL/
    RLWMD or scan the following QR code:

Weapons of Mass Destruction

The Search for Global Security

Joseph M. Siracusa and Aiden Warren

ROWMAN & LITTLEFIELD
Lanham • Boulder • New York • London

Published by Rowman & Littlefield
A wholly owned subsidiary of The Rowman & Littlefield Publishing Group, Inc.
4501 Forbes Boulevard, Suite 200, Lanham, Maryland 20706
www.rowman.com

Unit A, Whitacre Mews, 26-34 Stannary Street, London SE11 4AB

British Library Cataloguing in Publication Information Available

Library of Congress Cataloging-in-Publication Data Available

ISBN: 978-1-4422-4236-4 (cloth : alk. paper)
ISBN: 978-1-4422-4237-1 (pbk. : alk. paper)
ISBN: 978-1-4422-4238-8 (electronic)

∞ ™ The paper used in this publication meets the minimum requirements of American
National Standard for Information Sciences Permanence of Paper for Printed Library
Materials, ANSI/NISO Z39.48-1992.

Printed in the United States of America

Contents

Abbreviations/Acronyms   vii

Introduction   xi

1   World War II and the Race for the A-Bomb   1

2   The Cold War   27

3   Other UN Security Council Nuclear Weapon States: United Kingdom, France, and China   59

4   Non–UN Security Council Nuclear Weapon States: Israel, India, Pakistan, North Korea (and Iran)   89

5   The Global Nuclear Non-Proliferation Regime   125

6   The Modern Era: The Post–Cold War and Beyond   167

7   Biological and Chemical Weapons and Nuclear Terrorism   193

Conclusion   221

Bibliography   227

Index   245

About the Authors   257

Abbreviations/Acronyms

ABM — Antiballistic Missile
ABMT or ABM Treaty — Antiballistic Missile Treaty
ACDA — Arms Control and Disarmament Agency
BJP — Bharatiya Janata Party
BMEWS — Ballistic Missile Early Warning System
BTWC — Biological and Toxin Weapons Convention
BW — Biological Weapons
BWC — Biological Weapons Convention
C3 — Command, Control, and Communication
C/B — Chemical/Biological
CBW — Chemical and Biological Weapons
CD — Conference on Disarmament
CFE — Conventional Forces in Europe
CIA — Central Intelligence Agency
CNS — James Martin Center for Non-Proliferation Studies
CPPNM — Convention on the Physical Protection of Nuclear Materials
CTBT — Comprehensive Nuclear Test Ban Treaty
CTR — Cooperative Threat Reduction
CW — Chemical Weapons
CWC — Chemical Weapons Convention
DC — Disarmament Commission
DPRK — Democratic People's Republic of Korea
DSP — Defense Support Program
EAM — Emergency Action Messages
ENDC — Eighteen Nation Disarmament Committee
EU — European Union
FAS — Federation of American Scientists
FATF — Financial Action Task Force
FDR — Franklin Delano Roosevelt
FMCT — Fissile Material Cut-Off Treaty
GICNT — Global Initiative to Combat Nuclear Terrorism
GLCM — Ground-Launched Cruise Missiles
GTRI — Global Threat Reduction Initiative
HEU — Highly Enriched Uranium
HMS — Her Majesty's Ship
IAEA — International Atomic Energy Agency

ICBMs — Intercontinental Ballistic Missiles
ICSANT — International Convention for the Suppression of Acts of Nuclear Terrorism
IMS — International Monitoring Systems
INF Treaty — Intermediate Nuclear Force Treaty
ISIS — Islamic State of Iraq and Syria
JCPOA — Joint Comprehensive Plan of Action
KAL — Korean Air Lines
KGB — Komitet Gosudarstvennoy Bezopasnosti (Russian Secret Police)
LEU — Low-Enriched Uranium
LTBT — Limited Test Ban Treaty
MENWFZ — Middle East Nuclear Weapon Free Zone
MIDAS — Missile Defense Alert System
MIRV — Multiple Independently Targeted Re-Entry Vehicle
MLF — Multilateral Force
NAS — National Academy of Sciences
NATO — North Atlantic Treaty Organisation
NDRC — National Defence Research Committee
NNA — Non-Aligned States
NNSM — National Security Study Memorandum
NNWS — Non-Nuclear Weapons States
NORAD — North American Aerospace Defense Command
NPR — Nuclear Posture Review
NPT — Nuclear Non-Proliferation Treaty
NSA — National Security Agency
NSC — National Security Council
NSC 20 — National Security Council Report 20
NSC 68 — National Security Council Report 68
NSCWMD — National Strategy to Combat Weapons of Mass Destruction
NSG — Nuclear Suppliers Group
NSPD — National Security Presidential Directive
NSS — National Security Strategy
NWFZ — Nuclear-Weapon-Free Zone
OPCW — Organisation for the Prohibition of Chemical Weapons
OPENAL — Agency for the Prohibition of Nuclear Weapons in Latin America and the Carribean
P5 + 1 — Five Permanent Members of the UN Security Council plus Germany
PNE — Peaceful Nuclear Explosions
PNET — Peaceful Nuclear Explosions Treaty
PRC — Peoples Republic of China
PSI — Proliferation Security Initiative
RDD — Radiological Dispersal Device
RRW — Reliable Replacement Warhead
SALT — Strategic Arms Limitation Talks
SDI — Strategic Defense Initiative
SLBM — Submarine-Launched Ballistic Missile
SLCM — Sea-Launched Cruise Missiles
SORT (also the Moscow Treaty) — Strategic Offensive Reductions Treaty
SSBN — Strategic Submarine Ballistic Nuclear
START — Strategic Arms Reduction Treaty
TNT — TriNitro Toluene
TTBT — Threshold Test Ban Treaty
TTNT — Tactical Targeting Network Technology
U-235 — Uranium 235
U-238 — Uranium 238
UK — United Kingdom
UN — United Nations

UNAEC — United Nations Atomic Energy Commission
UNSC — United Nations Security Council
UNSCOM — United Nations Special Committee on Iraq
UNSCR — United Nations Security Council Resolution
USSR — Union of Soviet Socialist Republics
WMDs — Weapons of Mass Destruction
WMDFZ — Weapons of Mass Destruction Free Zone

Introduction

Whether possessed by a state or non-state actor, the specter of weapons of mass destruction (WMDs), and more specifically, nuclear weapons and their associated material, present a significant threat to global security.[1] While many in the international community regard such devices as being a Cold War vestige that have limited impact on global stability, this somewhat skewed assessment cannot be further from the truth. Notwithstanding the significant reductions in nuclear arsenals, there is ample evidence to suggest that the risks deriving from nuclear security have actually expanded: where more states in more unstable regions have attained such weapons, terrorists continue to pursue them, and the command and control systems in even the most sophisticated nuclear-armed states remain susceptible to not only system and human error but, increasingly, cyberattack. Even a limited regional nuclear war would have calamitous global consequences.[2] Moreover, the failure of existing nuclear-armed states to disarm, the inability to impede new states obtaining nuclear weapons, the potential of non-state actors gaining access to such weapons and their concomitant material, and the challenge presented by the expansion of nuclear energy plants all present serious security challenges in the twenty-first century.[3]

There is a positive note: the number of nuclear weapons has declined markedly since the Cold War's demise—down from a peak of approximately 70,300 in 1986 to an estimated 15,350 in early 2016.[4] However, their very presence remains a global strategic/political driver, evident in their storage and possession across ninety-eight sites in fourteen nation-states. Some 10,000 of these weapons are in military arsenals, while the others are either in the process of being retired or awaiting dismantlement. Roughly 4,000 are operationally available, and some 1,800 are on high alert and gauged toward potential use within a very short time frame. The largest possessors of nuclear weapons are Russia and the United States, which together hold 93 percent of the total global suite. Significantly, the United States "houses" its nuclear weapons on eighteen sites, including twelve sites in eleven states within the United States, and a further six sites in five European countries.[5] Given the recent deterioration of U.S.-Russian bilateral relations and the reemergence of NATO into the United States' EU security calculi, the positioning and strategic consideration of such weapons remains a potential source of ongoing consternation.

In the context of regulating such threats and adhering to the obligations of Article VI of the nuclear Non-Proliferation Treaty (NPT), there appears to be an apparent stalling, if not breaking down of the non-proliferation regime based on state ambivalence at the very least, but perhaps best described as state recalcitrance. Indeed, despite many forebodings—not to mention the non-participation of France and China until 1992—the regime has held together moderately well for the first thirty years of its existence, defined by the overarching NPT. However, with India and Pakistan, who had never signed the treaty, joining the undeclared Israel as fully fledged nuclear-armed states in 1998, North Korea's ongoing nuclear and missiles tests and withdrawal from the NPT, and, until recently, Iran's uranium enrichment program, the regime has been well and truly under strain. With such developments taking place in some of the most unpredictable regions, a diminishing confidence in weapons security and the command systems of the longer-established nuclear powers, and the continuance of proliferation in new nuclear weapons states, there is much to be concerned about. Additionally, as the modernization drives of the United States, Russia, and China[6] continue to expand, the notion of adhering to the NPT core principle of pursuing "negotiations in good faith on effective measures relating to cessation of the nuclear arms race at an early date and to nuclear disarmament" seems a long way off.

With the events of 9/11 and the discovery of the AQ Khan ring, an added dimension of horror became a significant component of any assessment apparatus pertaining to mitigating nuclear threats. Indeed, there can no longer be any misconceptions of the rationale of certain clandestine actors and their preparedness to wield massive destruction on non-combatant civilians. And while the likelihood is minimal and lower than many overstated accounts have signified, their capacity to construct and detonate a rudimentary nuclear device does not necessarily distend the limits of our imagination. Of course, for such actors, a much easier pathway in creating destruction is contained in the simple device referred to as the "dirty bomb": a combination of conventional explosives and radioactive materials.[7] While the dirty bomb does not have the capacity to cause the same sort of devastation as a fission or fusion bomb, the psychosomatic impact would be enormous, and no doubt it has been a central motivation behind the four Obama-championed Nuclear Security Summits of 2010–2016. Additionally, the likely growth of civil nuclear energy, not least in response to climate change concerns, will pose some further proliferation and security risks, particularly if accompanied by the building of new state amenities for enrichment at the front end of the fuel cycle and reprocessing at the back end. This entails a substantial amount of fissile material that could potentially become accessible for destructive intent.[8]

For many analysts and scholars in the WMD domain, the only unconditional resolution to the issue of nuclear weapons is to push for their comprehensive abolition, and to secure the very stockpiles of the highly enriched uranium or separated plutonium on which they are dependent. This is—and will continue to be—an elongated and multilayered route, and its end will require all existing nuclear-armed states to reassert their obligation toward eventual elimination, and actually mean what they say. Indeed, if one contemplates the disarmament and non-proliferation efforts[9] over the last two decades, it is quite evident that new impetus for change has been difficult to sustain when positive developments can so easily be erased. The Cold War's end ushered in a brief but relatively industrious period of nuclear disarmament and threat reduction deeds. This included the decommissioning and removal of thousands of warheads from the astonishing level of seventy thousand weapons that "peaked in the mid-1980s."[10]

Additionally, there were assertive unilateral reductions undertaken by states on their respective arsenals in the United States, Russia, the United Kingdom, and France. These cuts were evident in initiatives such as the 1991 Strategic Arms Reduction Treaty (START), which produced significant reductions in the number of offensively deployed strategic weapons;[11] the elimination of Intermediate Range Nuclear Forces; the removal of ground-based battlefield nuclear weapons from Europe; and the French and UK removal of all ground-based nuclear weapons of all ranges from their inventories. In 1992, the United States sanctioned the progressive threat reduction programs designed to secure perilous weapons and materials and, specifically, to diminish the possibility of such materials being attained by terrorist groups or states that permitted terrorism.[12] Further positive developments were also evident when South Africa relinquished its weapons program and joined the NPT, while three states of the former Soviet Union—Belarus, Kazakhstan, and Ukraine—abandoned nuclear weapons and also joined the NPT as non-nuclear-weapon states. In addition, the nuclear enmity between Argentina and Brazil was controlled when Argentina ratified the regional nuclear-weapon-free zone (the Treaty of Tlatelolco) and both subsequently joined the NPT. Of course, one of the definitive successes for non-proliferation proponents was the indefinite extension of the NPT, formalized during the 1995 conference of NPT parties.[13]

Notwithstanding some of the aforementioned positives, such weapons continue not only to exist but also remain central to the security doctrines of those states who possess them. Additionally, in 1998, having rejected repeated appeals for them to join the NPT, India and Pakistan became unambiguous nuclear-armed states, while it was clearly evident that Israel was nuclearly active despite never confirming its status. In the same year, multilateral discussions relating to a fissile material production cut-off treaty at the Geneva Conference on Disarmament (CD) failed and have remained off the broader agenda for well over a decade and a half. In 1999, the U.S. Senate did not ratify the Comprehensive Nuclear Test Ban Treaty (CTBT) and, despite Obama's Prague declarations, the treaty is still a long way from being a real consideration within the U.S. Congress. While the Moscow Treaty of 2002 provided, albeit imperfect, legal forte to earlier announced unilateral cuts, it was the last action displayed in arms control by the Bush administration, which would later pursue new avenues of reinvigorating the nuclear option via "bunker busters" and a Reliable Replacement Warhead (RRW) program. Moreover, Bush unilaterally seceded from the Antiballistic Missile Treaty, guaranteeing that many problems for future disarmament negotiations would again arise.

While there was a concentrated effort to reinvigorate new non-proliferation regulations in the wake of the 9/11 attacks, such efforts—as indicated above—were greatly challenged with the revelation of the AQ Khan clandestine ring, concerns over the alleged Iraq nuclear program, and the materialization of the North Korea and Iran issues.[14] But even more than this, when it came down to firm and robust disarmament decisions, responses from the core nuclear-armed states were nothing short of neglect and, in some instances, absolute disinterest. This was clearly evident with the 2005 NPT Review Conference, which produced no substantive consensus on any proliferation items and was defined by Harald Müller as "the biggest failure in the history of this Treaty."[15] Similarly, at the UN World Summit of the same year, there was nothing in the form of consensus, or even a well-intentioned nuclear non-proliferation or disarmament statement.[16]

With the nuclear non-proliferation regime under immense challenge, the impetus for change came in the form of the 2007 seminal opinion piece put together by four U.S. statesmen: Secretaries Henry Kissinger, George Shultz, William Perry, and Senator Sam Nunn. Published in the *Wall Street Journal*, the article argued that while nuclear weapons were central to maintaining international security during the Cold War, the doctrine of mutual Soviet-American deterrence was now obsolescent. Although deterrence would continue to be a pertinent consideration for many states—with regard to threats from other states—the dependence on nuclear weapons for this purpose was becoming increasingly perilous and ineffective. As a means to revitalize the non-proliferation regime for the twenty-first century and work toward the ultimate goal of "global zero," a joint initiative encompassing a series of steps would need to be undertaken.[17] The steps, they argued, would entail changing the Cold War posture of deployed nuclear weapons to one that encompassed an increase in warning time and, therefore, markedly reducing the danger of an accidental or unauthorized use of a nuclear weapon. Naturally, the steps should also include the continued and substantial reduction in the size of nuclear forces in all states that possess them, and the elimination of short-range nuclear weapons designed to be forward-deployed.[18]

Moreover, the pursuit of the highest possible standards of security for all stocks of weapons, weapons-usable plutonium, and highly enriched uranium everywhere in the world should also be an imperative. Similarly, attaining control of the uranium enrichment process combined with the guarantee that uranium for nuclear power reactors could be obtained at a reasonable price—via the Nuclear Suppliers Group and then from the International Atomic Energy Agency (IAEA)—was also flagged.[19] Further steps pertaining to halting the global production of fissile material for weapons were canvassed, involving phasing out the use of highly enriched uranium in civil commerce and removing weapons-usable uranium from research facilities around the world. Realizing the goal of a world free of nuclear weapons, they continued, would also require proficient actions to thwart or counter any nuclear-related conduct that was potentially threatening to the security of any state or peoples. Pointing to the impact U.S. leadership could have in this context, Kissinger, Shultz, Perry, and Nunn maintained that reasserting the vision of a world free of nuclear weapons and practical measures toward achieving that goal would be a "bold initiative" that "could have a profoundly positive impact on the security of future generations."[20]

In extending on such nuclear ambitions, Barack Obama attempted to redefine the pathway ahead during his speech at Hradčany Square, Prague, on April 5, 2009. He pledged to "set a new direction in U.S. nuclear weapons policy and show the world that America believes in its existing commitment under the Nuclear Non-Proliferation Treaty (NPT) to work to ultimately eliminate all nuclear weapons."[21] In this push for nuclear disarmament, Obama argued that a leadership role for the United States was needed not only because of its global standing or the size of the U.S. nuclear arsenal, but as a matter of "moral responsibility." Having set up the imperative for action, which itself was a remarkable change in the presidential "lexicon for international security policy," Obama made a dual pledge.[22] On the one hand, his administration would "take concrete steps towards a world without nuclear weapons" and to "put an end to Cold War thinking" by reducing "the role of nuclear weapons in our national security strategy, and [urging] others to do the same." On the other, Obama pledged to "maintain a safe, secure and effective arsenal to deter any adversary, and guarantee that defense to our allies." As a means to reduce U.S. warheads and stockpiles, his administration would negotiate a new Strategic Arms Reduction Treaty with the Russians in 2010; to achieve a global ban on nuclear testing, the administration would immediately and "aggressively" pursue U.S. ratification of the CTBT; and finally, Obama would attempt to strengthen the NPT as a basis for cooperation.[23]

The president described the victorious election of 2008 as both a juncture and an opportunity to redefine international security and the future of nuclear weapons in the twenty-first century. In an attempt to separate himself and his administration from their predecessors, Obama pointed to the existence of thousands of nuclear weapons as the unbridled perilous legacy of the Cold War. Of course, while no nuclear war was ever fought between the United States and the Soviet Union, several generations from both states carried the knowledge that their lives could have been "erased in a single flash of light." Indeed, despite the Cold War's demise and the diminished threat of a global nuclear war, the specter of a nuclear attack had actually increased. Additionally, he argued, more states had acquired these weapons, tests had continued, and the black market trade "in nuclear secrets and nuclear materials abounded." As a significant plank in his nuclear strategy, Obama pointed to how the technology to build a bomb had transcended borders and that non-state actors were determined more than ever "to buy, build or steal one." Therefore, stronger efforts to thwart such dangers must involve an emboldened global non-proliferation regime, otherwise, "as more people and nations break the rules, we could reach the point where the center cannot hold."[24]

In simpler terms, Obama's vision called for a stronger global effort to curb the spread of nuclear weapons, greater progress on long-overdue disarmament measures, more unified efforts in mitigating nuclear terrorism, and, ultimately, the abolition of nuclear weapons.[25] According to Daryl G. Kimball of the Arms Control Association, "The U.S. nuclear-weapons policy can and must change and the United States must lead by example, or else the global effort to reduce the risk of nuclear war, curb proliferation, and prevent catastrophic terrorism will falter."[26] There is no doubt that political impetus forged via the election of Barack Obama as president of the United States in November 2008 spurred a series of diplomatic initiatives seeking nuclear non-proliferation and disarmament. He negotiated a START follow-on treaty with Russia, pressed for the U.S. ratification of the CTBT, and changed the U.S. stance on fissile material cut-off treaty negotiations, agreeing that it should be verifiable. Additionally, he presided over a meeting of the UN Security Council in September 2009, which fashioned the important consensus Resolution 1887, and was responsible for the U.S. hosting a world summit on nuclear security issues early in 2010. As a result of these efforts, a wave of optimism came to the fore, evident in the 2010 NPT Review Conference, "a much better atmosphere than anyone recalling the meltdown of 2005 had a right to expect."[27]

Of course, the reality is that by the end of his tenure in office—notwithstanding the Iran nuclear deal of 2015—much of these efforts had fallen short. In fact, it is evident that in recent times the United States has been moving *away* from these pronouncements. Aside from slowing down its nuclear stockpile reductions during its second term in office, the Obama administration embarked on an overhaul of its entire nuclear weapons enterprise, encompassing the development of new weapons delivery systems and modernizing its enduring nuclear warhead types and nuclear weapons production facilities in a program that scholars estimate could cost more than a trillion dollars.[28] Additionally, recent substantial investments by other nuclear weapon possessor states in the upkeep and modernization of their nuclear postures indicate a return of the nuclear factor in international politics—where deterrence is clearly taking precedence over nuclear arms control and disarmament, and the ultimate global goal of nuclear abolition.[29] The nuclear reductions of Russia and the United States are slowing; U.S. offers to resume bilateral arms control negotiations with Russia have been ignored; France reduced its arsenal by a third after 2008 but seems determined to retain its capability for the long-term; India and Pakistan continue to upgrade their delivery and weapons capabilities; and China is also adding to its arsenal and is believed to be deploying multiple warhead (MIRVed) missiles. In short, there has been a decisive shift toward modernizing and sustaining nuclear arsenals for the indefinite future. At present, it is unclear whether the global nuclear non-proliferation regime will survive the fractures that are opening up as a result of these developments. If nuclear force modernization programs continue apace without a renewed focus on arms control and disarmament, the future prospects of the NPT—which is almost universally acknowledged to be the cornerstone of the nuclear non-proliferation regime and one of the most important pillars of international security—look increasingly bleak.

As the subtitle of this book suggests, the "search for global security," if at all attainable or legitimately pursued, is precariously dependent on delicate conditions that require the presence of cogent decision makers behind each nuclear arsenal, as well as the "absence of any rogue launches, human-error incidents, or system malfunctions."[30] For nuclear stability to be assured, deterrence and fail-safe mechanisms must work every single time; for a nuclear devastation to take place, they only have to fail once. Clearly this is not a reassuring calculation, particularly as states evidently continue to attain nuclear weapons, and even more so, continue to busily modernize their stockpiles.[31]

In providing both a background and the core monograph from which the Rowman & Littlefield WMD Series is based, we seek to provide emerging scholars, analysts, and students in the international security domain with a foundational book that provides an understanding on how we arrived at this juncture in time. While the focus is mainly on the defining arm of WMDs—that being nuclear weapons—it also considers the security concerns pertaining to chemical and biological weapons, as well as the associated ramifications relating to nuclear terrorism. As indicated, notwithstanding the fact that there are fewer weapons today than the massive stockpiles that existed in the 1960s and 1970s, the complexities relating to nuclear security have in many ways intensified amid globalization and porous borders—where more states in volatile regions possess such weapons and non-state actors have made clear their intention to use them should they attain them. Additionally, the emerging specter of cyberattack, or a misunderstanding that could potentially evolve into a limited regional nuclear war, would both have dire global ramifications. Overall, the monograph seeks to inform and advance policy debate in ways that support international security, while also filling gaps in the academic analysis of nuclear weapons and non-proliferation, and adding important connective tissue between analytical areas in the IR and historical domains that often remain separate.

NOTES

1. "Global Governance Monitor: Nuclear Proliferation," Council for Foreign Relations, 2016, http://www.cfr.org/global-governance/global-governance-monitor/p18985#!/nuclear-proliferation?cid=soc-facebook-in-ggm_nuclear_prolif-082916.

2. Gareth Evans and Yoriko Kawaguchi, *Eliminating Nuclear Threats: A Practical Agenda for Global Policymakers*, International Commission on Nuclear Non-Proliferation and Disarmament (Canberra/Tokyo, 2009), 3–6; Brian Martin, "Nuclear Winter: Science and Politics," *Science and Public Policy* 15, no. 5 (1988); Peter King, "Undermining Proliferation: Nuclear Winter and Nuclear Renunciation," The Centre for Peace and Conflict Studies, Working Paper No. 09/1, October 2009.

3. Evans and Kawaguchi, *Eliminating Nuclear Threats*, 3–6.

4. Hans M. Kristensen and Robert S. Norris, "Status of World Nuclear Forces," Federation of American Scientists (FAS), October 2016, http://fas.org/issues/nuclear-weapons/status-world-nuclear-forces/.

5. Hans M. Kristensen and Robert S. Norris, "Worldwide Deployments of Nuclear Weapons," *Bulletin of the Atomic Scientists*, September 2014, http://thebulletin.org/2014/september/worldwide-deployments-nuclear-weapons-20147595.

6. Evans and Kawaguchi, *Eliminating Nuclear Threats*, 3.

7. "What Are the Risks of Nuclear Weapons?" Global Security Institute, September 2012, http://www.gsinstitute.org/dpe/docs/FactSheetRisks.pdf.

8. Evans and Kawaguchi, *Eliminating Nuclear Threats*, xviii.

9. See "Nuclear Non-Proliferation Chronology of Key Events," IAEA.org, http://www.iaea.org/Publications/Factsheets/English/npt_chrono.html#2000.

10. Melissa Gillis, *Disarmament: A Basic Guide* (New York: United Nations Office for Disarmament Affairs, 2009), http://www.un.org/disarmament/HomePage/ODAPublications/AdhocPublications/PDF/guide.pdf.

11. *Strategic Arms Reduction Treaty (START I)*, Federation of Atomic Scientist (FAS), http://www.fas.org/nuke/control/start1/index.html.

12. Evans and Kawaguchi, *Eliminating Nuclear Threats*, 5.

13. Ibid., 6.

14. "What Are the Risks of Nuclear Weapons?" Global Security Institute.

15. Harald Müller, *The 2005 NPT Review Conference: Reasons and Consequences of Failure and Options for Repair*, Weapons of Mass Destruction Commission (WMDC), UN Secre-

tariat, Stockholm, Sweden, 2005, http://www.blixassociates.com/wp-content/uploads/2011/03/No31.pdf.

16. Evans and Kawaguchi, *Eliminating Nuclear Threats*, 3.

17. George P. Schultz, William J. Perry, Henry A. Kissinger, and Sam Nunn, "A World Free of Nuclear Weapons," *Wall Street Journal*, January 4, 2007, http://online.wsj.com/article/SB116787515251566636.html.

18. See Aiden Warren, *The Obama Administration's Nuclear Weapon Strategy: The Promises of Prague* (New York: Routledge, 2014).

19. Schultz, Perry, Kissinger, and Nunn, "A World Free of Nuclear Weapons."

20. Ibid.

21. Barack Obama, "Remarks by President Barack Obama," Hradčany Square, Prague, Czech Republic, The White House, Washington, DC, Office of the Press Secretary, April 5 2009, http://www.whitehouse.gov/the_press_office/Remarks-By-President-Barack-Obama-In-Prague-As-Delivered/.

22. Paul Meyer, "Prague One Year Later: From Words to Deed," *Arms Control Today*, May 2010, http://www.armscontrol.org/act/2010_05/LookingBack.

23. Obama, "Remarks by President Barack Obama."

24. Ibid.

25. Ibid.

26. Daryl G. Kimball, "Arms Control Association Praises Obama's Commitment to a Nuclear Weapons Free World," *Arms Control Association*, April 5, 2009, http://www.armscontrol.org/print/3616.

27. Evans and Kawaguchi, *Eliminating Nuclear Threats*, 7.

28. Jon B. Wolfsthal, Jeffrey Lewis, and Marc Quint, "The Trillion Dollar Nuclear Triad," James Martin Center for Non-Proliferation Studies, January 2014; Kingston Reif, " U.S. Nuclear Modernization Programs," *Arms Control Association*, October 2016, https://www.armscontrol.org/factsheets/USNuclearModernization; William J. Broad and David E. Sanger, "U.S. Ramping Up Major Renewal in Nuclear Arms," *New York Times*, September 22, 2014.

29. Reif, "U.S. Nuclear Modernization Programs."

30. Ramesh Thakur, "Why Obama Should Declare a No-First-Use Policy for Nuclear Weapons," *Bulletin of the Atomic Scientists*, August 19, 2016, http://thebulletin.org/why-obama-should-declare-no-first-use-policy-nuclear-weapons9789.

31. Ibid.

Chapter One

World War II and the Race for the A-Bomb

In the lead-up to World War II in September 1939, physicists in many states had recognized that if a chain reaction could somehow be tamed, nuclear fission could lead to a promising, and potentially devastating, new source of energy. Scientists in several belligerent nations—including the Axis partners Japan and Germany, as well as the Allied states of Britain, France, Russia, and the United States—understood that at least theoretically, this energy could also be used to create an atomic bomb. Indeed, there was mounting concern among some scientists in the Allied states that Nazi Germany may have been well on the way to developing fission-based weapons. While the engineering and technical challenges needed to create a bomb were not insurmountable, the task would require substantial funding, materiel, and skilled technicians. As became evident, it was only the United States who clearly possessed the commitment and necessary resources to capture the fission process. It also had the requisite geographic isolation needed to avoid hostile enemy assault, and thereby was able to pursue the nuclear design and related logistics that would ultimately "terminate" the Pacific theater of the war.

One of the technical hurdles U.S. physicists encountered was finding a substance that could "moderate" the energy of neutrons emitted in radioactive decay, so that they could be captured by other fissionable nuclei. Heavy water and graphite were prime candidates for the task. This process could occur in an "engine device"—later defined as a reactor—that would allow the chain reaction to provide useable heat. However, according to McGeorge Bundy in *Danger and Survival*, "a reactor was not and never would be a bomb." In discussing the matter of World War II decisions and the quest for nuclear weapons in lay terms, he stated that "a bomb would be something else, as different from a reactor as TNT from a bonfire." Of course, the

1

difference was not fully grasped. The prospect in 1939 of obtaining a bomb from uranium required the separation of U-235 from U-238; the use of plutonium, a by-product of the transformation of U-235 neutrons in a reactor, would come later.[1] Bundy explained the challenging process:

> To choose that path one must acquire confidence that the properties of U-235 would be so significant that the recognized difficulty of separating it out would be acceptable. One must have confidence that one or another method of separation could be made to work. One must understand that when the stuff was separated it would produce a chain reaction if it reached a certain "critical" size, and one must believe that "subcritical" amounts of separated material could be brought together in some almost instantaneous way, so as to produce a true explosion and not a fizzle.[2]

GERMANY'S NUCLEAR DRIVE

With its scientists perceived to be at the forefront of this vital research, it was generally expected by many in the international community that Germany would be the first nation to harness nuclear fission. Late in 1938, Lise Meitner, Otto Hahn, and Fritz Strassman discovered the phenomenon of atomic fission. Meitner had worked in Germany with physicists Hahn and Strassman until fleeing to Sweden to escape Nazi persecution. From her work in Germany, Meitner knew the nucleus of uranium-235 splits (fission) into two lighter nuclei when bombarded by a neutron, and that the sum of the particles derived from fission was not equal in mass to the original nucleus. She speculated that the release of energy—energy a hundred million times greater than normally released in the chemical reaction between two atoms—accounted for the difference. In January 1939, Frisch substantiated these results and, together with Meitner, calculated the unprecedented amount of energy released. Frisch first applied the term *fission*, from biological cell division, to name the process. This "very sensational new development," wrote physicist Leo Szilard to Lewis L. Strauss during the same month, was being discussed as a means to "provide a new source of energy." Szilard acknowledged this, but feared that the "potential possibilities" of this discovery might also lead "to atomic bombs."[3]

After the discovery of fission, German physicists informed various governmental authorities of its potential benefits, and while agreeable to a coordinated research program and accepting of military sponsorship, they nonetheless remained at their university laboratories and focused on their own research. Even so, in their independent labs such physicists were able to make steady progress in the understanding of nuclear science. Otto Hahn, whose independence was recognized by a government that supplied needed materials, continued to experiment in his modest laboratory with nuclear fission materials and achieved impressive results. His work, although listed as "decisive for the war effort," was not related to military products, for he apparently desired this arrangement to preserve the future high status of German science. Indeed, it was evident that the German physicists clearly grasped the "science," the theoretical significance of separated U-235, and the potential of what the young American chemist Glenn Seaborg—while working with Ernest Lawrence's cyclotron at Berkeley—defined as "plutonium." Here were the two principal ingredients either of which could be used to build an atomic bomb.[4]

Werner Heisenberg, Germany's leading nuclear theorist, was recruited to work on a chain-reacting pile in September 1939. A Nobel Prize laureate whose lectures included Einstein's scientific contributions, the twenty-seven-year-old Heisenberg struggled to gain the confidence of older scientists. Publicly acknowledging his patriotism, he nevertheless often assisted scientists being persecuted by the Nazis. While British and American scientists were motivated to cooperative action by an interaction of scientific insights and political concerns, their German counterparts were never so moved. The Americans, led by Italian-born physicist Enrico Fermi at the University of Chicago, would choose pure graphite to slow down or moderate the neutrons produced by the fission in uranium-235 so that they could cause further fissions in a chain reaction. Heisenberg, who experimented with impure graphite to no avail, would ultimately choose heavy water. He calculated the critical mass for a bomb in a December 6, 1939, report for the German Arms Weapons Department. Heisenberg's formula for a bomb, with the nuclear parameters assumed at that time, required a critical mass in the hundreds of tons of "nearly" pure uranium-235 for an exploding reaction. This greatly exceeded what Germany could hope to produce. Anticipating commercial production two decades in the future, Heisenberg wrote that sufficient knowledge existed to indicate that the fission process could "be used for large-scale energy production," but this would require the construction of a reactor "to enrich the uranium 235 isotope."[5]

As early as 1940, Carl-Friedrich von Weizsäcker, the leading Nazi physicist, reasoned that a new fissionable element could be created in a reactor that would provide the necessary ingredient for an "atomic explosive." Subsequently, in June 1942, Heisenberg informed the senior German officials that, "given the positive results achieved up until now it does not appear impossible that, once a uranium burner [reactor] has been constructed, we will one day be able to follow the path revealed by von Weizsäcker to explosives that are more than a million times more effective than those currently available."[6] It was agreed that Heisenberg and his staff would concentrate their efforts on the construction of a reactor that would provide both a source of power and create plutonium for weapons. Despite the efforts of Heisenberg, however, the Nazi nuclear physics program was never able to produce the essential nuclear reactor.[7] Not surprisingly, senior German physicists hesitated approaching Hitler directly for his support in making an atomic bomb because if they promised this magnificent, yet untested, weapon, they would have to either produce it or face unpleasant ramifications should they fail.[8]

In 1941, Heisenberg became aware of the possibility that America might launch a crash program to develop an atomic bomb. Although he did not believe that Germany could build a nuclear bomb before the war ended, he wondered if German nuclear insights might result in a bomb. Could physicists worldwide halt any such effort? While his intent remains unclear, Heisenberg decided in October 1941 to visit Niels Bohr. "Did he go as a loyal German," Warren Strobel writes in a review of Michael Frayn's award-winning play *Copenhagen*, "to learn how much Bohr (and the Allies) knew about atom bombs? Or as a scientist-hero, trying to stall Nazi research and naively hoping to persuade Bohr to restrain the Allies?" The setting of the meeting probably ensured that it would go badly, for how was Heisenberg, a German, to breach the wariness of Bohr living in Nazi-occupied Denmark? Since Heisenberg chose to approach the matter obliquely, Bohr gained the impression that the Germans were putting great effort into developing a bomb. When he passed this impression on to Allied officials in 1943, it infused the Manhattan Project with an added urgency.[9]

EVALUATING THE GERMAN NUCLEAR PROGRAM

As Germany crumbled in the spring of 1945, Allied agents, led by Dr. Samuel A. Goudsmit, were desperate to learn how close Heisenberg and his program had come to making a bomb and, in particular, to keep the scientists and their data out of Soviet hands. Heisenberg and others were quickly rounded up, questioned, and finally interned for six months at a country manor in Britain called Farm Hall, where microphones secretly recorded many of their conversations. Judging from the data, the war's end found the German program to be significantly behind the Manhattan Project. Yet the question persisted, why? Robert Jungk's initial 1956 version of *Brighter than a Thousand Suns* found German scientists suggesting they had downplayed the possibility of an atomic bomb to Nazi officials based on ethical and moral grounds, thus preventing Hitler from obtaining one such device. Jungk concluded that Heisenberg and the other German scientists had deliberately misled him. Likewise, in Thomas Power's 1993 biography, *Heisenberg's War*, the German physicist was portrayed as purposely withholding significant calculations indicating that a bomb was possible.[10]

Notwithstanding substantive evidence to the contrary, German historian Rainer Karlsch posited that the Nazis were actually fairly advanced in their nuclear development. In 2005, he argued that Nazi scientists tested a "hybrid tactical nuclear weapon," albeit much smaller than those dropped on Hiroshima or Nagasaki. He also insisted that the Germans had constructed an atomic reactor near Berlin that operated for a short time, perhaps days or a few weeks, which provided the material for "Hitler's bomb." Karlsch told the BBC News in Berlin that a successful test was carried out on March 3, 1945, at Thuringia, on the Baltic Sea, destroying an area of some five hundred square meters and resulting in the deaths of several hundred prisoners of war and concentration camp inmates. This account aroused considerable interest and skepticism in Germany. "The eyewitnesses he puts forward are either unreliable or they are not reporting first-hand information," the influential news weekly *Der Spiegel* stated, and "allegedly key documents can be interpreted in various ways." "Karlsch displays a catastrophic lack of understanding of physics," according to physicist Michael Schaaf in the *Berliner Zeitung* newspaper. Acknowledging that he did not possess absolute proof to substantiate the existence of a Nazi atomic bomb, Karlsch hoped that his account would nonetheless stimulate further research. [11]

Contrary to this speculative report, John Newhouse writes that the Nazi "uranium fission program never moved much beyond the talking stage." German officials apparently never developed a plan to turn the discovery of fission into an atomic bomb since they were unwilling or unable to collect their physicists together for a major nuclear project. Moreover, they lacked qualified engineers and large experimental instruments such as a cyclotron and faced a shortage of manufacturing facilities and materials. Finally, if the Germans had been able to even construct major U-235 processing facilities, these would have been subjected to constant Allied aerial attacks because when compared to the standard allied aerial targets—rail yards, oil refineries, and ball-bearing factories—nuclear installations would have had a much higher priority. Thus, as McGeorge Bundy concluded, many factors contributed to Nazi Germany's inability to develop a nuclear weapon: "Because their best physicists were not zealous for weapons, because they made uncorrected mistakes, because Hitler was Hitler, and because men like [Albert] Speer always had more urgent production priorities, the Germans never really tried to make an atomic bomb, but if they had, they would have failed. Their country was in the wrong place at the wrong time." [12]

BRITAIN'S INITIAL CONTRIBUTIONS

In the context of the United States' wartime allies, the British effort in its own quest for an atomic device can be considered belated, significant, and limited. While British scientists did not immediately join the scientific activity in early 1939 following the Hahn-Strassmann discovery of fission, they nevertheless fully appreciated what was taking place. Their scientific community, prior to the outbreak of war, agreed to press forward with uranium research and established a single governmental bureau headed by G. P. Thomson to facilitate the work. When hostilities broke out in September 1939, these efforts somewhat lagged as other immediate wartime needs took priority. Moreover, many government officials, including Sir Henry Tizard, did not believe uranium could be manipulated to form a useful bomb, a view shared by Winston Churchill and his scientific adviser Frederick Lindemann, and later Lord Cherwell. Such skepticism might have prevailed had only British-born scientists been involved, but fortunately Hitler's policies had created an abundance of brilliant refugees with outstanding scientific credentials. [13]

Two of the refugees, Otto Frisch and Rudolf Peierls, wrote a theoretical paper in early 1940 that ranked in significance with the Hahn-Strassmann discovery, for it suggested an alternative to using large amounts of natural uranium to make a bomb. Rather, they theorized, a small amount of U-235, perhaps a pound or two processed from U-238, could be brought quickly together to make a sphere "of critical size" where it would provide a destructive force equivalent to thousands of tons of ordinary explosives. They had drawn on Niels Bohr's earlier insight regarding U-235 as a fissile isotope of uranium and applied their own mathematical skill and intuition to arrive at their findings. Margaret Gowing, the British official historian of nuclear activities, has emphasized that the Peierls-Frisch paper "stands as the first memorandum in any country which foretold with scientific conviction the practicality of making a bomb and the horrors it would bring. The two scientists had performed one of the most important and difficult tasks in the development of science—they had asked the right questions . . . [and] they had also answered them correctly from theory without any experimental aid." [14] Yet occasionally they had erred, but even their errors prompted close attention. One of their major fears was that scientists in Germany already were privy to their insights and were striving to be the first to build the bomb. [15]

THE MAUD COMMITTEE

The closely held Peierls-Frisch memorandum underwent scrutiny by a newly formed (but misnamed) M.A.U.D., or Maud, Committee. The name was derived from a curious telegram sent by Lise Meitner from Sweden to her nephew Frisch assuring him that the Niels Bohr family was safe after German occupation of Denmark. The message concluded: "Tell Cockcroft [later Sir John] and Maud Ray Kent." The latter mentioned name was erroneously perceived to be a code for uranium disintegration. It was not until after the war that Meitner could explain that the message was also for Maud Ray, who lived in Kent and had been a governess to the Bohr children. Happily ignorant that its name was due to an error, the committee nevertheless would play a major role in the quest for the bomb. Although overseen by British nationals, Maud initially relied heavily upon refugee scientists, most who had not yet been cleared by security; one of which was Klaus Fuchs, a brilliant young German involved in calculating the size of the first atomic bomb. In 1950, Fuchs was discovered to be a Soviet agent and, perhaps, the only agent to contribute significantly to their fission project. [16]

A major challenge confronting the Maud Committee was how to separate the U-235 isotope from U-238, an activity that would require new innovative technology. Two refugee scientists—French citizens and former associates of Joliot-Curie—Hans von Halban, an Austrian, and Lev Kowarski, a Russian, experimented with heavy water as a moderator to slow down the neutrons during a chain reaction. They possessed most of the world's supply of this precious commodity—a product that was only with great difficulty separated from normal water—which had traveled from a plant in Norway to Paris and then to Britain to escape the Gestapo. Efforts by the British—such as employing spies, commandos, and bombers—to prevent German occupation forces from gaining control of additional supplies from the Norwegian plant present their own involved and heroic story. Still, had the Germans actually obtained the heavy water, it probably would not have meant much because their fission project never developed to where it would have been needed. In America, Szilard and Fermi were experimenting with graphite instead of heavy water as a moderator. Although not quite as efficient, graphite was much more readily available. Peierls and Frisch ultimately decided that a gas diffusion process—one that separated mixed gases by diffusing them through ultrafine membranes—would provide the most efficient method of retrieving U-235. Again, in the United States, Ukrainian-born chemist George B. Kistiakowsky, who fought the Bolsheviks as a member of the White Army and later served as President Dwight Eisenhower's science advisor, also had concluded that gas diffusion was the appropriate method. [17]

By the middle of 1941, the distinguished senior scientists of the Maud Committee had thoroughly reviewed the Peierls-Frisch paper and found it to be persuasive. In their report, the committee argued that constructing a uranium bomb was practical, estimated that sufficient U-235 would be available by 1943, insisted the project be given the highest priority, and urged that a bomb be developed as quickly as possible. Churchill handed over to Sir John Anderson—member of the war cabinet, scientist, and long-time civil servant—the next phase of the nuclear project. At first both impressed and skeptical, Anderson grasped the deep void between a brilliant theory and a finished product—but he never considered he was charged with producing a nuclear weapon to be used during the war. The Maud Committee had suggested, while the project rated the highest priority, it should be accomplished in logical phases. No final decision to undertake extensive construction of manufacturing facilities would be made until results were received from the initial pilot projects. While Churchill, Cherwell, and the chiefs of staff agreed that the project should proceed, the location was still a point of discussion. Their initial thoughts were that the work should be done in Britain so that the British would control not only the bomb but also the technology for postwar civilian uses. Several scientists, especially Tizard and P. M. S. Blackett, argued otherwise, concerned that such a large-scale undertaking would seriously interfere with other necessary wartime production. Then, too, an extensive separation facility would become a target for German bombers. In the end, Anderson and the Scientific Advisory Panel concluded that the work should be done in North America. Politically, the British favored establishing the essential facilities in Canada; however, the necessary technical and industrial support needed to build the bomb inevitably pointed toward the United States. By choosing to share their scientific findings with the Americans, the British would make a major contribution toward the ultimate goal.[18]

After an uneasy beginning, London and Washington agreed to pool their resources and information; however, the other Allied partner—the Soviet Union under Joseph Stalin—was not officially informed. Given communist espionage, this proved not to be a major concern for Stalin, who some have argued may have been better informed about his partners' nuclear activities than either American or British leaders.

AMERICA'S NUCLEAR DRIVE

Nuclear physics was not a mystery to American scientists. Indeed, even though the United States was suffering through the Great Depression, in more than a dozen places strong science departments were engaged in significant research. "The country was dotted with well-appointed laboratories and had more cyclotrons than the rest of the world combined," historian Daniel Kevles had noted. Ernest Lawrence at Berkeley possessed the largest laboratory and his cyclotron permitted examination of the nucleus; however, an equally significant contribution was his fostering of cooperative team research into the larger questions of physics. Thus, while in the late 1930s prominent foreign scientists fleeing persecution and war in Europe added greatly to the atomic adventures of the interwar years, it should not be overlooked that many American physicists had achieved equal status and shared in the ever-expanding nuclear research. Still, America welcomed such top-ranking physicists as Hans Bethe, Felix Bloch, Enrico Fermi, James Franck, Leo Szilard, Edward Teller, Victor Weisskopf, and Eugene Wigner, as well as many other refugee scientists, all of whom would contribute to the enrichment of science in the United States.[19]

Some of the physicists, especially Szilard and Wigner, worried about what their German counterparts might be doing with the possibilities of nuclear fission now that war had broken out in Europe. Szilard, who had fled ultimately to America in the late 1930s to escape Nazi and Fascist repression, was among the most vocal of those advocating a program to develop weapons based on recent findings in nuclear physics and chemistry. He met with Albert Einstein at the latter's home on Long Island to find a way to alert U.S. officials to the possibility that German scientists might win the race to build an atomic bomb, and to warn that Hitler would be more than willing to resort to using such a weapon. Although Einstein had not yet learned of chain reaction, he grasped its significance and agreed that American officials ought to be alerted to its importance. Though no single decision created the American atomic bomb project, most accounts begin with the discussion of a letter drafted by Szilard and signed by the most famous scientist of the twentieth century, Albert Einstein, on August 2, 1939. Alexander Sachs, Wall Street economist and unofficial advisor to President Franklin D. Roosevelt, was selected to deliver Einstein's letter. With Europe in flames during September, Sachs had to wait until October 11, 1939, to meet with the president. Einstein wrote that recent research had made it "probable . . . that it may become possible to set up a nuclear chain reaction in a large mass of uranium, by which vast amounts of power and large quantities of new radium-like elements could be generated," leading "to the construction of bombs, and it is conceivable—though much less certain—that extremely powerful bombs of a new type may thus be constructed." This was all likely to happen "in the immediate future." In the letter, Einstein stated his fear that the Nazi government was actively supporting research in the area and urged the American government to do the same. Although presidential files contain no record of the meeting, Sachs apparently briefed FDR on the main points contained in Einstein's letter. Initially, the president was noncommittal and expressed concern over the necessary funds, but at a second meeting over breakfast the next morning Roosevelt became persuaded of the value of exploring atomic energy. He could hardly do otherwise. Turning to his aide, Major General Edwin Watson, he declared: "This requires action."[20]

Although preoccupied with events in Europe, Roosevelt informed Einstein on October 19, 1939, that an Advisory Committee on Uranium had been created. Lyman J. Briggs, a government scientist and director of the Bureau of Standards, headed the committee made up of representatives from the army and navy, Sachs, and the Hungarian trio of Szilard, Wigner, and Teller to explore the prospects of uranium. Briggs, operating without a presidential mandate for a crash program, moved cautiously, awaiting results of the step-by-step approach to experiments designed by an equally cautious Fermi. Despite the urgency shown by Szilard and a few others, Washington at first failed to come to grips with the seriousness of the Peierls-Frisch paper. It was nearly a year later that Vannevar Bush, director of the Carnegie Institution and confidant of FDR, convinced Roosevelt to establish a new agency—the National Defense Research Committee (NDRC)—to replace Briggs's group. Even with Bush as the chairman of the NDRC, and James B. Conant, president of Harvard University as head of the Explosives Division, little progress was made toward meeting the challenges of nuclear fission. Initially both men sought to discount the feasibility of atomic weaponry even though London's Maud Committee had correctly determined that a nuclear bomb was practical. In late spring 1941, Bush worried that the nuclear project could absorb "a very large amount of money." A month later, in June, he said, "This uranium business is a headache" and again expressed doubts on whether nuclear fission could result in an atomic bomb. There were ample reasons to be reluctant to allocate the considerable amount of capital required to aggressively pursue the nuclear program, for at this time there were many other urgent military needs to be met. Newhouse, in his *War and Peace in the Nuclear Age*, suggests that the nuclear "program might well have been scrapped but for Britain's Maud Committee." Maud's mid-July report, Bush having received an informal version two weeks earlier, confirmed the feasibility of a nuclear weapon and, as noted above, urged its attainment be given the highest possible priority as it could figure decisively in terminating the war.[21]

While Conant still registered some hesitation during the summer, Ernest Lawrence among others spoke up and called for an aggressive nuclear program. Glenn Seaborg, working at UC Berkeley with Lawrence's cyclotron, had demonstrated a few months earlier that U-238 bombarded by neutrons issued a new, intensely radioactive element. He had discovered plutonium, which when bombarded was very fissile and could provide another, easier to obtain, source of material for a bomb. George Kistiakowsky, one of the country's leading explosive authorities, added his voice in support of the bomb and, in the process, convinced Conant of its feasibility. By mid-summer Bush was persuaded as well. The end of the beginning came on October 9 when Bush outlined the Maud Committee's report for Roosevelt and Vice President Henry Wallace. The requirements for launching the quest of the atomic bomb was addressed, including an estimate of the bomb's required amount of uranium, the cost of constructing a U-235 processing facility, and the time needed to build and deliver the bomb. Roosevelt gave the approval to move ahead with the nuclear project, while restricting the list of individuals Bush would keep fully involved to himself, Wallace, Conant, Henry L. Stimson, secretary of war, and General George C. Marshall, army chief of staff. Although America was two months away from becoming a full-fledged belligerent, FDR had made a pivotal decision, the consequences of which would reach far beyond the war.[22]

THE TRINITY AUGMENTATION

The American atomic bomb program began taking shape during the summer of 1942. The Anglo-American relationship, which Churchill sought to establish as a partnership, had been discussed in June when Churchill and Roosevelt met at Hyde Park, New York. The British reluctantly conceded that the atomic energy facilities—referred to in all correspondence as "Tube Alloys"—would be constructed in the United States; but the two leaders continued to see their undertakings as a joint arrangement. While the British had contributed much scientific expertise early and actively stimulated the quest for a nuclear weapon, the American share would become larger as it involved an ever-growing number of workers and increasing consumption of financial resources. During the summer the atomic program acquired its code name—the Manhattan Engineer District or simply the Manhattan Project. Now that a full-scale government commitment had been made, as a wartime measure, control of the project was transferred from the scientists to a Military Policy Committee so as to provide the necessary cover and secrecy. Brigadier General Leslie R. Groves, who had earlier supervised the construction of the Pentagon, took charge of the Manhattan Project in September 1942.[23]

The Manhattan Project became a massive industrial and scientific undertaking scattered across the United States and Canada, eventually employing sixty-five thousand workers and involving many of the world's great physicists in its scientific and development aspects. The project was essentially located at four main sites: the University of Chicago's Metallurgical Laboratory (the Met Lab), whose primary contribution came early; Hanford (code named W) near Richland, Washington; Oak Ridge (X) in eastern Tennessee; and Los Alamos (Y), near Santa Fe, New Mexico. At Hanford, where reactors would produce the highly radioactive plutonium, large-scale facilities were constructed, including a 386-mile, eight-lane highway (to allow workers and their families to escape if a disaster occurred) and 158 miles of railway track. This site alone employed thousands of individuals. The separating of U-235 from U-238 by the gaseous diffusion technique took place at Oak Ridge. "Just one of the electromagnetic plants" at Oak Ridge, Garry Wills has written, "had 200 buildings, residing on 825 acres." The Los Alamos Laboratory, an isolated site atop a seven-thousand-foot mesa, was where the atomic bomb was designed and put together. The remote super-secret facility, previously a small ranch school, by 1945 housed some "3,500 people—scientists, soldiers, construction workers, staff and families—living inside a triple ring of fences, with sentries on horseback or in jeeps patrolling the circuit twenty-four hours a day. The tech area, inside the innermost ring of fencing, had 37 buildings, and the support structures totaled 350 buildings and 200 trailers."[24]

In many ways the Manhattan Project operated like any other large con-struction company. It purchased and prepared sites, let contracts, hired per-sonnel and subcontractors, built and maintained housing and service facil-ities, placed orders for materials, developed administrative and accounting procedures, and established communications networks. By the end of the war, General Groves and his staff had spent approximately $2.2 billion on production facilities and towns in the states of Tennessee, Washington, and New Mexico, as well as on research in university laboratories from Columbia University, in New York City, to the University of California at Berkeley. What made the Manhattan Project clearly unlike other companies performing similar functions was that, because of the necessity of moving quickly, it invested hundreds of millions of dollars in unproven and hitherto unknown processes, and did so entirely in secret. Secrecy dictated remote site loca-tions, required subterfuge in obtaining labor and supplies, and compartmen-talized its activities so completely, in fact, that many of the staff did not know exactly what they had been working on until they heard about the bombing of Hiroshima on the radio.

Selected personally by Groves, J. Robert Oppenheimer, at Los Alamos, headed the work of a group of theoretical physicists he called the "luminar-ies," which included Felix Bloch, Hans Bethe, Edward Teller, and Robert Seber, while John H. Manley assisted him by coordinating nationwide fission research and instrument and measurement studies from the Metallurgical Laboratory in Chicago. Bush was initially worried about Groves's insensitiv-ity regarding the scientists who would be working on the project. "Having seen Groves briefly," he declared, "I doubt whether he has sufficient tact for the job." His concern was not without cause, for Groves warned his Army staff at Los Alamos, "At great expense we have gathered here the largest collection of crackpots ever seen." Obsessed with secrecy, he demanded that access to information should be only on a need-to-know basis that would prevent most of his employees from discovering the purpose of the project. Because he had the support of the highest authorities, Groves usually had things his way. When the issue of compartmentalization arose, his demands carried at Oak Ridge and Hanford but not at Los Alamos, where the scien-tists, including Oppenheimer, demanded that they work the way they always had—with a free flow of ideas and information. When Groves sought to organize the site along military lines, including putting the scientists in uni-form, he encountered a wall of resistance.[25]

In April 1943, Oppenheimer brought the key bomb designers together at Los Alamos to inform them of their objective and hasten the process of arriving at it. Robert Serber began the conference by flatly stating: "The object of the project is to produce a practical military weapon in the form of a bomb in which the energy is released by a fast neutron chain reaction in one or more of the materials known to show nuclear fission."[26] He proceeded to state that the current belief was that critical mass for U-235 required a thirty-three-pound core, roughly the size of a melon, while plutonium would need twelve pounds, about the size of a tennis ball. Uranium would be used to encase both in a heavy shell. The purpose of the uranium was to "reflect the neutrons back into the heart of the bomb," as P. D. Smith described the process, "increasing the number of potential fission reactions and thus the explosive yield of the bomb." There was little need for more theoretical physics, as the work remaining focused largely on the engineering of the bomb. The remaining major challenge was to develop the means of bringing together a critical mass while avoiding a premature or muted explosion. Two bomb designs emerged, one for U-235 that utilized a gun barrel effect in which an explosive charge fired a slug of uranium into another. An implosion design was required for a plutonium bomb. Here a plutonium core was surrounded with high explosive that was, in turn, ringed with a detonator. With hundreds of pounds of high explosives pressing upon the center, the plutonium was to set off a chain reaction that would be sustained sufficiently to release huge amounts of energy.[27]

For any large organization to take laboratory research into design, construction, operation, and product delivery in two and half years (from 1943 to August 1945) was a major industrial achievement. The need for alacrity clarified priorities and shaped decision-making. Unfinished research on three separate, unproven processes had to be used to freeze design plans for production facilities, even though it was recognized that later findings could dictate changes. The pilot stage was eliminated entirely, violating all manufacturing practices and leading to intermittent shutdowns and endless troubleshooting during trial runs in production facilities. Not surprising, the inherent problems of collapsing the stages between the laboratory and full production created an emotionally charged atmosphere, as optimism and despair alternated with confusing frequency.

At precisely 5:30 a.m., on Monday July 16, 1945, at "Trinity," the code name for the Manhattan Project test site near Alamogordo, New Mexico, a group of officials and scientists led by Groves and Oppenheimer witnessed the first explosion of an atomic bomb. As Isidor Rabi wrote, "There was an enormous flash of light, the brightest light I have ever seen or that I think anyone has ever seen. It blasted; it pounced; it bored its way right through you. . . . Finally it was over, diminishing, and we looked toward the place where the bomb had been; there was an enormous ball of fire which grew and grew and it rolled as it grew; it went up into the air, in yellow flashes and into scarlet and green. It looked menacing."[28] The explosion had vaporized the tower, turned asphalt around the base of the tower to green sand, and released an explosive force of nearly nineteen thousand tons of TNT. Some observers suffered temporary blindness even though they looked at the brilliant light through smoked glass. Seconds after the explosion came a huge blast, sending searing heat across the desert and knocking some observers, standing a thousand yards away, to the ground. A steel container weighing over two hundred tons, standing a half-mile from ground zero, was knocked ajar. As the fireball stretched up and flattened into a mushroom cloud, it provided the atomic age with a symbol that has since become imprinted on the human consciousness. [29]

As the light dimmed and the mushroom cloud rose, Oppenheimer was reminded of fragments from the *Bhagavad-Gita*, the sacred Hindu text, "I am become Death / The shatterer of worlds." Less quoted but more memorable perhaps was the comment by test site manager Kenneth Bainbridge to Oppenheimer: "Oppie, now we're all sons of bitches." The terrifying destructive power of atomic weapons and the uses to which they could be put were to haunt some of the Manhattan Project scientists for the remainder of their lives. Others would go on to build bigger and better bombs. [30]

HIROSHIMA AND THE DEFEAT OF THE JAPANESE

With the defeat of Nazi Germany in May 1945, the Allies' most pressing matter was to persuade Japanese leaders to surrender unconditionally. Having successfully executed the "Europe first" part of U.S. war strategy, American military might was being diverted to the Pacific. At the Potsdam Conference in July, Stalin, who was then technically still at peace with Tokyo, agreed to enter the war in the Pacific on August 15, making good a pledge given earlier that the Soviet Union would do so three months after the war in Europe had been won. Also at Potsdam, the British, Chinese, and Americans (since the USSR was technically not yet at war with Japan, Stalin took no part in discussions concerning the war in the Pacific) reissued their ultimatum of the unconditional surrender of Japan. American B-29s had for some time struck at many Japanese targets, including urban areas, but still Tokyo officials refused to surrender. Although there were elements within the Japanese government that had long recognized that the war was lost, the military, led by the army, dedicated to defending the homeland, was preparing the islands' defenses. Faced with such determined resistance, the Joint Chiefs of Staff and other administration officials estimated that the human costs of invading the Japanese home islands could result in many thousands of U.S. and Allied casualties. At the same time, President Harry S. Truman, who succeeded to the presidency after the sudden death of Franklin D. Roosevelt on April 12, 1945, was becoming aware of the Manhattan Project's accomplishments and promise. [31]

On April 25, Secretary of War Henry Stimson and General Groves gave the new president a lengthy briefing on the weapon we now know as the atomic bomb. Here Groves reported on the genesis and current status of the atomic bomb project, while Stimson presented a memorandum explaining the implications of the bomb for international relations. Stimson addressed the terrifying power of the new weapon, declaring that "within four months, we shall in all probability have completed the most terrible weapon ever known in human history, one bomb which could destroy a whole city." He went on to allude to the dangers that its discovery and development foreshadowed, even warning the president that a small and cunning state might be able to build an atomic bomb with which to defeat or at least blackmail larger democratic nations. At that point in time, Stimson noted, no adequate controls existed in the international community to restrict the bomb's destructive capacity. "On the other hand," Stimson continued, "if the problem of the proper use of the weapon *can be* solved, we would have the opportunity to bring the world into a pattern in which the peace of the world and our civilization can be saved." Truman seemed to focus less on the geopolitical implications of the possession of the atomic bomb and more on the personal burden of authorizing the possible use of the awesome weapon. "I am going to have to make a decision which no man in history has ever had to make," he reportedly said to a White House staffer, the very next person he saw after Stimson and Groves left his office. "I will make the decision, but it is terrifying to think about what I will have to decide."[32]

The president was at the Potsdam Conference—which had been postponed until the bomb was tested—when General Groves conveyed word of the successful Trinity test to Secretary of War Henry Stimson's aide, George Harrison, who in turn cabled Stimson in cryptic fashion: "Operated on this morning. Diagnosis not yet complete but results seem satisfactory and already exceed expectations." Stimson could hardly contain himself, giving Truman a preliminary report in the evening after the president returned from his tour of Berlin. While the success of the test took a great load off his mind, Truman casually informed Stalin that the United States "had a new weapon of unusual destructive force." Stalin, who had spies on the ground in New Mexico, simply replied that he hoped the president would use it well. Certainly, with the success of Trinity, many U.S. officials may have believed that America could probably conclude the war without Russian assistance; but earlier Truman's "one objective," Secretary of Commerce Henry Wallace had recorded, "was to be sure to get the Russians into the Japanese war so as to save the lives of 100,000 American boys." Later, he showed less enthusiasm for the Soviet's speeded up invasion of Manchuria. Nonetheless, from Potsdam, Truman sent an ultimatum to Tokyo to surrender immediately, unconditionally, or face "prompt and utter destruction."[33]

In any case, the United States now had in its arsenal a weapon of unparalleled destruction; Stimson even suggested that it would create "a new relationship of man to the universe." Truman's advisers agreed that the atomic bomb could end the war in the Pacific, but they could not agree on the best way to use it. There is a certain irony here: the scientists who developed the bomb wanted it used against the Nazis but were horrified when it became clear it would be used against Japan. Some proposed a public demonstration on an uninhabited region, while others argued that it should be used against Japanese naval forces and should never be used against Japanese cities. Still, the objective according to others was not so much to defeat Japan but as to employ "atomic diplomacy" against the Soviet Union, thereby providing a demonstration to make it "more manageable" in Eastern and Central Europe after the war. Of course, one certainty that Truman *did* know was that the Japanese still remained a difficult adversary in a very present conflict. Early in the year, in their unsuccessful effort to hold the tiny island of Iwo Jima, over 25,000 Japanese gave up their lives, with only a fraction taken prisoners; to secure this vital stepping-stone, 750 miles from Tokyo, 8,000 American sailors and marines lost their lives, with an additional 20,000 wounded. The battle for Okinawa of April–May, together with Japanese kamikaze tactics, cost the Americans another 50,000 casualties, along with eighty-eight sunk and damaged ships. Okinawa, the costliest battle of the Pacific War—110,000 Japanese were killed and just 7,800 taken prisoner— made it evident what the Allies would likely encounter in a full-scale assault on the Japanese home islands. Indeed, U.S. intelligence knew that the Japanese were preparing for the expected U.S. invasion.[34]

Nonetheless, after considering the various options, Truman concluded that the only way to shorten the war, while avoiding an invasion of Japan, was to use the bomb against Japanese cities. On the morning of August 6, 1945, shortly after 8:15 a.m., a lone B-29 bomber named the *Enola Gay* dropped "Little Boy" over the city of Hiroshima (population 350,000), Japan's second most important military-industrial center, instantly killing 80,000 to 140,000 people and seriously injuring 100,000 or more. The first (never before tested) uranium 235-based bomb to be used had the explosive force of 14,000 tons of TNT—puny and primitive by later thermonuclear standards. Still, in that one terrible moment, 60 percent of Hiroshima, 4 square miles, an area equal to one-eighth of New York City was destroyed. The burst temperature was estimated to reach over a million degrees Celsius, which ignited the surrounding air, forming a fireball some 840 feet in diameter. Eyewitnesses more than 5 miles away said its brightness exceeded the sun tenfold. The blast wave shattered windows for a distance of ten miles and was felt as far away as 37 miles. Over two-thirds of Hiroshima's buildings were demolished. The hundreds of fires, ignited by the thermal pulse, combined to produce a firestorm that had incinerated everything within about 4.4 miles of ground zero. Hiroshima had disappeared under a thick, churning foam of flame and smoke. Three days later, on August 9, another lone B-29 bomber, named *Bock's Car*, dropped "Fat Man" (the Trinity test bomb) on Nagasaki (population 253,000), home to two huge Mitsubishi war plants on the Urakami River, instantly killing 24,000 and wounding 23,000. Unlike Hiroshima, there was no firestorm this time, but the blast was more destructive to the immediate area due to the topography and greater power of "Fat Man." However, the hilly, almost mountainous terrain limited the total area of destruction, as well as the loss of life, at least when compared to Hiroshima. With Japanese doctors at a loss to explain why many civilian patients who had not been wounded were now wasting away, in the following weeks the death counts in both cities rose as the populations succumbed to radiation-related sickness.[35]

The shockwaves were felt well beyond the Japanese home islands. Western newspapers struggled to explain to a triumphant but mystified public how thousands of American, British, and Canadian scientists had managed to harness the power of the sun to such deadly effect. No easier to explain was that the U.S. government could undertake a military and scientific program as massive and prolonged as the Manhattan Project with such absolute secrecy. This paradoxical view of the government's achievement was typical of the American public's response to the bomb. The elation of the prospects of imminent peace was tempered by a growing recognition of the awesome responsibilities of possessing such a powerful weapon. Opposition to nuclear weaponry emerged almost immediately after the bomb was built. The Franck Report of June 11, 1945, signed by a number of the Manhattan Project scientists, warned Secretary of War Stimson that an unannounced attack would surely lead to an arms race. Both the report and scientists were ignored. The impact of the new weapon spread well beyond the military and scientific circles in which it had been developed; to an extent unprecedented, it began to seep into the popular imagination as images of mushroom clouds became symbolic of the new destructive potential that had been developed. What Truman called "the greatest scientific gamble in history" had paid off with devastating effectiveness, and there was no doubt that a turning point in the history of the contemporary world had been reached. Indeed, "the bomb," as it was quickly dubbed, became the defining feature of the post–World War II world.[36]

Truman, apparently under the impression that the atomic bombs would be used against only military targets, halted use of the third scheduled atomic bomb. The "thought of wiping out another 100,000 people was too horrible," he explained. Yet in a strategic sense, the atomic bombing of Hiroshima and Nagasaki represented only a technological improvement in the strategy of city-busting that the Allies had developed in Europe at Hamburg and Dresden, and practiced at Tokyo on March 9, 1945, with 334 B-29s, each carrying nearly six tons of incendiary bombs. Long before August 6, aerial bombardment had eroded away the distinction between combatants and noncombatants as targets. A couple of years later David Lilienthal, chairman of the U.S. Atomic Energy Commission, aptly described the new situation:

Then we burned Tokyo, not just military targets, but set out to wipe out the place, indiscriminately. The atomic bomb is the last word in this direction. All ethical limitations of warfare are gone, not because the *means* of destruction are more cruel or painful or otherwise hideous in their effect upon combatants, but because there are no individual combatants. The fences are gone.[37]

Of course, the subsequent planned use of nuclear weapons during the Cold War traversed the same new path of targeting.

With a Japanese surrender imminent, and recognizing that if it was going to play a part in postwar Asia it would need to enter the fray quickly, the Soviet Union declared war on Japan on August 8, a week sooner than Stalin had pledged at the Potsdam conference. Nine minutes after its declaration, the Soviet Union's Far Eastern Army and Air Force launched a massive offensive against the Japanese forces in Manchuria and the Korean peninsula. The seizure of the Kurile Islands and southern Sakhalin also constituted part of the Soviet continental campaign. The overwhelming nature of the Soviet attack caused very high casualties among the Kwantung Army, killing 80,000 Japanese soldiers (against 8,219 Soviet dead and 22,264 wounded) in less than a week. Yielding to the reality of the situation, Emperor Hirohito, supported by civilian advisers, finally overcame the militarists and ordered surrender on August 14. For its part, the United States agreed to retain the institution of the emperor system, stripped of pretension to divinity and subject to American occupation headed by General Douglas MacArthur. On September 2, thereafter known as V-J Day, a great Allied fleet sailed into Tokyo Bay. Aboard the *USS Missouri*, General MacArthur accepted Japanese surrender on behalf of the Allies. With this simple ceremony, World War II was finally brought to a close.[38]

Looking back, historians have engaged in a prolonged, occasionally antagonistic historical debate over what was the dominant factor that finally compelled Japan to surrender. Was it the terrible destruction of the atomic bombing of Hiroshima? Of Nagasaki? Was it the combination of the two and fear that more such attacks could be forthcoming? Could the Soviet decision to intervene have been a more important factor? Did the prospect of the impending U.S. invasion play a role? Historian Andrew Rotter's response to these questions seems most appropriate: "It may be nothing more than a historian's common sense to suppose that the infliction of death on many thousands—no one yet knew even roughly how many—by a mere two bombs was, along with Soviet intervention, decisive in ending the war. Given the mix of evidence available, and in the absence of any 'smoking gun,' common sense may be the best measure possible."[39] Among critics of the various reasons given for dropping the bomb, British scientist Patrick M. S. Blackett argued that Hiroshima and Nagasaki could best be seen as the first chapter of the Cold War rather than the last chapter of World War II.

THE USSR AND THEIR OWN NUCLEAR DRIVE

During the 1930s, Russian scientists were widely respected, especially the physicists, and recognized as part of the international scientific fraternity. As it did their Western colleagues, the discovery of fission excited Soviet physicists, particularly in terms of power generation. They undertook research with renewed energy even though, as David Holloway points out in his valuable account *Stalin and the Bomb*, as late as 1939 many were still skeptical as to whether it was possible to create an atomic bomb any time soon. Yet in light of some promising research, one prominent Soviet scientist was reported to have suggested in August 1939 that "a bomb can be built that will destroy a city out to a radius of maybe ten kilometers." Peter Kapitsa, an acknowledged leading experimental physicist, thought that the amount of energy required for separation of uranium isotopes would exceed that produced. Consequently he doubted that atomic energy would prove to become a reality, at least in the near future.[40]

With Britain, France, and Germany at war after September 1939, and the United States indirectly assisting Britain, London and Washington were receiving warnings from their nuclear scientists about the danger of a possible German atomic bomb. Soviet scientists, however, functioned in a different political sphere following the Nazi-Soviet Pact of August 1939, as it seemed to remove the USSR from the hostilities. Consequently, they did not bombard Moscow with warning of a possible Nazi nuclear threat; instead, they continued with their nuclear fission research and published their results until the summer of 1940. Among the more prominent scientists, in addition to Peter Kapitsa, were: Lev Landau, a world-class theoretical physicist; Igor Kurchatov, who constructed Europe's first cyclotron; and Konstantin Petrazhak and Georgi Flerov, who discovered spontaneous uranium fission.[41] Flerov, visiting a library in February 1942 to see if foreign journals had commented on his and Petrazhak's 1940 discovery of spontaneous fission, found no response or any mention of research being conducted by internationally known physicists. Such censorship, he concluded, indicated that Britain and America were engaged in the quest for the bomb. In an example of unintended consequences, Professor Martin Zuberi notes, "secrecy itself gave the secret away."[42]

Meanwhile, Soviet secret intelligence agencies began receiving classified information after the German invasion of the USSR in June 1941, including the British decision to create a program to research and develop an atomic bomb. Soon after, a copy of the Maud report appeared in Moscow. During the next year many scientific documents were sent predominantly by physicist Klaus Fuchs, John Cairncross, a secretary to Lord Hankey of the War Cabinet, and Bruno Pontecorvo, a collaborator of Enrico Fermi. Much of the clandestine material was collected by Lavrenti Beria, head of the KGB, who reported directly to Stalin, worried that the data was deliberately misleading so as to obstruct Soviet efforts. Indeed, only a few select Soviet scientists saw the data because of the fear that their agents might be compromised. Stalin apparently received brief oral summaries of the bomb material, but given the devastation caused by Germany's assault on the Soviet Union that began in late June 1941 and destroyed much of its existing industrial base, it was not surprising that the data drew little immediate government attention. As the military situation became less desperate, Stalin finally agreed on February 11, 1943, to a proposal by the State Committee of Defense to launch the Soviet atomic bomb project. It fell to long-time Stalin associate V. M. Molotov, head of the new project, to recommend a scientific leader. Molotov later wrote that he spoke with Kapitsa, who believed that "the atomic bomb was a weapon not for this war, but something for the future." Finally, after interviewing various candidates, Molotov was sufficiently impressed with Igor Kurchatov to permit him to review the secret intelligence reports.[43]

After going through the secret documents for several days, Kurchatov reported that they were of "huge, incalculable significance" for the Soviet program. He concluded his report, stating that "the totality of intelligence materials indicates the technical possibility of resolving all the uranium problems in significantly shorter time than our scientists thought who were not familiar with the progress of the work on this problem abroad." On March 10, 1943, Stalin appointed Kurchatov to direct the scientific work of the USSR's atomic energy project, and little more than a month later he assumed the leadership of the secret scientific institute, code named "Laboratory No. 2," while No. 1 remained in the Kremlin or Beria headquarters. Fending off Beria's opposition, Kurchatov ultimately succeeded in distributing the secret materials to several of his department heads—Abram Joffe, Abram Alikhanov, Isaac Kikoin, Lev Artsimovich, Yulii Khariton, and Kirill Shchelkin—each of whom led the research into a particular scientific-technical problem. Kurchatov focused on constructing a uranium-graphite reactor to isolate plutonium, Alikhanov concentrated on building a reactor employing heavy water, and Kikoin sought to separate uranium isotopes by gas diffusion, while Artsimovich hoped to achieve the same goal by using magnetic force. Khariton and Shchelkin were challenged with constructing uranium and plutonium bombs. Since these "trusted physicists" could not reveal the sources of their information, they could only present a particular significant aspect of the secret documents as their own discovery, giving them "a halo of genius."[44]

If Soviet scientists gained access to a substantial volume of data describing what their counterparts in America were accomplishing, they were unable to make much progress toward their ultimate goal—an atom bomb—because, in part, they possessed little uranium. In another example of unintended consequences, William Laurence, the *New York Times* science correspondent writing to warn government officials of his suspicions that German nuclear research was aimed at developing an atomic bomb, actually prompted activity in Russia. His story appeared on May 5, 1940, and dealt with the research and possibilities of U-235 and its "tremendous implications" as a new source of power. Geologist Vladimir Vernadskii, upon receiving a copy of the article from his son who was at Yale University, with radiochemist Vitalii Khlopin immediately urged the Department of Geological and Geographical Sciences of the Academy of Sciences to survey the Soviet Union for deposits of uranium. The subsequent Commission on the Uranium Problem, created on July 30, 1940, found it extremely difficult to supply Soviet physicists with the various forms of uranium required for their research. In any case, the commission collapsed with the Nazi invasion in June 1941. Two years later a former commission member, Dmitrii Shcherbakov, revisited the subject of Soviet uranium deposits, what was required to develop them, and noted that Central Asian deposits had not been adequately studied. Later in 1943, Vernadskii and Khlopin joined with others to not only continue the quest for deposits in the USSR, but also to record the geological conditions of uranium deposits for future prospecting. The lack of early systematic exploration, as David Holloway has noted, resulted in geologists not knowing "what uranium reserves the country had."[45]

Kurchatov, frustrated by what he perceived as a lack of support from Molotov, sent a critical progress report to Beria on September 29, 1944. He began by noting that America and Britain's "concentration of scientific and engineering-technical forces on a scale unseen in the history of world science . . . has already achieved the most valuable results." Reviewing Soviet activity, Kurchatov wrote, "In spite of great progress in developing the work on uranium in 1943–1944, the state of affairs remains completely unsatisfactory. The situation with raw materials and questions of separation is particularly bad. The research at Laboratory No. 2 lacks an adequate material-technical base. Research at many organizations that are cooperating with us is not developing as it should because of the lack of unified leadership, and because the significance of the problem is underestimated in these organizations." He believed that the lack of cooperative effort and the insufficient support extended by Soviet leaders was due primarily to the failure to assign the nuclear project a high priority. Kurchatov understood, perhaps better than anyone else, the gap between the progress and support of the Soviet program and the American Manhattan project. Information supplied by Klaus Fuchs and others in 1945 substantially assisted (or in some instances verified) Soviet research. On April 7 Kurchatov wrote that Fuchs's data was of "great value." In particular, information of significance related to spontaneous fission and that related to the fission cross-sections of U-235 and plutonium 239 for the various energies of fast neutrons. Learning about Anglo-American research concerning the implosion technique also greatly aided Soviet research.[46]

In the context of the data supplied to the Soviets, according to Holloway, "Fuchs was by far the most important informant in the Manhattan project." Some Western scientists have agreed, arguing that Fuchs played a vital role in achieving the bomb. "All things were available to Fuchs," General Kenneth D. Nichols had noted. "He sat in on all the policy meetings on the fission bomb with people like Fermi, Bacher, and Rabi. . . . Knowing what worked and what didn't was very useful to the Soviets." Disagreeing with this view, Carson Mark, who replaced Hans Bethe as chief of the Theoretical Division, declared: "I don't think Fuchs was of any use to them at all. They were probably fascinated but not dependent on him. They didn't need him or other spies. They'd have come out at the same place at the same time if he had sent them nothing." I. I. Rabi was also skeptical of Fuchs's contribution, although informing the Soviets that the United States was working on a bomb would have been quite important. Thus, some Western scientists believed that except for the disruptive effects of the war, Soviet scientists were equal to the challenge and might well have tested an atom bomb before 1949. While the usefulness of the various spies' scientific information may be questioned, the political impact cannot. Public disclosure of their duplicity would contribute significantly to America's anticommunist resurgence.[47]

At the end of March 1945, members of the Czechoslovakian government in exile visited Moscow on their way home to Prague. The Soviets improved their supply of uranium via a secret agreement reached at Moscow that gave them control of Czechoslovakia's uranium mines that early in the twentieth century had provided most of the world's supply of uranium. If gaining access to the Czechs' uranium was important, the occupation of Germany provided even greater benefits. In May, after Germany's surrender, Moscow sent a mission to examine the Nazis' nuclear activities—much like U.S. general Groves's Alsos mission. While the Soviet mission quickly recognized they had little to learn from the Nazis' wartime research, they were able to recruit (or draft) some German scientists to assist with their program. Even more important to Moscow than German scientists or laboratory equipment was the estimated 240–340 tons of uranium oxide seized in Germany and Czechoslovakia as the war ended. Groves succeeded in removing another 1,200 tons before it fell into Soviet hands—an amount that would have been of highly significant value to the Soviet program. For the long term, the Soviets benefited from the enormously valuable uranium sites in occupied East Germany.[48]

During the war years British and American nuclear programs were driven by the fear that German scientists were also making a determined effort to create an extremely destructive atomic device to use *against* the Allies. While the period across 1940 and 1941 specifically saw scientists in Germany, Britain, America, the Soviet Union, and even Japan pursue similar lines of research, in actuality the German, Japanese, and Soviet governments did not make the attainment of a nuclear weapon the utmost priority to their respective state security. It was only President Franklin D. Roosevelt who committed the substantial resources necessary to transform and configure the scientists' findings into a weapon of war. As the hostilities ended, Moscow had yet to place a high priority on their nuclear project; bureaucratic inertia, lack of adequate funding, and concerns about reconstruction were still at play. Of course, all of this would significantly change once the destruction of Hiroshima demonstrated the awesome power of the atomic bomb. A few weeks later, with the new postwar order seemingly revealing a new set of international tensions and acrimony, the possession of such a weapon became of essential importance to the strategy and security of the Soviet Union.

NOTES

1. McGeorge Bundy, *Danger and Survival: Choices About the Bomb in the First Fifty Years* (New York: Random House, 1988), 10. Elements of this chapter have been adapted from Professor Siracusa's study (with Richard Dean Burns) *A Global History of the Nuclear Arms Race: Weapons, Strategy, and Politics*, 2 vols. (Santa Barbara, CA: Praeger, 2013).

2. Ibid.

3. Robert Jungk, *Brighter than a Thousand Suns: A Personal History of the Atomic Scientists*, trans. by James Cleugh (New York: Harcourt, Brace and World, 1958), 67–69; Szilard's letter in Philip L. Cantelon, Richard C. Hewlett, and Robert C. Williams, eds., *The American Atom: A Documentary History of Nuclear Policies from the Discovery of Fission to the Present*, 2nd ed. (Philadelphia: University of Pennsylvania Press, 1991), 8–9.

4. Bundy, *Danger and Survival*, 14–15; John Newhouse, *War and Peace in the Nuclear Age* (New York: Knopf, 1989), 8–10, 23.

5. Heisenberg's 1939 report in David Irving, *The German Atomic Bomb: The History of Nuclear Research in Nazi Germany* (New York: Simon & Schuster, 1968), 53.

6. Heisenberg, quoted in P. D. Smith, *Doomsday Men: The Real Dr. Strangelove and the Dream of the Superweapon* (New York: St. Martin's Press, 2007), 283.

7. Ibid.

8. Albert Speer, *Inside the Third Reich: Memoirs by Albert Speer*, trans. by Richard and Clara Winston (New York: Macmillan, 1970), 228, 336.

9. Warren P. Strobel, "Absence of A-Bomb: Were the Nazis Duped—or Simply Dumb?" *U.S. News and World Report*, July 24, 2000, U.S. News Online, http://www.usnews.com/usnews/doubleissue/mysteries/nazi.htm; Jungk, *Brighter than a Thousand Suns*, 99–102. Heisenberg later wrote to Jungk attempting to explain his visit and purpose; see Margaret Gowing, *Britain and Atomic Energy, 1939–1945* (London: Macmillan, 1964), 248.

10. James Glanz, "Of Physics, Friendship and Nazi Germany's Atomic Bomb Efforts," *New York Times*, March 21, 2000; David C. Cassidy, "Germany and the Atomic Bomb: New Evidence," *Scientific American*, February 1993: 120; see Strobel, "Absence of A-Bomb," *U.S. News and World Report*.

11. Ray Furlong, "Hitler 'Tested Small Atom Bomb,'" *BBC News*, Berlin, http://news.bbc.co.uk/go/pr/fr/-/2/hi/europe/4348497.stm; Rainer Karlsch, *Hitler's Bombe: die geheime Geschichte der deutschen Kernwaffenversuche* (Munchen: Deutsche Verlags-Anstalt, 2005).

12. Newhouse, *War and Peace in the Nuclear Age*, 9; Bundy, *Danger and Survival*, 23.

13. The Peierls-Frisch Memorandum is in Cantelon et al., *The American Atom*, 11–15; Gowing, *Britain and Atomic Energy, 1939–1945*, 42; Bundy, *Danger and Survival*, 223–25; Newhouse, *War and Peace in the Nuclear Age*, 17–18.

14. Ibid.

15. Ibid.

16. Newhouse, *War and Peace in the Nuclear Age*, 18–20.

17. Ibid.

18. Part I of the Maud Report is in Cantelon et al., *The American Atom*, 16–20; Bundy, *Danger and Survival*, 27–29.

19. Kevles quoted in Bundy, *Danger and Survival*, 30.

20. Richard G. Hewlett and Oscar E. Anderson Jr., *The New World, 1939–1946, Vol. I: A History of the United States Atomic Energy Commission* (University Park, PA: Pennsylvania State University Press, 1962), 17; Spencer Weart and Gertrude Weiss Szilard, eds., *Leo Szilard: His Version of the Facts: Selected Recollections and Correspondence* (Cambridge, MA: MIT Press, 1978), 82–84, 94–96.

21. Richard Rhodes, *The Making of the Atomic Bomb* (New York: Random House, 1986), 338, 362; James B. Conant, *My Several Lives* (New York: Harper & Row, 1970), 277; Newhouse, *War and Peace in the Nuclear Age*, 22–23.

22. Newhouse, *War and Peace in the Nuclear Age*, 23.

23. Ibid., 24–25.

24. Smith, *Doomsday Men*, 305; Garry Wills, *Bomb Power: The Modern Presidency and the National Security State* (New York: Penguin, 2010), 14–15.

25. Smith, *Doomsday Men*, 307–8; Stephen M. Younger, *The Bomb: A New History* (New York: Harper-Collins, 2009), 22–24.

26. Quoted in Smith, *Doomsday Men*, 307–8.

27. Ibid.

28. Rabi, quoted in Smith, *Doomsday Men*, 310–11.

29. Newhouse, *War and Peace in the Nuclear Age*, 41.

30. Ibid.

31. Sadao Asada, "The Shock of the Atomic Bomb and Japan's Decision to Surrender: A Reconsideration," *Pacific Historical Review* 67 (November 1998): 475–512; Rhodes, *The Making of the Atomic Bomb*, 617.

32. Greg Herken, *The Winning Weapon: The Atomic Bomb in the Cold War, 1945–1950* (New York: Knopf, 1980), 15–16; Wilson D. Miscamble, *From Roosevelt to Truman: Potsdam, Hiroshima, and the Cold War* (New York: Cambridge University Press, 2007), 28, 127.

33. Herken, *The Winning Weapon*, 15, 17, 21; Miscamble, *From Roosevelt to Truman*, 195.

34. Richard B. Frank, *Downfall: The End of the Imperial Japanese Empire* (New York: Random House, 1999), 337–34, assesses potential U.S. casualties during an invasion of Japan; Joseph M. Siracusa, *Nuclear Weapons: A Very Short Introduction* (Oxford, UK: Oxford University Press, 2008), 22; Gary R. Hess, *The United States at War, 1941–1945*, 2nd ed. (Wheeling, IL: Harlan Davidson, 2000), 78–83.

35. For the full impact of the two bombs, see *Hiroshima and Nagasaki: The Physical, Medical, and Social Effects of the Atomic Bombings*, trans. by Eisei Ishikawa and David L. Swain (New York: Basic Books, 1981); Paul Boyer, *By the Bomb's Early Light: American Thought and Culture at the Dawn of the Atomic Age* (New York: Pantheon, 1985), especially 3–26.

36. Ibid.

37. Lilienthal, quoted in Andrew J. Rotter, *Hiroshima: The World's Bomb* (New York: Oxford University Press, 2008), 147.

38. Rotter, *Hiroshima*, 220; see Michael Kort, *The Columbia Guide to Hiroshima and the Bomb* (New York: Columbia University Press, 2007).

39. Ibid.

40. David Holloway, *Stalin and the Bomb: The Soviet Union and Atomic Energy, 1939–1956* (New Haven, CT: Yale University Press, 1994), 53–54.

41. A more extensive list, with brief biographies, may be found in Holloway, *Stalin and the Bomb*, 447–52.

42. Ibid., 58, 76–79; Martin Zuberi, "Stalin and the Bomb," *Strategic Analysis* 23, no. 7 (October 1999).

43. Stephen M. Younger, *The Bomb: A New History* (New York: HarperCollins, 2009), 33; Zhores A. Medvedev, "Stalin and the Atomic Bomb," trans. by Tony Simpson (1999), 50–54, http://www.spokesmanbooks.com/Spokesman/PDF/medvedev.pdf.

44. For Soviet organization structure, see Holloway, *Stalin and the Bomb*, 86–88; Medvedev, "Stalin and the Atomic Bomb," 54–56.

45. Holloway, *Stalin and the Bomb*, 59–63; Medvedev, "Stalin and the Atomic Bomb," 56–57.

46. Quotes in Holloway, *Stalin and the Bomb*, 102–3, 107–8.

47. Newhouse, *War and Peace in the Nuclear Age*, 33–34.

48. Holloway, *Stalin and the Bomb*, 108–15.

Chapter Two

The Cold War

PART A: THE NUCLEAR ARMS RACE AND NSC 68

Throughout the late 1940s, Soviet actions tended to confirm the Truman administration's worst fears. Two events in 1949, however, greatly shaped the direction of the U.S. defense effort: the revelation that the Kremlin had exploded its first atomic bomb on August 29, and the Chinese Communists' completion of its conquest of the mainland in October. On April 7, 1950, President Harry Truman received from the National Security Council a report entitled "United States Objectives and Programs for National Security." It suggested four possible courses of action open to the United States: (a) continuation of current policies, with current and projected programs for carrying out these policies; (b) isolation; (c) "preventive" war; or (d) a rapid build-up of political, economic, and military strength in the free world. [1]

On January 31, 1950, several months after America's atomic monopoly had been broken, and in line with the president's decision to determine the technical feasibility of a thermonuclear weapon, Harry S. Truman had directed Secretary of State Dean Acheson and Secretary of Defense Louis Johnson "to undertake a re-examination of our objectives in peace and war and of the effect of these objectives on strategic plans, in the light of the probable fission bomb capability and possible thermonuclear capability of the Soviet Union." Moreover, the terms of reference continued: "It must be considered whether a decision to proceed with a program directed toward feasibility prejudges the more fundamental decision (a) as to whether, in the event that a test of a thermonuclear weapon proves successful, such weapons should be stockpiled, or (b) if stockpiled, the conditions under which they might be used in war." Truman, acutely sensitive to the potential pressure to produce and stockpile such weapons in the event that tests proved affirmative, regarded the question of "use policy" in the broadest possible terms. Specifically, the president noted, "the question of our policy can be adequately assessed only as a part of a general re-examination of this country's strategic plans and its objectives in peace and war," a position that also took into consideration the incipient arms race with the USSR as well as related social, psychological, and political questions.[2] No one could doubt the gravity of the exercise. "The outcome," concluded Truman, "would have a crucial bearing on the further question as to whether there should be revision in the nature of agreements, including the international control of atomic energy, which we have been seeking to reach with the USSR." The final joint State–Defense report, "United States Objectives and Programs for National Security," was submitted to the president on April 7, 1950.[3] Thus was born Policy Paper Number 68 of the National Security Council—NSC 68.

Implementation of NSC 68

Contrary to the view that President Truman and the National Security Council officially "approved" the document for implementation in April 1950, NSC 68 had as yet a long road to travel. Comments on the draft were requested from atomic physicists Chester Barnard, Henry Smyth, J. Robert Oppenheimer, James B. Conant, Ernest Lawrence, and Under Secretary of State Robert Lovett. Only Oppenheimer and Conant raised serious objections to the draft. While he accepted the need for an increased defense effort, Oppenheimer called for a shift away from "complete dependence on the atomic bomb" and expressed concern at the high level of government secrecy regarding technical information. He also exhibited concern at the unanswered questions regarding the stockpiling and control of nuclear weapons, and the projected motives of the Soviet Union, questioning if it actually was such a clear distinction between "jet black and pure white." James Conant, president of Harvard University, believed that the United States had set its sights "much too high," arguing instead for some kind of accommodation with the Soviet Union and its satellites. He also called for greater emphasis on land forces and tactical air power rather than strategic air power. Paul H. Nitze, director of the States Department Policy and Planning staff, considered Oppenheimer and Conant's concerns as "peripheral issues," particularly Conant's "unrealistic" suggestion to put one million troops indefinitely in Europe so as to avoid reliance on atomic weapons.[4]

Louis Johnson, newly appointed secretary of defense, presented a difficult obstacle. The president was determined to hold down the defense budget at $12.5 billion. The ambitious Johnson had been appointed with that brief and he considered its fulfillment to be his means of obtaining the Democratic presidential nomination when Truman stepped down. Nitze recalled that Johnson had objected to the review all along, "probably because he knew that such a review would undermine his credibility by exposing critical deficiencies in our military posture." While the secretary of state had been appraised daily on the group's work, the secretary of defense claimed in a meeting on March 22 that he had only just received the report and refused to participate in the meeting, claiming to be the victim of a State Department conspiracy. Later, however, Johnson saw little option but to add his approval to the report after recognizing that most of the Pentagon and many of the physicists backed Nitze. As Nitze recollected, "Johnson may have suffered from numerous defects of character, but he knew when he was beaten; in this instance he tried to make the best of the situation by adding his approval to the report and by recommending that Mr. Truman accept it."[5]

State Department representatives most concerned with securing congressional support of the broad analysis contained in NSC 68 had initially hoped, in the words of one representative, to make "public a large part of it, taking it out of the Top Secret category, and making it general knowledge." As Nitze put it, it was an essential issue to make a vetted version of the report available to the public "because it was perfectly clear that you weren't going to get even a seventeen or eighteen or twenty billion dollar appropriation and the kind of a program which could be financed thereby, unless you made available to the public at least the substance [in the paper] . . . and we couldn't get the President's approval of that." Truman chose to retain sole responsibility for any disclosure of the document. The president has requested, noted the executive secretary of the NSC, "that this report be handled with special security precautions . . . [and] that no publicity be given to this report or its contents without his approval." In retrospect, Truman's decision to keep the entirety of NSC 68 from Congress was probably a mistake. Nitze estimated that only a single paragraph in NSC 68—the American intelligence community's crude four-year projection of the Soviet Union's fission bomb production capability—fell into the category of "secret information"; and, even here, Oppenheimer believed it was "not a cardinal one percent."[6]

While Truman did not disagree with the intellectual framework of the report, he was concerned with the fiscal issues. The budgetary implications of NSC 68 were deliberately unclear. Five days later, therefore, when Truman passed the unsigned report on to the NSC, he wrote: "I am particularly anxious that the Council provide me with clear indication of the programs which are envisaged in the Report, including estimates of the probable costs of such programs." Acheson recalled in his memoirs, "NSC 68 lacked, as submitted, any section discussing costs. This was not an oversight. To have attempted one would have made impossible all those concurrences and prevented any recommendation to the President." Acheson wanted to get the president and the top bureaucracy "signed-on" before he went to the Congress and the people. Including a figure around the $40 billion mark, he feared, would have dire implications for the document. Nitze, who initially wanted to include this estimated figure, recalled a warning from Acheson: "Paul, don't put any such figure into this report. It is right for you to estimate it and to tell me about it, and I will tell Mr. Truman, but the decision on the amount of money to be requested of the Congress should not be made until it has been costed out in detail."[7] In the ad hoc interagency committee designed to assess the budgetary implications of NSC 68, representatives from the Bureau of Budget and Council of Economic Advisors seriously attacked the document. A deadlock was forming and it appeared that NSC 68 would not survive. It was only the North Korean invasion of South Korea on June 25, 1950, with Soviet complicity, that ultimately solved the problem of how best to sell NSC 68. It is probably safe to conclude along with Herbert Feis that without the communist attack, the proposed rearmament program would have been defeated by its opponents.[8]

As noted, it was not until September 30, 1950, that the president and the National Security Council actually adopted "the Conclusions of NSC 68 as a statement of policy to be followed over the next four or five years." It was also agreed at that time that the implementing programs would be put into effect as rapidly as possible, with the understanding that the specific nature and estimated costs of these programs were to be decided as they were more firmly developed. During the next several months the NSC staff, with the assistance of the relevant departments and agencies participating in the NSC 68 project, revised an earlier action paper that had been prepared in September but had been deferred for further study. On December 14, 1950, with Truman presiding, the National Security Council together with the secretaries of the Treasury and of Commerce, the Economic Cooperation Administrator, the director of the Bureau of Budget, and the chairman of the Council of Economic Advisers approved the final draft (NSC 68/4) "as a working guide for the urgent purpose of making an immediate start." And, again, Truman evidenced special caution with regard to the manner with which the report was to be handled.[9]

Briefly, "United States Objectives and Programs for National Security," or NSC 68/4, began with the assumption that "the invasion of the Republic of Korea by the North Korean Communists imparted (yet) a new urgency to the appraisal of the nature, timing, and scope of programs required to attain the objectives outlined in NSC 68." Furthermore, the substantial intervention of Mao's "volunteers" in late November "had created a new crisis and a situation of great danger"; consequently, "our military build-up must be rapid because the period of greatest danger is directly before us." The several programs described in NSC 68/4 were conceived as mutually dependent. In agreement with the underlying concept of NSC 68, they represented an effort to achieve, under the shield of a military build-up, an integrated political, economic, and psychological offensive designed to counter the current threat to the national security posed by the Soviet Union. Among the report's numerous directives, none loomed larger than accelerating the nation's military build-up. "It is evident," underscored the document, "that the forces envisaged earlier for 1954 must be provided as an interim program as rapidly as practicable with a target date of no later than June 30, 1952." Other goals dealt, inter alia, with such matters as civilian defense, stockpiling of strategic and critical materials, the uses of psychological warfare, intelligence activities, and internal security. In this way, then, and at an estimated cost of hundreds of billions of dollars—projections reaching "a peak annual rate of 70 billion dollars during the second half of the Fiscal Year 1952, or about 25 per cent of total national output"—the implementation of the conclusions reached in NSC 68 was soon to be realized. [10]

In summary, the basic American strategic position taken toward the USSR in NSC 68 in 1950 had, with minor modifications, remained relatively unchanged from that taken in late 1948 in the wake of the Berlin crisis. The only appreciable, though most dramatic, change in those years—if the NSC 20 Series may serve as a guide—was the Truman administration's shift in its perception of the Soviet acquisition of the atomic bomb, which, with its presumed first-strike character, led to the decision to pursue further the feasibility of a thermonuclear bomb, though no one knew for certain what it would cost. This much was certain: for the second time within ten years, the scientific community had received a blank check, this time based on the justification found in NSC 68, which had always been Nitze's brief. Equally significant, the available evidence indicates that the case for the direct relationship between the recommendations contained in NSC 68 and the final U.S. commitment to the UN police action in Korea was, at best, tenuous. The views of policymakers such as Truman, General Omar N. Bradley, chairman of the Joint Chiefs of Staff, and Admiral Forrest P. Sherman, chief of naval operations, as to the origin of the decision to draw the line against perceived communist imperialism make it probable that Korea was an opportunity in search of a policy, rather than the other way around.

Building Up

Over the course of the Cold War political officials frequently justified the construction of thousands of nuclear warheads and their delivery vehicles in order to "negotiate from strength," to build up, before building down. But rarely was it mentioned just what would be negotiated: would it be the contested political, economic, or territorial issues at the heart of the Cold War? Or were the superpowers, as Mikhail Gorbachev later concluded, "mesmerized by ideological myths"? When negotiations occurred, they rarely sought to define the Cold War's fundamental differences; instead, they focused on the strategic weaponry itself. All American nuclear weapons strategists, at least until the late 1960s, held as self-evident that the United States must possess a superior military prowess over the Soviet Union. Likewise, Soviet leaders of its military-industrial complex, Andrei Grechko and Dmitry Ustinov, persistently and vigorously resisted efforts to restrict the expansion of Soviet military strength, opposed any attempt to limit the nation's strategic missiles, and strove for parity if not superiority. As arsenals and delivery systems expanded, military chiefs of both superpowers worried about the other's first strike or preventive capability. "Thus, each side feared the other's strategy and believed that a preemptive option was essential for nuclear planning," as William Burr posited for the National Security Archive, "even if it was difficult to implement successfully and highly dangerous, for example, the risk of a false warning leading to an accidental and horrific nuclear exchange." Nuclear warheads and delivery systems became disconnected from the political and economic dimensions separating the two superpowers. These weapons of mass destruction had taken on a life of their own in each country as their scientific-military-industrial bureaucracies pressed for the development and production of newer weapons. In the process, was each nation actually increasing its security, or had they somewhere along this road, as early critic Ralph Lapp wrote, lost their way and became "guided by the compass of technology" without consideration of its consequences?[11]

Whether the bomb has been a force for peace is still frequently debated. Even seventy-plus years after the beginning of the Cold War—including the twenty-five years plus after its demise—there is still no unanimity on how important nuclear weapons have been in keeping the peace. For the forty-five years of the Cold War, or what historian John Lewis Gaddis referred to as "the long peace," there was not an outbreak of direct, major conflict between the major powers, an unprecedented accomplishment.[12] But how much of that peace was due to nuclear weapons and how much despite them? Political scientist John Mueller stirred controversy in 1988 by suggesting that nuclear weapons were "essentially irrelevant" to keeping the peace, that even without these new, devastating weapons, a major war had simply become too costly for any rational power to enter into.[13] It is an argument that goes against the grain of most thinking on the Cold War. Superpower statesmen certainly believed that nuclear weapons were, indeed, relevant and that they fundamentally altered their adversaries' policies and decisions. As more and more documents and records become available in international archives, the conclusion that the bomb had profoundly affected the course of international history over the past seven to eight decades is inescapable.

As historian John Lewis Gaddis put it, "Prior to that moment, improvements in weaponry had, with very few exceptions, increased the costs of fighting wars without reducing the propensity to do so."[14] Marc Trachtenberg has written that "the nuclear revolution was like a great earthquake, setting off a series of shock waves, that gradually worked their way through the world political system."[15] Conversely, Michael Mandelbaum has argued that although nuclear weapons were revolutionary in several important respects and had significant effects on political behavior, "they have not produced a revolutionary change in the international system" and had "not produced a political revolution comparable to the technical revolution they represent." As such, like many of the major issues concerning nuclear weapons, the debate about whether nuclear weapons have helped or hindered the cause of peace remains unresolved. One American diplomat who dealt with nuclear technology and weapons, Gerald C. Smith, offered a definite opinion: "Myth, misconception and plain ignorance have often influenced U.S. policy" and surely its adversaries as well. "We have avoided nuclear cataclysm as much through providence as through wise or well-informed policy."[16]

Initially, several nations possessed rudimentary knowledge of the theoretical basis of an atomic bomb, but only the United States with Britain's scientific assistance poured the resources into the quest for technology to develop the atomic bomb. After the devastation at Hiroshima, the "race" for more efficient nuclear weapons began in earnest, and during the next four decades that contest was primarily between the United States and the Soviet Union as the two technologically driven superpowers constructed enormous nuclear arsenals during their Cold War. A corresponding and equally significant "race" involved the development and refinement of delivery systems, first long-range bombers and then ballistic missiles—the latter greatly increased the reach and potential destructiveness of nuclear weaponry. Consequently, any nation seeking to use nuclear weapons as a serious lever in international politics found its influence substantially governed by the means it had available to deliver them. During various stages of the nuclear era, aircraft, land- and sea-based ballistic missiles, and other generally discounted means—suitcases, trucks, merchant ships, etc.—became factors of equal concern with the nuclear weaponry itself. Aircraft carrying nuclear bombs—between take-off and reaching their targets—initially provided an opportunity for a lengthy warning of their impending delivery. As told in such dramatic episodes as *Dr. Strangelove* and *Fail-Safe*, the fictious adversaries had ample time to consider political and military alternatives. The advent of the intercontinental ballistic missiles (ICBMs) and submarine-launched ballistic missiles (SLBMs) allowed no such luxury. These weapons drastically reduced the time between launch, actual or suspected, and delivery of nuclear warheads required leaders to respond quickly, within minutes of warning.

Ultimately, retaliatory nuclear forces were expected to be ready to "launch on warning," thus greatly increasing the possibility that erroneous information from one's warning system might cause an unintended nuclear exchange. Indeed, the race to create more sophisticated missiles and components soon engaged as much or more political concern than the cargo they carried. Even before long-range guided ballistic missiles became partnered to nuclear cargoes, both superpowers were pressing to devise countermeasures. The quest for antiballistic missile systems, confronted as it has been with serious technical challenges, found many supporters and perhaps even more critics. As the various races for more effective nuclear weapons, ballistic missiles, and antiballistic missiles appeared to threaten the stability of the Cold War's environment, the superpowers and other nations simultaneously began looking for political (arms control) measures to lessen the prospects of an unintended holocaust. This process, which began in the 1960s, gradually took on increasing importance and even managed to result in the reduction of, and restrictions on, certain nuclear weaponry and delivery systems in the final years of the Cold War.

In his farewell address to the American people, delivered on January 17, 1961, President Eisenhower noted the conjunction of an immense military establishment and large arms industry, each in itself necessary, was new in the American experience. Recognizing the imperative need of basing American security on possession of the latest scientific and military technology, he warned his fellow citizens that they must not fail to comprehend its grave implication. Specifically, he went on, "In the councils of government, we must guard against the acquisition of unwarranted influence whether sought or unsought, by the military-industrial complex. The potential for the disastrous rise of misplaced power exists and will persist." In the circumstances, the president concluded, "only an alert and knowledgeable citizenry can compel the proper meshing of the huge industrial and military machinery of defense with our peaceful methods and goals, so that security and liberty may prosper together." He also wanted to mention their congressional allies but chose not to do so, out of a sense of political propriety. As a citizen-soldier, and because of his long experience in both the army and the presidency, Eisenhower knew firsthand the invidious connection between industrialists and bureaucrats in their domination of the American defense establishment. He himself presided over the growth of America's nuclear arsenal from a thousand warheads in 1953 to more than eighteen thousand when he left. His message was clear; his remedy, less so.

Eisenhower's warning about the potential of the military-industrial complex has surely come to pass. The waste produced by the American defense establishment—not to mention the Soviet/Russian defense establishment, and the others—has amounted to a policy of national profligacy. Taking just one example, from 1940 to 1996, according to the Brookings Institution's *Atomic Audit*, the United States spent almost $5.5 trillion (in constant 1996 dollars) on nuclear weapons and weapons-related programs. This was 29 percent of all military spending from 1940 (beginning with the Manhattan Project) through 1996 ($18.7 trillion). Put another way, this figure exceeded all other categories of government spending except non-nuclear national defense ($13.2 trillion) and social security ($7.9 trillion) amounting to almost 11 percent of all government expenditures through 1996. During this period, American administrations spent on average nearly $98 billion a year developing and maintaining nuclear capabilities. Yet there was another dimension to these costs. Most of this spending was done in secret, encompassing the use of untraceable and unreported budgets, and costing in the vicinity of some $3.4 billion. Indeed, "the nuclear secrecy system," according to the authors of *Atomic Audit*, "has had adverse implications for informed congressional and public debate over nuclear policy, constitutional guarantees, government accountability, and civilian control over the military." The result of this unprecedented secrecy, professor Janet Farrell Brodie argues, contributed greatly to the emerging security state as "the U.S. civilian society became increasingly militarized during the Cold War." Eisenhower was well to worry.[17]

The Soviet Union's nuclear (and foreign) policies were largely driven by its gigantic military-industrial complex. Dmitry Ustinov, the brilliant technocrat who oversaw the moving and rebuilding of Soviet industries during World War II, was "a tireless leader of the Soviet military-industrial complex." He and the minister of defense, Andrei Grechko, were persuaded beyond peradventure that Moscow faced another world war and they were determined that the USSR would emerge victorious. Soviet leader Brezhnev also believed in negotiating from a position of strength. Professor Vladislav Zubok writes that these two men pursued an "unrelenting arms race," and under Brezhnev's leadership, by the mid-1970s, total defense-related expenses, especially for missiles, grew at an alarming rate with a detrimental impact on the Soviet standard of living. Mikhail Gorbachev complained that he was unaware of "the true scale of the militarization of the country" until after he became general secretary. Initially informed that military expenditures comprised 16 percent of the nation's budget, he soon learned that it was around 40 percent and that of the 25 billion rubles marked for science, the military took 20 billion for technical research and development. The state's emphasis on centralization, secrecy, and the military-industrial complex had destabilized the Soviet economy.[18]

PART B: REAGAN, GORBACHEV, AND THE END OF THE COLD WAR

Most strategists assumed that the Cold War, in large measure shaped by the nuclear bomb, would be resolved in a string of mushroom clouds. That this critical period ended without such a clash was due in large measure to the efforts of American president Ronald Reagan and Soviet leader Mikhail Gorbachev in spurring the process to reduce nuclear arsenals. These two charismatic leaders, who differed in so many ways, were an oddly matched pair who sought to lessen the prospects of a nuclear war. Reagan, the older of the two, was a convinced, outspoken anticommunist who came to the White House with little understanding of the Soviet Union and largely uniformed about the intricacies of nuclear weaponry. Without intellectual or analytical pretensions, his fear that these destructive weapons might be used would lead him to urge the development and deployment of a questionable missile defense system, and seek a halt to building nuclear weaponry. Gorbachev, a dedicated communist bent on domestic reform, provided the imaginative leadership that redirected Moscow's relations with the West even while it led to the collapse of the Soviet Union. Overriding the opposition in the Politburo, professor Robert English has recorded, Gorbachev sincerely believed "that he could end the Cold War solely by cutting weapons and halting the arms race." Both men put great stock in personal contact and their ability to persuade others of their programs. Gorbachev felt that his initial face-to-face meeting with Reagan would break the deadlock on arms limitation; when it did not, he would upset the Cold War hawks on both sides by offering extensive Soviet concessions. He gained the Nobel Peace Prize in 1990 for his role in ending the Cold War. [19]

Leaving Washington hours after his presidency ended in March 1989, Reagan declared flatly: "The Cold War is over." Weeks ahead of most policymakers, and decades ahead of those who continued to act as though a Cold War still existed, the American public first grasped the possibility of the Cold War's demise after hearing Gorbachev's December 1988 speech at the United Nations. Public opinion polls revealed that 60-odd percent of Americans now believed the Soviets were essentially focused on their own security, and only 28 percent thought they were still seeking world domination. Frances Fitzgerald summed it up best: "Gorbachev launched a political revolution in the Soviet Union. Few in Washington understood what he was doing or where he was going, and the Cold War was over before the American policy establishment knew it." "I know of *no one* in or out of government," onetime chief of the Central Intelligence Agency Robert Gates wrote in his memoirs, "who predicted early in 1989 that before the next presidential election Eastern Europe would be free, Germany would be unified in NATO, and the Soviet Union an artefact of history." Ambassador Jack F. Matlock Jr., Reagan's former expert on Soviet affairs, has argued that individuals who give the American president full credit for ending the Cold War do so "out of a sense of partisanship." And, one might add, those who extend total credit to Gorbachev fall into the same trap. How to apportion the credit is still in the hands of the historical jury, yet it may be possible to reach an interim judgment. [20]

Reagan, Gorbachev, and Their Views on Nuclear Arms

In his initial press conference on January 29, 1981, President Reagan declared, "I know of no leader of the Soviet Union . . . including the present leadership" who have denied that "their goal must be the promotion of world revolution and a one-world Socialist or Communist state." And since these leaders "have openly and publicly declared that the only morality they recognize is what will further their cause" and "reserve unto themselves the right to commit any crime, to lie, to cheat" to gain that goal, thus, when you "do business with them . . . keep that in mind." This fierce anticommunism drive would see the administration's frequently irrational military build-up, virtually tripling the U.S. national debt from $907.7 billion in 1980 to $3,233 billion in 1990. Yet, at the same time, Reagan's strong conviction that communism was inherently immoral and evil was matched by his fascination with the dramatic biblical story of "Armageddon"—the world's final struggle between good and evil. The Armageddon story that Reagan envisioned as a nuclear holocaust never reconciled him to the necessity or possibility of nuclear war; indeed, he declared often "a nuclear war can never be won, and must never be fought." It was prudent, he contended, to seek means to avert or mitigate such a possibility by the elimination of nuclear weaponry. "The purpose of a negotiation is to get an agreement," the president once declared, yet he found it difficult to even marginally compromise his missile defense or "Star Wars" program that was, at best, very far in the future.

This rigidity, together with his administration's staunch adherence to the institutionalized precepts of the Cold War, prevented the formulation of realistic policies to substantially reduce strategic nuclear weapons—aside from intermediate missiles—during his presidency. Significant reductions would begin with his successors. Reagan did shift away from his initial diplomatically inconsiderate and provocative anti-Soviet rhetoric during his second term, especially after meeting Gorbachev. In his final years in the White House, Reagan came to think of Mikhail Gorbachev as a friend and proclaimed a "new era" in American-Soviet relations. Reagan had changed, according to his biographer Lou Cannon, "even though he did not recognize any ideological odyssey." "It became a cruel irony of fate that President Reagan's desire to banish the nuclear specter on the one hand opened up the prospect for nuclear disarmament," Raymond Garthoff has rightly observed, "while foreclosing it with the other through stubborn dedication to the quixotic pursuit of his SDI illusion."[21]

Nevertheless, former Pentagon official Richard Perle, and most Cold War hawks for that matter, attributed the passing of the Cold War to U.S. nuclear and conventional military superiority that compelled the Soviet leadership "to choose a less bellicose, less menacing approach to international politics. . . . We're witnessing the rewards of the Reagan policy of firmness." To

Harvard historian Richard Pipes, Ronald Reagan was the champion of those who believed the Soviet Union was "a totalitarian state driven by a militant ideology and hence intrinsically expansionist." No less than for hardliners generally, it was the "policy of containment, reinforced by a technological arms race, economic denial, and psychological warfare, that brought down the Soviet Union and communism." Pipes's assault on those who favored a more modest response to Soviet behavior, however, ignored the close relationship between official public condemnation and silence in the absence of affordable policy choices. Reagan clung to his conviction, much to the dismay of skeptical neoconservatives, that the Soviet leader's efforts at domestic reform and international cooperation were genuine. Moreover, he willingly met and negotiated with the Soviet leader. By continuing to negotiate with Gorbachev in spite of the abusive criticism of so many supporters, Michael Beschloss placed Reagan in his pantheon of courageous presidents. [22]

Gorbachev represented a new Soviet generation, especially by his embracing of intellectuals who espoused a "new thinking" regarding foreign affairs. Since he was not burdened by the horrific experiences of the Great Patriotic War, it was easier for him to put aside the "old thinking" steeped in the Stalinist concept of a hostile capitalist encirclement and the prospect of a final, apocalyptic conflict with the imperialist nations. He could thus greatly expand on Nikita Khrushchev's program of "peaceful coexistence." Although often not recognized in Washington, Gorbachev's selection as general secretary in March 1985 was a close run affair. It was much aided by the fortuitous death three months earlier of longtime Defense Minister Dmitri Ustinov, a hawkish conservative and staunch supporter of the armed forces. Powerful reactionary forces, if they had gained power, could have instituted repressive policies to deal with dissent at home, heightened confrontational ones abroad, and, in spite of the severe economic problems, readily prolonged the Cold War for at least a few more decades. However, while making no secret of his desire for reforms, Gorbachev withheld his radical ideas to end the confrontation with the West and was elected by a disorganized majority of conservatives. During 1986, Gorbachev met frequently with foreign leaders and their representatives seeking to deflate their fears of the Soviet Union, and through these discussions he came to understand "the other world" and to formulate his bold foreign initiatives. [23]

The deadly nuclear reactor explosion and fire at Chernobyl in the Ukraine on April 26, 1986, causing the worst nuclear catastrophe since Hiroshima and Nagasaki, had a severe emotional and political impact on Gorbachev and his associates. Shocked by the devastation, embarrassed by the international scandal, and indignant at the bureaucratic rigidities, Gorbachev placed the blame on the Soviet military-industrial complex. Not only had this event revealed the inefficiency and corruption of the Stalinist system and the hardliners' efforts to cover up such events, it graphically demonstrated the damage nuclear weapons could cause. The spread of radiation killed 8,000 men and women, as well as affecting the health of an additional 435,000 people and the future-held casualties still to be counted. Not since the Cuban missile crisis had Soviet political leaders been so shaken by an event. Chernobyl's impact rattled Soviet military scientists and military commanders as the notion of "victory" in a nuclear conflict now rang hollow. Marshal Sergei Akhromeyev recalled that after Chernobyl the prospect of a nuclear conflict "for our people ceased to be abstraction. It became a palpable reality." The thousands of deaths and devastation of the surrounding countryside prompted Gorbachev to declare: "We learned what nuclear war can be." Instead of continuing to wait for more conciliatory leadership in the United States, he committed himself to resolving the contemporary nuclear limitation impasse. The reduction, if not the elimination, of the nuclear arsenals—and thus sharply cutting back the bloated Soviet military-industrial budget—was for Gorbachev not only the way to end the Cold War, but equally important to a solution of his country's serious internal economic problems.[24] Unlike Stalin, Khrushchev, and Brezhnev, who were closely involved with the military-industrial complex and grasped the "nuts and bolts" of Soviet military force, Gorbachev confronted nuclear issues only when he became the general secretary and, by tradition, head of the Defense Council.

Furthermore, Professor Vladislav Zukok has noted, as late as 1987, Gorbachev apparently showed little "interest in or knowledge of missile technology." Even so, he had long questioned the Soviet-Western reliance on nuclear deterrence, both because it rationalized limitless expenditures on weapons and because it legitimized nuclear war should deterrence fail. He understood, moreover, that the USSR could never achieve nuclear supremacy over the United States and that an intensified arms race, based on scientific and technological advances, would demand greater human and material resources than the Soviet Union possessed. The United States and the Soviet Union had reached an effective strategic parity of power in the 1970s, giving them the means to destroy each other many times over. In pursuing its continued arms build-up, Gorbachev observed, the United States gained nothing; the Soviet Union retained sufficient strength to destroy it in war. As a result, the international nuclear environment had become both dangerous and irrational. The Americans and Soviets, therefore, had no choice but to eliminate their competition in arms and live in peace. He insisted, therefore, that Moscow needed to engage the Reagan administration in meaningful discussions to end the arms race and reduce the threat of a nuclear holocaust. As his foreign minister, Eduard Shevardnadze, recalled, "The point at issue was to stop the arms race. It was true that the Americans were ahead of us on some weapons. But there was no stopping them unless we signed an agreement." And, according to a close observer, Gorbachev had "already decided, come what may, to end the arms race. He's taking this gamble because [he believes that] nobody is going to attack us even if we disarm completely."[25]

Geneva, Reykjavik, and Washington Summits

Shortly after Gorbachev arrived at the Kremlin he sought to engage Reagan in negotiating nuclear arms reductions; however, the president and his advisers were slow to respond. This delay stemmed, in part, from the fact Reagan had never endorsed any previous arms limitation treaty. He opposed the 1963 Test Ban pact, the 1968 Non-Proliferation Treaty, and the 1972 SALT I and ABM agreements; criticized the Helsinki Accords; and denounced SALT II as "fatally flawed." Additionally, during in his first term in office, he terminated negotiations for a comprehensive test ban treaty. Unfortunately, Reagan's "allergy to detail" contributed to his inability on several occasions to grasp the basics of nuclear arms issues. He shocked congressional leaders with the revelation in the fall of 1983 that he had not understood that most of the Soviet's nuclear-tipped intercontinental ballistic missiles were land-based. Only later did he understand why Moscow labeled as "non-negotiable" his 1982 proposal to reduce all land-based missiles by one-half. Then, too, Reagan had to acknowledge that he "forgot" America's long-range bombers and cruise missiles carried nuclear warheads.[26]

Yet, Reagan's opposition to earlier arms limitation pacts, ignorance of factual data, or anticommunist rhetoric never really denied his ultimate intention to seek improved relations with the Soviet Union. In his inaugural speech, he recognized the American concern for peace. "We will negotiate for it, sacrifice for it," he told the nation, but "we will not surrender for it, now or ever." Embracing the need for dealing from strength, building up to build down, as it were, Reagan assured his critics that his expanding and modernizing U.S. forces were aimed at producing successful negotiations with the Kremlin. Although whether the president even then lacked the power to negotiate from strength was doubtful, this emphasis on building more military forces clashed with the public's growing fear that nuclear weapons had become a serious global threat. Pressure from antinuclear protesters in NATO countries and the nuclear freeze movement at home forced Reagan, in late 1981, to review the ongoing intermediate nuclear forces (INF) negotiations. The INF discussions had been prompted by a NATO decision, late in Carter's administration, to deploy 108 Pershing II and 464 ground-launched cruise missiles (GLCMs) to West Germany, Belgium, Britain, the Netherlands, and Italy in order to offset the Soviet's new SS-20s. The solid-fueled, mobile SS-20s were a significant improvement over the aging SS-4 and SS-5s as they carried three warheads a longer distance and with greater precision. The Reagan administration opened INF discussions with the Soviets as early as the fall of 1981, but made no progress. Then, on November 18, in an address before the National Press Club in Washington, the president offered the zero sum option of canceling "deployment of Pershing II and ground-launch cruise missiles if the Soviets [would] dismantle their SS-20, SS-4, SS-5 missiles." In March 1982, the NATO defense ministers reaffirmed the plan to deploy the U.S. cruise and Pershing II missiles in Europe, beginning in 1983. They still faced the task of persuading their antinuclear publics that Europe's security required the new missiles. Schmidt favored the emplacement of theater weapons if the arms talks stalled, but, he argued, there "might have been fewer demonstrations in Europe if there had been less loose talk out of the United States, telling the Europeans we were not living in a post-war period but in a pre-war period. That had a psychologically devastating effect."[27]

Meanwhile, in May 1982, Reagan finally outlined his plan for the long promised Strategic Arms Reduction Treaty (START), which he insisted would bring about "practical phased reduction" of strategic nuclear weapons in two stages. In Phase I, warheads would be reduced by a third, with significant cuts in ballistic missiles, followed by Phase II where a ceiling would be put on ballistic missile throw-weights and other elements. While the American public response was enthusiastic, analysts who examined the proposal found, as with the "zero option," that it was so one-sided, it was nonnegotiable. Phase I would require the Soviets to substantially reduce their land-based ICBMs—their most effective strategic weapons—while the United States would retain most of its land-based Minutemen and could proceed with its planned emplacement of a hundred new, large MX missiles in similar silos. In addition, the United States could deploy its cruise missiles and modernize its submarine and bomber fleets. During Phase II, the Soviets would be required to reduce by almost two-thirds the aggregate throw-weight of their missiles, while the United States offered no cuts at all. "This proposal is so stacked against the Soviets," the sponsor of the House's nuclear freeze resolution, Congressman Edward J. Markey, complained, "there is little chance they will accept it." Not surprisingly, Moscow ignored Washington's proposal and negotiations on strategic weaponry staggered along as predicted.[28]

To the Geneva Summit

Before the end of 1982, strategic arms reduction talks had opened in Geneva only to be side-tracked by Reagan's dramatic proposal, on March 23, 1983, for a Strategic Defense Initiative (SDI) to provide a space-based defense against incoming missiles. Soviet leaders, conscious of their country's economic and technological inferiority, feared further U.S. pressures on the weakening Soviet system, but they were not prepared for the president's unprecedented technological challenge. If SDI could neutralize all nuclear-armed ballistic missiles aimed at U.S. targets, it would also neutralize the deterrent effect of Soviet nuclear forces. Reagan's "Star Wars" program may well have failed to impress many U.S. military leaders and most of its scientists; however, it created consternation in Moscow.[29] Yuri Andropov, the Soviet leader since November 1982, was troubled by the Soviet Union's inability to compete with the United States at the higher levels of technology. He therefore viewed SDI as a program to bury the ABM treaty of 1972, Moscow's only means to limit the ever-widening security and technology gap with the West. In a *Pravda* interview of March 27, Andropov charged that Reagan's space-based missile defense would unleash an arms race in offensive and defensive weapons. "Engaging in this is not just irresponsible, it is insane," he said. "Washington's actions are putting the entire world in jeopardy." As the strategic arms limitation talks in Geneva stalled, states of Western Europe carried out their threat to accept U.S. Pershing II and cruise missiles. The Kremlin responded by breaking off both the INF and the START negotiations. In the absence of agreement, the number of missiles in Europe began to mount.[30]

Finally, Secretary of State George Shultz's lengthy conversations with Soviet foreign minister Andrei Gromyko in Geneva, on January 7–8, 1985, committed both powers to strive for greater cooperation. Their formula included a comprehensive three-talk process, one for long-range missiles and bombers, one for mid-range missiles, and one for space and defensive weapons. In Washington, the vast changes in the Soviet Union's world position registered slowly and divisively. In large measure, the problem of recognition lay in the widespread supposition that Gorbachev was too ubiquitous, cunning, and appealing to be trusted. Still, during the late summer and autumn of 1985, both Washington and Europe's capitals had no choice but to shift their attention from continuing a stalemate on arms limitation to the forthcoming Geneva Conference, scheduled for late November. As Gorbachev marched toward the summit amid televised press conferences and meetings with world leaders, U.S. officials, even as they declared Soviet proposals old and unacceptable, acknowledged Gorbachev's success in establishing the Soviet positions as moderate and reasonable. Reagan tried to put the Soviets on the defensive by adding regional conflicts to the summit agenda. Despite the maneuvering, the propaganda, and the struggle for advantage, the European press predicted smiles but meager results.[31]

Outside Geneva's Chateau Fleur d'Eau, on a wintry November 19, a coatless Ronald Reagan awaited the approaching Mikhail Gorbachev. The president, as the official host on this opening day of the Geneva Summit, had set the stage for his first meeting with the Soviet leader with great care. He led Gorbachev and their two interpreters to a small meeting room for a private conversation. The people in the neighboring conference room, Reagan began, had given them fifteen minutes "to meet in this one-on-one. . . .

They've programmed us—they've written your talking points, they're writing my talking points. We can do that, or we can stay here as long as we want and get to know each other." The private conversation lasted one hour. During a break in the afternoon session, Reagan steered Gorbachev to the chateau's summer house for a continuing tête-á-tête. The summit itself, the first in six years, was essentially a media event as it achieved little substantive progress. What concerned Gorbachev was Reagan's known attachment to the expensive and technologically sophisticated SDI program. He argued that the 1972 Antiballistic Missile Treaty permitted the two states one land-based defense system.[32]

In broadening the American defense capability, however, SDI challenged the effectiveness of the Soviet nuclear deterrent. Gorbachev concluded that the Soviets could compete only by building additional offensive weapons; for his part, Reagan refused to accept any arrangement that would deny the United States the right to defend itself from nuclear attack. At the end the two leaders achieved little, yet both regarded the summit a success. Separated by twenty years, they recognized in each other a warmth and sincerity that promised future success. Reagan observed that Gorbachev scarcely resembled his predecessors in his intelligence, knowledge, and openness. The new Soviet foreign minister, Eduard Shevardnadze, noted, "We had the impression that [the president] is a man who keeps his word and that he's someone you can deal with . . . and reach accord." The failure to obtain agreement on SDI produced no recriminations. In explaining the U.S. position to the Supreme Soviet, Gorbachev used only moderate language. The two leaders agreed to meet in Washington in 1987 and in Moscow during 1988. Not since the Nixon-Brezhnev summits of 1972 and 1973 did Soviet-American relations appear more hopeful.[33]

At the Reykjavik Summit

If the predictable damage of nuclear war decreed that it could not be won, the same was not true for the propaganda war over its elimination. For Moscow and Washington, the arms debate continued to revolve around Euro-missiles and the Strategic Defense Initiative. The Soviets, always looking for a way to drive a wedge between Washington and its NATO allies, still hoped to reverse their failure to block the deployment of Pershing II and cruise missiles in Europe. Reagan, promising Americans and Europeans alike an impenetrable fortress in the sky, continued to proclaim his support for SDI against Soviet complaints that Washington was actually attempting to regain offensive supremacy. Gorbachev, recognizing Europe's nuclear anxiety, put forward new arms proposals while Pentagon officials, reading the fine print, rejected them. *New York Times* writer James Reston, who favored Shultz's plea for quiet diplomacy to break the deadlock, noted the preference for "ideological confrontation and warrior diplomacy . . . at the Pentagon and the White House." Columnist Andrew J. Glass feared that the Reagan administration would never succeed in assuring the Soviets of its goodwill. "The national security apparatus in the White House," he observed, "remains thoroughly fractionated. With so many hawks and pseudo-hawks flapping about in the Reagan aviary, it will muster all the administration's ability in diplomatic falconry merely to fashion a cogent response to the latest Soviet initiative." Europeans who favored negotiations found hope in the prospect that Reagan, unlike many of his Pentagon advisers, favored an arms agreement as the one means still available to him for reducing international tension. Meanwhile, as Gorbachev swept the European polls as a man of peace, he pleaded with Reagan to meet with him for a day or two in Iceland or London.[34]

In late August 1986, Reagan announced that the United States would not exceed the limits imposed by the 1979 SALT II treaty, paving the way for a summit with Gorbachev at Reykjavik, Iceland, on October 11–12. Secretary Shultz and national security adviser Admiral John Poindexter, who had guided Reagan's extensive preparations for the Geneva meeting, downplayed the significance of the forthcoming meeting, convinced that there would be no new initiatives. Believing that the Soviets would be talking from "our script," Shultz urged the president to "convince Gorbachev of the wisdom of our step-by-step approach." In preparing for the meeting, however, Gorbachev explained to his aides that "our goal is to prevent the next round of [the] arms race. . . . And if we do not compromise on some questions, even very important ones, we will lose the main point: we will be pulled into an arms race beyond our power, and we will lose this race, for we are presently at the limit of our capabilities." Rejecting the underlying basis of existing strategic weapons treaties, SALT I and II, "the leitmotif here is the liquidation of nuclear weapons, and the political approach prevails here, not the arithmetical one." Gorbachev came to the meeting hoping to obtain the comprehensive nuclear test ban, seeking to prevent Reagan's SDI program from developing space weapons using nuclear explosions, and eliminating intermediate-range nuclear weapons from Europe. This brief meeting, which one writer called "the most bizarre summit in the history of the Cold War," saw a "startling and far-reaching exploration of the possibilities for the drastic reduction or even elimination of nuclear weapons."[35]

Unexpectedly, Gorbachev and Chief of the Soviet General Staff Marshal Sergey Akhromeyev opened the meeting with a series of significant concessions. They offered a 50 percent reduction in strategic weapons, including their own heavy missiles, to remove French and British forces from the proposed INF treaty cuts, to exclude U.S. short-range forward based systems from the list of strategic weapons, to consider Reagan's proposed 7.5-year non-withdrawal from the ABM treaty, and withdrew their demand for a ban on SDI research, asking instead that testing be restricted to laboratories. Caught up in each other's enthusiasm for a nuclear-free world, Reagan and Gorbachev, as well as their key negotiators, moved toward the elimination of all nuclear weapons from their arsenals. In their last session, Reagan and Gorbachev tentatively agreed to reduce 50 percent of their strategic offensive weapons, not just missiles, within five years and "to eliminate all nuclear explosive devices, including bombs, battlefield systems, cruise missiles, submarine weapons, and intermediate-range systems, by 1996." The deal, however, collapsed as Reagan's devotion to his SDI program would not permit him to accept any restrictions or adjustments, a promise he presumably had made to the American people.

When the president offered to share SDI technology with the Kremlin, a disappointed Gorbachev responded sharply, "You won't even share milking machines. For the U.S. to give the products of high technology would be a second American Revolution, and it would not happen." The fact that the discussions were not translated into action resulted in a sharply divided assessment of the summit's outcome, with some individuals seeing it as "a spectacular missed opportunity" and others viewing it as "a perilous near disaster." Western and Soviet military strategists were shaken by news of the near-agreement aimed at eliminating nuclear weapons and equally thankful it had failed. Although major participants viewed the meeting outcome differently, both leaders agreed that their frank talks had set the stage for moving forward toward arms limitation and potentially the end of the Cold War. Gorbachev wrote in his memoirs that Reykjavik had shaken "the foundations on which the post-war world was built," while Reagan remarked that "the progress that we made would've been inconceivable just a few months ago." Substantive progress on arms limitation would take considerably more time.[36]

Reviewing the conversations, one is left with the impression that Reagan had confused his priorities. He had long spoken of a desire to eliminate "nuclear weapons," but when this opportunity loomed, he clung to his Strategic Defense Initiative. It is not clear whether Reagan understood the extent to which most components of the U.S. missile defense systems were still on the drawing board or largely untested prototypes. What is certain is that he had no evidence that any of the systems would work and, if they should, when they might be available for deployment. "Frankly I have no idea what the nature of such a defense might be," he wrote in a private letter a few months after announcing his plan. "I simply asked our scientists to explore the possibility of developing such a defense." Earlier he acknowledged to reporters that it might be "20 years down the road" before a workable missile defense system arrived. Faced with such uncertainty, he might have been expected to compromise and satisfy his frequently stated desired to rid the planet of the nuclear threat. He did not.[37]

The Washington Summit / INF Treaty

Aside from being an international media show, the Washington summit in December 1987 finally focused on arms limitation with the signing of the Intermediate Nuclear Forces (INF) treaty. It had its origins in the so-called "zero option" proposal that asked the Soviets to remove all of their SS-20s based in Europe, and the West would not deploy their scheduled weapons. This June 1981 proposal, according to long-time arms control agency official Thomas Graham, "was devised by Assistant Secretary of Defense Richard Perle and was intended to be unacceptable." In an April 1987 meeting, acting with the Politburo's endorsement, Gorbachev and Shevardnadze surprised Secretary of State Schultz by announcing that the Kremlin now accepted Reagan's "zero option" relating to intermediate-range ballistic missiles. They also added that Moscow would reduce its force of SS-23 short-range missiles. Surprised American officials accepted the offer and agreed with the Soviets to work out the technical features of a formal treaty. Although Gorbachev still fumed about the United States' missile defense activities, SDI would no longer hinder progress. Soviet nuclear physicist Andrei Sakharov had undertaken to gradually persuade Gorbachev that Reagan's antimissile systems could never stop a full-scale attack with ICBMs carrying decoys and multiple warheads. He argued that SDI should not stand in the way of reducing offensive nuclear weapons, because it was a kind of "Maginot line in space," a line that could not defeat concentrated missile attacks any more than the French Maginot defense line stopped the German blitzkrieg in 1940.[38]

Just as Moscow's SS-20s could target Western Europe, NATO's intermediate-range missiles had very short flight time to targets in the Soviet Union. These weapons were most threatening because they could readily spur escalation from any local hostile use of these nuclear-armed missiles to a general nuclear war. As such, they were perceived as most threatening by the Soviet leadership and the Soviet military. There was a significant opposition among the military of both nations to include the shorter-range weapons; the Soviets were most outspoken at what they viewed as a hasty squandering of assets. Nevertheless, under the final terms of the INF Treaty, the Soviet Union and the United States would remove and destroy, under supervision, all of their intermediate-range (1,000–5,500 kilometers) missiles and shorter-range (500–1,000 kilometers) missiles.

The treaty's remarkably extensive and intrusive inspection and monitoring arrangements were based on the "any time and place" proposal of March 1987. Gorbachev's acceptance of such verification caught Washington by surprise and unprepared, even though earlier U.S. arms limitation proposals had insisted on it. Cold War hawks in the past always counted on Moscow's rejection of on-site inspection demands to kill any arms limitation offer, but now the Pentagon, National Security Agency, and CIA had to consider the price of verification. The dual implications of on-site inspections had these officials bristling at the thought of Soviet inspectors prowling U.S. defense plants, nuclear-armed submarines, and missile sites. As Secretary of Defense Frank Carlucci admitted, "Verification has proven to be more complex than we thought it would be. The flip side of the coin is its application to us. The more we think about it, the more difficult it becomes." At every meeting with Soviet leaders, Reagan had repeated the Russian proverb "trust but verify." Now, however, the United States willingly accepted less intrusive procedures. Nonetheless, the INF's on-site inspection regime lasted for thirteen years, during which time the United States would conduct over 511 inspections in Russia, and Russia would conduct 275 similar inspections in the United States. The new Soviet position on verification not only removed the hurdle that long had seemed insurmountable but, according to the U.S. ambassador to Moscow Jack Matlock, became a symbol of the new trust developing in U.S.-Soviet relations, which made the treaty and further progress on arms control possible. Robert Gates of the CIA placed responsibility for making the INF treaty possible where it was due: "thanks almost entirely to continuing concessions from Gorbachev."[39]

The Washington summit of December 1987 was itself another Reagan-Gorbachev triumph. Gorbachev arrived, Secretary Shultz recounts, "upbeat, positive, animated, and eager." He was concerned about the criticism that Reagan was receiving from hardliners, but Shultz reassured Gorbachev that "the vast majority of Americans support what President Reagan is doing." The Soviet leader need not have worried, for he and his wife were so enthusiastically greeted in the normally blasé capital that it prompted *Washington Post* columnist Tom Shales to observe that the city was seized by "Gorby fever." Shortly after arriving in Washington, the Gorbachevs met with a wide-ranging group of celebrities that included Billy Graham, Henry Kissinger, and Yoko Ono. The signing of the INF treaty occurred on December 8, with an exchange of pens and a brisk handshake. "For the first time in history," Reagan declared, "the language of 'arms control' was replaced by 'arms reduction' in this case, the complete elimination of an entire class of U.S. and Soviet nuclear missiles." For his part, Gorbachev responded that this treaty "offers a big chance at last to get onto the road leading away from the threat of catastrophe. It is our duty . . . to move forward toward a nuclear-free world . . . [that is] without fear and without a senseless waste of resources on weapons of destruction." Although only some 4 percent of the superpowers' nuclear arsenal would be eliminated by the INF pact, it did initiate the process of arms reductions.[40]

False Nuclear Attack Warnings

A continuing downside to modern technology that could not easily be re-solved was the real-life "close call" missile-related incidents that took place during the Cold War. The 1962 missile crisis, of course, immediately comes to mind as a most dangerous event. Yet, until the arrival of Michael Dobbs's *One Minute to Midnight: Kennedy, Khrushchev, and Castro on the Brink of Nuclear War* (2008), the truly close calls during October were generally not fully appreciated. Two decades later, in the fall of 1983, a combination of events occurred that Steven Zaloga has argued "came close to activating the Soviet strategic forces and starting a nuclear war." In the weeks after Sep-tember 1, when a Soviet fighter shot down a South Korean airliner that had strayed into Soviet airspace, killing 269 people, superpower relations were nearly as tense as any time during the Cold War. President Ronald Reagan's earlier "evil empire" speech and subsequent harsh denunciation of the KAL incident may have appeased domestic feelings, but these remarks only fur-ther exacerbated an already hostile political climate. In the midst of the controversy, a Soviet early warning satellite on September 26 mistook sun-light glinting off clouds over a Montana missile site and reported, three times, the launch of perhaps five U.S. ICBMs. Given the past problems with the satellite and reasoning that a U.S. first strike would involve many more missiles, Lt. Colonel Stanislav Petrov, the duty officer at the early warning center, checked ground radar and other information before concluding the satellite's reports were false. He decided not to pass on the warning, which could have put Soviet strategic nuclear forces on full alert "with dangerous and unpredictable consequences." Petrov was later condemned for his lack of action and forced into retirement. The danger, however, was not over. A high-level NATO military command exercise, Able Archer 83, planned for early November to test the release and use of nuclear weapons worried Mos-cow's senior political leaders. Given the political climate, Soviet intelligence officers tracking the event worried that it might be a cover for the long-feared nuclear first strike and ordered KGB agents to report any signs that might pertain to a nuclear attack. Moscow was on a strategic intelligence alert. When made aware of the fears in high Soviet circles, neither British nor American officials could believe Soviet leaders actually thought the West would launch a first strike.[41]

American early warning systems, the National Security Archive reported in 2012, produced a number of false alerts in 1979–1980. President Jimmy Carter's national security adviser, Zbigniew Brzezinski, was awakened at 3 a.m. on November 9, 1979, by the North American Aerospace Defense Com-mand (NORAD)—a combined U.S.–Canada military operation—that warned of an approaching Soviet missile attack. Just as Brzezinski prepared to call the president, NORAD called off its alert. The apparent cause of the false alarm? The routine testing of an overworked computer system. Other false warnings of approaching Soviet missiles sent to the Pentagon and military commands by NORAD's computers during these two years resulted from computer tests and worn-out computer chips. Commenting on the Brzezinski incident, senior State Department adviser Marshal Shulman wrote that "false alerts of this kind are not a rare occurrence" and that there is a "complacency about handling them that disturbs me." Understandably disturbed by these events, Soviet general secretary Leonid Brezhnev secretly complained to Carter that these erroneous warnings and false alerts were "fraught with a tremendous danger." Further, "I think you will agree with me that there should be no errors in such matters."

Secretary of Defense Harold Brown told the president that "human safeguards"—people reading data produced by warning systems—ensured that there would be "no chance that any irretrievable actions would be taken." Another serious episode, which one analyst called "the most dangerous moment of the nuclear missile age," occurred on January 25, 1995, when Russian radars in Latvia and Lithuania located a large missile somewhere over the North Sea. Its trajectory appeared to be on an identical flight path, Geoffrey Forden wrote, "as a U.S. Trident missile would take to mask a massive U.S. nuclear first strike by knocking out Russian detection systems with a high-altitude nuclear airburst." The Russian early warning radar system prompted the duty general at the General Staff headquarters to activate the strategic command and control network and notify the officers responsible for President Boris Yeltsin's Cheget briefcase. While Yeltsin was meeting with Defense Minister Pavel Garchev, the operators of the early warning system determined that the missile was not headed over Russia and ended the alert. It turned out that Norwegian scientists had launched the rocket to study the aurora borealis and had notified Russian authorities, but they apparently had failed to inform officers in their command-and-control network.[42]

These American and Russian incidents involved potentially dangerous consequences since officials in Washington and Moscow have always feared preemptive nuclear strikes. To counter such a threat, both nations' strategic nuclear-armed missile forces had established a launch-on-warning posture. Presidents Bill Clinton and Yeltsin, seeking to avoid future dangerous incidents or accidents, agreed to create a Joint Data Exchange Center in 1998 that would share early warning information. Soviet officers were given access to the U.S. early warning system in late 1999 due to fears that a Y2K computer glitch might occur on January 1, 2000. Although a permanent center was to be established later, the agreement was terminated when George W. Bush decided to abrogate the ABM treaty.[43]

From "Launch on Warning" to Doomsday Machine

Building nuclear weapons proved to be easier than the unanticipated and often underappreciated issue of managing their use. As aircraft-carrying nuclear bombs were gradually married to nuclear-tipped ICBMs and SLBMs, the delivery time between take-off or launch was drastically reduced, placing a heavy burden on strategic command, control, and communications (C3) systems. While the age of nuclear bomb carrying aircraft adversaries had sufficient time to contemplate political and military alternatives, ballistic missiles eliminated this luxury. Launching quickly, within minutes of warning, greatly increased the possibility that erroneous information from one's warning system might cause an unintended catastrophic nuclear exchange. "Despite the enormous investment in these [command, control, and communications] programs," Bruce Blair, John Pike, and Stephen Schwartz wrote of U.S. C3 efforts in *Atomic Audit*, "the systems to control the use of nuclear weapons have always been vulnerable to attack, set on a hair trigger, susceptible to false alarms, and dependent on dubious measures of control such as predelegating nuclear launch authority to military officials other than the president." Yet the circumstances of the Cold War presented a launch on warning option as a logical policy. Though, as Director of the Center for Defense Information Bruce Blair suggests, troublesome questions arise from the fact that both the United States and Russia have in the past, and still do, maintained such a dangerous hair-trigger alert posture.[44]

In May 2000, presidential candidate George W. Bush reflected Blair and other critics' concerns about the United States' launch on warning policy. "The United States should remove as many weapons as possible from high-alert, hair-trigger status," he declared. The ability to quickly "launch within minutes of warning" was an "unnecessary vestige of cold-war confrontation." The quick-launch policy was not only outdated, but it was dangerous: "Keeping so many weapons on high alert may create unacceptable risks of accidental or unauthorized launch." Once in the White House, however, he never mentioned this concern again. Much to the dismay of critics, the retaliatory nuclear forces of both superpowers readied their "launch on warning" option during much of the Cold War, even allowing it to persist after its demise.[45]

Although recognized as a potentially dangerous posture, the "launch on warning" policy grew largely out of strategic necessity. "Throughout the Cold War," reported *Atomic Audit*, "highly classified studies showed that a surprise attack by a small fraction of the Soviet [nuclear] arsenal could decapitate the U.S. command system and destroy the communication links used to send the go-code (formally known as emergency action messages, or EAMs) to retaliatory forces. . . . The top political leaders, the senior military commanders, their fixed and mobile command posts, and their communications links were all acutely vulnerable to sudden destruction by a few tens of Soviet weapons." To meet this threat, U.S. planners at first focused on pre-emptive nuclear strikes on Soviet targets, but preemption relied on an early warning whose availability was doubtful. With the introduction of ballistic missiles, political leaders came to prefer a strategy of deterrence and believed that it was greatly enhanced with the availability of a second-strike retaliatory threat. But military strategists recoiled at the idea of absorbing a Soviet first strike before launching their retaliatory forces. William Burr of the National Security Archive writes that by the late 1950s and early 1960s, "strategic planners recognized that if tactical warning information was available, there was another position that was just short of preemption but avoided 'retaliation after ride-out.'" Once the U.S. Ballistic Missile Early Warning System (BMEWS) radars were installed, White House adviser professor Jerome Wiesner suggested in mid-1959, they could be able to provide the "[warning] time necessary to ready our missiles so they can be fired before they are destroyed." When the BMEWS became operational in the early 1960s it provided command officials a fifteen-minute warning of an impending ICBM attack. By the early 1970s the prospect of a launch on warning option improved significantly with the deployment of the Missile Defense Alert System (MIDAS), later redesignated the Defense Support Program (DSP).[46]

Because of the option's complexity and sensitivity, the history of Washington's launch on warning policies remains highly classified. Indeed, it has not been revealed when nuclear planners made launch on warning a specific option, although documents obtained by the National Security Archive confirm "that a specialized launch-on-warning option entered into the Single Integrated Operational Plan, the U.S. nuclear war plan, in 1979." Moreover, it is not evident how long the high-alert strategic forces posture and a launch on warning option will continue since the president cannot unilaterally change it. The 1996 defense authorization legislation specifically denies the White House the authority "to de-alert the missile force." Although DSP satellites have been frequently augmented and enhanced, Schwartz and his coauthors have noted that from its inception, "launch on warning was a dangerous option from the standpoint of safety, and its feasibility was questionable in the event of a Soviet attack spearheaded by submarines patrolling off the American coasts. . . . [It] was . . . no panacea for the problem of command vulnerability. Under the best conditions, a president would have had only three or four minutes to get briefed and reach a retaliatory decision before Washington disintegrated. The danger of inadvertent war caused by false warning was as great as the risk that retaliation could not be authorized in time during an actual attack."[47]

End of the Cold War

The subsequent unraveling of the Soviet empire was an unintended side effect of Gorbachev's effort at reform—termination of the Cold War was not. Reagan deserves some credit for recognizing Gorbachev's sincerity and determination to significantly alter earlier Soviet foreign policies. For this, Reagan felt the wrath of anticommunist hawks for "doing business" with a communist leader. It was Gorbachev, however, who recognized that both of the superpowers had become "mesmerized by ideological myths," which ruled out any meaningful discussions of possible political accommodation for more than four decades. Even the long-time Soviet ambassador to Washington, Anatoly Dobrynin, acknowledged in his memoirs that Moscow's Cold War policies were "unreasonably dominated by ideology, and [that] this produced continued confrontation." Gorbachev broke the Cold War's ideological straitjacket that had paralyzed Moscow and Washington's ability to resolve their nuclear differences and, in doing so, faced greater political, even physical, risks. Considering all of this, it would be difficult to avoid the conclusion that without Gorbachev, the end of the Cold War could have played out much differently and very dangerously.[48]

With the end of the Cold War the nuclear arms race also virtually halted, but not the actual threat deriving from nuclear weaponry. The global concern with nuclear non-proliferation that took on a formal guise in the 1970s treaty was viewed with a renewed urgency in the twenty-first century. Once again the question is posed: Does the spread of nuclear weapons (and missiles) make the world safer or more dangerous? In regional rivalries such as the subcontinent, East Asia, and the Middle East, the bomb still has influence—great influence. Kenneth Waltz maintains, for example, that nuclear weapons preserve an "imperfect peace" on the subcontinent between India and Pakistan. Responding to reports that all Pentagon war games involving India and Pakistan always end in a nuclear exchange, Waltz argues: "Has everyone in that building forgotten that deterrence works precisely because nuclear states fear that conventional military engagements may escalate to the nuclear level, and therefore they draw back from the brink?"[49]

Whatever else one has to say—and not much has been left unsaid about the nuclear strategy of the past seventy-plus years—nuclear status still imparts extraordinary prestige and power. The threat of terrorists with a nuclear capability has given rise to new global concerns. The risk of nuclear weapons or fissile materials falling into the wrong hands seems greater since the terrorist attack on the United States on September 11, 2001. The smuggling of highly enriched uranium that could be used for a nuclear instrument of destruction has subsequently prompted great concern. In particular, there has been an ongoing concern pertaining to Russia's nuclear weapons or materials falling into the hands of terrorists. According to Graham Allison, "Thousands of weapons and tens of thousands of potential weapons (softball-size lumps of highly enriched uranium and plutonium) remain today in unsecured storage facilities in Russia, vulnerable to theft by determined criminals who could then sell them to terrorists." In the years since the end of the Cold War, there have been numerous cases of theft of nuclear materials in which the thieves were captured, sometimes in Russia, on other occasions in the Czech Republic, Germany, and elsewhere.[50] How effective are the methods employed to limit terrorist access to nuclear materials? How effective have the Cooperative Threat Reduction Program, Global Threat Reduction Initiative, and the Nuclear Suppliers Group been to this end? Prominent world leaders have suggested putting the genie back in the bottle—but is it possible? In this sense, then, our historical account may not provide an answer to every question or even to the basic question of whether nuclear weapons helped or hindered the search for stability during the Cold War. Yet as Bernard Brodie suggested in his *War and Peace*, we hope it may sharpen one's "receptivity to appropriate insights about these problems."[51]

According to his biographer, famed diplomat George F. Kennan had never heard of the Albert Einstein Peace Prize when he received a phone call on March 9, 1981, informing him that he had become the second recipient of the award—the first recipient was Alva Myrdal, Sweden's former minister for disarmament—and the $50,000 check that went along with it. The ceremony took place in May before members of the new Reagan administration as well as veteran Soviet ambassador to the United States, Anatoly Dobrynin. Long concerned with the nuclear question "How much is enough?" Kennan likened American and Soviet leaders to "men in a dream, like lemmings headed for the sea, like the children of Hamlin marching blindly behind their Pied Piper." Beginning with the assumption that American and Soviet arsenals were "fantastically redundant to the purpose in question"—deterrence—he urged "an immediate across-the-board reduction by 50 percent of the nuclear arsenals now being maintained by the two superpowers; a reduction affecting in equal measure all forms of the weapon, strategic, medium-range, and tactical, as well as their means of delivery." While Kennan's advice was ignored, the problem was, of course, not new. President Dwight D. Eisenhower, perpetually confronted with his own doubts and worries about underwriting America's technical superiority in the atomic age, was among the first to articulate the problem, informing his advisers that "we are piling up these armaments because we don't know what else to do to provide for our security." By the time Eisenhower left office, there were already more weapons than conceivable targets. Democratic senator George McGovern of South Dakota put it in plain language: "How many times is it necessary to kill a man or a nation?"[52]

A sample of statistics from the global nuclear age provides a sobering reminder of the scale of the problem. Upward of 128,000 nuclear weapons have been produced in the past seventy-plus years, of which about 93 percent are still "housed" by the United States and the former Soviet Union. The nine current members of the nuclear club—the United States, Russia, the United Kingdom, France, China, India, Pakistan, Israel, and North Korea—still possess 15,000-plus operational nuclear weapons between them, a thousand of which are ready to fire at moment's notice, enough to destroy the Earth's inhabitants many times over. At least another fifteen states currently have on hand enough highly enriched uranium for a nuclear weapon. In light of the failure of major players to act on the Comprehensive Test Ban Treaty, or on the treaty to cut off production of nuclear weapons material in recent years, is it any wonder that, in January 2017, the iconic Doomsday Clock of the *Bulletin of Atomic Scientists* has been set to two and a half minutes? As stated,

> Over the course of 2016, the global security landscape darkened as the international community failed to come effectively to grips with humanity's most pressing existential threats, nuclear weapons and climate change. . . . This already-threatening world situation was the backdrop for a rise in strident nationalism worldwide in 2016, including in a US presidential campaign during which the eventual victor, Donald Trump, made disturbing comments about the use and proliferation of nuclear weapons and expressed disbelief in the overwhelming scientific consense on climate change. For the last two years, the minute hand of the Doomsday Clock stayed set at three minutes before the hour, the closest it had been to midnight since the early 1980s. . . . In 2017, we find the danger to be even greater, the need for action more urgent. It is two and a half minutes to midnight, the Clock is ticking, global danger looms. Wise public officials should act immediately, guiding humanity away from the brink. If they do not, wise citizens must step forward and lead the way.[53]

NOTES

1. NSC 68, A Report to the National Security Council, "United States Objectives and Programs for National Security," April 14, 1950, 3, President's Secretary's File (PSF), Papers of Harry S. Truman, Harry S. Truman Library, Independence, Missouri (hereafter cited as NSC 68). See Harry S. Truman, *The Memoirs of Harry S. Truman: Years of Trial and Hope 1946–1953*, 2 vols. (New York: Doubleday, 1956), II: 326; "Report by the Special Committee of the National Security Council to the President," January 31, 1950, U.S. Department of State, *Foreign Relations of the United States: 1950*, Washington, DC: GPO, 1977, 513–23, hereafter cited as *FRUS*; David Holloway, *Stalin and the Bomb: The Soviet Union and Atomic Energy, 1939–1956* (New Haven, CT: Yale University Press, 1994), 196–223. Elements of this chapter have been adapted from Professor Siracusa's study (with Richard Dean Burns) *A Global History of the Nuclear Arms Race: Weapons, Strategy, and Politics*, 2 vols. (Santa Barbara, CA: Praeger, 2013).

2. The "Terms of the Reference" were framed by Nitze. Interview with Paul H. Nitze, Center for National Security Research, Arlington, Virginia, April 29, 1977. See "Memorandum by the Director of the Policy Planning Staff (Nitze) to the Secretary of State," January 17, 1950, *FRUS: 1950*, I: 13–17.

3. NSC 68/1. Minutes of the 55th Meeting of the National Security Council, PSF, Papers of Harry S. Truman, Truman Library.

4. Daniel Yergin, *Shattered Peace: The Origins of the Cold War and the National Security States* (Boston: Houghton Mifflin, 1977), 403; "Record of the Meeting of the State-Defense Policy Review Group," *FRUS: 1950*, I: 162–82; Nitze, "The Development of NSC 68," 176.

5. Paul H. Nitze, *From Hiroshima to Glasnost, at the Center of Decision: A Memoir* (New York: Grove/Atlantic), 91, 95.

6. Princeton Seminar, October 11, 1953; note by the executive secretary, James S. Lay Jr., to the National Security Council, April 14, 1950 (attached to NSC 68); NSC 68, 19; interview with Paul H. Nitze, April 29, 1977; exchange between Oppenheimer and Nitze, see Princeton Seminar, October 11, 1953.

7. "The President to the Executive Secretary of the National Security Council," *FRUS: 1950*, I: 235; Dean Acheson, *Present at the Creation* (Princeton, NJ: W. W. Norton, 1987), 374; Nitze, *From Hiroshima to Glasnost*, 96.

8. NSC 8/1, A Report to the National Security Council. "The Position of the United States with Regard to Korea," March 16, 1949, NSCF, Modern Military Records Division, National Archives. Soviet complicity is no longer in doubt; see Jonathan Haslam, "Russian Archival Revelations and Our Understanding of the Cold War," *Diplomatic History* 21 (Spring 1997): 224–25; and CWIHP, *Bulletin*, Winter 1995/1996: 6–7. For a different view, see Bruce Cumings, *The Origins of the Korean War*, vol. 2, *The Roaring of the Cataract, 1947–1950* (Princeton, NJ: Princeton University Press, 1990).

9. NSC 68/2, attached note by the Executive Secretary; NSC 68/4, note by the Executive Secretary. Since programs in NSC 68/4 were not definitive, Truman directed State and Defense "to undertake immediately a joint review of the politico-military strategy of their Government with a view to increasing and speeding up the programs outlined . . . as critical situation and submit to me appropriate recommendations, through the NSC, as soon as possible."

10. NSC 68/4, 1; various programs were described in NSC 68/3, A Report to the National Security Council, "United States Objectives and Programs for National Security," December 8, 1950, NSCF, Modern Military Records Division, National Archives; Samuel Huntington, *Common Defense: Strategic Program in National Politics* (New York: Columbia University Press, 1961), 54.

11. Nina Tannenwald, "Stigmatizing the Bomb: Origins of the Nuclear Taboo," *International Security* 29, no. 4 (Spring 2005): 5–49; Mikhail Gorbachev, *Perestroika: New Thinking for Our Country and the World* (New York: Harper & Row, 1987), 211; Vladislav Zubok, *A Failed Empire: The Soviet Union in the Cold War from Stalin to Gorbachev* (Chapel Hill: University of North Carolina Press, 2007), 151, 202; William Burr, "New Evidence on the Origins of Overkill," National Security Archive, *Electronic Briefing Book* No. 236 (updated October 1, 2009); Ralph E. Lapp, *Arms Beyond Doubt: The Tyranny of Weapons Technology* (New York: Cowles, 1970), 3–4.

12. John Lewis Gaddis, *The Long Peace: Inquiries into the History of the Cold War* (New York: Oxford University Press, 1987); Robert Jervis, "The Political Effects of Nuclear Weapons," *International Security* 13, no. 2 (Fall 1988): 80–90.

13. John Mueller, "The Essential Irrelevance of Nuclear Weapons: Stability in the Post-War World," *International Security* 13, no. 2 (Fall 1998): 55–79.

14. John Lewis Gaddis, *We Now Know: Rethinking Cold War History* (New York: Clarendon Press, 1997), 85.

15. Marc Trachtenberg, *History and Strategy* (Princeton, NJ: Princeton University Press, 1991), 146.

16. Michael Mandelbaum, *The Nuclear Revolution: International Politics before and after Hiroshima* (Cambridge: Cambridge University Press, 1981), 8–9; Gerald C. Smith, *Disarming Diplomat: The Memoirs of Gerald C. Smith, Arms Control Negotiator* (Lanham, MD: Madison Books, 1996), xiii.

17. Steven I. Schwartz et al., *Atomic Audit: The Cost and Consequences of U.S. Nuclear Weapons since 1940* (Washington, DC: Brookings Institution, 1998), 3, 434; Janet Farrell Brodie, "Learning Secrecy in the Early Cold War: The RAND Corporation," *Diplomatic History* 35, no. 4 (September 2011): 643.

18. Zubok, *A Failed Empire*, 205, 242–43, 277; Mikhail Gorbachev, *Memoirs* (New York: Doubleday, 1995), 215.

19. See Lou Cannon, *President Reagan: The Role of a Lifetime*, 2nd ed. (New York: Public Affairs, 2000); Robert D. English, *Russia and the Idea of the West: Gorbachev, Intellectuals & the End of the Cold War* (New York: Columbia University Press, 2000), 205.

20. France Fitzgerald, *Way Out There in the Blue: Reagan and Star Wars and the End of the Cold War* (New York: Simon & Schuster, 2000), 17–18, 466–71; Robert M. Gates, *From the Shadows: The Ultimate Insider's Story of Five Presidents and How They Won the Cold War* (New York: Simon & Schuster, 1996), 449; Jack R. Matlock Jr., *Reagan and Gorbachev: How the Cold War Ended* (New York: Random House, 2004), 323; see Director of Central Intelligence, "Soviet Policy Toward the West: The Gorbachev Challenge," NIE 11-4-89, in National Security Archive, *Electronic Briefing Book* No. 261, December 8, 2008.

21. Cannon, *President Reagan*, 241, 246–50; Cannon, "Reagan at the Crossroads Again, 1986," in *Leadership in the Reagan Presidency: Seven Intimate Perspectives*, ed. Kenneth W. Thompson (Lanham, MD: Madison Books, 1992), 125; Fred Barnes, "The Reagan Presidency: Moments," in *Leadership in the Reagan Presidency*, ed. Kenneth W. Thompson (Lanham, MD: Madison Books, 1992), 99; Raymond L. Garthoff, *The Great Transition: American-Soviet Relations and the End of the Cold War* (Washington, DC: The Brookings Institution, 1994), 524.

22. Richard Perle in Charles W. Kegley Jr., *The Long Postwar Peace* (New York: Harper Collins, 1990), 104; Richard Pipes, "Misinterpreting the Cold War: The Hardliners Had It Right," *Foreign Affairs* 74, no. 1 (1995): 154–60; Garthoff, *The Great Transition*, 524; see Michael Beschloss, *Presidential Courage: Brave Leaders and How They Changed America, 1789–1989* (New York: Simon & Schuster, 2007).

23. English, *Russia and the Idea of the West*, 196–98.

24. Vladislav M. Zubok, *A Failed Empire: The Soviet Union in the Cold War From Stalin to Gorbachev* (Chapel Hill: University of North Carolina Press, 2007), 288–89; English, *Russia and the Idea of the West*, 200, 205, 215–17.

25. Zubok, *A Failed Empire*, 283; English, *Russia and the Idea of the West*, 206.

26. Fitzgerald, *Way Out There in the Blue*, 88–96; Leslie Gelb, "The Mind of the President," *New York Times Magazine*, October 6, 1985, 21ff; Lou Cannon, "Dealings with the Soviets Raise Uncomfortable Questions," *Washington Post*, July 2, 1984, A13.

27. James Reston and Flora Lewis in the *New York Times*, November 15, 1981; Schmidt, quoted by Reston in ibid., January 3, 1982; Martin Walker, *The Cold War: A History* (New York: Henry Holt, 1993), 266–67.

28. Fitzgerald, *Way Out There in the Blue*, 153–54; Waller, *Congress and the Nuclear Freeze*, 94–97, 99; see Svetlana Savranskaya and Tom Blanton, eds., "To the Geneva Summit Perestroika and the Transformation of U.S.-Soviet Relations," National Security Archive *Electronic Briefing Book* No. 172, November 22, 2005.

29. Televised Strategic Defense Initiative speech, March 23, 1983, *Public Papers: Reagan, 1983*, I; Edward Reiss, *The Strategic Defense Initiative* (Cambridge: Cambridge University Press, 1992). For the debate over Star Wars, see John Tirman, "The Politics of Star Wars," in *The Empty Promise: The Growing Case against Star Wars*, ed. John Tirman (Boston: Beacon Press, 1986); Union of Concerned Scientists, *Empty Promise: The Growing Case Against Star Wars* (Boston: Beacon Press, 1986); Edward Tabor Linenthal, *Symbolic Defense: The Cultural Significance of the Strategic Defense Initiative* (Urbana, IL: University of Illinois Press, 1989).

30. John Newhouse, "Annals of Diplomacy: The Abolitionist—I," *The New Yorker*, January 2, 1989, 48–49; William Pfaff, *Barbarian Sentiments: How the American Century Ends* (New York: Hill & Wang, 1989), 113.

31. David Fouquet, *Christian Science Monitor*, December 13, 1984, 13, 15; George Shultz, "U.S.-Soviet Agreement on the Structure of New Arms Control Negotiations," *American Foreign Policy, Current Documents, 1985* (Washington, DC: U.S. State Department, 1986), 73; Editorial, *New York Times*, November 3, 1985, E20; *Daily Telegraph* in *World Press Review* 32, August 1985, 20; *Die Zeit* in ibid., January 3, 1986, 16.

32. Garthoff, *The Great Transition*, 234–39; Fitzgerald, *Way Out There In the Blue*, 306–13.

33. Ibid.

34. Reston in *New York Times*, April 6, 1986, E23; Andrew J. Glass in *The Daily Progress*, Charlottesville, VA, July 8, 1986, A4. European polls in 1986 consistently revealed Gorbachev's popularity. For a typical report, see Michael R. Gordon in *New York Times*, June 7, 1987, 7. Somewhat later Jimmy Carter proclaimed Gorbachev "by far the most popular person on Earth" (*Chicago Sun-Times*, April 14, 1989, 16).

35. Quotes are in Thomas Blanton and Sveltana Savranskaya, "Reykjavik: When Abolition Was Within Reach," *Arms Control Today*, October 2011, 46–51; see their "The Reykjavik File: Previously Secret Documents from U.S. and Soviet Archives on the 1986 Reagan-Gorbachev Summit," National Security Archive, *Electronic Briefing Book* No. 203, October 13, 2006.

36. Ibid., "The Reykjavik File," document 15; see Zubok, *A Failed Empire*, 293–95.

37. *Public Papers of the Presidents: Ronald Reagan, 1983*, I, 465; letter, June 20, 1983, in Kiron K. Skinner, Annelise Anderson, and Martin Anderson, eds., *Reagan: A Life in Letters* (New York: Free Press, 2003), 425. For an evaluation of SDI, see Richard Dean Burns, *The Missile Defense Systems of George W. Bush: A Critical Assessment* (Santa Barbara, CA: Praeger, 2010), esp. Chapter 2.

38. Svetlana Savranskaya and Thomas Blanton, eds., "The INF Treaty and the Washington Summit: 20 Years Later," National Security Archive *Electronic Briefing Book* No. 238, December 10, 2007; Thomas Graham Jr., *Disarmament Sketches: Three Decades of Arms Control and International Law* (Seattle: University of Washington Press, 2002), 107; Fitzgerald, *Out in the Blue*, 409–11, 412–15; Anatoly Dobrynin, *In Confidence: Moscow's Ambassador to America's Six Cold War Presidents* (Seattle: University of Washington Press, 2001), 620.

39. Zubok, *A Failed Empire*, 300–1; Newhouse, *New Yorker*, January 9, 1989, 65–66; Cannon, *President Reagan*, 694; Fitzgerald, *Way Out There in the Blue*, 444–45; Robert M. Gates, *From the Shadows: The Ultimate Insider's Story of Five Presidents and How They Won the Cold War* (New York: Simon & Schuster, 1996), 423; *Washington Post*, October 31, 1987, A1, A17; *Washington Post*, December 9, 1987, A1; Rowland Evans and Robert Novak, *Washington Post*, December 11, 1987, A27; Cannon, *President Reagan*, 695–98, Shultz, *Turmoil*, 1009–11.

40. Ibid.

41. Steven J. Zaloga, *The Kremlin's Nuclear Sword: The Rise and Fall of Russia's Strategic Nuclear Forces, 1945–2000* (Washington, DC: Smithsonian Institution Press, 2002), 200–1; Garthoff, *The Great Transition*, 138–39.

42. William Burr, ed., "Zbigniew Brzezinski Received 3 a.m. Phone Call Warning of Incoming Nuclear Attack," National Security Archive *Electronic Briefing Book* No. 371 (posted March 1, 2012); Geoffrey Forden, "Reducing a Common Danger: Improving Russia's Early Warning System," *Policy Analysis*, no. 399 (May 3, 2001); Zaloga, *The Kremlin's Nuclear Sword*, 225–28. Mention should be made of weapons-related aircraft incidents (U.S. incidents known as "Broken Arrows") that could have turned quite ugly. More than a dozen Broken Arrow incidents, from 1959 to 1980, involving U.S. aircraft carrying nuclear weapons have been described by Michael Krepon on his blog ArmsControlWonk, December 26, 2011.

43. Richard Dean Burns, *The Evolution of Arms Control: From Antiquity to the Nuclear Age* (Santa Barbara, CA: Praeger, 2009), 135.

44. Stephen I. Schwartz, ed., *Atomic Audit: The Costs and Consequences of U.S. Nuclear Weapons Since 1940* (Washington, DC: Brookings Institution Press, 1998), 198; see Chapter 3, "Targeting and Controlling the Bomb," for details of U.S. command centers; William Burr, ed., "Launch on Warning: The Development of U.S. Capabilities, 1959–1979," National Security Archive *Electronic Briefing Book*, April 2001, at http://www.gwu.edu/~nsarchiv/NSAEBB/NSAEBB43/. For Bruce Blair's writings, see his *The Logic of Accidental Nuclear War* (Washington, DC: Brookings Institution, 1993), and *Global Zero Alert for Nuclear Forces* (Washington, DC: Brookings Institution, 1995).

45. Ibid.

46. Schwartz, ed., *Atomic Audit*, 204–7; Burr, ed., "Launch on Warning." For information on the U.S. presidential nuclear "football," see Schwartz, ed., *Atomic Audit*, 222; for Soviet counterpart, see David E. Hoffman, *The Dead Hand: The Untold Story of the Cold War Arms Race and Its Dangerous Legacy* (New York: Doubleday, 2009), 149.

47. Schwartz, ed., *Atomic Audit*, 217–18.

48. Mikhail Gorbachev, *Perestroika: New Thinking for Our Country and the World* (New York: Harper & Row, 1987), 211; Dobrynin, *In Confidence*, 472.

49. Waltz, quoted in David G. Coleman and Joseph M. Siracusa, *Real-World Nuclear Deterrence: The Making of International Strategy* (Westport, CT: Praeger Security International, 2006), 108.

50. Graham Allison, *Nuclear Terrorism: The Ultimate Preventable Catastrophe* (New York: Times Books, 2004), 1.

51. Bernard Brodie, *War and Peace* (New York: Macmillan, 1973), 451.

52. John Lewis Gaddis, *George F. Kennan: An American Life* (New York: Penguin Press, 2011), 647–48; Eisenhower quote found in MemCon, January 26, 1956, *Foreign Relations of the United States, 1955–1957* (Washington DC: GPO, 1980), vol. 20, 297; and George McGovern, August 2, 1963, quoted in David Coleman, "Camelot's Nuclear Conscience," *Bulletin of the Atomic Scientists* 62, no. 3 (May/June 2006): 41.

53. Joseph M. Siracusa, *Nuclear Weapons: A Very Short Introduction*, 2nd ed. (Oxford: Oxford University Press, 2015), iii; *Bulletin of Atomic Scientist*, "It Is Two and a Half Minutes to Midnight, 2017 Doomsday Clock Statement," January 2017, http://thebulletin.org/timeline.

Chapter Three

Other UN Security Council Nuclear Weapon States

United Kingdom, France, and China

The superpower atomic duopoly did not sit well with some of the other great powers, and thus began the next phase in the quest for nuclear weaponry. If aimed, in large measure, at deterring the Soviet Union from "adventurism" in Europe, Britain and France's nuclear programs were also related to national pride. While it is often easy to overlook the driving force of the national interest, or even the national ego, perhaps it is worth considering the following statement. British Foreign Secretary Ernest Bevin, after being on the receiving end of condescending attitudes reflected by nuclear-armed American officials, declared in 1946, "I don't want any other foreign secretary of this country to be talked to or at by a secretary of state in the United States as I have just had in my discussions with Mr. Byrnes. We've got to have this thing [an atomic bomb] over here whatever it costs. We've got to have the bloody Union Jack on top of it." Frédéric Joliot-Curie in 1945 argued that "France and Britain together could 'hold the position *vis-à-vis* America' better than either one alone," anticipating French president Charles de Gaulle's subsequent belief that when Britain chose to keep its special arrangement with the United States, London chose *against* Europe. Of course, outside of such considerations, the reality was that these devices were designed to *be* deterrents, enhance national status, and to embolden each nation's international political and security interests. [1]

With the United Kingdom and France developing nuclear weapons in 1952 and 1960, respectively, the subsequent search for a negotiated, acceptable strategic stability in the 1970s and 1980s would see their independent nuclear forces inevitably create issues for Washington and, especially, Moscow. While U.S. Defense Secretary Robert McNamara sought to dissuade Britain and France from developing such forces, Soviet officials facing new nuclear states on their eastern and western border completely misread the British-American connection. They drew from the Truman-Attlee-King statement in November 1945 the conviction that an "anti-Soviet bloc" had been formed to conduct "atomic diplomacy." Thereafter, especially during the arms negotiations of the 1970s and 1980s, they consistently sought to have British and French forces counted in treaties designed to place limits on nuclear weaponry. Not surprisingly, American diplomats, exhibiting a remarkable display of hypocrisy, rejected such agreements that required the inclusion of their allies.

Communist China, politically isolated from the United States and initially aligned with the Soviet Union, sought Moscow's assistance in developing a nuclear capability. Sino-Soviet relations flourished during the years between 1953 and 1957, stimulated by Chairman Nikita Khrushchev's efforts to strengthen the alliance by providing the means for the Chinese to upgrade their own weaponry. Moscow aided in construction efforts, agreed to build 205 facilities, and sent hundreds of experts to instruct the Chinese in the use of various Soviet conventional weapons and in atomic energy. Initially, the technical nuclear information provided focused on peaceful applications, but later was expanded to include information necessary for building an atomic bomb. Mao Zedong's intense, personal dislike of Khrushchev, whom he considered boorish, inferior, and lacking in ability to lead the communist movement, contributed to bringing military cooperation—especially of the nuclear kind—to an abrupt end in 1959. Nonetheless, Mao proceeded to move forward, determined that China would have its own nuclear weapons and an effective delivery system. This pursuit for a deterrent power stemmed from what Beijing believed to be threatening behavior on the part of the United States and the Soviet Union/Russia. In response, the fear of Chinese nuclear weapons in the late 1960s and early 1970s enhanced the Johnson and Nixon administration's rationale in considering a missile defense system.[2] Overall, the period would see the remaining Security Council states, in the form of Britain, France, and China, scale the nuclear ladder—Britain tested a thermonuclear weapon in November 1957, China in June 1967, and France in August 1968—and force their way into the upper reaches of the strategic nuclear equation.

BRITAIN, FRANCE, AND THE UNITED STATES

Britain and France decided to join the nuclear club, but each adopted divergent strategies to gain American assistance that could reduce the costs and technical uncertainty in furthering their nuclear quests. London hoped to parlay their wartime role as a close ally of the United States to gain desired nuclear technology, whereas Paris chose to emphasize its independence and depend upon traditional diplomacy to demonstrate why America should assist its program. For years, nuclear issues often dominated the relations between the three governments, especially the determination shown by London and Paris to develop their own nuclear arsenal based on rationales that were as much political as strategic. "Schizophrenic" was how John Newhouse once described Washington's attitude toward these two independent programs. The United States initially did little to assist Britain and offered even less to France in their independent nuclear quests. Many in Washington during the immediate postwar years maintained the belief that providence had sanctified only the "peace-loving" American people with "the secret" to the making of atomic bombs. Congress was devoted to this idea. However, when the Soviets tested their own atomic device in August 1949, Secretary of State Dean Acheson later wrote, "A good deal of the senatorial nonsense about our priceless heritage" temporarily vanished. Within a decade, Washington came to look much more favorably upon British efforts to achieve nuclear independence, while President Charles de Gaulle's designs for nuclear force would prove to be a source of consternation.[3]

THE MULTILATERAL FORCE (MLF)

If an underlying rationale, not often stated in public, for the independent nuclear arsenals rested on national interest or international status, there was a second, perhaps more prominent argument publicly asserted in the 1950s and early 1960s—based on a suspected unreliability of the United States' total support of the Western alliance. In simple terms, fears arose in London and Paris that questioned the very dependability of the U.S. nuclear shield. "It was often presented as a simple assertion that in a cruel and uncertain world," observed Lawrence Freedman, professor of War Studies at King's College, London, "where others may get nuclear weapons and the United States' own willingness to engage in nuclear war on Europe's behalf was open to doubt, an independent British force was a necessary form of insurance." London handled the issue more diplomatically in its 1964 Statement on Defence: "If there were no power in Europe capable of inflicting unacceptable damage on a potential enemy he might be tempted . . . to attack in the mistaken belief that the United States would not act unless America herself were attacked." President Charles de Gaulle devised similar arguments when he pushed for a decision-making position within NATO and claimed that Europe's ability to deter nuclear attack rested on France's independent force alone.[4]

Meanwhile, Washington's inconsistent symptoms had become abundantly apparent in its efforts to address Europe's emerging independent nuclear forces. If the Truman administration largely ignored London's determination to construct its own atomic bomb, its successor would encounter the nuclear ambitions of not only Britain, but also France and West Germany. With NATO states resisting the expense of creating conventional forces during the 1950s, Eisenhower's New Look and the development of intermediate ballistic missiles carrying nuclear warheads led strategists to focus on nuclear weapons for the defense of Europe. In 1956, NATO commander American general Lauris Norstad suggested that Washington ought to create a nuclear weapons stockpile—short-range missiles and tactical nuclear weapons—in Europe, and that NATO should develop a ballistic missile force to counter the growing threat posed by Soviet intermediate ballistic missiles deployed in Central Europe. During 1960, the Eisenhower State Department presented an alternative to a NATO-controlled missile force. "Wary of encouraging national nuclear forces, fearful of German nuclear ambitions, and committed to European unification," McGeorge Bundy, a special assistant in the Kennedy and Johnson White Houses, noted that the State Department proposed and ardently pressed for what became known as a multilateral force (MLF). Initially, U.S. submarines, later surface ships, it was suggested, could be assigned to NATO with the prospect of multinational crews subsequently placed aboard these ships.

In the earlier stages, the incoming Kennedy administration demonstrated only a moderate interest in MLF. However, by May 1962, the president announced that "the United States will commit to the NATO command five—and subsequently still more—Polaris atomic-missile submarines, which are defensive weapons, subject to any agreed NATO guidelines on their control and use. Beyond this, we look to the possibility of eventually establishing a NATO sea-borne force, which would be truly multilateral in ownership and control." During the months following, Washington officials continued to encourage the MLF program, but insisted that the Europeans contribute support. According to Bundy, Kennedy, and later President Lyndon Johnson, eventually found that "the political leaders of Britain, France, and Germany steadily behaved in ways that frustrated" them. The British believed that plans designed for MLF would have limitations, while the French believed that the MLF would undermine their determination to become a nuclear power in their own right. Yet neither London, nor especially Paris, wanted the Germans to develop their own nuclear weapons. Chancellor Konrad Adenauer had earlier, in October 1954, unilaterally pledged that West Germany would not manufacture nuclear weapons; now West German officials declined to participate in MLF when they learned of France's determined opposition. The MLF's rocky political course aroused considerable attention, occasionally some enthusiasm, but found no lasting favor with

President Lyndon Johnson. In December 1965, he terminated the program in favor of pursuing a non-proliferation agenda.[5]

BRITAIN ATTAINS THE BOMB

It was Britain that led the way in the pursuit of a nuclear force independent of the superpowers. In 1941, the Maud Committee, a group of British scientists dedicated to fission research, estimated that they could develop an atomic bomb in two and a half years. The Churchill government decided, certainly by November 1945, that it must have its own bomb. "This I take it is already agreed," the prime minister declared unchallenged, "we should make atomic bombs." British independent efforts in the atomic energy field significantly slowed during World War II as London chose to impart its scientific findings to the United States where the bomb could be built well out of reach of Nazi bombers. British science and scientists continued to play an integral role in America's development of the atomic bomb; however, after the war, this reciprocity was not returned. Sparked by an erroneous belief there was a "secret" to the construction of an atomic bomb and fearful that Soviet spies were seeking it, American politicians refused to share atomic knowledge with other states under the Atomic Energy Act of 1946. This treatment of the British by the American public, Congress, the Joint Chiefs of Staff, and especially the head of the Atomic Energy Commission, Lewis Strauss, derived from a misunderstanding of British wartime contributions to the development of the atomic bomb. Acknowledging his ignorance of British scientific contributions, Senator Brien McMahon later told London officials, including Churchill, that had he known about it the prohibition in the McMahon Act might have been relaxed for Britain. At the time, however, the lack of appreciation was aggravated by the arrest in 1950 of physicist Klaus Fuchs, a former member of the British wartime team at Los Alamos, on charges that he stole secret atomic information for the Soviet Union.

Following the end of hostilities, work began without public notice on construction of British plants to produce fissile material. The British government, despite the McMahon Act, continued to seek a means of restoring cooperation with the United States to obtain information regarding building an atomic bomb. In January 1947, Prime Minister Clement Attlee formally, but secretly, decided it necessary to establish a military presence in this new field. Abandoning his earlier hope that international controls could govern atomic developments, Attlee rejected the isolated, dissenting argument of physicist P. M. S. Blackett that the United Kingdom abstain from building atomic weapons. The government's reasoning at the time for obtaining nuclear weapons, as described by the official British historian Margaret Gowing, apparently "had 'emerged' from a body of general assumptions." As further stated:

> It had not been a response to an immediate military threat but rather something fundamentalist and almost instinctive—a feeling that Britain must possess so climacteric a weapon in order to deter an atomically armed enemy, a feeling that Britain as a great power must acquire all major new weapons, a feeling that atomic weapons were a manifestation of the scientific and technological superiority on which Britain's strength, so deficient if measured in sheer numbers of men, must depend. A bomb would not be ready in any case for five years, so that the decision was of the variety that was impossible *not* to take rather than of the type that must be taken for urgent and immediate purposes.[6]

Essentially, most British officials believed that possessing nuclear weapons was necessary for Britain to retain its status as a world power. Prime Minister Harold Macmillan echoed this view in 1958: "The independent contribution . . . gives us a better position in the world, it gives us a better position with respect to the United States. It puts us where we ought to be, in the position of a Great Power." Interestingly, he downplayed the role of British nuclear weapons to deter the Soviet Union and, rather, emphasized their political significance. "The fact that we have it [the nuclear bomb] makes the United States pay a greater regard to our point of view, and that is of great importance." Macmillan's successor after 1962, Alec Douglas-Home, described his nation's atomic bomb as a "ticket of admission" that ensured "a place at the peace table as [a] right."[7]

As tensions increased between Washington and Moscow during 1947, the Truman administration, busily expanding its nuclear program, turned to London for assistance in two important matters. First, the U.S. program needed an additional supply of uranium from the Belgian Congo that would require the British to reduce their agreed allotment; second, Washington required London to abandon the clause in the 1943 Quebec accord that called for British approval before America could use its atomic bomb. The secret Quebec clause loomed as a significant political issue should Congress uncover it. Therefore, the president decided on a full disclosure to leading Republican senators who, incensed that U.S. bombs could be so shackled, demanded that the clause be canceled. American and British diplomats arranged a modus vivendi (the McMahon Act restricted any formal accord) that canceled the Quebec agreement, the Roosevelt-Churchill Hyde Park memorandum, and resumed cooperation on technical nuclear matters that did not include nuclear weapons. The Truman administration, John Newhouse has noted, "largely ignored both the letter and spirit of the Modus Vivendi." The depth of the cool relations between the former close allies became further apparent when the British asked Washington in 1951 to test an atomic bomb for them; however, the administration was too fearful of congressional reaction to even consider requesting its approval. For the moment, the British were alone in their nuclear quest.[8]

In 1952, the United Kingdom conducted its first nuclear test, entitled "Hurricane," at the Monto Bello Islands off the coast of Australia. The "Blue Danube" was the first nuclear weapon that Britain produced. Early models were transferred to the Royal Air Force in November 1953, using plutonium as the fissile material. The smaller and lighter "Red Beard" weapon came into service in 1958. During the same time, the megaton fission bomb "Violet Club" was produced, followed by its successor, "Yellow Sun" MK I. Yellow Sun MK II was the first British thermonuclear operational gravity bomb that possessed a yield in the megaton range and was ready for use in 1962. Coinciding with this release was the thermonuclear Blue Steel air-launched cruise missiles. Both used an Anglicized version of the U.S. MK-28 warhead and remained in the stockpile until 1970. The WE-177, joining the suite of British nuclear-gravity aircraft bombs, came into force on Royal Air Force strategic bombers in 1966 and was later deployed on Royal Navy and Air Force attack aircraft and helicopters. (The WE-177 was decommissioned between 1992 and 1998.) From the early 1960s to the mid-1990s, the U.K. nuclear stockpile of British-produced warheads was estimated to be in the vicinity of 250 and 350 warheads. U.S. weapons "complemented" the British stockpile under NATO nuclear-sharing provisions from 1958 to 1991. Three hundred to 400 of these warheads were accessible to the United Kingdom in the 1960s and 1970s, and 200 to 300 warheads in the 1980s. However, Lance warheads, artillery shells, and depth bombs for land-based maritime patrol aircraft were sent back to the United States for dismantlement in 1991.[9]

FROM SKYBOLT TO POLARIS

By 1958, the United States and the United Kingdom both recognized the advantage of a closer relationship and began sharing extensive nuclear information under their Mutual Defense Agreement that amended the McMahon Act. The significant shift in emphasis occurred between 1955 and 1965 as London and Washington focused less on competition in nuclear weapons and more on designing and deploying new missile systems. In the new age of ballistic missiles, these delivery systems clearly provided the best means of achieving strategic deterrence. After the British discarded plans to develop their own missile system (Blue Streak), President Eisenhower willingly agreed to sell them America's "Skybolt," an air-to-ground ballistic missile system currently in the design stage. In return, London agreed that the U.S. Navy could base nuclear-armed submarines at Holy Loch, Scotland. Although they had been warned of technical difficulties with Skybolt, British government officials were nonetheless dismayed when in November 1962 the Kennedy administration announced that it was being terminated. "The abrupt cancellation undermined Britain's nuclear programme," Lawrence Freedman has pointed out, and "underlined the extent to which nuclear weapons were creating a form of dependence on the United States rather than becoming a source of influence." This diminished influence had been clearly evidenced two months earlier by Washington's minimal consultation with London during the Cuban missile crisis.[10] Ken Young suggests that in terms of the Anglo-American atomic narrative, the so-called "special relationship" looked dramatically different when viewed from either side of the Atlantic: "While it would be a travesty to present this as a story of dominance and submission, it becomes clear that at every stage the initiative lay with the United States, simply because Americans had the clear and unambiguous understanding of their national security interests that Britain lacked. The British—ambivalent and equivocal—simply responded to American overture, sometimes reluctantly, sometimes in apparent absence of mind."[11]

The next month, at the Nassau meeting, President John F. Kennedy met with his friend Prime Minister Macmillan and, overruling his advisers, reluctantly offered to sell Britain the Polaris missile system that would be used "for the purpose of international defense of the Western Alliance in all circumstance." If he had traveled to the Nassau meeting unenthusiastic about bailing out Macmillan, Kennedy was even less disposed to reopen a dialogue aimed at assisting President Charles de Gaulle. However, a letter arriving from Nikita Khrushchev that suggested he was willing to reconsider a nuclear test ban prompted Kennedy to place the current dilemma in a global context. The president responded to Macmillan as he did for several reasons: he recognized the prime minister had been placed in a difficult political position by the demise of Skybolt; feared jeopardizing the "special relationship" enjoyed by both nations; and welcomed Macmillan's political skills in the forthcoming test ban negotiations. Kennedy offered de Gaulle the Polaris system with little expectation that it would be accepted since the French as yet possessed neither the thermonuclear warheads for the Polaris nor the submarine technology to use it. He hoped that further discussions might lead to a nuclear partnership with Paris that would persuade the French to sign the impending test ban, and that Moscow would pressure the Chinese to adhere to it. Neither objective was immediately attained.[12]

Beginning in 1960, the United Kingdom operated a nuclear-capable land force of Lance missiles and 166-millimeter Howitzers, based in Germany, with borrowed warheads and delivery devices from the United States under NATO nuclear-sharing arrangements. The Royal Air Force also had access to U.S. depth bombs for its long-range antisubmarine Nimrod aircraft. Bombers such as the Buccaneer, Jaguar, and Tornado were capable of delivering WE-177 bombs. The Royal Navy operated Sea Harriers and antisubmarine helicopters capable of carrying WE-177s. In 1968, the British deployed the first four Polaris (or Resolution-class) submarines, carrying six-teen A3T submarine-launched ballistic missiles (SLBMs) supplied by the United States. The Polaris A3T missile carried a delivery system that incor-porated three warheads, each believed to have a yield of 200 kilotons. The Polaris A3TK or Chevaline missile replaced the A3T in 1982, and was de-signed to penetrate the Soviet antiballistic missile system around Moscow. The fleet of Polaris submarines was phased out by the end of 1996, and replaced by four Vanguard class submarines (SSBNs) with a life expectancy of twenty-five years. The HMS Vanguard entered service in 1994, HMS Victorious in 1995, HMS Vigilant in 1998, and the Vengeance in 2001. These submarines carried the Trident II D-5 inertial guided SLBM, which had a greater payload capability, range, and accuracy than its precursor, the Polaris SLBM. The three-stage, solid propellant missile has a range of more than 7,400 kilometers at full payload and was accurate to within a few feet. The Trident II re-entry vehicle carries warheads that have a yield of 100 kilotons. In 1998, the Trident missiles aboard the Vanguard class ballistic missile submarines took over the sub-strategic role replacing the WE-177 bombs. Fiscal restraints necessitated employing only one nuclear submarine on patrol at a time, each carrying sixteen Trident missiles with forty-eight warheads or half of the planned number; additionally, crews were reduced to one for each boat.[13]

BRITAIN AND THE END OF THE COLD WAR

By October 1991, the United Kingdom's nuclear forces were losing diver-sity: warheads for Lance missiles, Nimrod bombers, and nuclear artillery were transferred from Europe to the United States when NATO's nuclear forces were drastically reduced after the fall of the Soviet Union. In June 1992, the United Kingdom announced the removal of all WE-177 bombs from navy surface ships. The remaining WE-177s were planned for replace-ment in or about 2005 with tactical air-to-surface cruise missiles, but in 1993 the British dropped the idea. The production of Trident warheads apparently ended in 1999 and in 2001 it was estimated that the United Kingdom pos-sessed fewer than two hundred operational warheads. Since the end of the Cold War, Britain has cut its nuclear weapons explosive capacity by 70 percent.[14]

Budgetary issues arose in the first decade of the twenty-first century that challenged London's traditional nuclear position. In 2006–2007, Labor prime minister Tony Blair raised the issue of a replacement for the four Vanguard-class nuclear submarines and their Trident missile system, pointing out that nuclear weapons had held a uniquely important role in Britain's approach to international affairs. "During the Cold War, they provided the ultimate insurance against Soviet attack," as one British writer put it. "These days, they are seen as ensuring a seat at the 'top table' for a mid-sized, mid-ranking country whose influence wanes a little more with every passing year." Aside from fiscal restraints, critics immediately questioned the notion of pressing ahead with the replacements without consideration of Britain's commitments regarding nuclear non-proliferation, and whether such weapons were relevant for the twenty-first century. In a wide-ranging report entitled "Worse than Irrelevant? British Nuclear Weapons in the 21st Century," Rebecca Johnson, Nicola Butler, and Stephen Pullinger argued that a full public and parliamentary debate should precede any government decision to replace the Trident system. Such a debate, they suggested, "should start with a reappraisal of Britain's role in the world and an evaluation of the security challenges relevant to the 21st century. . . . [I]t is necessary to analyse the efficacy of nuclear deterrence in the transformed security environment and re-examine the circumstances, if any, in which it might be justifiable to use nuclear weapons." The debate should also clarify Britain's non-proliferation policies and objectives.[15]

With the replacement decision yet to be resolved, Conservative prime minister David Cameron inherited the issue and even greater concern about the costs. Where in the past funds for strategic weapons had emanated from a special allocation by the Treasury, in July 2010, Cameron's chancellor of the exchequer George Osborne announced that the entire cost of replacing the submarine nuclear deterrent, perhaps 20 billion pounds over a couple of decades, had to be found within the Ministry of Defence's budget. It would be "very difficult" to absorb these costs, Defense Secretary Liam Fox said; but he insisted that renewing the Trident system was the most "cost-effective way of maintaining Britain's nuclear deterrent." Arguing the prospect of Iran followed by Saudi Arabia, Egypt, and Turkey all becoming nuclear weapons states, he believed it was increasingly likely that "we could see ourselves in a new nuclear arms race."[16]

Notwithstanding such words of warning, it must be said that of all the nuclear weapons states, the United Kingdom is the one state that has advanced furthermost toward possible nuclear abolition. Its existing amass of approximately 225 weapons is scheduled to reduce to somewhere in the vicinity of 180 by the mid-2020s. After the United Kingdom's removal of its air- and sea-based tactical nuclear weapons in the 1990s, there has been extensive debate on the extent to which the state actually requires nuclear weapons. That said, however, the government has nonetheless continued its drive to replace the current suite of four Vanguard-class nuclear-armed submarines with a new class of three to four submarines in the mid-2020s. As of December 2015, the HMS *Vengeance* had been refitted with a new reactor and received updated defense systems.[17] Commenting on the refit of the *Vengeance*, then-Defense Secretary Philip Hammond stated, "As well as securing 2,000 U.K. jobs, this contract will ensure the nuclear deterrent submarine fleet can continue to operate safely and effectively to maintain a continuous at-sea deterrent."[18] Additionally, the United Kingdom leases its Trident II D5 SLBMs from the United States; these are currently being equipped with the W76-1/Mk4A, a form of the existing warhead that has augmented targeting proficiencies. The W76-1 is believed to have been modified by U.K. warhead designers for use on U.K. missiles.[19] Overall, while the United Kingdom has made the most positive movements toward meeting the requirements of Article VI of the NPT, the deterrent option also remains an important component of its strategic calculi.

FRANCE PURSUES THE BOMB

France launched its nuclear program incrementally during the Fourth Republic (1945–1958). Before World War II, French scientists were at the forefront of nuclear science, but the German occupation stymied this activity. General Charles de Gaulle, speaking to the press on October 12, 1945, spoke of France's relationship to the "immense consequences" of the atomic bomb. After noting that the French government in exile played no role in the allies' development of the bomb, he suggested that this might not have been the best way to handle things. "That the Anglo-Saxons pursued this grand enterprise without France (though not without the help of French scientists)," Philip Gordon, an authority on de Gaulle's France, has written, "and that they would continue to refuse to share their knowledge and responsibility with de Gaulle, was perfectly consistent with the General's wartime (and pre-war) experience." "As for the bomb," he told the media, "we have time." Although not a direct statement of intent, given past events, it could be taken to imply that if France wanted to join the nuclear community it would probably have to go it alone. A few days later General de Gaulle created the French Atomic Energy Commission, charged with exploring civilian uses of atomic energy. It had no explicit goal of developing an atomic bomb, but as Gordon has suggested, "the door to nuclear weapons" was left open, for the Commission's charter "specifically mentioned 'national defence' as one of its areas of competence."[20]

Headed by Frédéric Joliot-Curie and aided by some members employed in Canada in conjunction with the United States' atomic program, the commission tackled the problem of creating nuclear weapons without any outside assistance. Annoyed by Washington's emphasis on secrecy and London's inward atomic effort, de Gaulle's goal in establishing the commission was "to give his country the means of catching up in the nuclear field, and also of breaking the atomic isolation in which the Anglo-Saxon powers enclosed themselves." If he found the Anglo-Saxons irritating, he was more driven to reestablishing France's position of power and influence. "France is not really herself in the front rank," he declared in the opening paragraph of his wartime memoirs. "France cannot be France without greatness." While the pursuit of the "front rank" meant that France must have its own nuclear weapon, the atomic weapons program would generate a great deal of opposition. For many, such as even Joliot, the promise of atomic energy to expand industrial applications seemed more viable than military purposes. A member of the French Communist Party, Joliot did not much endear himself to Cold War hawks in Washington, but he managed to hold his position until 1950. By that time, the harsh Stalinist policies of the French Communists had backfired, with the effect of stymying dissident political parties opposed to the government's measured expansion of its atomic program.

Paris's experience during the 1956 Suez crisis was a key turning point in its nuclear assessment. Many French leaders, including Prime Minister Guy Mollet, reconsidered their tepid support of the nuclear weapons program. If France were to deal with such situations in the future, it needed to join the nuclear club. As such, according to Bertrand Goldschmidt, the government's "previous hostility toward atomic weapons was transformed overnight into a determined and positive interest in national nuclear armament." Compared with the three nuclear powers, the commission's work progressed slowly but skillfully. De Gaulle returned to power in 1958, surprised and pleased with the commission's advance toward a French atomic bomb and welcomed the decision to test a nuclear device during the last weeks of the Fourth Republic in 1958.[21]

FRANCE BECOMES A NUCLEAR STATE

Washington was generally unsympathetic to independent forces. President Truman and Eisenhower's decision against directly aiding France in obtaining nuclear weapons greatly irked de Gaulle. Moreover, he had little confidence in the wisdom of Anglo-Saxon diplomacy, especially the hostile manner Washington demonstrated in dealing with communist China during the Formosa Straits crisis and its intervention in Lebanon. Consequently, de Gaulle, seeking for France a position as a full nuclear partner, complained in a confidential letter to Eisenhower on May 25, 1959, that the U.S. refusal to share nuclear secrets had forced the French "to discover them for ourselves and at great expense." De Gaulle went much further and expressed his basic concern that

> America reserves entirely to itself the decision to use or not to use the nuclear forces at her disposal. For the consequences that could follow, for us, from any unilateral action you might undertake in such a field could lead us to formulate explicit demands, and to adopt, as far as possible, measures of our own for our

safety. If there were no alliance between us, I would agree that your monopoly of the possible unleashing of nuclear conflict was justified. But you and we are bound together to a point where the opening of this sort of war, whether by you or against you, would automatically expose France to total and immediate destruction. She obviously cannot leave her life and death entirely in the hands of any other state whatever, even the most friendly. That is why France insists that it is essential for her to participate, if the case should arise, in any decision that might be taken by her allies to use atomic weapons and to launch them against give places at given times.[22]

De Gaulle also declared that none of NATO's nuclear weapons could be stored in France without some form of joint control. After Eisenhower reiterated his request to store America's nuclear weapons in France, de Gaulle spelled out his position even more explicitly in a February 1960 speech at Grenoble. "France considers that if, unfortunately, atomic bombs were launched in the world, none would be launched from the free world without her having accepted it, and that no atomic bomb be launched from her soil unless she herself makes the decision." In Washington, no empathy existed for de Gaulle's demand for joint control of U.S. nuclear weapons, wherever placed, and his statements were taken as evidence of France's continuing uncooperative attitude toward the NATO planning process.

Of course, there was some legitimacy to de Gaulle's argument. The basic disagreement between Washington and Paris, as Bundy has pointed out, was not trivial: "Who can wish his country's survival to be dependent on the good sense of others? Who can wish to increase his country's danger by accepting dangerous weapons on his territory without any control over the decisions that might bring them under attack?" Just stationing the United States' (or NATO's) nuclear weapons on French soil obviously made France a target of Soviet weapons in any outbreak of nuclear hostilities. Every American president, certainly Eisenhower and his successors, was equally determined to keep control of the decision to use nuclear weapons, and not to share this process with anyone else. Surely, de Gaulle understood that his principal demand—shared responsibility for any decision to use the West's nuclear weapons—would not be forthcoming. In building a public case for France's nuclear strike force (*force de frappe*) he certainly never suggested that an American president should have a veto over its use. In February 1960, France tested its first weapon in then-French Algeria. During the debate that immediately followed, a French Catholic newspaper expressed the opinion that "France has constructed the atomic bomb and is prepared to construct an H-bomb not in order to use it against those who would become her adversaries, but to be able to be respected in the camp to which she belongs." For de Gaulle, it simply allowed it to ignore American leaders in determining its own destiny. The nuclear arsenal became operational in 1964, with the entry into active service of the first Mirage IVA nuclear bombers.[23]

The Kennedy administration was dismayed with various issues brought on by independent nuclear forces. Academic strategists and government officials arrived at the conclusion that there was little value in these forces; indeed, they denigrated France's nuclear efforts. Albert Wohlstetter's widely read 1961 essay, "Nuclear Sharing: NATO and the N + 1 Country" in *Foreign Affairs,* labeled any attempt by Washington to engage in nuclear sharing as being foolish. Efforts by Britain and France to obtain their own nuclear forces he viewed as costly, both initially and in the long run, and insufficient to establish a meaningful deterrent because these nations could not afford an adequate second strike capability. Not only did he criticize the arguments of French strategic theorists, he repeated an uncomplimentary comment, suggesting that it was no accident that the first French delivery vehicle was named Mirage.

At Ann Arbor, Michigan, on June 16, 1962, Defense Secretary Robert McNamara laid out the Kennedy administration's position on independent nuclear forces—aimed essentially at France. He explained that the United States believed it was necessary to have large and varied nuclear forces, capable of maintaining a second strike reserve so as to establish a credible deterrent policy. "Relatively weak national nuclear forces with enemy cities as their targets," he added, "are not likely to be sufficient to perform even the function of deterrence. If they are small, and perhaps vulnerable on the ground or in the air, or inaccurate, a major antagonist can take a variety of measures to counter them. . . . Meanwhile the creation of a single additional nuclear force encourages the proliferation of nuclear power with all of its attendant dangers." McNamara concluded by discounting the emerging "weak national nuclear forces" because such forces "are not likely to be sufficient to perform even the function of deterrence . . . [and] are dangerous, expensive, prone to obsolescence and lacking in credibility as a deterrent." However, Khrushchev, in his communications with Kennedy, did not appear to be disturbed by the new independent forces. As Secretary of State Dean Rusk has noted, the Soviet leader "never expressed serious concern about the British and French programs." Apparently it was that obvious. [24]

In 1970–1971, the Nixon and Ford administrations began secretly assisting the French in the development of its nuclear weapons and ballistic missile projects. The Nixon administration had concluded that it was in America's interest for the French to possess a more effective nuclear force. France's Armaments Ministry approached the Pentagon in December 1969, requesting assistance with developing their ballistic missiles. President Nixon met with French president Georges Pompidou in February 1970, at which time, according to National Security Archive senior analyst William Burr, "the two tacitly agreed on the possibility of 'nuclear cooperation' which led Nixon to make a 'decision to be forthcoming' to French requests." The administration agreed to "minimal" assistance, especially with matters involving nuclear safety and computer exports; however, while the United States would aid in improving the reliability of France's existing missiles, Washington would not provide direct help in developing new systems. Paris officials appreciated the missile technology guidance extended to them but, during 1972 and early 1973, the documents presented by Burr showed that they requested additional information about "warhead miniaturization and 'physics package' and the submarine-launched ballistic missile technology, so they could move into the 'next generation' of ballistic missiles."[25]

French Defense Minister Robert Galley twice met secretly with high-level U.S. officials, including National Security Adviser Henry Kissinger and Secretary of Defense James Schlesinger during mid-1973 to explain his nation's need for the advanced technology. To circumvent U.S. atomic energy laws, American officials sought to provide the French indirect assistance. Kissinger went along with the idea of employing "negative guidance" that would allow Washington "to critique what you are doing." With this approach American experts could review French data and respond, "That's the wrong way." Kissinger apparently was intrigued by this method, for it provided the means of whetting Galley's desire for additional information—making him "drool." According to Burr, some in the administration found the use of "negative guidance" to be controversial and the documents do not indicate when it was introduced; however, eventually it did assist the French in refining their nuclear warheads. President Gerald Ford continued the Nixon administration's policy of assisting the French, and in June 1975 even enhanced the 1971 understanding. The Ford administration's guidance helped "to decrease the vulnerability of French missiles, including re-entry vehicles and missile hardening and information on multiple re-entry vehicle technology."[26]

FRANCE'S NUCLEAR APPROACH AFTER THE COLD WAR

During the Cold War, France pursued a "three-circles" approach aimed at protecting its vital interests against outside threats (principally the Soviet Union) through nuclear deterrence, contributing in the broad defense to Western Europe within the Atlantic Alliance, and by upholding an active role outside Europe (mainly in Africa and the Middle East). In this regard, the French arsenal expanded to a triad of sea-, air-, and land-based weapons systems with a few hundred warheads, positioned within a national policy of "sufficiency" (*suffisance*) and relying on the threat of massive retaliation. With the Cold War's demise, France revised its nuclear strategy. Its 1994 defense white paper (the first since 1972) acknowledged French security as being steered by the likely intensification in the weaponry and military of other states, including the proliferation of weapons of mass destruction, and

Russia's continuing strong military power in Europe. Additionally, the document sought to emphasize a decrease in the significant role French nuclear weapons would play in its security assessments, while still maintaining a deterrence stance. Nuclear weapons would nonetheless continue to safeguard the protection of France's "vital interests," predominantly against the "resurgence of a major threat against Western Europe."[27]

In 1995–1996, newly elected Gaullist president Jacques Chirac introduced the restructuring of the French nuclear arsenal. Entering office after a period of "coexistence" with a socialist president and a Gaullist prime minister, Chirac encountered challenging defense issues. He adhered to much of the white paper's recommendations for France's defense, but altered funding priorities from nuclear weaponry to intelligence, force projection, and a professional army. In contrast to extensive international opinion, Chirac briefly recommenced nuclear weapons testing with a series of six tests in 1995–1996 (after a moratorium from 1992 to 1995) and began to restructure the national arsenal. He decided to dismantle two ground-to-ground missile systems: the S-3D, based in Albion, and the shorter-range Hades missiles. He continued to adjust reductions in nuclear spending from the Cold War level of more than 30 percent of the procurement budget to about 20 percent. Extensive debate took place as policy moved from the Cold War era "weak to the strong" posture against the Soviet Union to a "strong to the weak," or "strong to the crazy" posture, to counter other developing nuclear threats and the proliferation of unconventional weapons. The concept, however, retained its original rationale: that being conserving French vital interests vis-à-vis all potential threats. As stated by President Chirac in June 2001:

> Nuclear deterrence is the crux of the resources enabling France to affirm the principle of strategic autonomy from which derives our defence policy. Thanks to the continuous efforts made since the time of General de Gaulle, nuclear deterrence today is an essential foundation of our security and will remain so for many more years in the new strategic context, where it remains fully meaningful and effective. Nuclear deterrence is above all an important factor of global stability. It is thanks to nuclear deterrence that Europe has been protected for more than 50 years from the ravages it experienced during the twentieth century. By imposing restraint and inciting [others] to exercise reason, a credible nuclear threat commands peace. Our nuclear forces are not directed against any country, and we have always refused [to accept] that nuclear weapons should be regarded as weapons of war to be used as a part of military strategy.

In this and other ways, France has always brought a European focus to its nuclear forces. Paris also sought to reengage with NATO's nuclear strategies, but always on terms that recognized France's national interests. Thus, Paris has made several more formal openings to Europeanize its nuclear capabilities, for example, calling for a "concerted deterrence" in 1995. Yet, beyond increasing France–United Kingdom cooperation, these attempts have not met with much success. [28]

According to a 2011 report, France's twenty-first-century nuclear force consisted of sea- and air-based elements, and contained some 300 weapons. The majority of these nuclear devices, perhaps 240, were assigned to France's four nuclear power Le Triumphant–class submarines, one of which is on patrol at any given time. The deployment of these much quieter second-generation boats, only completed in 2010, created a superior fleet that was designed to last well into the 2010s. Three of the boats carried sixteen M-45 sea-launched ballistic missiles that have a range of 4,000 kilometers, armed with as many as six TN-75 warheads. The fourth boat carries up to sixteen newer M-51 missiles, armed with up to six TN-75 warheads, which had ranges from 6,000 to 9,000 kilometers depending upon their payload. The report noted, "Only 48 missiles are available in total, however, and it is not known what the distribution of those missiles across the four submarines actually is." Two squadrons of Mirage 2000N aircraft make up the air-based component of the French nuclear force. These aircraft are equipped with medium-range, 300-kilometer, air-launched missiles armed with a single TN-81 warhead or a newer version. The French Navy deploys ten Super Etendard aircraft—armed with the ASMP with a TN-81 warhead—that operate from the aircraft carrier Charles de Gaulle. Beginning in 2009, France started replacing the older Mirages with Rafale 3s armed with new missiles and having a greater range. A carrier-based version of the Rafale 3 is replacing the Super Etendard. [29]

In a March 2008 speech, President Nicolas Sarkozy largely repeated the 1994 white paper's justification for an independent nuclear force as a deterrent that protects the nation's "vital interests." These interests were defined as "the integrity of the national territory, including the mainland as well as the overseas departments and territories, the free exercise of our sovereignty, and the protection of the population." His subsequent 2008 "French White Paper on Defence and National Security" argued that France's nuclear force further protected "our identity and our existence as a nation-state." The nuclear doctrine also consistently rejected any pledge of "no-first-use" of nuclear weapons and placed less significance on negative security assurances such as those given to non-nuclear nations party to the Non-Proliferation Treaty. [30]

Like many states today, France continues to plan for the elongated haul. It is in the final stage of a wide-ranging modernization of its nuclear forces envisioned to prolong its arsenal well into the 2050s. Most noteworthy is the deployment during 2010–2018 of the new M-51 SLBM on the abovementioned Triumphant-class submarines. The innovative missile has superior range, payload capability, and greater precision than its predecessor, the M-45. Beginning in 2015, the existing TN75 warhead will be supplanted with

the new TNO (Tête Nucléaire Océanique) warhead. The modernization of
the sea-based leg of the arsenal trails the conclusion in 2011 of the replacement of the ASMP (Air-Sol Moyenne Portée) air-launched cruise missile,
which had a range of 300 kilometers, with the new ASMPA (Air-Sol Moyenne Portée Amélioré), and could reach the distance of approximately 500
kilometers. The missile has been assimilated with two fighter-bomber regi-
ments—Mirage 2000N K3 aircraft at Istres on the Mediterranean coast, and
Rafale F3 aircraft at Saint-Dizier northeast of Paris. In due course, the Istres
wing will also be upgraded to Rafale aircraft. The ASMPA possesses the new
TNA (Tête Nucléaire Aéroportée) warhead. A navy version of the Rafale
aircraft is deployed on the Charles de Gaulle aircraft carrier located at Tou-
lon. The wing was improved to carry the ASMPA missile in 2010, but the
weapons are warehoused on land during regular circumstance and not deployed on the carrier during times of stability.[31] Overall, according to the
Nuclear Threat Initiative, "France's commitment to retaining its nuclear deterrent remains strong and the new administration has no plans for further
reductions."[32]

THE PEOPLE'S REPUBLIC OF CHINA (PRC) AND NUCLEAR WEAPONS

Drawing his views from the lessons taught by the ancient Chinese strategist
Sun Tzu, Mao Zedong initially saw little difference between the atomic
bomb and conventional weaponry. Speaking to the sympathetic American
journalist Anna Louise Strong in August 1946, Mao for the first time put
forth publicly his famous description: "The atomic bomb is a paper tiger"; a
"tiger" used by "U.S. reactionaries to scare people. It looks terrible, but in
fact it isn't. Of course, the atomic bomb is a weapon of mass slaughter, but
the outcome of a war is decided by people, not one or two new types of
weapon." Although drawing his thoughts on war and strategy from a different source, his initial conclusion was quite similar to that of Joseph Stalin.
The major difference, of course, is that Stalin immediately ordered the highest priority be given to building a Soviet bomb, while it would be some time
before Mao recognized that China might profit by joining the nuclear club.

The Chinese decision to deploy forces against the U.S. and UN troops
during the Korean hostilities revealed Mao's lack of concern about the bomb.
If some Chinese military leaders worried that such action might prompt the
United States to retaliate with atomic bombs, Mao exhibited little fear. At the
ninth meeting of the Central People's Government Council on September 5,
1950, he declared: "You may bomb [us] with the atomic bomb, but we will
respond with our hand-grenades. We then will catch your weakness to tie you
and finally defeat you." While subsequent Communist Chinese propaganda

efforts conceded that atomic bombs could inflict mass destruction and raise great psychological fear, they would have little impact on battlefield operations. Apart from normal civil defense activities, a major advantage of China was its vast territory that allowed for the dispersal of factories and population. This notion of defense "in depth" was similar to arguments that Nikita Khrushchev came to adopt.[33]

Although PRC commanders insisted they had broken the myth of American invincibility when their forces had driven U.S. and UN forces out of North Korea, they understood that there were lessons to be learned from the experience. On September 12, 1953, the commanding general of Chinese forces in Korea, Peng Dehaui, acknowledged that although his troops with "inferior equipment have achieved a brilliant victory in fighting the invading forces of superior equipment, [we must pay closer attention to the] new weapon's 'omnipotence' with which U.S. imperialists have applied in bluffing, threatening, and scaring people." Thus, throughout the early 1950s, the Chinese military focused on developing a modern air force, heavy artillery, tanks, and other accoutrements of conventional weaponry with considerable Soviet assistance. Mao's concentration on conventional weapons was realistic because that was what he had. Nevertheless, PRC leaders paid serious attention to the design and location of defensive projects, particularly in attempting to make them antinuclear. With the Soviets constructing 150 defense plants during this period, senior Chinese official Zhou Enlai frequently cautioned that where possible care should be given to place them out of reach of American bombers.

Washington's responses to the bombardment of Quemoy and Matsu in late 1954 caused Chinese leaders to take seriously the possibility of nuclear hostilities. They had noted an article appearing in the U.S. press that reported ships in the American 7th Fleet carrying tactical nuclear weapons and that should communist forces invade Formosa they would face these weapons. From March 15 to March 17, 1955, Secretary of State John Foster Dulles, President Dwight E. Eisenhower, and Vice President Richard Nixon each had publicly mentioned the potential use of nuclear weapons "to fight a war against China in the Far East." Following the first Taiwan Strait crisis, Beijing's fears of nuclear war greatly increased. The enthusiasm in Washington during 1958 for diminishing the role of massive nuclear responses in favor of limited nuclear hostilities, using various tactical weapons, further compounded Chinese fears that such a strategy might loosen America's restraints on the use of nuclear weapons.[34]

MAO DECIDES TO BUILD THE BOMB

Given increasing concerns about the U.S. nuclear threat, PRC leaders chose to construct their own nuclear weapons early in 1955. Two factors greatly aided the activity: first, in 1954, uranium had been discovered in Guangxi province; and second, as Shu Guang Zhang has pointed out, "a number of Western-educated Chinese scientists returned during the early 1950s. Many of them had studied nuclear, high-energy, and experimental physics, and some were specialists in accelerator, computer, and vacuum technology, as well as radioactivity and geology. From America, England, and France, they brought back nuclear science literature and equipment for nuclear research of which most were on the US list of items embargoed against shipment to the PRC." At the conclusion of a meeting to discuss the prospects of establishing a nuclear program on January 15, 1955, Mao stated that because of other matters "there has not been enough time for us to pay attention to this matter [of nuclear weapons]. . . . Now, it is time for us to pay attention to it." While the Chinese leadership was launching its atomic bomb project, it also began to give attention to delivery systems, especially missiles, though there is no evidence that any overarching strategic doctrine had informed Chairman Mao's thinking on the matter. In any case, in early 1956, Qian Xuesen, a PhD from the renowned California Institute of Technology with experience at the Jet Propulsion Laboratory, emphasized in a report that "developing missiles and developing atomic energy should be two key projects in China's defence modernization." In October, after the Central Military Commission endorsed the development and manufacture of strategic missiles, the Ministry of National Defense established China's first missile research agency with Qian as its director.

In April 1955, the Soviets promised to help Beijing with basic nuclear technology for peaceful uses, and in 1957, as the Soviet advisers helped the Chinese master Russian-made conventional weapons, Soviet leader Nikita Khrushchev even promised to provide a sample atomic bomb and assist with the development of ballistic missiles. Between 1957 and 1959 Soviet advisers provided the technology for the medium-range R-12 missile and cruise missiles. They also provided the technical insights necessary to construct nuclear weapons. The days of Sino-Soviet cooperation soon ended, however, as egos and personalities of the top leaders clashed over the direction of the communist bloc. Mao's strident approach to the West clashed with Khrushchev's proposed strategy of peaceful coexistence. His rejection of Khrushchev's offer to commit to Soviet nuclear protection so as to deter the United States during the 1958 crisis in the Formosa Straits involving Quemoy and Matsu islands finally aroused in Khrushchev concern about Mao's brinkmanship and his approach toward a nuclear conflict. Other concerns were also evident: Would a Chinese independent nuclear force pose a danger to Sino-

Soviet relations and to broader superpower strategic stability? The Khrushchev-Mao dispute would soon sever relations. In a letter to Mao on June 20, 1959, Khrushchev informed Beijing that the promised prototype atomic bomb and further nuclear technology would not be arriving, and that the PRC would have to develop its nuclear weapons without further Soviet assistance. With the advantage of hindsight, the Soviet leader had probably overreacted, for Mao did understand the threat posed by the presence of American nuclear weaponry. He understood that China must proceed with caution and not let the episode escalate out of control. At the same time, Mao was unsure about the Soviet offer of extended deterrence and became even more determined to join the nuclear club: "If we are not to be bullied in the present-day world, we cannot do without the bomb."[35]

The Chinese moved quickly to create the needed facilities to deliver the bomb. In 1958, Beijing established the Nuclear Weapons Research and Design Academy (later the Ninth Academy) and the Tongxian Uranium Mining and Hydrometallurgy Institute. It also began construction of the Baotou Nuclear Fuel Component Plant and the Lanzhou Gaseous Diffusion Plant. Finally, in early 1960, construction commenced on a plutonium production reactor at the Jiuquan Atomic Energy Complex, whose facilities provided vital components for atomic weapons. A nuclear test site was also being built by 1960 in western China at Lop Nur. Following its first nuclear test in 1964, China began a slow but steady process of developing a full-fledged arsenal holding strategic and tactical nuclear weapons. Immediately afterward, Beijing announced in October 1964 its "no-first-use" nuclear policy.[36]

THE UNITED STATES' CHINA POLICIES

Perhaps the most serious failing of hawkish senior advisers during significant Cold War episodes, certainly evident in Washington, was their rush to worst-case scenarios without sufficient analysis of the consequences, intentional and unintentional, of aggressive action. The worst-case fears of President Kennedy and his National Security assistant Bundy gravitated toward consideration of preventive strikes—perhaps with a cooperative strike authorized by Khrushchev—aimed at eliminating the PRC's nuclear facilities. Officials from the Central Intelligence Agency and State Department offered their considered opinion that communist China would not be an aggressive threat, that the United States should show restraint, and that Beijing would likely follow suit. The State Department's China expert Robert Johnson, in a memorandum for President Johnson, suggested that Beijing officials viewed their impending nuclear capability as a deterrent rather than a means of undertaking high-risk adventures. He minimized China's potential military threat and argued against preemptive strikes against the PRC's nuclear facilities, except in "response to major ChiCom aggression." His assessment proved to be accurate. Surely, most analysts today would agree that a unilateral or cooperative military assault on PRC nuclear facilities prior to their first nuclear test would undoubtedly have resulted in far more harm than good. The restraint shown by Washington during the emergence of Beijing's nuclear program, moreover, should hold meaning for its twenty-first-century non-proliferation policies.[37]

"The Johnson administration's restrained approach toward the Chinese nuclear program is significant not because it suggests that restraint is always the best choice," William Burr and Jeffrey T. Richelson wisely emphasized,

> but because it highlights the different variables that must be considered in choosing among diplomatic, economic, and military (including preventive action and missile defense) options. Those variables include the limits of intelligence collection and uncertainties in intelligence analysis concerning the nature and status of a WMD [weapons of mass destruction] program, the likely impact a specific WMD capability will have on the conduct of a nation and its leadership, probable overseas reactions to various U.S. decisions, the possibility of international action, and the deterrent effect of U.S. nuclear capabilities on decisions to develop or employ WMD.[38]

President Johnson and Defense Secretary McNamara did later reluctantly agree to establish an antiballistic missile system, publicly introduced as a means of protecting American cities from communist China's strategic threat. Later, President Nixon revised the system and focused on protecting the U.S. intercontinental ballistic missile sites. It was evident, however, that in both instances, despite announced objectives, the adversary raising the greatest concern was the Soviet Union. Some four-plus decades later, the potential threat of the PRC's "massive" military build-up has again generated heated discussions among national security officials and members of Congress. Reviewing the arguments regarding the U.S. defense budget, Tammy Schultz reports that "many who support boosting defense spending, especially in heavy weaponry, use the possibility of a rising China using its military buildup for aggressive purposes as a justification." Even though most assessments of any "upcoming war with China will be a conventional one," like the early 1960s and 1970s, some analysts view China's nuclear forces as a dire threat, while others see Beijing's nuclear policy as one of deterrence.[39]

U.S.-CHINESE BILATERAL NUCLEAR TALKS

By the end of 2011, more than a decade of efforts by Washington and Beijing officials to discuss their nations' respective nuclear weapons programs, participants on both sides had become increasingly frustrated and disappointed at the lack of progress. They have been unable to move beyond "the first item on their agenda," according to Gregory Kulacki, because "U.S. security analysts and military planners discount China's pledge not to be the first to use nuclear weapons. Their Chinese counterparts resent this derision of the nuclear taboo. Moreover, they see U.S. incredulity as a way to deflect attention from Chinese questions about why the United States is unwilling to provide the same assurance." The Americans involved in the discussions refused "a no-first-use pledge seriously. To them, the pledge is an expression of naïveté or mendacity." This general attitude originated early in the Cold War and has continued as American officials persistently downplayed the political dimension of issues dealing with nuclear weaponry and the strategy that other nations view as significant. As a result, these bilateral discussions have floundered because the Americans suspect that their Chinese counterparts cannot or simply will not provide accurate information about their nuclear weapons policy. For their part, the Chinese participants believe that the American mistrust stems from "hegemonic arrogance that has led the United States to use nuclear threats as part of a broader U.S. policy intended to intimidate and contain China." Indeed, Washington's 2002 "Nuclear Posture Review" intimated that U.S. forces might initiate the use of nuclear weapons should hostilities arise over Taiwan.[40]

American participants, seeking to bypass officials from Beijing's foreign ministry, have hoped to restart discussion with representatives from Second Artillery (sometimes referred to as China's strategic rocket forces) that has responsibility for China's land-based intercontinental ballistic missiles. Officials in the Obama administration apparently were convinced that these senior military leaders would offer "a different and more authoritative voice" than Beijing's civilian representatives. An examination of the Second Artillery's classified texts used to train its missile forces, Kulacki argues, "suggests U.S. analysts and administration officials are mistaken" since Chinese civilian and military both function "under the assumption that China will continue for the foreseeable future to operate a small nuclear arsenal that is kept off alert and is to be launched only in retaliation after a nuclear attack." In fact, the Second Artillery's closely held text, entitled *The Science of Operations of the Second Artillery*, fails to challenge China's current nuclear policy. Moreover, it insists that this policy "is a political decision that lies with the Chinese leadership, not with the Second Artillery." It is Kulacki's position that American representatives ought to "accept that China's nuclear weapons policy is fundamentally different from that of the United States and that the Chinese policy deserves U.S. attention and respect, despite understandable U.S. doubts about its viability." Perhaps then Chinese participants might come to understand America's uncertainty about its nuclear weapons policy as reflecting "legitimate differences" in the approach needed to avoid nuclear hostilities. That said, at the end of the first decade of the twenty-first century, the mutual respect required to revive meaningful discussions appeared to be missing.[41]

Some of the problems between the participants arose from problems with the vocabulary dealing with nuclear weapons. The original lexicon was developed in the discussions between American and Soviet diplomats during the Cold War arms limitation negotiations, and it usage continues to dominate such talks and writings. The Chinese imported this vocabulary to use in arms control conferences; however, by 2006, American and Chinese negotiators finally agreed that they needed to devise a mutually accepted bilingual dictionary of terms to reduce misinterpretations that had been found in translations from one language to the other. A year and a half of study resulted in mutual agreement on about a thousand terms, but no consensus emerged on some basic concepts. One of the more significant areas of confusion affecting participants of the nuclear weapons bilateral discussions has been various Chinese definitions of the phrases *minimal deterrence* and *limited deterrence*. As American analysts interpreted the two phrases, the differences focused on China's efforts either to deter or to wage and win a nuclear conflict. These differences as interpreted by the Americans were, according to Kulacki, that "limited deterrence imagines pre-emptive or retaliatory nuclear strikes against enemy forces and victory on the battlefield using 'counterforce' targeting. Minimal deterrence imagines retaliatory strikes against enemy population centers, the political leadership, or critical economic infrastructure, otherwise known as 'countervalue' targeting." In the bilateral talks Chinese participants used *minimal deterrence* to describe their official policy.

Although an American analyst examining Second Artillery military texts occasionally found the phrase *limited deterrence*, the Chinese participants rejected this phrase as defining their nation's nuclear policy. Moreover, they insisted that it was not authoritative and the U.S. definition of the phrase was erroneous. To Washington officials, however, these two phrases suggested that in Beijing *minimal deterrence* was being used to project a public or diplomatic policy, while a separate secret policy, *limited deterrence*, was being used by the military. In spite of miscommunication and misunderstanding, the textual evidence favors Beijing's definition of the three essential aspects of its nuclear weapons policy. These three basic policy characteristics are to be found in the pages of *The Science of Operations of the Second Artillery*—(1) a small nuclear force; (2) keep off alert; and (3) launch only in retaliation. Regardless of their frequently intense disagreements, American and Soviet (later Russian) diplomats contemplating nuclear weapons issues were focused on the basic desire to diminish the prospect of either side launching a disarming first strike. China did not possess a first strike capability that would neutralize the United States' nuclear forces nor, most observers believe, has it shown a desire to seek such an arsenal.[42]

CHINESE MODERNIZATION

Some members of Congress rejected this assessment of China's intentions and believed that the United States should be concerned with the modernization of Russian and Chinese delivery systems and nuclear arsenals. During congressional hearings on October 14, 2011, the chairman of the House Subcommittee on Strategic Forces, Republican congressman Michael Turner of Ohio, warned against reducing the budget for the modernization of U.S. nuclear weapons. He called such action tantamount to "unilateral disarmament." Also objecting to the possible reduction of U.S. nuclear capabilities in Asia, Richard Fisher, a senior fellow at the International Assessment and Strategy Center, stated that any "perceived weakness in the United States" military deterrent will "embolden [China] to take risks." Republican representative Doug Lamborn of Colorado, among others, expressed concern about China's Second Artillery 5,000-meter-long series of tunnels apparently used to house its nuclear weapons. Lamborn found the tunnels to be a "very destabilizing factor," because China might use these tunnels to hide a sizeable increase in its nuclear arsenal, without being detected. Several experts cautioned against the notion, prevalent in some circles, that China was secretly preparing to build to parity with Russia and the United States as these two nations reduced their nuclear forces. Noting that the Chinese military had long used tunneling as a basic defensive technique, Jonathan Pollack said that he was not surprised by the underground network, nor was he convinced with estimates of the length of these facilities. Finding it difficult to offer a definitive assessment of China's nuclear ambitions, Robert Hathaway, nevertheless, did not believe that it was very likely the Chinese were secretly building a large nuclear arsenal: "I don't think the Chinese believe they need a numerical parity with the U.S. or Russia," he stated. "Once you reach a certain level . . . everything else is simply redundant."[43]

Of course, the fact remains that China is the only one of the five nuclear weapon states recognized under the NPT that does not posit any sanctioned data on its prevailing and envisaged nuclear forces. Moreover, it is the only member of the five original nuclear weapon states that has actually been increasing its nuclear arsenal. It validates this by elucidating that its nuclear forces are substantively less than those of other nuclear powers, and concealment of such numbers has been necessary for maintaining a vigorous deterrence. Still, China's opaqueness regarding its military force—not to mention budgets, expenditure, and the "remarkable rate" of its modernization—has been a source of consternation for both the Bush and Obama administrations. Indeed, Chinese nuclear forces are in the latter phase of a two-decades-long upgrade that includes deployment of new land-, sea-, and air-based nuclear delivery vehicles. This exertion is taking place in parallel with a wider modernization of China's general military forces. Dissimilar to the other nuclear members of the NPT, China is growing the size of its nuclear arsenal, which is presently estimated to be around 250 warheads.[44]

In contrast to some of the above views, China, in recent times, does not seem to be planning a significant increase in the size of its nuclear forces, but is changing the configuration of that force and placing more importance on mobile systems. The ICBM force is "intensifying" with deployment of the solid-fueled, road-mobile DF-31 and DF-31A in limited numbers to accompany the old silo-based, liquid-fueled DF-5A. The DF-31 and DF-31A do not appear to have been very successful; deployment of the DF-31 has been delayed, and China may produce a new ICBM to replace the DF-31A.[45] A further development is the Jin-class SSBN with the JL-2 SLBM, a marked improvement over the old Xia/JL-1 weapons system, which never became completely operational. It is difficult to ascertain the role of the small fleet of Jin/JL-2 SSBNs under manufacture given the disinclination of the Chinese government to permit deployment of nuclear warheads on missiles under standard conditions. Considering the geographical restraints and the preeminence of U.S. attack submarines, it will be difficult for China to operate SSBNs efficiently. Hitherto, the navy seems to have secured consent to construct the fleet so as to at least maintain some semblance of national stature. There are also unverified reports that China is adding a nuclear capability to ground- and air-launched cruise missiles. If so, it would signify a vital addition to the Chinese nuclear posture, particularly given Beijing's specified observance to a doctrine of minimum deterrence.[46]

As indicated, aside from now possessing a strong fleet of modern diesel submarines—not to mention developing an advanced nuclear submarine—China also has new short-, intermediate- and long-range ballistic missiles (both conventional and nuclear), alongside a medium range of missiles that can already reach many parts of Asia (including Japan and several U.S. airbases). Indeed, China's growing capabilities have caused concerns in the Asia-Pacific region. In particular, Japan and Southeast Asian nations have been worried about how they might counter China's expanding capacity to deploy forces in the region, and what this could mean in the context of the territorial and resource issues in the South China Sea and East China Sea. In response, Japan has shifted the deployment of its military southward, while Southeast Asian states have been acquiring greater offshore capabilities. This has also led to calls for the United States to counterbalance China's outward actions, and in response, the Obama administration acted accordingly.[47] It deployed more forces to Guam, attained an "understanding" with Japan about the use of force during crises, increased surveillance and patrolling along China's coast, sold more arms to Taiwan to deter Beijing from using coercive means, and undertaken classified efforts to counter China's missile threat to U.S. warships. However, as the two militaries become more suspicious of one another, particularly in the context of the South China Seas, there is a chance that the tensions and adversarial dimensions may impinge greatly upon the bilateral relationship. The concern has been that perceptions on both sides—Washington can increasingly see a more assertive and aggressive China, and Beijing can see a United States in a prolonged period of decline—will spur the strategic rivalry to a potentially dangerous level. The assumption is that military competition and its obvious spill over into the nuclear weapon realm will ultimately lead to a Cold War–type situation, and pose a significant threat to regional and global stability.[48]

NOTES

1. Bevin quote in "Britain's Nuclear Weapons: Accounting and the Bomb," *The Economist*, July 30, 2010, 1, http://www.economist.com/blogs/blighty/2010/07/britains_nuclear_weapons; McGeorge Bundy, *Danger and Survival: Choices about the Bomb in the First Fifty Years* (New York: Random House, 1988), 475. Elements of this chapter have been adapted from Professor Siracusa's study (with Richard Dean Burns) *A Global History of the Nuclear Arms Race: Weapons, Strategy, and Politics*, 2 vols. (Santa Barbara, CA: Praeger, 2013).

2. Shu Guang Zhang, "Between 'Paper' and 'Real Tigers': Mao's View of Nuclear Weapons," in *Cold War Statesmen Confront the Bomb: Nuclear Diplomacy Since 1945*, ed. John Lewis Gaddis et al. (New York: Oxford University Press, 1999), 195–97.

3. John Newhouse, *War and Peace in the Nuclear Age* (New York: Knopf, 1989), 58–61, 130.

4. Lawrence Freedman, *The Evolution of Nuclear Strategy*, 2nd ed. (London: Macmillan, 1989), 311–12.

5. Bundy, *Danger and Survival*, 488–89, 492–98; Richard Dean Burns, *The Evolution of Arms Control: From Antiquity to the Nuclear Age* (Santa Barbara, CA: Praeger, 2009), 69.

6. Margaret Gowing, assisted by Lorna Arnold, *Independence and Deterrence: Britain and Atomic Energy, 1945–1952*, vol. 1: *Policy Making* (London: Macmillan, 1974), 194–206.

7. Bundy, *Danger and Survival*, 464, 468–70; Gowing, *Independence and Deterrence: Britain and Atomic Energy, 1945–1952*, 184, 194–206; Freedman, *The Evolution of Nuclear Strategy*, 311.

8. Bundy, *Danger and Survival*, 465–70; Newhouse, *War and Peace*, 60–61.

9. Joseph Cirincione, Jon B. Wolfsthal, and Miriam Rajkumar, *Deadly Arsenals: Nuclear, Biological, and Chemical Threats*, 2nd ed. (Washington, DC: Carnegie Endowment for International Peace, 2005), 198–201; Robert Norris, Andrew Burrows, and Richard Fieldhouse, *British, French, and Chinese Nuclear Weapons*, vol. 5 (Boulder, CO: Westview Press, 1994), 54–60, 63.

10. Freedman, *The Evolution of Nuclear Strategy*, 310–11; Bundy, *Danger and Survival*, 490–92.

11. Ken Young, *The American Bomb in Britain: US Air Forces' Strategic Presence, 1946–64* (Manchester: Manchester University Press, 2016), 3. See also John R. Walker, *British Nuclear Weapons and the Test Ban, 1954–1973: Britain, the United States, Weapons Policy and Nuclear Testing, Tensions and Contradictions* (Surrey, UK: Ashgate, 2010).

12. Freedman, *The Evolution of Nuclear Strategy*, 311; Newhouse, *War and Peace in the Nuclear Age*, 185–86.

13. Joseph M. Siracusa, *Nuclear Weapons: A Very Short Introduction* (Oxford: Oxford University Press, 2008), 115–16; "Britain's Nuclear Weapons: The Current British Arsenal," April 30, 2001, http://nuclearweaponarchive.org/Uk/UKArsenalRecent.html.

14. House of Commons, Defence Committee, *The Future of the UK's Strategic Deterrent: the White Paper*, vol. 1 (London: The Stationery Office Limited, March 7, 2007).

15. "Britain's Nuclear Weapons: Accounting and the Bomb," 1; Rebecca Johnson, Nicola Butler and Stephen Pullinger, *Worse than Irrelevant? British Nuclear Weapons in the 21st Century* (London: Acronym Institute for Disarmament Diplomacy, 2006).

16. "Trident Costs Must Come from MoD Budget, Osborne Says," BBC News, July 20, 2010, http://www.bbc.co.uk/news/uk-10812825; Eben Harrell, "Britain Takes another Look at Its Nuclear Subs," *Time World*, July 30, 2010, http://www.time.com/time/world/article/0,8599,2007441,00.html.

17. "British Jobs Secured Through Upgrade to Nuclear Deterrent Submarine," Royal Navy, December 7, 2015. http://www.royalnavy.mod.uk.

18. Svenja O'Donnell, "U.K. to Sign Contract to Refit Royal Navy Nuclear Submarine," Bloomberg, March 25, 2012, www.bloomberg.com.

19. Hans M. Kristensen, "Nuclear Weapons Modernization: A Threat to the NPT?" *Arms Control Association*, https://www.armscontrol.org/act/2014_05/Nuclear-Weapons-Modernization-A-Threat-to-the-NPT.

20. Philip H. Gordon, "Charles de Gaulle and the Nuclear Revolution," in *Cold War Statesmen Confront the Bomb: Nuclear Diplomacy Since 1946*, ed. John Lewis Gaddis et al. (New York: Oxford University Press, 1999), 219–20.

21. Lawrence Scheinman, *Atomic Energy in France under the Fourth Republic* (Princeton, NJ: Princeton University Press, 1965), 40–57, 78–85, 171–74; Wilfrid Kohl, *French Nuclear Diplomacy* (Princeton, NJ: Princeton University Press, 1971), 35–37; Bertrand Goldschmidt, *Atomic Complex: A Worldwide Political History of Nuclear Energy*, trans. by Bruce M. Adkins (La Grange Park, IL: American Nuclear Society, 1982), 37.

22. Quoted in Richard D. Burns and Joseph M. Siracusa, *A Global History of the Nuclear Arms Race: Weapons, Strategy, and Politics*, 2 vols. (Santa Barbara, CA: Praeger, 2013).

23. Quotes in Bundy, *Danger and Survival*, 477–82; French newspaper quote in Kohl, *French Nuclear Diplomacy*, 105.

24. Albert Wohlstetter, "Nuclear Sharing: NATO and the N + 1 Country," *Foreign Affairs* 39 (April 1961): 355–87; Bundy, *Danger and Survival*, 484–86; Newhouse, *War and Peace in the Nuclear Age*, 187, 191.

25. William Burr, ed., "The French Bomb, with Secret U.S. Help: Documents from Nixon and Ford Administrations," National Security Archive *Electronic Briefing Book* No. 346, posted May 26, 2011.

26. Ibid.

27. Norris, Burrows, and Fieldhouse, *British, French, and Chinese Nuclear Weapons*, 183–84.

28. Transcript of President Jacques Chirac's speech before the Institute of Higher National Defence Studies in Paris, June 8, 2001, quoted in Cirincione, Wolfstahl, and Rajkumar, *Deadly Arsenals*, 190–91.

29. Ian Kearns, *Beyond the United Kingdom: Trends in the Other Nuclear Armed States*, Discussion Paper 1 of the Trident Commission, London: British American Security Information Council [BASIC], November 2011, 20.

30. Ibid., 21.

31. Kristensen, "Nuclear Weapons Modernization."

32. "France," *Nuclear Threat Initiative*, October 2016, http://www.nti.org/learn/countries/france/nuclear/.

33. Shu Guang Zhang, "Between 'Paper' and 'Real Tigers': Mao's View of Nuclear Weapons," in *Cold War Statesmen Confront the Bomb*, ed. John Lewis Gaddis et al., 195–97.

34. Ibid., 198–202.

35. Ibid., 203–9; John Wilson Lewis and Hua Di, "China's Ballistic Missile Program: Technologies, Strategies, Goals," *International Security* 17, no. 2 (Fall 1992): 5–40; William Taubman, *Khrushchev: The Man and His Era* (New York: Norton, 2003), 336–37, 392–93; John Wilson Lewis and Xue Litai, *China Builds the Bomb* (Stanford, CA: Stanford University Press, 1988), 11–46; Vladislav M. Zubok, *A Failed Empire: The Soviet Union in the Cold War from Stalin to Gorbachev* (Chapel Hill: University of North Carolina Press, 2007), 136.

36. Lewis and Xue, *China Builds the Bomb*, 90, 140–41, 177–78; Norris, Burrows, and Fieldhouse, *British, French, and Chinese Nuclear Weapons*, vol. 5, 338, 340, 345; William

Burr and Jeffrey T. Richelson, "Whether to 'Strangle the Baby in the Cradle': The United States and the Chinese Nuclear Program, 1960–64," *International Security* 25, no. 3 (2000/2001): 57–60.

37. "The United States, China, and the Bomb," National Security Archive *Electronic Briefing Book* No. 1, Document 1, "Implications of a Chinese Communist Nuclear Capability."

38. Burr and Richelson, "Whether to 'Strangle the Baby in the Cradle,'" 94.

39. Ibid.; Tammy S. Schultz, "The U.S. Defense Budget and Strategic Overmatch," *World Politics Review*, November 7, 2011, 1.

40. Gregory Kulacki, "Chickens Talking With Ducks: The U.S.-Chinese Nuclear Dialogue," *Arms Control Today*, October 2011: 15–16.

41. Ibid., 15–17; see Alastair Iain Johnson, "China's New 'Old Thinking': The Concept of Limited Deterrence," *International Security* 20, no. 3 (1995–1996): 5–42; Michael S. Chase, Andrew S. Erickson, and Christopher Yeaw, "Chinese Theater and Strategic Missile Force Modernization and Its Implications for the United States," *Journal of Strategic Studies* 32, no. 1 (February 2009): 67–114.

42. Kulacki, "Chickens Talking With Ducks," 17–20.

43. Kathleen E. Masterson, "China Cited by Foes of Nuclear Budget Cuts," *Arms Control Today*, December 2011, 48.

44. Kristensen, "Nuclear Weapons Modernization"; Office of the Secretary of Defense, U.S. Department of Defense, "Annual Report to Congress: Military and Security Developments Involving the People's Republic of China 2013," May 2013, 6.

45. Ibid.

46. Kristensen, "Nuclear Weapons Modernization."

47. See Aiden Warren, *The Obama Administration's Nuclear Weapon Strategy: The Promises of Prague* (New York: Routledge, 2014), 187–94; Michael Swaine, "Avoiding U.S.-China Military Rivalry," *The Diplomat*, February 27, 2011, http://thediplomat.com/whats-next-china/avoiding-us-china-military-rivalry.

48. Ibid.

Chapter Four

Non–UN Security Council Nuclear Weapon States

Israel, India, Pakistan, North Korea (and Iran)

In the years following the Security Council states' attainment of nuclear weapons, a further five states would also make the leap to address what they perceived were their regional and broader security interests. Israel came to view its nuclear arsenal as its ultimate insurance policy, as well as its most effective means of deterring its Arab neighbors. Of course, some of the nearby states—such as Iran, and perhaps Syria—felt sufficiently threatened to launch their own nuclear programs, although Iran and Syria regularly denied seeking a nuclear weapons capability. Even so, with the Middle East's myriad political and religious differences, the potential for multiple independent nuclear forces in the region posed many concerns for the international community. In the context of India, its officials viewed China's nuclear program as threatening and ultimately decided that they must develop one for themselves. While the New Delhi decision provided a deterrence strategy vis-à-vis China, it also aroused fears in Pakistan sufficient enough for its officials to develop its own nuclear and missile programs. The competition between India and Pakistan soon sparked a nuclear and missile arms race in South Asia that even today has the capacity to engender disastrous results far beyond their respective borders. North Korea's expanding nuclear ambitions and provocations present a more complex set of circumstances: the desire for additional security vis-à-vis the United States and greater international recognition of their status.

Long after the Cold War drifted into history, regional nuclear ambitions have continued and alliances with great powers have sometimes been uncertain. While some observers doubted that the nuclear equation could ever become so complex,[1] when looking at the actions of the above states, the regions within which they are situated, and the Security Council states they have relations with, it is evident that nuclear weapons will continue to play an influential role in shaping international security deep into the twenty-first century.[2]

ISRAEL'S NUCLEAR WEAPONS

Very early in Israel's existence, David Ben-Gurion, according to Michael Karpin's account, was "the man who conceived the idea of the Jewish doomsday weapon." However, he argued, "there is no available record of any official decision ever taken by any competent governmental body to endorse Ben-Gurion's personal wish to acquire the nuclear option." If Ben-Gurion had established the basic objective, Israel's nuclear program gradually unfolded as the product of improvised strategies and opportunism. Initially, his search for all types of weaponry was stymied by the United States, Britain, and France's Tripartite Agreement (1950) that sought to balance the supply of weapons to Israel and the neighboring Arab states. When these three nations refused to allow the Soviet Union's participation, Moscow independently arranged for Egypt to obtain conventional weapons from the Soviet bloc, thus repealing the 1950 pact and allowing Israel to obtain arms from France. Israel's formal introduction to the nuclear world took place as part of President Dwight D. Eisenhower's "Atoms for Peace" program. In July 1955, the signed agreement committed the United States to provide "an experimental, low-powered reactor of up to 5,000 kilowatts of the 'swimming pool' type (in which uranium rods are immersed in a pool of heavy water that serves mainly to moderate the chain reaction process and as a coolant)." While technically too small to provide the basic material needed for an atomic bomb, it did train Israeli scientists and provide radioactive isotopes used by medical and industrial facilities.[3]

The Suez Crisis of 1956 provided Jerusalem with the opportunity to obtain the powerful nuclear reactor it needed from France, which would deliver the required material needed for the bomb. This connection developed earlier in 1955 when French officials agreed to supply Israel with conventional weapons in exchange for intelligence regarding Egypt's assistance to Algerian insurgents. In an intriguing tripartite arrangement that gradually focused on the Suez Canal, England sought to prevent Egypt's seizure of the canal, France hoped to terminate Egypt's aid to the Algerian rebels, and Israel aimed to obtain the nuclear reactor and scientific assistance it desired from France. While London and Paris' desired goals were thwarted in 1956 by

U.S. and Soviet actions, the Israelis gained their objective. Ben-Gurion had taken a major step toward obtaining his "nuclear option."

The Dimona site in the Negev Desert began to take shape by the end of 1957, as French scientific technicians arrived to assist the construction of a reactor similar to the French G-1, activated on the Rhône River in early 1956. A main differential was that France's version was moderated by graphite, while the Dimona version operated via heavy water and did not produce electricity. Despite Israeli claims that the Dimona reactor had a 24-megawatt capacity, other experts have argued that it was built for a 40-megawatt capacity and was additionally upgraded in the 1970s. The former Dimona technician, Mordechai Vanunu, who provided a London newspaper with the site's secrets, prompted American and British specialists to believe at the time that Israel had produced at least 40 kilos of plutonium yearly—sufficient for some ten bombs. For many years, Ben-Gurion, as defense minister and later prime minister, kept knowledge of the development of the nuclear weapons program covert and limited to very few associates, excluding most members of the government. Some political leaders were provided with information about Israel's relations with France and about the construction of the reactor at Dimona, but nothing substantive pertaining to the site's bomb production.[4]

Henry Jacob Gomberg, a Jewish nuclear professor at the University of Michigan, told American intelligence officials in December 1960 that "Israel, with French assistance is building a powerful nuclear reactor in the Negev, with the intention of producing weapons-grade plutonium." Moreover, he speculated, Israel could have a bomb within a decade. Karpin suggests that this episode was part of a carefully developed scheme to let Washington know what was taking place without irritating the French. After all, the Defense Ministry had begun to realize it could not indefinitely keep the huge project a secret as too many foreign individuals were making "trips to the desert." When the Kennedy administration quietly queried Israel on its nuclear program, Prime Minister Ben-Gurion replied that Washington "must accept" his word that Israel had no plans to build an atomic bomb as its projects were for "peaceful purposes." However, believing that Tel Aviv was developing nuclear weapons for the purpose of creating a deterrent, Ambassador Paul C. Warnke concluded: "I do not think that the U.S. had the feeling that it could physically stop Israel from developing a nuclear weapon." In Washington, officials were coming to look upon Israel as a partner in the Cold War and were warming to making the requisite concessions.[5]

On July 18, 1970, *New York Times* lead writer Hedrick Smith revealed to the American public Israel's status as an opaque nuclear weapons state, that is, a state that neither confirms nor denies it has the bomb. In simpler terms, it had no formally stated declaratory policy, the classic "don't ask, don't tell" situation. "To this day," observed Avner Cohen and William Burr, "all Israeli governments of the left and right have been faithful in keeping secrecy over their nuclear activities, making great efforts to ensure that nothing would be visible, politically, technologically, militarily, or otherwise." Although unclear who leaked the information, the article was principally based on comments made by Democratic senator Stuart Symington, a leading member of Congress and former secretary of the air force. Smith also revealed much of what the U.S. government had known about Israel's nuclear program, emphasizing: "For the past two years the United States Government had been conducting its Middle East policy on the assumption that Israel either possesses an atomic bomb or has component parts for quick assembly." What Smith could not have known was the extent to which Nixon and Kissinger had already pushed the Israeli nuclear issue with Israeli prime minister Golda Meir and Israeli ambassador Yitzhak Rabin, in September 1969, or that, for all practical purposes, the debate was fairly much over before it started.[6]

Smith covered many of the highly sensitive issues that had dogged Johnson and Nixon in their negotiations with Jerusalem over Israel's nuclear program. These included disagreement within the highest levels of government as to whether Israel should be regarded as being a nuclear state before "the last piece of mechanism is hooked up," otherwise known as the "last wire issue." As late as the early 1960s, the CIA had concluded that Israel was well within reach of developing a nuclear capacity within twelve to eighteen months, subsequently lowered to between six and nine months, and then dropped entirely. According to "well-informed sources," wrote Smith, the absence of a reference to any time delay "indicated the official belief that Israel [already] had the fissionable material and the mechanisms for rapid assembly, if not actual weapons as well." This information was presumably so sensitive that the U.S. government had "not developed a fully coordinated national intelligence estimate that [said] directly that Israel does have atomic bombs." Still, background papers prepared by the State Department for Nixon's meeting with Prime Minister Meir, in September 1969, including an intelligence update with clearance by all the relevant agencies—including the CIA, the Pentagon, and even the Arms Control and Disarmament Agency and the Atomic Energy Commission—made it clear beyond peradventure that the threshold had already been passed: "Israel might very well now have a nuclear bomb" and certainly "already had the technical ability and material resources to produce weapon-grade uranium for a number of weapons."[7]

Israel's response to the *New York Times* allegations, penned by an unnamed Israeli source, was swift: "The report in the *New York Times* is speculative, unauthoritative, and inaccurate. . . . Israel is not a nuclear state and it will not be the first country to introduce nuclear weapons in the Middle East." According to the disclaimer published by the newspaper, Israeli officials informed the international community "this means Israel would not be the first Middle Eastern country to test or use nuclear weapons." It was progress of a sort. In any case, Smith's article in the *New York Times* marked the beginning of a new era in the public discourse of Israel's nuclear weapons program, revealing the worst-kept secret in the history of the global arms race. Israel was, indeed, a nuclear weapons state and should be regarded as such. The State Department went so far as to incorporate this development in its negotiations with the Soviets apropos the NPT, suggesting that despite the fact that Israel was "moving forward with a nuclear weapons and missile program," it might still be possible to persuade the Israelis and Egyptians to ratify the NPT as part of a larger peace settlement. There was never much chance of that happening. Israel now had the best of all possible worlds—it had the widely accepted status as a de facto nuclear weapons state, it had a strict policy of nuclear opacity, and it was seemingly free to exploit its official ambiguity.[8]

While U.S. intelligence agencies continued to collect data on Israel's nuclear program, it was uncertain what conclusions were reached after January 1970, other than confirming Israel had acquired the bomb. What was known was the purpose of the Dimona nuclear research site, an underground plutonium-processing plant in the Negev Desert used in the production of the necessary fissile materials to make nuclear weapons. Whatever nuclear information American intelligence agencies collected at this point was not communicated outside the highest levels of government. Nor did any useful information filter down to U.S. embassy staff around the world, or to its allies, who took American assurances at face value that the Israelis would not be the first to introduce nuclear weapons into their region. National Security Advisor Henry Kissinger had earlier confirmed to President Nixon, in October 1969, following Golda Meir's visit in September, that Israeli ambassador Rabin had gone so far to as to define "introduce" as meaning "not to test and not publicize."[9]

PRODUCTION AND PROLIFERATION

By 1974, the CIA reported that Israel had developed between ten and twenty nuclear weapons, an estimate derived from the Federation of American Scientists that calculated Israel could have separated enough plutonium to produce at least six nuclear weapons and had probably stolen enough uranium for four more bombs. This estimate became public knowledge in 1976 when the CIA's deputy director for science and technology, Carl Duckett, conveyed this information at a local meeting of the American Institute of Aeronautics and Astronautics.[10] Israeli leaders have long contended that science could compensate them for what nature had denied them. Surrounded on all sides by historical enemies sworn to drive them into the sea, it was only natural that Israel would turn to the ultimate weapon as a way of compensating for its demographic, geographic, and conventional military weakness relative to its Arab neighbors. In this sense, then, the original motivation for Israel's nuclear weapons program was, simply put, to possess a weapon of last resort. It would not be of much use otherwise. Even the experience of near conventional defeat in the Yom Kippur War in 1973 suggested that a weapon of this magnitude had very little military application.

While subsequent peace agreements between Israel and both Egypt and Jordan somewhat lessened fears, these were replaced with concerns pertaining to Iraqi weapons of mass destruction and the nascent Iranian nuclear program. Such developments in the region would spur the Begin Doctrine (after Menachem Begin, the leader of the right-wing Likud party) under which Israel took dramatic military action against secret nuclear facilities at Osirak, in Iraq, in 1981, and then at Al Kibar, in Syria, in 2007. These "preemptive" attacks left a legacy that echoes today, where the "all options are on the table" drumbeat emanating from Washington and Jerusalem remains a consideration of both states' security calculi. Of course, the effectiveness of military strikes, especially the one at Osirak, is certainly open to question given Iraq's subsequent extensive expansion of its facilities as discovered after the First Gulf War by IAEA inspectors.[11]

More recently, it has been estimated that Israel has an arsenal ranging from 100 to 200 nuclear warheads, in which approximately 50 of them are missile warheads, and the rest deliverable by aircraft. Analysts now believe that the size of Israel's nuclear stockpile is either comparable to or exceeds the nuclear arsenal of Britain, as well as that of India and Pakistan. In terms of the specific make-up, Israel has fifty medium-range ballistic missiles (1,500–1,800-kilometer range) with the capacity to strike that extends to the south of Russia. In 2008 Israel tested an extended range Jericho III missile with a maximum range of 4,800–6,500 kilometers, taking it across the line to an intercontinental ballistic missile. Apart from missiles, Israel has one of the most powerful air forces in the world, including 205 U.S.-made fighter planes capable of carrying nuclear weapons. Independent analysts also believe that having bought the first two Dolphin-class submarines from Germany in the 1990s and securing the purchase of the sixth submarine in 2011–2012, Israel has in effect developed a nuclear triad.[12] Additionally, according to a Global Fissile Material report, Israel may still produce plutonium for weapons and may already house approximately 820 ± 150 kilograms of weapons-grade plutonium at its underground Dimona production reactor. While Israel is believed to still be operating the reactor, its exact status is uncertain. Additionally, it is also believed that Israel may have produced highly enriched uranium in the past for military purposes,[13] with the stockpile estimated at approximately 0.3 metric tons.[14]

Like all nuclear states, Israel is clearly in for the long haul, evident with persistent information, albeit unsubstantiated, pertaining to its modernization program. One such development is the continual upgrading and refinement of the abovementioned land-based ballistic missile force, from the current Jericho II to a longer-range Jericho III missile contained on the Shavit space launch vehicle. The air-based arm of Israel's nuclear force could possibly also undergo modernization as the Israeli air force obtains the F-35 Joint Strike Fighter from the United States. Additionally, there is information that Israel may have transformed a cruise missile to nuclear weapons capability for its new Dolphin-class attack submarines, with specific attention given to the Popeye Turbo or Harpoon missiles; however, this status still remains ambiguous. That said, if this transition has been taking place, the submarines would deliver Israel with a new limited-range offensive proficiency and more secure reactive capability. [15]

IRAN'S NUCLEAR PROGRAM

Iranian officials began considering a nuclear program during the 1950s, with its U.S.-supplied research reactor going critical in 1967. After securing increased petroleum funds in the 1970s, Tehran explored the prospect of 10–20 nuclear power reactors that would provide more than 20,000 megawatts of electrical power by 1994. As it considered obtaining uranium enrichment and reprocessing technology, Tehran demonstrated it was not interested in seeking nuclear weapons by signing the Non-Proliferation Treaty, in 1968, and proposed to the UN General Assembly a plan for creating a nuclear-weapons-free zone in the Middle East. In spite of close relations with the shah's government, Washington officials during the 1970s began worrying about Iran's interest in nuclear weaponry. A 1975 State Department memorandum suggested "uncertainty" over Iran's "long-term objectives despite its NPT status." The Central Intelligence Agency's 1988 report entitled *Middle East-South Asia: Nuclear Handbook* asserted that Tehran had undertaken nuclear weapons "design work" prior to the 1979 Islamic revolution. The same report indicated that the revolutionary government had initially halted the nuclear program only to reinstitute it in 1982. By 1985, a National Intelligence Council report identified Iran as a potential "proliferation threat" and declared that the new regime was "interested in developing facilities that . . . could eventually produce fissile material that could be used in a [nuclear] weapon." It was estimated that it would take at least a decade for Tehran to produce a weapon. [16]

Thereafter, according to Paul Kerr, "Tehran's construction of a gas-centrifuge-based uranium enrichment facility" aroused proliferation fears, while Iranian officials insisted that they desired only "to produce low-enriched uranium (LEU) fuel for its planned light-water nuclear reactors." While these officials indicated interest in obtaining nuclear fuel from other nations, they stated that Iran ought to possess its own enrichment capability to guard against possible fuel supply disruptions. Additionally, Tehran's building of a heavy-water reactor at Arak also became an issue, because its spent fuel would contain plutonium suitable for producing nuclear weapons. For this latter stage to occur, the plutonium would have to be separated (reprocessed) from the spent fuel, an activity in which Iran stated it would not engage. An IAEA investigation, together with information supplied by Tehran after an October 2003 pact, showed that "Iran had engaged in a variety of clandestine nuclear-related activities, some of which violated Iran's safeguards agreement." These involved "plutonium separation experiments, uranium enrichment and conversion experiments, and importing various uranium compounds." The election of President Mahmoud Ahmadinejad, in 2005, was followed by Iranian intransigence regarding restrictions on their nuclear activities that resulted in a series of UN and nationally imposed economic sanctions.[17]

During this period, Western nations, and of course Israel, viewed Iran as posing two potential threats: the construction of enhanced nuclear enrichment facilities as a first step in obtaining nuclear warheads, and an ambitious missile program. The Supreme Leader Ayatollah Ali Khamene'i attempted to dispel their fears, declaring on June 3, 2008, that Iran was opposed to nuclear weapons "based on religious and Islamic beliefs as well as based on logic and wisdom." Moreover, he said: "Nuclear weapons have no benefit but high costs to manufacture and keep them. Nuclear weapons do not bring power to a nation because they are not applicable. Nuclear weapons cannot be used." In the same vein, a spokesman for the Iranian Foreign Ministry noted, on November 10, 2008, "pursuance of nuclear weapons has no place in the country's defense doctrine." Even President Ahmadinejad chimed in on April 9, 2009, asserting that "those who accumulate nuclear weapons are backwards in political terms." Unconvinced Western leaders turned to the UN Security Council for economic sanctions, resulting in Resolutions 1803 (2006) and 1747 (2007) that were supplemented by Resolution 1696 (2006) and Resolution 1929 (2010), as well as a variety of national restrictive policies. Essentially, these resolutions were intended to halt or regulate Iran's nuclear enrichment programs and allow its facilities to be inspected by the International Atomic Energy Agency. These sanctions stimulated intermittent diplomatic activities that found it difficult to acknowledge Iran's sovereign rights while applying coercive action.[18]

With diplomacy and sanctions in play, the West and the United States, particularly, continued searching for ways to persuade or coerce Iran not to join the nuclear weapons club. For example, the U.S. Nuclear Posture Review Report in April 2010 stated: "We seek to bolster the nuclear nonproliferation regime and its centerpiece, the NPT, by reversing the nuclear ambitions of North Korea and Iran, strengthening International Atomic Energy Agency safeguards and enforcing compliance with them." By late 2011, diplomatic activity and sanctions appeared unable to achieve the UN and IAEA's desired goals—neither did the clandestine assassination of several Iranians involved in its nuclear program or anonymous cyberattacks, including the Stuxnet computer virus. On November 8, the IAEA issued a sharply critical report that declared:

> While the Agency continues to verify the non-diversion of declared nuclear material at the nuclear facilities and LOFs [located outside facilities] declared by Iran under its Safeguards Agreement, as Iran is not providing the necessary cooperation, including by not implementing its Additional Protocol, the Agency is unable to provide credible assurance about the absence of undeclared nuclear materials and activities in Iran, and therefore to conclude that all nuclear material in Iran is in peaceful activities.

After further extensive analysis of information in another report, the agency concluded that Iran had "carried out activities relevant to the development of a nuclear explosive device" before 2003. Therefore, the agency urged Iran without delay to provide "clarifications regarding possible military dimensions to its nuclear programme."[19] Even though the IAEA report failed to surprise most observers, those individuals stimulated by what professor Francis Gavin referred to as "nuclear alarmism," rushed to the media demanding preventive military strikes to destroy its nuclear facilities. The alarmism was essentially grounded on several fears, ranging from the conviction that nuclear proliferation had arrived at a "tipping point" and, thus, "a nuclear Iran might drive Egypt, Saudi Arabia, and Turkey into the nuclear club" as they would be concerned that a nuclear Iran would become more aggressive. In Washington, concerns focused on the prospect that a nuclear-armed Iran would alter the balance of power in the Middle East and diminish America's ability to influence affairs in that region. However, as Thomas Barnett pointed out, "Once the U.S. went into both Iraq and Afghanistan, the question went from being, 'How do we prevent Iran from getting the Bomb?' to 'How do we handle Iran's Bomb?'" Perhaps nuclear weapons in Iranian hands was "not the system-changing event so many analysts are keen to portray."

Ayatollah Khamene'i together with high-ranking Revolutionary Guard commanders were considered the individuals that would likely have control over any Iranian nuclear weapons. Reviewing deterring factors operating during the seven-plus decades of the nuclear age, Michael Cohen, writing in *Global Policy,* argued that these Iranian leaders "may be revisionists but they are not suicidal: a bolt out of the blue attack on Israel or other American allies would be suicidal and unlikely." Therefore, "the most dangerous consequences of an Iranian bomb is conventional or, more likely, sub-conventional aggression. . . . After developing nuclear weapons, Iran can slowly but steadily increase the cost of U.S. influence in the Persian Gulf and threaten to respond to American or Israeli retaliation with nuclear escalation." Matthew Kroenig did not regard Iran's "movements" as being a forecast for an incremental (peaceful) ascendency. In fact, a nuclear-armed Iran would pose immense danger to U.S. interests in the Middle East and beyond. Nonetheless, skeptics of military action fail to understand, he argued, that "the cure would be worse than the disease—that is, that the consequences of a U.S. assault on Iran would be as bad as or worse than those of Iran achieving its nuclear ambitions. But that is a faulty assumption. The truth is that a military strike intended to destroy Iran's nuclear program, if managed carefully, could spare the region and the world a very real threat and dramatically improve the long-term national security of the United States."[20] While these controversial sentiments of Kroenig engendered extensive debate, many observers, and policy makers for that matter, believed that the military option would not necessarily provide the desired solution.[21] Instead, the diplomatic option backed with firm sanctions, as espoused by the Obama administration, would remain the chosen path.

OBAMA, THE P5+1, AND IRAN

Indeed, the first significant public materialization of President Obama's approach to Iran policy came in a March 21, 2009, speech to the Iranian people on Nowruz, the Persian New Year. He stated that the United States "is now committed to [a form of] diplomacy that addresses the full range of issues before us, and to pursuing constructive ties among the United States, Iran, and the international community."[22] Additionally, he referred to Iran as "The Islamic Republic of Iran,"[23] a symbolic recognition of the Islamic revolution in Iran. Coinciding with such rhetoric, administration officials were less forthright in endorsing hardline options such as military action or regime change—although no option was explicitly "taken off the table." The aggressive Iranian response to the 2009 election-related unrest and its refusal to agree to technical terms of the October 1, 2009, nuclear agreement shifted the Obama administration's focus toward employing greater economic and diplomatic pressure. Despite the subsequent implementation of UN Resolution 1929 on June 9, 2010, the key priority for the administration was to work toward a deal via the P5+1 (the five permanent members of the United Nations Security Council—China, France, Russia, the United Kingdom, and the United States—plus Germany) to halt Iran's accumulation of 20 percent enriched uranium (which is above normal fuel grade and closer to weapons grade) in exchange for fuel assemblies for its Tehran Research Reactor and medical isotopes. This was consistent with the principle that Iran had the right under the NPT to only enrich in full compliance with safeguards and only for genuine civilian purposes, thereby allowing it to work as a platform for a broader arrangement to limit the size and scope of its enrichment program.[24] In essence, the employment of the "two track" approach emphasized imposing and implementing additional sanctions, while continuing to offer dialogue and negotiations if Iran was willing to negotiate on the key issues pertaining to its nuclear program.[25] This was reiterated by Obama during his first post-election press conference on November 6, 2012, when he said he would "try to make a push in the coming months to see if we can open up a dialogue between Iran and—not just us but the international community—to see if we can get this thing resolved."[26]

However, developments in 2012 signified that the Iran security issue would continue to challenge the administration's dual approach. Fordow site revelations in the said year clearly illustrated how Iran had continued to make progress toward a nuclear weapon capability, notwithstanding demands from the UNSC that it suspend uranium enrichment and other sensitive nuclear activities.[27] Iran publicized these developments even while there were reports that such sanctions contributed to an 80 percent reduction in the value of its currency, the rial; caused Iranian exports of crude oil to fall by more than half; led to a 60 percent cut in Iranian crude oil production; and blocked Iranian banks, including the central bank, from access to the international banking system.[28] During the earlier stages of its second term, the deflection of Iran's nuclear course became the most pressing foreign policy issue for the Obama administration. In staying the course between firm sanctions and a more receptive leadership in Iran under the moderate President Hassan Rouhani, the P5+1 was able to reach a detailed framework that would ultimately secure a decisive agreement two months later.[29]

A FRAMEWORK AND THEN AN AGREEMENT

On April 6, 2015, the framework agreement posited by the P5+1 and Iran laid a crucial and detailed foundation. It articulated an effective, verifiable, enforceable, long-term plan to mitigate the development of a new nuclear-armed state in the Middle East. The framework comprehensively addressed the key avenues by which Iran could attain material for nuclear weapons. These included: limiting Iran's capability to enrich uranium to the point where it would take at least twelve months to accumulate the requisite uranium enriched to weapons grade for one bomb; necessitating Iran to adjust its Arak heavy water reactor so as to implicitly decrease its proliferation capacity and ban Iran from developing any proficiency for extricating plutonium from spent fuel for weapons; implementing improved international inspections and monitoring that would hinder attempts to contravene the agreement, and if Iran did, embolden the international community's capacity to identify quickly and, if necessary, impede future efforts by Iran to construct nuclear weapons, including at potential clandestine sites; and requiring Iran to conjoin with the IAEA in concluding the investigation of Iran's previous efforts to develop a nuclear warhead, and provide pellucidity sufficient to facilitate any such efforts.[30]

The detailed nature of the April framework enabled a final agreement to take place on July 14, 2015, between Iran, the P5+1, and the European Union, achieving "what no amount of political posturing and vague threats of military action had managed to do before." Formally known as the Joint Comprehensive Plan of Action (JCPOA), the agreement established a set of robust verifiable limits on Iran's ability to develop a nuclear weapon for at least the next ten to fifteen years, and was potentially one of the "most consequential accords in recent diplomatic history, with the ability not just to keep Iran from obtaining a nuclear weapon but also to reshape Middle East politics."[31] The outcome of twenty laborious months of negotiations articulated a phasing approach to lifting of international economic sanctions, and in return, Iran would reduce by 98 percent its stockpile of lowenriched uranium, which can be processed further into bomb-grade fuel, and reduce the number of operating centrifuges used to enrich that fuel by two-thirds, to 5,060. Such limitations meant that if Iran decided to undermine the agreement and make a push for a nuclear bomb, it would take at least a year to produce the requisite weapons-grade fuel. Many of the restrictions of the agreement will be in force for ten to twenty-five years. However, other stipulations pertaining to IAEA monitoring would remain in place indefinitely, including access to ambiguous sites "where necessary, when necessary." As conveyed by President Obama, "There will be 24/7 monitoring of Iran's key nuclear facilities. For decades, inspectors will have access to Iran's entire nuclear supply chain—from the uranium mines and mills where they get raw materials, to the centrifuge production facilities where they make machines to enrich it."[32] In simple terms, if Iran contravenes the agreement, there will be ample time to quickly re-implement sanctions, ratchet up firm diplomacy, and/or, as a last resort, pursue a military strike option.[33] As further stated:

> So this deal is not just the best choice among alternatives—this is the strongest non-proliferation agreement ever negotiated. And because this is such a strong deal, every nation in the world that has commented publicly, with the exception of the Israeli government, has expressed support. The United Nations Security Council has unanimously supported it. The majority of arms control and non-proliferation experts support it. Over 100 former ambassadors—who served under Republican and Democratic Presidents—support it. I've had to make a lot of tough calls as President, but whether or not this deal is good for American security is not one of those calls. It's not even close.[34]

A MIDDLE EAST NUCLEAR-WEAPON-FREE ZONE?

As early as the mid-1970s, when it became apparent that Israel had devel-oped nuclear weapons, spurred by Iran, the United Nations General Assem-bly issued the first of its almost annual resolutions calling for a nuclear-weapon-free zone (NWFZ) in the Middle East. Through the intervening decades many discussions took place and proposals were offered, but with little political movement toward the basic goal. Israel maintained a policy of ambiguity toward its nuclear weapons capability, although everyone assumes that it possessed a nuclear arsenal and effective delivery system. Since it was evident that Iran had previously been developing a nuclear base that could produce a weapon capability, many observers have experienced an even greater sense of urgency at finding a formula to remove nuclear forces, existing and potential, from the Middle East. However, gaining any traction toward a NWFZ in the Middle East, as a draft report by the Monterey Non-proliferation Strategy Group in 2009 put it, "will require finding resolution on a host of seemingly intransigent issues, including questions ranging from maritime passage and security assurances, to the difficulty of facilitating engagement between Arab states, Iran and Israel." It should also be noted that "in addition to the Israel-Arab relationship, any discussion on the Middle East Zone also involves Iran, Turkey, the United States, Russia and the European Union."[35]

In 2011, an opinion poll of 510 Israeli Jews conducted by the Program on International Policy Attitudes and the Anwar Sadat Chair at the University of Maryland, fielded by the Dahaf Institute in Israel, appeared to suggest that a substantial majority of Israeli citizens supported the idea of a nuclear-weap-on-free zone as a means of defusing Iran's potential nuclear threat. Their government, however, continued to resist the idea. This poll also found that the Israelis "not only expressed support for the long term goal of eliminating nuclear weapons from the region but also for an interim step of making their nuclear facilities transparent together with Iran." As there has been so little progress made in the past, there are "many reasons to be skeptical" that the various states will—for the foreseeable future—lack adequate motivation to move forward on such a NWFZ proposal. There are basic disagreements over how to begin approaching the issue. For example, "Israel believes that an incremental approach best suits the situation, starting with confidence build-ing measures that will lead to an improvement in relations, followed by reconciliation, mutual recognition, and conventional arms control measures. However, Arab states view this position as a means of permanently delaying substantive discussions on a [Middle East NWFZ]."[36]

Notwithstanding these sentiments, the 2010 NPT Review Conference did appear to actually yield some positive movement in regard to a WMDFZ. For the first time, state parties were able to agree to five applied steps advancing toward implementing the 1995 NPT Review Conference Middle East resolution. The United States, Russia, and the United Kingdom, the treaty core powers and sponsors of that resolution, agreed to collaborate with the UN secretary general to summon a regional conference so as to discuss the issue in 2012. Additionally, measures agreed upon encompassed the appointment of a WMDFZ expediter, as well as designation of a government that would convene the conference during the 2015 NPT Review Conference. Egypt led the Arab League in driving a new proposal to bestow with the facilitator and three of the conveners (Russia, the United Kingdom, and the United States), leaving the UN secretary general as the solitary authority for holding the conference inside 180 days of the Review Conference's conclusion. The Egyptian proposal also stipulated the formation of two working groups: Working Group I would orchestrate the scope, geographic differentiation, exclusions, and interim measures; Working Group II would be responsible for verification actions and implementation mechanisms.[37]

An amended version of the Egyptian application appeared in the draft final document of the 2015 NPT Review Conference. The document called for the UN secretary general to summon a conference by March 1, 2016, aimed at "launching a continuous process of negotiating and concluding a legally binding treaty" that inaugurates a WMD-free zone in the Middle East.[38] It also requested that the secretary general assign a special representative to expedite the process by July 1. The facilitator would work with the secretary general, as well as Russia, the United Kingdom, and the United States, to liaise with applicable states in the region on the itinerary/structure for the conference. Within the terms of the draft document, if an agenda for the conference was approved before the March deadline, the secretary general would have to organize the conference within forty-five days of agreement on the agenda. Ultimately, based on some of the language pertaining to the Middle East WMD-free zone, the United States, the United Kingdom, and Canada did not support the draft final document from the NPT review conference. Speaking at the conference, the United States said it withheld its approval because the disposition to set an agenda and hold a conference was not based on "consensus and equality," and that the document proposed "unworkable conditions" and "arbitrary deadlines."[39] Aside from these concerns pertaining to the terms of a WMDFZ, Francisco Galamas succinctly illustrated the broader impediments:

> Although Syria's accession to the Chemical Weapons Convention (CWC) and Iran's suspension of most of its nuclear activities may sound like good omens for the establishment of a WMDFZ in the Middle East, the chances of an agreement remain remote. . . . Even taking into consideration its policy of nuclear ambiguity, news related to the acquisition of new nuclear-capable submarines make clear that Israel intends to keep its nuclear weapons and reinforce its second strike capability, which places an added hurdle in front of

this disarmament effort. Other challenges for a WMDFZ are linked to the Egyptian lack of accession to the CWC and the Biological and Toxin Weapons Convention (BTWC). Hence, in spite of several meetings held over the past few years to debate the adoption of a WMDFZ, there is no evidence of progress.

THE SUBCONTINENT'S NUCLEAR DILEMMA

Beginning in the 1970s, the nations of India and Pakistan began developing nuclear weapons to meet a triangular strategic relationship. India's decision was in response to what it perceived as a threat from China's nuclear program that, in turn, stimulated Pakistan's program aimed at deterring India's nuclear force. In the process, both of the superpowers, ambivalent in their support of the two nations, became frustrated with the South Asia nuclear dilemma. "In the time period between the negotiations for the Nuclear Non-Proliferation Treaty (NPT) in 1967 through the end of the Cold War in 1989," Balazs Szalontai has written, "Soviet policy vacillated between disapproval (during the NPT negotiations), silence (in the aftermath of India's May 1974 nuclear test), and gradually increasing technical support for India's civilian nuclear program (from 1976 onward)." During the NPT negotiations, while Moscow's primary objective was to prevent West Germany from obtaining nuclear weapons, Szalontai notes that "Soviet leaders expressed their displeasure with India's nuclear policies in no uncertain terms. In contrast, in the 1970s and early 1980s, when the Kremlin sought to offset Chinese or U.S. influence in Asia, they turned a blind eye to New Delhi's nuclear ambitions, even going so far as to express their approval of an Indian plan to launch a preventive air strike on Pakistan's nuclear research center."

Conversely, White House officials paid little concern to nuclear affairs in South Asia. Their major focus was on ending the Vietnam War while developing a wide-ranging strategy involving China and the Soviet Union. Indeed, India's refusal to sign the Nuclear Non-Proliferation Treaty did not privately concern President Nixon or his foreign affairs adviser, Henry Kissinger, since neither placed more than a secondary priority on nuclear proliferation. The latter's secret visit to Beijing underscored the difficulty Washington had in improving relations with India, especially when later, in 1971, New Delhi signed a treaty with Moscow. The Indian nuclear test in 1974, consequently, took the Nixon administration by surprise.[40] In broader terms, it is evident that the increasingly dangerous nuclear arms race in the South Asia subcontinent emerged during the Cold War and would become a matter of increasing concern in the twenty-first century. As stated by Vipin Narang, "The catalytic, assured retaliation, and asymmetric escalation postures cover the substantive empirical variation in South Asia's two major powers. Critically, all three have been adopted during the region's nuclear period, whose de facto beginning occurred in the late 1980s, when India and Pakistan are believed to have weaponized their nuclear capabilities."[41]

INDIA'S DECISION FOR NUCLEAR WEAPONS

Until March 1971, India's official nuclear policy essentially remained the same as it had been in the early 1950s—in favor of nuclear power but opposed to nuclear weapons. The previous international actions of India to pursue global nuclear disarmament and support non-proliferation efforts were presumably based upon a strong moral premise. Within a year of having affirmed the previous policy, however, Indira Gandhi decided to pursue a peaceful nuclear weapon; as a result, India's nuclear status became much more ambiguous. In choosing to develop nuclear weapons, India clearly evaded the spirit of the Atoms for Peace program under which the Canadians and the United States had provided the CIRUS reactor. It apparently was this reactor that produced the plutonium for the initial test, and raised several questions when the U.S. government sought to again supply India with nuclear fuels.[42]

While there appeared to be significant interest and support within India regarding the potential development of nuclear weapons around 1965, by the early 1970s this interest had significantly waned. Thus, the 1974 explosion took many by surprise, catching the United States and the international community at large unaware; particularly given that the United States had been collecting data on areas pertaining to uranium exploration within India, the Indian civilian nuclear program and new nuclear power plants, as well as India's interest in developing a nuclear weapon. After the border clash with the Chinese in 1962 and China's 1964 entry into the nuclear club, the Americans were aware that India was becoming increasingly interested in developing a deterrent gauged toward its nuclear-armed neighbor. One year prior to Richard Nixon becoming president in 1969, the Bhabha Atomic Research Centre embarked on an intensive effort to develop an Indian nuclear explosive, while politicians, including Prime Minister Indira Gandhi, focused upon negotiating the NPT, apparently unaware of the scientists' unilateral decision to move Indian nuclear technology toward the next step. As George Perkovich states, "While Prime Minister Gandhi concentrated on politics and diplomats wrangled over the NPT, a small team of scientists at the Bhabha Atomic Research Centre initiated the most concerted effort yet to develop nuclear explosives." It was only when the scientists were actually ready to build and test a nuclear weapon that they sought prime ministerial approval.[43]

In 1968, Gandhi and her cabinet had confirmed that they would not sign the NPT, ostensibly on the grounds that the United States and USSR had not addressed India's concerns pertaining to latent inequality in the redrafting of the treaty. While India had been previously adamant in its policy of non-alignment, the non-signature of the NPT was seen as a diplomatic expression of its determination not to be subordinate to the major powers. India also revealed the shift in its policy to the international community, reflected in a reduced sense of urgency regarding international disarmament and non-pro-liferation agreements, as well as withdrawal from many negotiations on arms limitation issues; all indications that it was becoming more interested in pursuing national security through increased military power. Although the Indian government argued publicly that it refused to sign the NPT because the treaty treated nuclear and non-nuclear nations differently, keeping its nuclear option open was possibly the most important guide pertaining to its decision. [44]

American analysts and policy makers estimated at this time that India's nuclear research, development, and manufacturing capabilities had pro-gressed significantly beyond the level of a legitimate civilian nuclear energy program. In November 1970, the United States and India began discussions concerning peaceful nuclear explosions (PNEs). Knowing that India was interested in exploring nuclear technology in a considerably broader capac-ity, the Americans warned the Indians that conducting a PNE did not consti-tute a "peaceful use of nuclear materials," as defined in two previous agree-ments on the subject (Tarapur and CIRUS). In turn, India rejected the inter-pretation of the previous agreements, informing the United States that it had the sovereign right to test PNEs. To deter the Indians from reaching even this stage, the United States supported a universal embargo to prevent India from obtaining nuclear technology and enriched uranium. While Washington had hoped that such supply barriers would spur India toward suspending their nuclear weapons activities, the Indians persevered. [45]

In February 1971, senior American officials met with allies to discuss the issue of the Indian nuclear program. The meeting noted assertions made by the Pakistanis in the United Nations General Assembly, late in 1970, about both India's ability and intention to explode a nuclear device. While the entire record of the meeting is not available, it was concluded that India doubtless had the technical base and enough unsafeguarded plutonium— though restricted by agreement to peaceful uses—to now develop a simple fission device. The relationship between the United States and India grew increasingly tense after Gandhi's visit to Washington. Despite continuing to insist that India remained neutral in August 1971, the Indian prime minister proceeded to sign a twenty-year treaty of "peace, friendship and cooperation" with the Soviet Union. Included in the treaty was a virtual guarantee of Soviet-provided security for the Indians. There was also speculation within the National Security Council that the treaty might provide nuclear-capable bombers to the Indian government. Although American officials did not regard this as being highly plausible, they did believe that it was probable that the Indians and Soviets were conducting arms negotiations in order for the Indian government to "guarantee a continuing and secure source of military aid."[46]

Despite India's victory in the Indo-Pakistani War of 1971, which had resulted in India cementing its place as the dominant power on the subcontinent, the war (and possibly the United States' support for Pakistan during the war) further persuaded the Indian prime minister of the importance of emboldening her country's military capabilities. U.S. support of Pakistan angered the Indians, especially after Nixon had dispatched an aircraft carrier task force toward the Bay of Bengal—a move that the Indians regarded as a modern version of gunboat diplomacy.[47] In July 1972, Kissinger commissioned another examination of Indian nuclear developments. National Security Study Memorandum (NSSM) 156 was specifically designed to "examine the implications of an Indian nuclear test for US interests and the policy options open to the United States in these circumstances with respect to India, India's sub-continent neighbors, and other affected states." While unsure about a specific timeframe, the committee acknowledged that India was close to being in a position to "explode a device."[48] By 1973, Indian scientists had resolved any remaining technical problems involved in developing a nuclear weapon and proceeded to select a test site for their explosion in the Rajasthan desert—a sparsely populated area of northwest India.[49]

The May 18, 1974, test of a "peaceful nuclear device" was clearly a sign of India's determination to deter *the use* and *threat of use* of nuclear weapons against its territory and its forces, as well as a clear rejection of foreign influence in its nuclear affairs and associated decision-making processes. U.S. intelligence agencies such as the CIA, the National Reconnaissance Office, the NSA, and the Department of State, among others, failed to warn the administration's senior officials of the impending test.[50] The test was condemned by many states as a contravention of the peaceful-use agreements fundamental to U.S.- and Canadian-supplied nuclear technology and material transfers, and was a defining factor in the creation of the Nuclear Suppliers Group (NSG).[51] The United States responded to the test by applying a number of sanctions on India.[52] However, notwithstanding international apprehension about the military consequences of its nuclear explosion, India did not follow the 1974 test with subsequent tests, nor did it proceed to weaponize the device design it had tested.[53] Itty Abraham argues that it was not until approximately 1986 that India could be viewed as a "nuclear weapons-capable state."[54] At that time, progress in Pakistan's efforts to obtain nuclear weapons, and the nuclear threats posited by Islamabad in the context of the 1986 to 1987 Brasstacks crisis, appear to have been the driving factor in Prime Minister Rajiv Gandhi ultimately approving the weaponization of India's nuclear capability.[55]

In 1995 the Narasimha Rao government considered pushing for an augmented program of nuclear tests. However, its test provisions were noticed by U.S. intelligence agencies, and the subsequent U.S. diplomatic weight persuaded the Rao government to delay the tests.[56] While plans for testing were reintroduced when the Hindu-nationalist Bharatiya Janata Party (BJP) led by Atal Bihari Vajpayee came to power for a short-lived interval in 1996, the BJP decided not to proceed.[57] When it did return to government in 1998, however, the BJP sanctioned two sets of nuclear tests on May 11 and 13, 1998, after which it officially declared India as being a nuclear-weapon state.[58] Many commentators and analysts external to India did not predict the test; however, a geospatial examination by Vipin Gupta and Frank Pabian had recognized a probable site and timeframe for the test.[59] After the 1998 tests the Indian government created a National Security Advisory Board and delivered a Draft Report on Indian Nuclear Doctrine in 1999, positing India's nuclear no-first-use policy and defensive posture of "credible minimum nuclear deterrence."[60] In January 2003, a Ministry of External Affairs media release reaffirmed its observance to no-first-use, but with the qualification that nuclear weapons could also be used in reprisal for a biological or chemical attack, or to protect Indian forces operating in Pakistan.[61] Domestic debates pertaining to the status of nuclear weapons continued on, and saw the establishment of a task force by the Ministry of External Affairs to appraise India's nuclear posture in 2007, recommending "a comprehensive and integrated nuclear defense capability" that factors in the obstinate political volatility in the region and China's continual nuclear cooperation with Pakistan.[62]

OBAMA AND INDIA

Notwithstanding the many concerns articulated by the United States over the course of the last fifty years, there has also been an evidentiary paradox in the way it has viewed India's proliferation, very much apparent across all three post–Cold War administrations of Clinton, Bush, and Obama. For instance, during his tenure in office, Obama agreed to cooperate further in "space, civil nuclear, defense, and other high-end sectors," while also announcing the administration's support for a permanent Indian seat on the UN Security Council. Additionally, it attained a waiver from the Nuclear Suppliers Group (NSG) that allowed India to conduct nuclear commerce with the group's members, while remaining steadfastly outside the Nuclear Non-Proliferation Treaty (NPT), and also, not being required to subject all of its nuclear facilities to International Atomic Energy Agency (IAEA) safeguards—a stipulation under the NSG's non-binding guidelines for nuclear trade with the group's members.[63] Nonetheless, India maintained that it was a dependable nuclear power, pointing to its positive record on non-proliferation and active support for complete nuclear disarmament. [64] It kept a unilateral moratorium on nuclear testing and, at most intervals, supported negotiations of a Fissile Material Cut-Off Treaty (FMCT) that is "universal, non-discriminatory, and internationally verifiable." [65] Further, India established a set of export controls, such as the Weapons of Mass Destruction and Their Delivery Systems (Prohibition of Unlawful Activities) Act in June 2005. [66] That said, New Delhi has emphasized repeatedly that "nuclear weapons are an integral part of our national security and will remain so pending the global elimination of all nuclear weapons." [67] It has not signed the CTBT, and continues to produce fissile material for its nuclear weapons program. While it has reaffirmed its pledge on no-first-use of nuclear weapons, the nuclear posture of credible minimum deterrence continues to develop, encompassing a strategic triad of nuclear delivery systems. [68]

In the context of his broader Prague vision of reducing nuclear (in)security, Obama has been prepared to work with what his administration has referred to as a user-friendly state. However, to what extent will such compromises toward India—no doubt part of the United States' rebalance/ pivot into Asia—engender further complex security scenarios at both a regional and global level, particularly as it modernizes. [69] Indeed, India's nuclear modernization is moving into a new and multifaceted stage. After the preliminary introduction of the Prithvi and Agni missiles, India is developing several long-range Agni systems on new launchers. The first SSBN has been launched and it is estimated to have undertaken sea trials as the first of a class of three to five boats with a new SLBM. The construction of a new plutonium-production reactor has begun, together with "speedy breeder reactors" that can yield more plutonium than they ingest, as well as upgrades to reprocessing facilities. India's existing arsenal is in the vicinity of approximately 110 warheads. Unlike Pakistan's nuclear posture, which is directed wholly against India, India's posture is focused against Pakistan and China. As such, most of India's missile development is gauged toward producing long-range missiles that can reach all key cities in China. There is a protuberant inside debate on the extent to which India needs to deploy canistered launchers—a system in which the missile is carried inside a climate-controlled canister— and provide ballistic missiles with the capacity to embody multiple warheads. [70] Of course, this type of activity will only continue to embolden other states' resolve not to get left behind. In a 2016 report to Congress detailing China's nuclear trajectory, the Pentagon highlighted the intensified deployment of new command, control, and communications capabilities in the PRC nuclear suite. Interestingly, the report indicated that part of the PRC's defense calculi was India's modernizing and expanding nuclear force and a "driver behind China's [own] nuclear force modernization." [71]

PAKISTAN AND NUCLEAR WEAPONS

In January 1972, Pakistani president, later prime minister, Zulfiqar Ali Bhutto "called a meeting of eminent scientists . . . and announced his desire and decision to make Pakistan a nuclear weapons state." This was deeply troubling to New Delhi as it indicated that Pakistan's military aspirations had not been stymied by its 1971 defeat, but instead, spurred it to "raise the stakes" in the "race in the subcontinent." While Indira Gandhi was not particularly anxious about Pakistan's nuclear capabilities per se, she was alarmed about what the nuclear decision revealed about the Pakistani leaders: that Pakistan could potentially become a dangerous pawn of the nuclear powers (who Gandhi regarded as being India's "real peers"). For Pakistan, the government's long-term goal from the late 1960s was to "establish a nuclear deterrent to the aggression by India," its greatest security concern. In 1969, President Bhutto discussed the utility of the nuclear option in his book *The Myth of Independence*. The Pakistani president bluntly stated, "We have to find an effective deterrent . . . [and] obtain such a weapon in time before the crisis begins, because India can choose that timing due to technological advantage."[72]

Tensions between India and Pakistan emanated from the British carving up of the subcontinent in 1947. Since then there has been four military conflicts between the two states and each time India has won. The 1971 defeat in particular, together with the subsequent secession of East Pakistan as the independent state of Bangladesh, proved a bitter experience and source of insecurity. With this increasingly asymmetric nature of the military balance taking place within the subcontinent, the Pakistani president ordered its scientific community to begin development of nuclear arms in earnest. Even before "Buddha smiled" upon India, analysts were troubled about the impact an Indian nuclear weapons program would have on Pakistan's own ambitions. In 1972, William Brands argued that in light of the Indian program, Pakistan had four options: to accept Indian hegemony; to seek guarantees from the United States and the United Kingdom; to obtain nuclear protection from the Chinese; or, finally, to develop their own nuclear weapons. With India's nuclear advantage in place and the historic rivalry between the two states looking to diminish further, Islamabad believed it was left with only one real option—to develop its own nuclear device.[73]

With Pakistan's first nuclear power plant at Karachi completed in 1972 and the public declaration that they would "go nuclear," it seemed from this early stage that there was nothing that the U.S. government could do to prevent further proliferation in South Asia. Perhaps the only hope for the United States to entice Pakistan to join the NPT would have been to assure India's accession to the treaty prior to 1971; however, like India, they too cited the inequalities in the treaty as a major reason for their own non-signature. While the 1971–1972 period provided a turning point in strengthening Pakistan's resolve to develop its own nuclear weapon, it was really only after the Indian nuclear test of 1974 that a distinct line was drawn, after which Pakistan accelerated its program and the nature of their nuclear activities became clear.[74] Prime Minister Bhutto responded to the test by saying that, if necessary, Pakistan would "eat grass" if it were the only way to meet India's newly found nuclear status. India's response to this statement was typical of the Indian attitude toward its neighbor, when Prime Minister Gandhi's chief secretary stated: "If by eating grass one can produce atom bombs, then, by now, cows and horses would have produced them. But, of course, the people of Pakistan, under the great charismatic leadership to which they are now exposed, might produce a bomb on a diet of grass." The Pakistani foreign office responded to the successful Indian test by deeming it an intensification of relations that "cannot but be viewed with the degree of concern matching its magnitude by the world and more especially by India's neighbours."[75]

The Indian nuclear test was conducted in Rajasthan, not far from the India-Pakistan border. Aside from the close proximity, Pakistan viewed the nuclear explosion as the defining moment tipping the balance of power in the region against them, and permanently establishing India's dominant position. Just months after the Indian explosion in October, Pakistan signed a contract with France for a plutonium reprocessing plant, which would produce fuel for a series of nuclear power stations. By 1975, Bhutto, now prime minister, put Pakistani metallurgist and centrifuge enrichment expert Abdul Qadeer Khan (recognized as the "Father of Pakistan's nuclear bomb") in charge of a secret program to manufacture nuclear weapons. The infamous, vainglorious Khan brought much needed designs for gas-centrifuge technology from Europe as he relocated in Pakistan. As posited in a U.S. Defense Department report, gradually the Pakistanis developed a nuclear infrastructure that provided "for uranium conversion and enrichment and the capacity to produce nuclear weapons." Unlike the Indian program, rather than using plutonium Khan's unit focused on developing highly enriched uranium. Their efforts were enhanced by the discovery in December 1973 of large uranium deposits in the southern Punjab province. Initially, China provided Pakistan's military-controlled nuclear program with vital nuclear materials and expertise, while significant nuclear-related and dual-use equipment was additionally obtained from the Soviet Union and Western European sources. In September 1974, the CIA estimated that Pakistan would need at least ten years to design and develop nuclear weapons.[76]

Two incompatible events during the 1980s—Pakistan's nuclear program and the Reagan administration's desire to aid the Mujahedin guerrillas, fighting Soviet forces in Afghanistan—challenged Washington's non-proliferation objectives. Pakistani leader General Zia ul-Haq, according to declassified documents obtained by the National Security Archive, "repeatedly lied" to U.S. officials "about his country's nuclear program." In a secret meeting, former CIA deputy director General Vernon Walters informed Zia that the United States had "incontrovertible intelligence" that Pakistan representatives had "transferred designs and specifications for nuclear weapons components to purchasing agents in several countries for the purpose of having these nuclear weapons components fabricated for Pakistan." While Zia agreed that this "must be true," he subsequently denied everything. Walters concluded that either the Pakistani leader "did not know the facts" or was the "most superb and patriotic liar I have ever met." Forced to choose between non-proliferation and assisting Mujahedin resistance, the Reagan administration gave a higher priority to the latter. Hoping that creating a strong bilateral relationship would lead Pakistan to abandon its nuclear weapons program, administration officials obscured Pakistani nuclear activities as long as it did not "embarrass" the president. Nor did they really want Zia to disclose his country's true nuclear activities, because it would then become impossible for Secretary of State George Shultz to certify that Pakistan did not have a nuclear program and thus allow the continued flow of support to the Mujahedin.[77]

International public acknowledgment of Pakistan's nuclear weapons program really came to the fore when, in a 1987 interview with an Indian journalist, A.Q. Khan unexpectedly admitted that Pakistan was capable of producing nuclear weapons. By 1990, further progression seemed evident when Washington concluded that Islamabad had achieved the capability of assembling a first-generation nuclear device; from this point on Pakistan moved firmly down the path of developing nuclear weapons. In May 1998, India tested five nuclear weapons. Before the month was out, Pakistan had hastily responded with six nuclear tests of its own, becoming the next member in the nuclear weapons club. Following the terrorist attacks of September 11 on the United States and the shifting political situation in Pakistan, many observers were alarmed about Islamabad's ability to keep its nuclear arsenal out of the hands of various extremist groups. This concern has not lessened over time, despite the Pakistan government's repeated assurances that they can maintain control of these weapons.[78] As stated by Paul K. Kerr and Mary Beth Nikitin:

> Instability in Pakistan has called the extent and durability of these reforms into question. Some observers fear radical takeover of the Pakistani government or diversion of material or technology by personnel within Pakistan's nuclear complex. While U.S. and Pakistani officials continue to express confidence in controls over Pakistan's nuclear weapons, continued instability in the country could impact these safeguards.[79]

Of course, such concerns will only intensify as the world's fastest prolife-rator continues to modernize and refine its nuclear forces. New devices under construction include the Ra'ad air-launched cruise missile, Babur ground-launched cruise missile, Shaheen II medium-range ballistic missile, and Nasr short-range rocket. Infrastructural advancements comprise construction of the third and fourth plutonium-production reactors, and upgrades of uranium-enrichment and spent fuel reprocessing facilities. Pakistan's existing arsenal is estimated to be in the vicinity of 120 weapons. That said, the Shaheen II missile has been under construction for an extensive period of time and has only just become operational, signifying some technical limitations in pro-ducing the road-mobile, solid-fueled, medium-range ballistic missile. Simi-larly, while India has been pursuing an SSBN program, there is so far no indication that Pakistan is following suit. For many commentators, this is surprising given the usual tit-for-tat responses long evident in Pakistani-Indian nuclear rivalry. Whether this signifies that there has been some form of financial limitation is uncertain, and it remains to be seen if the Babur cruise missile will ever actually be deployed in a sea-based version. Develop-ment of the nuclear-capable Nasr short-range missile launcher, whose range is estimated to be 60 kilometers, represents an important and concerning strategic addition to Pakistan's nuclear posture as the weapon is produced for a strategic nuclear exchange.[80] Indeed, for Special Representative for Af-ghanistan and Pakistan, Ambassador Richard Olson, there is much to be concerned about. As conveyed to the House Committee on Foreign Affairs on December 16, 2015, the uncertainty pertains to "the pace and the scope of the Pakistan's missile program, including its pursuit of nuclear systems" as well as the possibility that "a conventional conflict in Southwest Asia could escalate to include nuclear use as well as the increased security challenges that accompany such growing stockpiles."[81]

NORTH KOREA AND NUCLEAR WEAPONS

It is vital to begin any discussion of North Korea's nuclear program by understanding the limits of available information regarding its development. "North Korea has been very effective in denying the outside world any significant information on its nuclear weapons program," Bruch W. Bennett of RAND's National Defense Research Institute has noted. "As a result, the outside world has little direct evidence of the North Korean efforts and mainly [relies on] indirect inferences, leaving substantial uncertainties." Since its nuclear weapons program was not self-contained, it has been espe-cially difficult to determine how much external assistance arrived, and from where, to assess the program's overall sophistication. That said, it is evident that Pyongyang has tested five nuclear devices—in 2006, 2009, 2013, and

2016—with varying degrees of success, and that North Korea has put considerable effort into developing and testing missiles as possible delivery vehicles. Many foreign observers have come to believe the otherwise desperate, hungry population and failing regime that make up North Korea is best symbolized by its nuclear and missile programs, which gives rise to the basic question: What is Pyongyang's motivation for its nuclear/missile programs? Is it, as Victor Cha once asked, for swords, shields, or badges? In other words, are the programs intended to provide offensive weapons, defensive ones, or symbols of status? In spite of the prolonged diplomatic negotiations with Pyongyang officials over the past two decades, the question of motivation still remains elusive.[82]

Indeed, two intense political crises arose, from 1989 to 1994, pitting North Korea's nuclear programs against the concerns of its neighbors, the United States and the IAEA. The first protracted crisis that dominated the early 1990s arose over charges that Pyongyang was developing a plutonium reprocessing plant, and ended in the 1994 Agreed Framework. Only two substances have proven to be suitable to manufacture into a fissionable, bomb-making material: uranium 235 and plutonium 239, with U-235 thought to be the more expensive and difficult to produce. Pyongyang followed the path of Israel and India in employing plutonium as its primary material, although it is troublesome to handle and requires a demanding implosion device to provide the necessary explosive trigger. Yet, with North Korea's existing, extraordinary large reserves of natural uranium, it only had to find the means of transforming raw U-235 to 90 percent purity to obtain weapons-grade material. Up until 1992, intelligence reports indicated that Pyongyang planned to use plutonium rather than uranium in its nuclear bomb production process. Of the said year, evidence also pointed to the construction of a huge third reactor at Yongbyon that could possibly produce sufficient amounts of plutonium for several bombs.

Of course, it was preceding political factors that pushed events to a crisis stage. There was the new but fragile North-South dialogue, which had been underway since 1988, and Moscow's 1990 decision to recognize South Korea. To Soviet foreign minister Eduard Shevardnadze fell the difficult task of informing North Korean officials of Moscow's decision to open formal diplomatic relations with Seoul—a devastating political blow to Kim Il Sung's regime. Desperately seeking to change Moscow's position, Pyongyang threatened to build its own nuclear weapons to provide for its own security. Unimpressed, Shevardnadze wondered what North Korea would do with nuclear weapons, when if used would also result in the North being covered in radioactivity. "What good is an ultimate deterrent," he allegedly asked, "if it will destroy the very thing you are trying to protect?"[83]

Meanwhile, U.S.–South Korean efforts to design a non-proliferation program aimed at drawing out Pyongyang drew impetus from President George

H. W. Bush's 1991 initiative to unilaterally recall to the United States all tactical nuclear weapons. During the development of their non-proliferation plan, the basic question that plagued American and South Korean authorities was the terms and advantages of the various incentives suggested to entice the North Koreans to cooperate with IAEA inspections. In September 1991, the twenty-three-member nations of the IAEA formally requested North Korea's permission to conduct "special" inspections—that is, inspections on demand, as opposed to regularly scheduled ones. Since in December Pyongyang agreed in principle to denuclearization of the Korean Peninsula, its officials agreed to a May 1992 IAEA inspection that was to affirm that North Korea's nuclear weapons program had been halted. Ahead of the inspector's visit, the North Koreans submitted a detailed report of its nuclear facilities, one that closely matched the West's assessment. The actual IAEA inspection from May 25 to June 7, 1992, appeared at first to go well. By February 1993, however, frustrations arising from the inability to implement the bilateral inspections called for in the North-South Denuclearization Agreement became evident. This was compounded by IAEA evidence that North Korea had at least three times reprocessed plutonium, had refused to accept, challenge, or demand inspection, and was overall being difficult in its general compliance to negotiations. On February 22, under the direction of the new U.S. president, Bill Clinton, Washington finally released highly sensitive satellite photos that revealed North Korean nuclear waste sites indicating that Pyongyang had lied about the nature of its nuclear program. In March 1993, the North Korean regime shocked the international community by announcing it was withdrawing from the Nuclear Non-Proliferation Treaty. [84]

During the inconsistent status of discussions, South Korean and American officials, despite the occasional muted call for a violent solution in the background, maintained a careful and calm diplomatic approach. Additionally, negotiations took on a multilateral level as it was recognized China might have influence in Pyongyang and, in a worst case, would be a key player in any effort to economically and politically isolate the North. While Beijing had no interest in a nuclear-armed Pyongyang, neither did it support the idea that any global institution, such as the IAEA, could dictate policies that might in any way impinge on China's sovereignty. As such, Beijing stipulated boundaries on South Korean, Japanese, and American diplomatic endeavors. During March 1994, IAEA officials were allowed to return to North Korea for a routine series of inspections, but what they found was concerning. Despite Kim Il Sung's pledge that "we have neither the need to make nuclear weapons nor the will and ability to do so," the inspectors found that North Korea was in fact "poised to go forward" in a new phase of developing nuclear weapons. While a crisis mounted and discussions regarding military strikes and economic sanctions against Pyongyang ebbed and flowed around Washington, former president Jimmy Carter was asked by the Clinton administration to visit the North Korean leader in early June. Ambassador Robert Gallucci seized upon the essentials of Carter's discussions to work out a pact with North Korea on October 16, 1994, known as the Agreed Framework, that ended the immediate crisis. Briefly, this accord through a series of steps, as the future U.S. secretary of state Madeleine Albright noted, "required the North to shut down its reactor, seal eight thousand fuel rods containing reprocessed plutonium, and freeze its plutonium production under IAEA inspection. In return, the United States and its allies [especially South Korea and Japan] agreed to help North Korea cope with its immediate fuel shortages and pay for the construction of two civilian nuclear power plants." Moreover, Washington promised to issue a formal statement of non-aggression and to normalize its relations with Pyongyang. [85]

An optimistic view can draw on the fact that after the revelations of Pyongyang's surreptitious activities, President Bill Clinton negotiated the Agreed Framework in 1993–1994. Indeed, for eight years the agreement was able to maintain its core goal of freezing North Korea's plutonium production program, and—while it is apparent that Pyongyang did not fully adhere to its requirements, not least in its covert links with the AQ Khan network to acquire centrifuge technology during this period—its demise was not necessarily an entirely one-sided responsibility. In simple terms, the Agreed Framework of 1994 floundered because of a continuing aura of mistrust. According to American officials, North Korea abrogated the pact by returning to its nuclear weapons program, but the reality was more complicated. Neither side fulfilled many of the various agreed stages, David Kang argues, with both the Clinton and George W. Bush administrations having "violated the letter and the spirit of the agreement."

One of the more significant features of the framework was that the United States would construct two light water reactor power plants by 2003; however, at that date these projects were four years behind schedule, even though South Korea and Japan had supplied a portion of the funds. Additionally, Washington agreed in Article II.3.1 "to provide formal assurance to the DPRK [North Korea] against the threat or use of nuclear weapons by the U.S." However, the U.S. "Nuclear Posture Review" in 2001 continued to target North Korea with nuclear weapons. Domestic political confrontations and repeated issues with Iraq greatly reduced the Clinton administration's interest in dealing with the terms of the Agreed Framework. George W. Bush's administration, clearly hostile to the accord and to the government of North Korea, had no intention initially of seeking a negotiated halt to Pyongyang's nuclear weapons program. While North Korea did at first suspend the activity in its reactors and allowed IAEA monitoring, it formally withdrew from the framework in December 2002, expelled inspectors, and restarted its uranium enrichment. Additionally, Bush's labeling of North Korea as one of the "axis of evil" and other comments by administration officials severely impaired diplomatic efforts. Finally, in 2002, Secretary of State Colin Powell made controls on North Korea's missile program an additional condition required for any political progress.[86]

The North Koreans obviously felt the new Bush administration had little interest in undertaking "balanced" negotiations. On June 9, 2003, they formally declared that they were pursuing a nuclear weapons capability. A series of six-party talks, involving North and South Korea, the United States, Russia, China, and Japan, throughout 2004 and 2005, sought a "verifiable denuclearization of the Korean Peninsula." The inability to reach an agreement centered in large part on Pyongyang's insistence on what it called a peaceful nuclear energy program, and Washington's refusal to endorse North Korea's possession of light-water reactors. In October 2006, the North Koreans detonated a nuclear device that apparently had a yield of less than 1 kiloton, disappointing its designers who claimed the explosion was an accomplished device with 2 kilograms of plutonium—an amount less than normally contained in a nuclear weapon. Following the failure of renewed discussions and the U.N. Security Council's condemnation of its missile launch in 2009, North Korea withdrew from the six-party talks and set off a second underground nuclear test on May 25. The second test resulted in a larger yield that was similar to regular designs that yielded 12 kilotons. At the time, many challenged the reliability of the two tests. Bruce Bennett of RAND's National Defense Research Institute wondered whether the North Koreans had yet designed a nuclear weapon—"if so, what form have they taken? Are they bombs, missile warheads, or just nuclear devices?" After all, developing a nuclear warhead that would fit on a ballistic missile "requires significant expertise in nuclear weapons design and explosions." Then, too, there is the matter of guidance systems and accuracy. Do the North Koreans have the terminal guidance technology that would substantially improve the accuracy of the NoDong missiles?[87]

OBAMA AND NORTH KOREA

Of course, North Korea has proceeded to address these questions. At the time of the writing of this book, it has undertaken five nuclear weapons tests: in the abovementioned 2006, 2009, 2013, and two 2016 tests, claiming that the January 2016 test was a thermonuclear device (although this has been highly disputed by analysts).[88] These claims were also posited back in December 2015 where Kim Jong Un, on a visit to the Pyongchon Revolutionary Site, stated that his regime had thermonuclear capabilities.[89] After making the bold declaration following the January 6, 2016, nuclear assertion, many suggested that while the test could have been a boosted fission device, it was not possible to ascertain its specific nature without captured particles in the atmosphere for analysis from a radionuclide monitoring station.[90] Not surprising, the test impelled extensive international condemnation, where even China, a traditional ally of the regime, supported a UN resolution to apply further sanctions against the hermit state.[91] For the international community, the 2016 tests continue a long line of obfuscation by the regime, where it has veered from a periodical willingness to negotiate, on the one hand, to recalcitrant, provocative, and strange behavior on the other.

This behavior has been very much on display during Obama's tenure in office. For instance, after extensive diplomatic meetings during the first presidential term—a visit from former President Jimmy Carter to North Korea in April 2011, a July 2011 meeting between U.S. Special Representative for North Korea Policy Stephen Bosworth and North Korean First Vice Foreign Minister Kim Gye Gwan, and a February 2012 bilateral meeting in Beijing—an agreement to halt uranium enrichment in exchange for U.S. food aid was reached in early 2012.[92] In an apparent conciliatory shift, North Korea subsequently announced its suspension of uranium enrichment at the Yongbyon Nuclear Scientific Research Center and said that it would not conduct any further tests of nuclear weapons while such productive negotiations involving the United States were taking place. The agreement required the cessation of long-range missile tests and also included permission for IAEA inspectors to monitor operations at Yongbyon. In affirming this move, the United States said that it had no aggressive intentions toward North Korea and was prepared to improve the bilateral relationship.[93] However, in what can be viewed as a microcosm of both North Korean actions and the bilateral relationship over the last decade, Pyongyang launched a provocative long-range missile test in April 2012, two months after the agreement. While not necessarily surprising, the agreement and backflip signify the many challenges that have worn down the Obama administration's "strategic patience" approach to Pyongyang.[94]

Indeed, if anything, North Korea's fifth nuclear test has all but dispelled such patience completely. On September 9, 2016, the anniversary of the founding of North Korea, the U.S. Geological Survey detected a 5.3-magnitude earthquake at the regime's nuclear testing site. North Korea swiftly acknowledged it had executed a nuclear test in a provocative pronouncement, stating that it had successfully constructed a warhead small enough to place onto the end of a missile and had the capacity to counter or impede any attacks from its adversaries. Analysts believed the explosion's yield to be between 10 and 20 kilotons as the explosion was significantly larger than all previous tests carried out by the regime.[95] The test drew immediate international condemnation. President Obama called the test "a grave threat" and stated that the regime's actions have only destabilized the region. Until two years ago the considered consensus on the North's nuclear program was that it was predominantly a political symbol, and the only power asset it had that could garner tangible economic and diplomatic responses. However, with the pace of both nuclear and missile testing intensifying, the prospect of North Korea actually unifying a nuclear warhead and missile technology onto one device can no longer be considered as being farfetched. As stated by Kelsey Davenport, the director for non-proliferation policy at the Arms Control Association, "It is likely now that North Korea could at this point put a nuclear warhead on a short- or medium-range missile which could reach South Korea, Japan and US military installations in the region." That said, she continued, this advancement would require at least another decade before Pyongyang was able to construct a dependable intercontinental ballistic missile capable of reaching the United States.[96]

As indicated, the recent nuclear test comes after a sequence of missile advancement, with the launch of a two-stage, solid-fueled, and submarine-launched missile in August and September (both in 2016) of three new aluminium-bodied versions of Scud missiles with a 1,000 km range. As Davenport again states, "All this activity is aimed at expanding the size of North Korea's nuclear arsenal and expanding its delivery options. . . . It is taking steps to quality-improve its missiles, using solid fuel so they can be deployed more quickly, and extending their range. The trajectory points to a growing North Korean nuclear threat and the next U.S. administration will have to prioritize that threat."[97] The procession of North Korean activity does not appear to be slowing in the near to distant future, nor does the broader specter of the nuclear threat emanating from such developments. Notwithstanding the global condemnation of its fifth nuclear test, the North has been again making further military overtures at the time of writing: South Korea's Defense Ministry spokesman said the rogue state was preparing to undertake a sixth test. As stated by Moon Sang-gyun, "Assessment by South Korean and U.S. intelligence is that the North is always ready for an additional nuclear test in the Punggye-ri area," the site of Pyongyang's five nuclear explosions.[98] In a sardonic yet frank assessment of the status of the North Korean nuclear drive and where this could perhaps end up, Jeffrey Lewis admonishes:

> We don't really know how big North Korea's nuclear arsenal is, or will be once the "standardized" warheads are deployed to the missile forces. But it's not a small number, and certainly not just a handful. It's a nuclear force, one that poses a threat to South Korea, Japan, and U.S. forces in the region. And it's likely to keep growing. If we do nothing, I suspect it will grow in number, grow to threaten the continental United States, and eventually grow to include very powerful staged-thermonuclear weapons. And all this is going to happen sooner that you think. That nuclear weapons program is going to grow quickly—much like the toddler who decorated my television in lotion. Before I know it, he'll be off to college. I wonder how big Kim Jong Un's nuclear arsenal will be by then.[99]

NOTES

1. Jacques E. C. Hymans, *The Psychology of Nuclear Proliferation: Identity, Emotions, and Foreign Policy* (Cambridge: Cambridge University Press, 2006), 181–82.

2. Elements of this chapter have been adapted from Professor Siracusa's study (with Richard Dean Burns) *A Global History of the Nuclear Arms Race: Weapons, Strategy, and Politics*, 2 vols. (Santa Barbara, CA: Praeger, 2013).

3. Michael Karpin, *The Bomb in the Basement: How Israel Went Nuclear and What That Means for the World* (New York: Simon & Schuster, 2006), 13, 51, 52; see Burns, *The Evolution of Arms Control*, 91–92.

4. Karpin, *The Bomb in the Basement*, 76, 108–9, 120–21; for Dimona's development, see Chapters 5 and 6.

5. Ibid., 179–81.

6. Hedrick Smith, "U.S. Assumes the Israelis Have the A-Bomb or Its Parts," *New York Times*, July 18, 1970, 1; Avner Cohen and William Burr, "Israel Crosses the Threshold," *Bulletin of the Atomic Scientists*, May/June 2006, 29; see Avner Cohen, National Security Archive *Electronic Briefing Book* No. 189, posted April 28, 2006; and Avner Cohen, *Israel and the Bomb* (New York: Columbia University Press, 1998), 316–19. See Yitzhak Rabin, *The Rabin Memoirs* (Berkeley, CA: University of California Press, 1996), 131–34.

7. Smith, "U.S. Assumes the Israelis Have A-Bomb or Its Parts," 1, 8. [Secretary of State William] Rogers to Nixon, "Suggested Position for You to Take with Israeli Prime Minister Golda Meir During Her Forthcoming Visit, September 18, 1969"; Theodore L. Eliot to Henry Kissinger, "Briefing Book—Visit of Mrs. Gold Meir," September 19, 1969, enclosing "Background—Israel's Nuclear Weapons and Missile Programs," in Record Group 59, General Records of the Department of State, Top Secret Subject-Numeric Files, 1967–69, Pol lsr, National Archives, College Park, Maryland.

8. "Israelis Criticize Article in the Times," *New York Times*, July 19, 1970; Cohen, *Israel and the Bomb*, 271, 338. See Shlomo Aronson, *The Politics and Strategy of Nuclear Weapons in the Middle East: Opacity, Theory, and Reality, 1960–1991* (Albany, NY: Albany State University of New York Press, 1992).

9. Jeffrey T. Richelson, *Spying on the Bomb: American Nuclear Intelligence from Nazi Germany to Iran and North Korea* (New York: W. W. Norton, 2006), 271; Henry A. Kissinger, "Memorandum for the President, Subject, Rabin's Proposed Assurances on Israeli Nuclear Policy," October, 8, 1969. DF 18—Arms Control and Disarmament, Record Group 59, General Records of the Department of State, NSC Files, Country Files, Middle East; Folder 4—Israeli Nuclear Program; Box 612, 1, National Archives.

10. Richelson, *Spying on the Bomb*, 272; David Binder, "CIA Says Israel has 10-20 A-Bombs," *New York Times*, March 16, 1976, A1; Kenneth S. Bower, "A Propensity for Conflict: Potential Scenarios and Outcomes of War in the Middle East," *Jane's Intelligence Review*, Special Report Number 14, February 1997, 14–15; and Robert S. Norris, Wiliam M. Arkin, and Hans M. Kristensen, "Israeli Nuclear Forces, 2002," *Bulletin of the Atomic Scientists*, September/October 2002, 75.

11. Simon Peres, *Battling for Peace: Memoirs* (London: Weidenfeld and Nicolson, 1995), 132; Joseph M. Siracusa, *Nuclear Weapons: A Very Short Introduction* (Oxford: Oxford University Press, 2008), 114; Bennet Ramberg, "Redemption Paradox," *Bulletin of Atomic Scientists*, July/August 2006, 50–56. See Richard Betts, "The Osirak Fallacy," *The National Interest*, Spring 2006, 22.

12. Tom Z. Collina, "Israel Has Nuclear-Armed Sub, Report Says," *Arms Control Today*, July/August 2012, http://www.armscontrol.org/2012_07-08/Israel_Has_Nuclear-Armed_Sub_Report_Says.

13. *Global Fissile Material Report 2011: Nuclear Weapon and Fissile Material Stockpiles and Production*, The International Panel on Fissile Materials, Princeton, NJ, January 2012, 18, http://fissilematerials.org/library/gfmr11.pdf.

14. "Arms Control and Proliferation Profile: Israel," *Arms Control Today*, July 2012, http://www.armscontrol.org/factsheets/israelprofile.

15. Hans M. Kristensen, "Nuclear Weapons Modernization: A Threat to the NPT?" *Arms Control Association*, https://www.armscontrol.org/act/2014_05/Nuclear-Weapons-Modernization-A-Threat-to-the-NPT.

16. Paul K. Kerr, "Iran's Nuclear Programs: Status," *CRS Report for Congress*, RL34544, Washington, DC: Congressional Research Service, September 18, 2009, 1–3. See William Burr, "A Brief History of U.S.-Iranian Nuclear Negotiations," *Bulletin of the Atomic Scientists*, January/February 2009.

17. Kerr, "Iran's Nuclear Programs," 3.

18. Anthony H. Cordesman and Adam C. Seitz, *Iranian Weapons of Mass Destruction: The Birth of a Regional Nuclear Arms Race?* (New York: Praeger, 2009); Kenneth Katzman, "Iran Sanctions," *CRS Report for Congress*, RS20871, Washington, DC: Congressional Research Service, June 23, 2010, 1–10.

19. Department of Defense, *Nuclear Posture Review Report* (Washington, DC: DoD, April 2010), vi; Director General, "Implementation of the NPT Safeguards Agreement and Relevant Provisions of Security Council Resolutions in the Islamic Republic of Iran," IAEA Report, GOV/2011/65, November 8, 2011, 10.

20. Matthew Kroenig, "Time to Attack Iran: Why a Strike Is the Least Bad Option," *Foreign Affairs* 91, no. 1 (2012): 77. See Matthew Kroenig, "Why Is Obama Abandoning 70 Years of U.S. Nonproliferation Policy?" *Tablet*, June 15, 2015; Matthew Kroenig, *A Time to Attack: The Looming Iranian Nuclear Threat* (New York: St. Martin's Press, 2014).

21. Francis J. Gavin, "Same as It Ever Was: Nuclear Alarmism, Proliferation, and the Cold War," *International Security* 34, no. 3 (Winter 2009/2010): 7–37; Thomas P. M. Barnett, "How to Stop Worrying and Live with the Iranian Bomb," *World Politics Review*, Special Issue: Iran, Playing With Fire, January 3, 2012: 11–12; Michael Cohen, "What Happens If Iran Gets the Bomb? *Global Policy Journal*, May 8, 2012.

22. Barack Obama, "Remarks by The President in Celebration of Nowruz," The White House, Office of the Press Secretary, Washington, DC, March 20, 2009, http://www.whitehouse.gov/video/The-Presidents-Message-to-the-Iranian-People#transcript. See Aiden Warren, *The Obama Administration's Nuclear Weapon Strategy: The Promises of Prague* (New York: Routledge, 2014), 122–44.

23. Ibid.

24. Daryl G. Kimball, "Pursue the Diplomatic Track on Iran," *Arms Control Today*, July/August 2012, http://www.armscontrol.org/act/2012_0708/Focus.

25. Kenneth Katzman, "Iran: US Concerns and Policy Responses," *CRS Report for Congress*, RS34544, Washington, DC: Congressional Research Service, October 17, 2012, 60–61.

26. "Obama Pledges Diplomatic Push on Iran," *Nuclear Threat Initiative*, November 15 2012, http://www.nti.org/gsn/article/obama-pledges-diplomatic-push-iran.

27. Leonard S. Spector, Chen Kane, Bryan L. Lee, Miles A. Pomper, Amy E. Smithson, Nikolai Sokov, Jessica C. Varnum, and Jon B. Wolfsthal, "Critical Questions: Urgent Decisions for the Second Obama Administration," *Nuclear Threat Initiative*, November 27, 2012, http://www.nti.org/analysis/articles/issues-obama-administration-its-second-term/.

28. Katzman, "Iran: US Concerns and Policy Responses," 60–61; "Iran's Rial Hits an All-Time-Low Against the US Dollar," *BBC News*, October 1, 2012, http://www.bbc.co.uk/news/business-19786662.

29. Spector et al., "Critical Questions: Urgent Decisions for the Second Obama Administration."

30. "Parameters for a Joint Comprehensive Plan of Action regarding the Islamic Republic of Iran's Nuclear Program," P5+1 (UN Security Council's five permanent members: namely China, France, Russia, the United Kingdom, and the United States, plus Germany), April 2, 2015, https://www.armscontrol.org/files/Parameters-for-a-Joint-Comprehensive-Plan-of-Action-regarding-the-Islamic-Republic-of-Irans-Nuclear-Program-2015-04-02.pdf.

31. Editorial Board, "An Iran Nuclear Deal That Reduces the Chance of War," *New York Times*, July 14, 2015, http://www.nytimes.com/2015/07/15/opinion/an-iran-nuclear-deal-that-reduces-the-chance-of-war.html.

32. Barack Obama, "Remarks by the President on the Iran Nuclear Deal," American University, Washington, DC: The White House, Office of the Press Secretary, August 5, 2015, https://www.whitehouse.gov/the-press-office/2015/08/05/remarks-president-iran-nuclear-deal.

33. Editorial Board, "An Iran Nuclear Deal That Reduces the Chance of War."

34. Obama, "Remarks by the President on the Iran Nuclear Deal."

35. "Nuclear Weapon Free Zones and the Middle East: A [draft] Report of the Monterey Nonproliferation Strategy Group," James Martin Center for Nonproliferation Studies, August 2009, 3–5, online.

36. Ibid., 5; "Israeli Public Supports Middle East Nuclear Free Zone," December 1, 2011, at World Public Opinion.Org.

37. Kelsey Davenport, "WMD-Free Middle East Proposal at a Glance," *Arms Control Association*, updated June 2015, https://www.armscontrol.org/factsheets/mewmdfz.

38. Agnieszka Nimark, "The Nuclear Deal with Iran, the NPT Review Deadlock and the Ukrainian Crisis," CIDOB Barcelona Centre for International Affairs, November 2015, http://www.cidob.org/en/.

39. Davenport, "WMD-Free Middle East Proposal at a Glance."

40. Balazs Szalontai, "The Elephant in the Room: The Soviet Union and India's Nuclear Program, 1967–1989," Washington, DC: Nuclear Proliferation International History Project, the Woodrow Wilson International Center, NPIHP Working Paper #1, November 2011, 1; "The Nixon Administration and the Indian Nuclear Program, 1972–1974: U.S. Post-Mortem on 1974 Indian Test Criticized Intelligence Community Performance for 'Waffling Judgments' and Not Following Up Leads," National Security Archive *Electronic Briefing Book* No. 367, December 5, 2011.

41. Vipin Narang, "Posturing for Peace? Pakistan's Nuclear Postures and South Asian Stability," *International Security* 34, no. 3 (2009/2010): 46, http://belfercenter.ksg.harvard.edu/files/Narang.pdf. See Vipin Narang, *Nuclear Strategy in the Modern Era: Regional Powers and International Conflict* (Princeton, NJ: Princeton University Press, 2014).

42. Daryl G. Kimball, "India's Choice, Congress' Responsibility," *Arms Control Today* 36 (January/February 2006): 3; Jacques E. C. Hymans, *The Psychology of Nuclear Proliferation: Identity, Emotions, and Foreign Policy* (Cambridge: Cambridge University Press, 2006), 181–82.

43. George Perkovich, *India's Nuclear Bomb: The Impact on Global Proliferation* (Berkeley: University of California Press, 2001), 139–42.

44. See K. Subrahmanyam, "India: Keeping the Option Open," in *Nuclear Proliferation: Phase II*, ed. Robert M. Lawrence and Joel Laurus (Lawrence: University of Kansas Press, 1973).

45. Michael J. Siler, "U.S. Nuclear Non-Proliferation Policy Towards India During and After the Cold War: A Conflict Bargaining Analysis," *Journal of the Third World Spectrum* 5, no. 2 (Fall 1998): 51. CIRUS is the Canada, India Research U.S. reactor at the Bhabha Atomic Research Centre at Trombay (near Mumbai); see David Hart, "India," in *A Non-Proliferation Policy: Prospects and Problems*, ed. Harald Muller (Oxford: Clarendon Press, 1987), 145.

46. Helmut Sonnenfeldt, "Memorandum for Mr. Kissinger, Subject: Implications of the Sino-Soviet Treaty," August 18, 1971. NSC Files, Country Files—Middle East, India Vol. IV 01/06-30/11/71 to India Vol. IV 1/07-30/11/7; Box: 597; Folder: India Vol. IV, 01/07-30/22/71 [December 1971] [2 of 4] 2; Nixon Presidential Materials Staff, National Archives and Records Administration, College Park, MD, 1.

47. Document 180, "Editorial Note," in *Foreign Relations of the United States*, 500, http://www.stategov/r/pa/ho/frus/nixon/xi/index.htm.

48. "The Nixon Administration and the Indian Nuclear Program, 1972–1974," National Security Archive *Electronic Briefing Book* No. 367; Henry A. Kissinger, "National Security Study Memorandum 156, Subject Indian Nuclear Developments," July 5, 1972, 1, http://nixonarchives.gov/virtuallibrary/documents/nationalsecuritystudymemoranda.php.

49. "The Buddha is smiling" was the prearranged coded telegraphic message that was sent by the scientists and Pokhran to Indira Gandhi, indicating the successful completion of the nuclear test. See Sumit Ganguly, *Conflict Unending: India-Pakistan Tensions since 1947* (New

York: Columbia University Press, 2001), 104, 111; Roberta Wohlsetter, *The Buddha Smiles: Absent-Minded Peaceful Aid and the Indian Bomb* (Los Angeles: Pan Heuristics, 1977).

50. J. N. Dixit, *Across Borders: Fifty Years of Indian Foreign Policy* (New Delhi: Picus Books, 1998), 437; Zulfiqar Ali Bhutto, *The Myth Of Independence* (Oxford: Oxford University Press, 1969), 152. Also cited in Haider K. Nizamani, *The Roots of Rhetoric: Politics of Nuclear Weapons in India and Pakistan* (Westport, CT: Praeger, 2000), 78.

51. "Historical Documents Regarding India's Misuse of Civilian Nuclear Technology Assistance," *Arms Control Association*, www.nci.org; "History of the NSG," *Nuclear Suppliers Group*, http://www.nuclearsuppliersgroup.org.

52. Steve LaMongagne, "India-Pakistan Sanctions Legislation Fact Sheet," The Center for Arms Control and Non-Proliferation, 2011, http://armscontrolcenter.org.

53. Itty Abraham, "Interpreting the Meanings of India's Nuclear Tests," in *Inside Nuclear South Asia*, ed. Scott D. Sagan (Stanford, CA: Stanford University Press, 2009).

54. Ibid.

55. George Perkovich, *India's Nuclear Bomb: The Impact on Global Proliferation* (Berkeley: University of California Press, 1999); "India," *Nuclear Threat Initiative*, http://www.nti.org/learn/countries/india/nuclear/.

56. Ibid.

57. Kanti Bajpai, "The BJP and the Bomb," in *Inside Nuclear South Asia*, ed. Scott D. Sagan (Stanford, CA: Stanford University Press, 2009).

58. Howard Diamond, "India Conducts Nuclear Tests; Pakistan Follows Suit," *Arms Control Today*, May 1998, www.armscontrol.org.

59. Vipin Gupta and Frank Pabian, "Investigating the Allegations of Indian Nuclear Test Preparations in the Rajasthan Desert," *Science & Global Security* 6 (1997): 101–88, www.princeton.edu.

60. "India's Draft Nuclear Doctrine," *Arms Control Today*, July/August 1999, www.armscontrol.org.

61. Scott D. Sagan, "Evolution of Pakistani and Indian Nuclear Doctrine," in *Inside Nuclear South Asia*, ed. Scott D. Sagan (Stanford, CA: Stanford University Press, 2009); Ministry of External Affairs of India, "The Cabinet Committee on Security Reviews Operationalization of India's Nuclear Doctrine," Press Release, January 4, 2003, www.mea.gov.in.

62. Rashme Sehgal, "Panel: Keep N-Arms Option Open," *The Asian Age*, October 21, 2007, www.lexis-nexis.com; "India," *Nuclear Threat Initiative*, http://www.nti.org/learn/countries/india/nuclear/.

63. Eric Auner, "Obama Easing Export Controls on India," *Arms Control Today*, December 2010, http://armscontrol.org/act/2010_12/Obama_India.

64. Pranab Mukherjee, "Statement by External Affairs Minister of India Mr Pranab Mukherjee on the Civil Nuclear Initiative," Embassy of India in Washington, DC, September 5, 2008, www.indianembassy.org.

65. Hamid Ali Rao, "Remarks by Ambassador Hamid Ali Rao of India," February 3, 2011, Reaching Critical Will, Women's International League for Peace and Freedom (WILPF), www.reachingcriticalwill.org.

66. "Communication from the Resident Representative of India to the International Atomic Energy Agency regarding India's Nuclear Export Policies and Practices," International Atomic Energy Agency, INFCIRC/647, June 25, 2005, www.iaea.org.

67. "Statement by India in the CD Plenary after the Adoption of Decision on Programme of Work Contained in CD/1863," Permanent Representative of India to the Conference on Disarmament, May 29, 2009, http://www.unog.ch/80256EDD006B8954/(httpAssets)/70F44FC9546F2038C12575C50044C565/$file/1139_India.pdf.

68. Bharat Karnad, *India's Nuclear Policy* (Westport, CT: Praeger Security International, 2008), 95.

69. See Aiden Warren, *The Obama Administration's Nuclear Weapon Strategy: The Promises of Prague* (New York: Routledge, 2014), 172–87; Auner, "Obama Easing Export Controls on India."

70. Kristensen, "Nuclear Weapons Modernization: A Threat to the NPT?" See Vipin Narang, "India's Nuclear Weapons Policy," in *Engaging the World: India's Foreign Policy since 1947*, ed. Sumit Ganguly (Oxford: Oxford University Press, 2015).

71. "U.S., Russia, India driving China's Nuclear Modernisation: Pentagon," *The Economic Times*, May 14, 2016, http://economictimes.indiatimes.com.

72. William J. Brands, *India, Pakistan and the Great Powers* (London: Pall Mall Press, 1972), 336.

73. See P. N. Haksar, *India's Foreign Policy* (New Delhi: Patriot Publishers, 1989).

74. Siracusa, *Nuclear Weapons*, 122–27; Office of the Secretary of Defense, *Proliferation: Threat and Response*, Washington, DC, January 2001, http://www.defenselink.mil; Volha Charnysh, *Pakistan's Nuclear Program* (Santa Barbara, CA: Nuclear Age Peace Foundation, September 3, 2009), www.wagingpeace.org/articles/pdfs/Proliferation_History.pdf.

75. Rekha Datta, "U.S. Security Policy in India and Pakistan and the Question of Nuclear Proliferation," *Journal of South Asian and Middle Eastern Studies* 21, no. 2 (1998): 27.

76. "Pakistan Nuclear Weapons: A Brief History of Pakistan's Nuclear Program," Federation of American Scientists (FAS), www.fas.org/nuke/guide/pakistan/nuke/; "Pakistan Profile," *Nuclear Threat Initiative*, 2011.

77. William Burr, "Reagan Administration Supported Sale of F-16," National Security Archive *Electronic Briefing Book* No. 377, April 27, 2012.

78. Joshua Pollack, "The Secret Treachery of A.Q. Khan," *Playboy Magazine*, January/ February 2012, online. See Adrian Levy and Catherine Scott-Clark, *Deception: Pakistan, the United States, and the Secret Trade in Nuclear Weapons* (New York: Walker, 2007).

79. Paul K. Kerr and Mary Beth Nikitin, "Pakistan's Nuclear Weapons," *CRS Report for Congress*, RL34248, Washington, DC: Congressional Research Service, August 1, 2016, https://www.fas.org/sgp/crs/nuke/RL34248.pdf.

80. Kristensen, "Nuclear Weapons Modernization: A Threat to the NPT?"

81. "Rep. Ed Royce Holds a Hearing on U.S.-Pakistan Relations," House Committee on Foreign Affairs, December 16, 2015; Kerr and Nikitin, "Pakistan's Nuclear Weapons."

82. Bruce W. Bennett, *Uncertainties in the North Korean Nuclear Threat* (Santa Monica, CA: RAND, National Defense Research Institute, 2010), 14; Victor Cha, "Badges, Shields or Swords? North Korea's WMD Threat," *Political Science Quarterly* 117, no. 2 (2002): 209–30.

83. Michael J. Mazarr, *North Korea and the Bomb: A Case Study in Nonproliferation* (London: Macmillan, 1995), 35–39, 42–43, 56.

84. Ibid., 46–47, 52, 81, 103; chapters 3, 4, and 5 provide a detailed description of these events.

85. Ibid., 154–55, 162–63, 173–75; Madeleine Albright with Bill Woodward, *Madame Secretary: A Memoir* (New York: Miramax Books, 2003), 456.

86. Victor D. Cha and David C. Kang, *Nuclear North Korea: A Debate on Engagement Strategies* (New York: Columbia University Press, 2003), 57, 134–39. See Charles L. Pritchard, *Failed Diplomacy: The Tragic Story of How North Korea Got the Bomb* (Washington, DC: Brookings Institution Press, 2007), chapter 1.

87. Bruce W. Bennett, *Uncertainties in the North Korean Nuclear Threat* (Santa Monica, CA: RAND, National Defense Research Institute, 2010), 18–21.

88. Anna Fifield, "North Korea Conducts Fifth Nuclear Test, Claims It Has Made Warheads with 'Higher Strike Power,'" *Washington Post*, September 9, 2016, www.washingtonpost.com; Joby Warrick, "A North Korean H-bomb? Not Likely, Experts Say," *Washington Post*, January 6, 2016, www.washingtonpost.com.

89. "Kim Jong Un Visits Reconstructed Pyongchon Revolutionary Site," *Rodong Sinmun*, December 10, 2015, http://rodong.rep.kp.

90. Declan Butler and Elizabeth Gibney, "What Kind of Bomb Did North Korea Test?" *Nature*, January 8, 2016.

91. "North Korea," *Nuclear Threat Initiative (NTI)*, http://www.nti.org/learn/countries/north-korea/.

92. Darly G. Kimball and Peter Crail, "Chronology of US-North Korean Nuclear and Missile Diplomacy," *Arms Control Association*, April 2012, http://www.armscontrol.org/factsheets/dprkchron.

93. Steven Lee Myers and Choe Sang-Hun, "North Korea Agrees to Curb Nuclear Work; US Offers Aid," *New York Times*, February 29, 2012, http://www.nytimes.com/2012/03/01/world/asia/us-says-north-korea-agrees-to-curb-nuclear-work.html?_r=1&hp.

94. See Aiden Warren, *The Obama Administration's Nuclear Weapon Strategy: The Promises of Prague* (New York: Routledge, 2014), 144–57.

95. Fifield, "North Korea Conducts Fifth Nuclear Test."

96. Julian Borger, "Kim Jong-un's Growing Nuclear Arsenal Could Force U.S. Back to Negotiating Table," *The Guardian*, September 9, 2016, https://www.theguardian.com/world/2016/sep/09/north-koreas-growing-ambition-nuclear-arsenal-force-us-negotiating-table.

97. Ibid.

98. Huileng Tan, "North Korea Prepares for Next Nuclear Test as UN, U.S. Weigh Sanction," *CNBC*, September 12, 2016, http://www.cnbc.com/2016/09/11/north-korea-prepares-for-next-nuclear-test-as-un-us-weigh-sanctions.html.

99. Jeffrey Lewis, "North Koreas Nuclear-Program Is Way More Sophisticated and Dangerous than You Think," *Foreign Policy*, September 9, 2016, http://foreignpolicy.com/2016/09/09/north-koreas-nuclear-program-is-way-more-sophisticated-and-dangerous-than-you-think/.

Chapter Five

The Global Nuclear Non-Proliferation Regime

Well before the destruction of Hiroshima and Nagasaki signaled the dawn of the nuclear age, many Manhattan Project scientists were deeply concerned about the challenges the atomic bomb would pose. Encompassing the fears of these scientists, the Franck Report of June 1945 warned that since a perpetual U.S. monopoly would be almost impossible to maintain, then the control or even the elimination of nuclear weapons should best be realized through international agreements. Not two months after Hiroshima, President Harry Truman told Congress in October 1945: "The hope of civilization lies in international arrangements looking, if possible, to the renunciation of the use and development of the atomic bomb." Those sentiments lay behind U.S. proposals made to the United Nations, in June 1946. Named the Baruch Plan after its chief American negotiator, Bernard Baruch, a financier and friend of the president, the core objective was to prevent the further spread of nuclear weapons by securing atomic technology and materials under the control of the newly created United Nations Atomic Energy Commission.

Unfortunately, the plan ignored the political realities that dominated the emerging Cold War. Established in 1946 "to deal with the problems raised by the discovery of atomic energy," the commission sought unsuccessfully to find an international agreement on control and usage. Most members of the United Nations wanted to promote the peaceful uses of atomic energy without disseminating its military technology and, thus, prevent the proliferation of atomic weapons. After the failure of the Baruch Plan and the development of hydrogen bombs in the early 1950s, the Disarmament Commission replaced the UN Atomic Energy Commission in carrying on the search for means of halting the spread of nuclear weapons. UN discussions to stem nuclear weapons proliferation have been productive on the margin; where a wide range of proposals have been offered, many of them have been formally discussed, and several have become signed agreements in piecemeal fashion.[1] Thus, the question arises: How does a nation—or a community of nations—seeking to enhance their security prevent the spread of nuclear weapons? Two approaches that have been contemplated and tried immediately come to mind—political (diplomatic) actions and punitive actions.

DEFINING THE NUCLEAR NON-PROLIFERATION REGIME

The diplomatic approach would gradually lead to establishing the pillars supporting a nuclear non-proliferation regime. Since the concept of a formal, structured international community has been unable to overcome most peoples' powerful-held allegiance to their own nation's sovereignty, the various pillars of the regime were necessarily built over the years by separate political agreements, conventions, and treaties—some multilateral, others bilateral, some formal, others informal—each one dealing with specific issues related to nuclear proliferation. Separately, these pacts may appear to have contributed little to rein in the awesome problem, but viewed together they may be seen, when fully implemented, as realistic pillars in the architecture of the non-proliferation regime.

The 1968 Treaty on the Non-Proliferation of Nuclear Weapons (NPT), sponsored by the UN, emerged as the central pillar of this informal regime even though it was preceded chronologically by seven significant building blocks. These included: (1) the Atoms for Peace program designed to share technology to non-nuclear states for peaceful uses; (2) the International Atomic Energy Agency (IAEA) needed initially to monitor Atoms for Peace activities but soon found to provide a vital role supporting other NPT activities; and (3) the nuclear-weapons-free zones (NWFZs), the first created in 1959, designed to control, monitor, or prohibit nuclear weaponry in a specific geographical area. Diplomatic efforts, beginning in the late 1950s, aimed at banning nuclear testing—long considered a vital pillar of non-proliferation—initially produced the (4) Limited Test Ban Treaty of 1963. Unfortunately, a comprehensive nuclear test ban (CTBT), although signed, is still not in force well into the twenty-first century. Restraints on transferring materials necessary for the development of nuclear weaponry were established, in 1974, by the informal (5) London Nuclear Suppliers Group. With the collapse of the Soviet empire at the end of the Cold War, the U.S.-sponsored (6) Cooperative Nuclear Threat Reduction program (1992) sought to prevent Russian and other states' nuclear materials and weapons from falling into the hands of rogue nations or terrorists. Additional measures have been added to strengthen IAEA safeguards in providing security for nuclear materials in transit and preventing a black market in weapons technology. The necessity of the latter was highlighted by the activities of Pakistani scientist Abdul Qadeer Khan's network. The tense situation in South Asia between India and Pakistan, and a March 2011 tsunami that destroyed Japan's Fukushima nuclear plant, have prompted recognition of the considerable dangers posed by an attack on civilian nuclear facilities during military hostilities leading to the need to revisit safety measures. The (7) Missile Technology Control Regime (1987), which seeks to restrict the traffic in missiles and missile technology—the nuclear weapons delivery systems—also complements nuclear non-proliferation activities.[2]

Is it possible to halt or at least slow global proliferation of nuclear weaponry? Washington's mostly unsuccessful efforts to thwart the British nuclear program in the postwar years consisted mainly of cutting off the flow of information and materials to their erstwhile atomic partners. As discussed in chapter 2, the Americans also tried to discourage the French from developing an independent nuclear option. Washington offered instead to create a multilateral nuclear force (MLF) that would incorporate U.S., British, and French weapons systems; however, French president Charles de Gaulle was quite adamant that France would never grant any other nation influence over French defense decisions. Moreover, journalist John Newhouse suggests, de Gaulle viewed the integration of nuclear forces as an opportunity for American control. Thus, external pressures were often not successful in reducing proliferation. "I am haunted," President John F. Kennedy conveyed in 1963, after the addition of the Soviet Union, Britain, and France to the nuclear club, "by the feeling that by 1970, unless we are successful, there may be 10 nuclear powers instead of four, and by 1975, 15 or 20." Of course, this did not occur. In addition to the original five nuclear weapons states— the United States, Britain, Russia, France, and China—only five other states during the next half century developed nuclear weapons: Israel, India, Pakistan, North Korea, and South Africa, with Iran suspected of moving precariously close to weaponization until the agreement of July 2015.[3]

What was it that occurred in the other states that Kennedy feared might go nuclear? Japan had a small, low-priority nuclear weapons program during World War II; however, after the war it was disarmed and Article 9 of its 1947 Constitution declared "land, sea, and air forces, as well as other war potential, will never be maintained." Of course, this unilateral decision prohibited Japan's manufacturing of nuclear weapons. Nazi Germany also made efforts to develop nuclear weapons during World War II, but in Paris on October 23, 1954, the chancellor of the Federal Republic (West Germany), Konrad Adenauer, unilaterally declared that his state would not manufacture weapons of mass destruction. While he did not rule out obtaining nuclear weapons in the future, he gradually came to understand that while "nuclear war is possible . . . it is also improbable." Foreign Minister Willy Brandt reiterated Adenauer's original pledge, on September 3, 1968, stating that "the

Federal Government has given an understanding to its allies not to manufacture nuclear weapons and has subjected itself to appropriate international controls. It does not seek any national control over nuclear weapons nor national possession of such weapons."[4]

Additionally, there were several other states that during varying other intervals had considered or even initiated a nuclear weapons program, only to have such efforts halted. Some of these same states decided to maintain low-level weapons research, while Canada became the first state to relinquish its opportunity to join the nuclear weapons club. Even though in 1945 the Canadians had all the materials and technology at hand—the uranium, the science, and the technical head start—they decided not to proceed with nuclear weapons production. They did, however, accept a small number of nuclear warheads from the United States during 1963–1984 for deployment "within the country" and with its NATO-assigned forces. In the 1950s and 1960s, Sweden undertook a serious study of the basic technical issues in nuclear weapons design and manufacture, but ultimately chose instead to pursue nuclear reactors for electricity purposes. Switzerland initially formed a scientific group to explore the prospects of the civil use of atomic energy, and during the 1960s seriously contemplated developing, testing, and manufacturing nuclear bombs, artillery shells, and rockets. Financial shortfalls prevented the execution of the project and on November 27, 1969, Switzerland signed the Non-Proliferation Treaty; however, a working committee continued to study its acquisition until its cancellation. Indonesia was suspected of pursuing a nuclear weapons program in the 1960s, but this did not materialize.[5]

Egypt attempted a nuclear weapons program in the 1960s, but gave it up in the 1970s and instead planned to pursue a nuclear power program. U.S. intelligence officials have since claimed that Cairo secretly acquired nuclear weapons technology from China, North Korea, and Pakistan from 1986, while in 2010 the IAEA posited that it believed Egypt had conduced sixteen secret nuclear experiments from 1990 to 2003. Taiwan, which started a plutonium-based nuclear weapons program in the 1960s, also opted out of the nuclear weapons hunt in the 1970s under strong U.S. counter-proliferation pressure. During the period 1976–1978, the Ford and Carter administrations secretly confronted Taipei officials regarding its clandestine nuclear activities, encompassing "uranium enrichment work and attempts to purchase reprocessing technology . . . clear ambition to develop a weapons capability." Ultimately, Premier Chiang Ching-kuo relinquished such ambitions and formally stated that his government had "no intention whatsoever to develop nuclear weapons or a nuclear device."[6]

South Africa's Atomic Energy Board established a nuclear weapons project in the 1970s and on September 22, 1979, a U.S. satellite detected a flash in the South Atlantic Ocean suspected of being a test of a nuclear device. Although the intelligence community could not conclusively verify that it was a South African nuclear test, its cooperation with nuclear-armed Israel sustained rumors that such was the case. In 1989, President F. W. DeKlerk ordered dismantlement of the nation's fully developed nuclear weapons program—including an arsenal of six weapons. South Africa proceeded to join the NPT in 1991, and the IAEA confirmed the closing of its nuclear weapons facilities. Argentina began building nuclear reactors but with no clear evidence of a military program, while its neighbor, Brazil, launched a nuclear weapons program in 1975, only to abandon it in the late 1980s. In 1991, throwing aside a legacy of rivalry, the two nations signed the Bilateral Agreement for the Exclusively Peaceful Uses of Nuclear Energy, which formally renounced any designs on developing nuclear weaponry. They additionally agreed to a monitoring regime by the International Atomic Energy Agency. Libya, although a signatory of the NPT, secretly acquired "thousands of parts for gas centrifuges as well as machine tools for making additional centrifuges," according to a report on Global Security.org. "Libya also had acquired designs for making a nuclear bomb. But key elements of the design were missing, and Libya's scientists lacked the expertise to evaluate the plans or build such a weapon." Consequently, following years of sanctions and British/American pressure, on December 19, 2003, long-time Libyan president Moammar Gaddafi abruptly renounced Libya's nuclear weapons program and invited international inspectors to oversee its new commitment. Belarus, Ukraine, and Kazakhstan returned nuclear weapons inherited at the end of the Cold War to Russia in the late 1990s. Iraq's nuclear weapons program was dismantled after the 1991 Gulf War by the United Nations Special Commission.[7]

NUCLEAR PROLIFERATION

Despite some seven decades of living with the bomb and constructing an international non-proliferation regime, the basic question still remains: Does the spread of nuclear weapons make the world safer or more dangerous? Most individuals usually have a quick response to this question: Of course, it makes things more dangerous. It might seem surprising, therefore, that not all nuclear experts agree on this sentiment and the debate continues unresolved. Like so many of the issues relating to nuclear weapons, the debate is built largely on speculation and ambiguous historical experience. Nuclear proliferation remains a critical security issue; not just because of the risk of a terrorist organization getting its hands on nuclear weapons, but because the proliferation of weapons may also mean a proliferation of nuclear deterrents. Nuclear weapons have long been viewed as a force multiplier, able to make up for imbalances in conventional military power. Paradoxically, then, the unassailable lead of the United States in military power and technology, owing largely to the so-called revolution in military affairs of precision-guided conventional munitions and advanced battlefield and strategic intelligence, might perforce invite other nations to acquire nuclear weapons as a way to influence or even deter American foreign policy. In response to the First Gulf War, an Indian general is reported as saying that you don't go to war with the United States without the bomb. It is a lesson American policymakers have been concerned about for some time, and one for which no easy solution seems likely. President Bill Clinton's secretary of defense, Les Aspin, outlined the problem in December 1993:

> During the Cold War, our principal adversary had conventional forces in Europe that were numerically superior. For us, nuclear weapons were the equalizer. The threat to use them was present and was used to compensate for our smaller numbers of conventional forces. Today, nuclear weapons can still be the equalizer against superior conventional forces. But today it is the United States that has unmatched conventional military power, and it is our potential adversaries who may attain nuclear weapons.

Chillingly, Aspin concluded, "We're the ones who could wind up being the equilizee."[8]

A central element of the proliferation debate revolves around the perceived effectiveness of nuclear deterrence. As John F. Kennedy acknowledged in the wake of the Cuban missile crisis, even a small number of nuclear weapons can deter the most powerful states. As its proponents argue, if deterrence works reliably then there is presumably less to be feared in the spread of nuclear weapons. But if nuclear deterrence does not work reliably, deterrence critics maintain, more nuclear weapons states will presumably lead to not only a more complicated international arena but also a far more dangerous one. Some commentators have made rational, well-argued cases that fears of nuclear proliferation, or the spread of nuclear weapons, are at the least exaggerated. Some go even further and argue that proliferation may actually increase global stability. It is an argument peculiar to nuclear weapons, as it does not apply and is not made with regard to other so-called weapons of mass destruction such as chemical and biological weapons. Nuclear weapons are simply *so* destructive that using them necessitates a crossing of a threshold where an irrational decision against a nuclear-armed foe is required. It is this strategic calculi that ultimately works in mitigating their use.

The argument has been evident in expansions both lateral—to other states—and vertical—in the growth of nuclear stockpiles. "Since 1945, the more nuclear weapons each has accumulated, the less likely, on the whole, it has seemed that either side would use them." Others have made similar arguments, combining both lateral and vertical elements. Kenneth Waltz maintains, for example, that nuclear weapons preserve an "imperfect peace" on the subcontinent between India and Pakistan. Challenging the views that all Pentagon war games involving India and Pakistan always end in a nuclear exchange, Waltz questions: "Has everyone in that building forgotten that deterrence works precisely because nuclear states fear that conventional military engagements may escalate to the nuclear level, and therefore they draw back from the brink?" This was an idea frequently debated during the Cold War. French military strategist General Pierre Gallois observed in 1960 that the path to greater stability lay in increased proliferation. "Few people are able to grasp that precisely because the new weapons have a destructive power out of all proportion to even the highest stakes, they impose a far more stable balance than the world has known in the past," he said. "Nor is it any easier to make people realize that the more numerous and terrible the retaliatory weapons possessed by both sides, the surer the peace . . . and that it is actually more dangerous to limit nuclear weapons than to let them proliferate." Gallois made this argument in the context of justifying the French bomb and increasing NATO nuclear capabilities. "These," Gallois said, "are the realities of our time, but no one is willing to accept them at first blush."[9]

Notwithstanding such notable proponents of the "proliferation equals more security" argument, the weight of opinion sits mainly at the other end of the spectrum. It has become an accepted norm—heightened especially since 9/11—that the spread of nuclear weapons actually engenders insecurity; where the greater the number of nuclear weapons and nuclear powers in the world, the more opportunities for disaster. Scott Sagan has highlighted the ways in which organizations and communications can fail, where rather than being anomalies, accidents are an inherent part of organizations. When nuclear weapons are thrown into the mix, the risks of catastrophic accidents or miscalculations are sobering. Sagan argues that a fundamental level of risk is inherent in all nuclear weapons organizations regardless of nationality or region. It is an element that further compounds the problem of nuclear weapons in regions still embroiled in religious, cultural, socio-economic, and ethnic tensions. All of these elements combine in a barely controllable milieu of states' nuclear weapons policy. Thus, the proliferation of nuclear weapons has posed, and continues to pose, multiple threats to major nuclear weapons powers. John Newhouse illustrates the dilemma:

> The use or threatened use of a nuclear bomb in a local conflict could increase the danger of a confrontation between them. Progress toward a bomb by one state goads other aspirants and may inspire new ones. . . . At the least, it poses a constant risk of accidental use of nuclear weapons since command and control in a country that has recently acquired the capability could be dangerously inadequate. Proliferation increases the risk of one state waging preventive nuclear war or striking preemptively against another country whose weapons are vulnerable.

In looking around the globe in the twenty-first century in regions in the Middle East, Northeast Asia, South Asia, and even Eastern Europe, notions of an escalation, misunderstanding, or accident that could lead to nuclear conflict should not be considered far-fetched.[10] While debates will continue to permeate the discourse, the main consensus appears to oppose the proliferation of nuclear weapons and, indeed, all weapons of mass destruction.

PREVENTIVE MILITARY ACTIONS

Of course, doubting the effectiveness of political non-proliferation measures, several policymakers have justified, or at least considered, the notion of taking preventive military action against an adversary's nuclear facilities. American officials engaged in serious discussions about launching preventive military assaults against both the Soviet and Chinese nuclear programs—prior to each nation's successful test of its first atomic device in 1949 and 1964, respectively. Although nothing materialized, Secretary of State Dean Rusk allegedly discussed the prospect of joint measures with the Soviets to "neutralize" the potential Chinese nuclear threat. Likewise, the Indian government of Prime Minister Indira Gandhi seriously considered, but ultimately rejected, plans for preventive military attacks on Pakistan's nuclear facilities in the early 1980s.[11] Israel also felt compelled to take action to halt Iraq's early efforts to develop a nuclear program that was suspected of military objectives. At first, they allegedly employed sabotage and assassination in their attempts to disrupt Baghdad's project. Ultimately, however, Israel carried out an aerial strike against the Iraqi nuclear power facility at Osirak on June 7, 1981, an attack that was officially condemned by the UN Security Council and the Reagan administration. British prime minister Margaret Thatcher also criticized the action: "Armed attack in such circumstances cannot be justified. It represents a grave breach of international law."

In commenting on how to deal with Iran's developing nuclear program, Bennett Rambert pointed to the applicability of the Osirak raid in a 2006 article. As stated, "A dramatic military action to prevent nuclear weapons proliferation, the June 7, 1981, strike left a legacy that echoes today in the 'all options are on the table' drumbeat emanating from Washington and Jerusalem. The seemingly straightforward message to Iran and other would-be proliferators was unequivocal: Abrogate nonproliferation pledges in this post–9/11 era or risk being 'Osiraked.'" Doubts over the effectiveness of such action, not to mention the possible ramifications, initially stymied enthusiasm for such action. In response to Rambert's article, Richard Betts offered a sharp rebuttal:[12]

> Contrary to prevalent mythology, there is no evidence that Israel's destruction
> of Osirak delayed Iraqis nuclear weapons program. The attack may actually

have accelerated it. . . . Recall the surprising discoveries after the [First] Iraq War. In 1991 coalition air forces destroyed the known nuclear installations in Iraq, but when UN inspectors went into the country after the war, they unearthed a huge infrastructure for nuclear weapons development that had been completely unknown to Western intelligence before the war. . . . Iraq's nuclear program [abandoned before the Second Iraq War] demonstrates how unsuccessful air strikes can be even when undertaken on a massive scale.

Nevertheless, Israel struck again on September 6, 2007, this time at a suspected nuclear facility in northern Syria. Israeli and American intelligence officers had decided that the site contained "a partly constructed nuclear reactor, apparently modeled on one North Korea has used to create its stockpile of nuclear weapons fuel." While the Syrian facility was actually years from being able to produce "the spent nuclear fuel that could, through a series of additional steps, be reprocessed into bomb-grade plutonium," the attack proceeded. This time there was no U.S. condemnation. [13]

Following the First Gulf War, the UN Security Council's Resolution 687 (1991) authorized the dismantling of Iraq's nuclear weapons program and systematic IAEA inspections to ensure that the program was not restarted. A special commission, the United Nations Special Commission on Iraq (UNSCOM), together with the International Atomic Energy Agency (IAEA), was mandated to oversee the destruction of these weapons. As with most imposed disarmament arrangements, the inspection process encountered domestic resistance, resulting in a September 1991 UN Security Council Resolution (715) that ordered Baghdad officials to "cooperate fully" with the weapons inspectors. Despite various obstacles, the UN teams were remarkably successful in their efforts to disarm Iraq of its weapons of mass destruction. In 2002/2003, contrary to the inspectors' reports, Washington and London officials vied for a pathway of "anticipatory" action. President George W. Bush, Prime Minister Tony Blair, and their spokespeople insisted that Iraq was expanding and improving its weapons of mass destruction facilities, including stepping up its quest for nuclear weapons, and rebuilding "much" of its banned missile production infrastructure. Following the capture of Baghdad in 2003 by U.S.-led forces, the Bush administration rushed two groups of inspectors to Iraq charged with uncovering Saddam Hussein's caches of banned weaponry but found nothing. In October 2004, the Iraqi Survey Group headed by Charles Duefler confirmed that Iraq's illicit arms had indeed been destroyed during the early 1990s, as earlier reported by UN and IAEA inspectors. While Iraq may have desired to reconstitute its programs to develop the banned weaponry, according to Duefler, there was no evidence that any such programs had been undertaken. [14]

Many political and legal questions accompanied these actions. Were both the Israeli military attacks and the U.S.-sponsored Second Gulf War, which have been labeled "preventive" and occasionally "preemptive" actions, in compliance with public international law? Only a preemptive strike, the burden of which, according to U.S. Secretary of State Daniel Webster's classic formulation of the customary right of self-defense in the aftermath of the British attack on American steamboat SS *Caroline*, in December 1837, must "show a necessity of self-defense, instant, overwhelming, leaving no choice of means, and no moment of deliberation," is generally considered legal. Therefore, the legality of Israel's claim of a preventive action remains dubious. Semantically speaking, the Bush administration did not distinguish between *prevention* and *preemption*, often using them interchangeably, nor did it believe that such delineation between the terms was important. On the political side, could the short-range benefits of such future military action be outweighed by long-range diplomatic difficulties? Would the political climate, in the long run, be seriously damaged by lingering hostile attitudes harbored by the injured adversary and its ethnic/religious neighbors? Of course, on the military side there remains the question of effectiveness should the threatened adversary take serious measures to protect its facilities. [15]

QUEST FOR A COMPREHENSIVE NUCLEAR TEST BAN

The search for political means to halt nuclear testing began early and was closely linked to the desire to restrict the spread of nuclear weapons. Indeed, most analysts have viewed the cessation of nuclear testing as a litmus test for achieving that goal. President John F. Kennedy and Soviet secretary general Nikita Khrushchev agreed to a partial or Limited Nuclear Test Ban in 1963 that most nations adopted. This treaty, while useful in reducing radioactivity in the atmosphere, did not halt the spread of nuclear weapons.

While the United States and Soviet Union sought to shelve the Comprehensive Test Ban Treaty (CTBT) after the signing of the partial ban, other nations took the issue to the Eighteen-Nation Disarmament Conference (1962–1968) at Geneva. It was evident that the non-nuclear states considered the CTBT as essential to halting proliferation. During the early years of Richard Nixon's presidency, the CTBT was generally avoided in superpower discussions so as not interfere with U.S.-Soviet bilateral negotiations on strategic arms limitations. At a Moscow summit meeting with Premier Leonid Brezhnev, in July 1974, Nixon dismissed his host's proposal for a multilateral CTBT on the grounds the U.S. Senate would not accept it. The two leaders, however, did agree on a bilateral Threshold Test Ban Treaty (TTBT) designed to limit underground tests to less than 150 kilotons, hold the number of tests to a minimum, not interfere with the other's efforts at verification, and exchange detailed data on all tests and test sites. Because the military chiefs on both sides wanted to complete some high-yield tests, the effective date of the pact was set at March 31, 1976. Brezhnev and President Gerald Ford signed a follow-up Peaceful Nuclear Explosions Treaty (PNET) in May 1976 that would allow nuclear explosives of less than 150 kilotons to be used for non-military projects. For the first time, the PNET provided for on-site inspections under certain circumstances. Both nations agreed to honor the two agreements even though ratification of both the TTBT and PNET continued to be delayed. [16]

When President Jimmy Carter shifted the focus from the TTNT back to a comprehensive test ban, the prospects for success were optimistic. In November 1977 the Soviet Union indicated that it was willing to accept a verification system based on national technical means (each nation's individual intelligence-gathering system), supplemented by voluntary challenge inspections and automatic, tamper-proof seismic monitoring stations known as "black boxes." However, in Washington, opponents fearful of Soviet motives defeated the administration efforts. The weapons laboratories, the Joint Chiefs of Staff, Secretary of Energy James Schlesinger, National Security Adviser Zbigniew Brzezinski, and other administration officials thwarted the initiative by emphasizing the old "safe guard" arguments that called for periodic tests to assure the reliability of the nuclear weapons stockpile. Brzezinski disclosed in his memoirs that he "was not very interested" in the CTBT negotiations and that he "saw CTBT as a likely embarrassment" to the administration's efforts to gain ratification of SALT II. The result contributed to heightened superpower tensions. As stated by Raymond Garthoff, "The course as well as the outcome of the CTBT negotiations in 1978–1979 contributed greatly to broader growing Soviet suspicion as to American lack of interest in arms control and preference for arms competition." [17]

The election of Ronald Reagan put a temporary end to American participation in discussions regarding the CTBT and, indeed, arms control generally. In July 1982, Reagan formally withdrew U.S. participants in the CTBT talks. Arguing that the Soviet Union was perhaps testing over the TTNT's 150-kiloton threshold, he insisted that verification issues of both the TTNT and PNET must be renegotiated before discussions of a CTBT could be considered. Critics noted that verifying that a test had taken place was much easier than determining its specific magnitude; therefore, the Reagan administration was slightly off track in its viewpoint. Pressure generated by the nuclear freeze movement and congressional resolutions failed to revive the stalled CTBT negotiations. In 1984, Konstantin Chernenko, who had just succeeded Yury Andropov as general secretary of the Communist Party of the Soviet Union, urged the United States to ratify the TTNT and PNET, as well as resume discussions on a comprehensive test ban. When Premier Mikhail Gorbachev wrote Reagan in December the next year indicating that the Soviet Union would accept on-site inspections as part of a CTBT agreement that too was rejected. In July 1985, the Soviet leader proceeded to unilaterally establish a moratorium on nuclear testing, and urged Reagan to stop testing. Without a positive answer from Washington, Moscow, on February 26, 1987, resumed nuclear testing; meanwhile, during Gorbachev's moratorium the United States had carried out twenty-six tests. Reagan's response to Gorbachev's various proposals suggested to Soviet officials that the president's frequently stated concern about verification was insincere and that he had used the issue in order to continue to increase America's nuclear arsenal. In September 1987, however, Secretary of State George Schultz and Soviet foreign minister Eduard A. Shevardnadze resumed talks on strengthening the verification procedures for the TTNT and PNET that would later bear positive results. [18]

NEGOTIATING A COMPREHENSIVE NUCLEAR TEST BAN

Despite attempts by many officials in Washington to ignore the fact, the non-nuclear nations had made it evidently clear that a comprehensive nuclear test ban had become a central tenet to maintaining the Non-Proliferation Treaty. As discussed later in the chapter, the four previous NPT Review Conferences repeatedly, and each time more stridently, emphasized the superpowers' apparent lack of effort to achieve a total ban on testing. Since the only conclusive evidence that a state had acquired or built a nuclear weapon would be a test explosion, it could secretly prepare a small stockpile of plutonium or of highly enriched uranium and, at a time of its choosing, embark on a testing program. As such, a total ban on testing, coupled with inspections by the IAEA, could greatly reduce this scenario.

In part a response to this demand, Soviet president Mikhail Gorbachev declared a unilateral nuclear test moratorium in 1991, followed by President Francois Mitterrand's surprise announcement of a French moratorium in 1992. President George W. H. Bush, however, continued to insist on America's right to test. He declared in January 1990 that his administration had "not identified any further limitations on nuclear testing . . . that would be in the United States' national security interest." Negotiations did proceed on verification protocols for the TTBT and PNET and, with the Soviets acceding to the American position, Bush and Gorbachev at their Washington summit meeting, in June 1990, signed new protocols clearing the way for their ratification. Yet, Bush remained reluctant to consider ratifying the CTBT in spite of America's increasingly isolated position. Congress finally urged the president to end underground nuclear testing and agree to a moratorium on all U.S. underground nuclear tests. The Senate enacted legislation in 1992—known as the Hatfield-Mitchell-Exon amendment—that called for an immediate unilateral nine-month moratorium, and requested the president to obtain a comprehensive test ban by September 30, 1996; if not obtained, an extended moratorium would take effect until "another nation" tested. The legislation, meanwhile, would allow the United States, after the expiration of the nine-month moratorium, to conduct five tests per year for three years for specified purposes—three tests were to check new safety devices for nuclear weapons, one test was to verify reliability, and one was allotted to Great Britain (who for some time had been using the Nevada Test Site). While the White House opposed the legislation, President Bush nevertheless signed it into law. With the United States joining the general unilateral moratorium, a cessation of testing has been maintained since 1993.[19]

The Hatfield-Mitchell-Exon amendment forced the Clinton administration to undertake efforts at the Conference on Disarmament, with the aim of achieving a comprehensive test ban treaty by 1996. The negotiations found only representatives from India and Pakistan opposed to a Comprehensive Test Ban Treaty (CTBT), doubtless because each was surreptitiously developing nuclear weapons. Still, the conference drafted a proposed treaty that would prohibit any nuclear explosion that generated a fission yield, or a "zero" yield ban. The treaty prohibited any nuclear test explosions or any other nuclear explosion at any location under the treaty's jurisdiction; moreover, there was no special withdrawal clause. In addition, the treaty would create an elaborate International Monitoring System (IMS) with a worldwide network of observational technology to "help to verify compliance with and detect and confirm violations." A U.S. State Department *Fact Sheet* explained: "When complete, the IMS will consist of 337 monitoring facilities. It will be complemented by an intrusive on-site [challenge] inspection regime applicable once the Treaty has entered into force." The IMS would employ four technologies in monitoring: seismological to check on shockwaves, radionuclide to measure atmospheric radioactive particles, hydro-acoustic to listen for sound waves traveling through water, and infrasound to detect ultra-low shockwaves.[20]

Thomas Graham, acting director of the Arms Control and Disarmament Agency (ACDA), confronted fierce bureaucratic opponents in Washington when seeking a continuation of a moratorium on testing. Since he was to lead the U.S. delegation to the crucial 1995 NPT review conference proposing to extend the treaty indefinitely, he feared that if the nuclear powers began testing, there would be little hope of gaining the requisite support of the non-nuclear countries. President Bill Clinton agreed in 1993 to continue the moratorium, with annual renewals as long as no other nation tested, until a CTBT had been achieved. After considerable wrangling, the draft was removed from the Conference on Disarmament, and in September 1996 Australia introduced a resolution in the UN General Assembly to open the draft treaty for signature. It was approved by a vote of 158–3, with India and Iraq voting against. The United States was the first to sign. The CTBT was, in President

Clinton's words, "the longest-sought, hardest-fought prize in arms control history."[21]

For the CTBT to enter into force, however, it had to be ratified by forty-four nuclear states and nuclear threshold states, many of which were waiting for the United States to act. Unfortunately for its supporters, the U.S. Senate rejected ratification on October 13, 1999, by a vote of 48 to 51—failing to gain even a majority in support of the treaty and, of course, significantly below the two-thirds needed for approval. The CTBT's defeat, according to one observer, was "an accident of politics, an executive-legislative stalemate that resulted from clashing institutional interests, partisan struggle, intraparty factionalism, and personal vindictiveness. Certainly it was a story of zealotry, conspiracy and incompetence in which all the key players share responsibility for an outcome that only a minority really desired." Underlying all of the political activity were issues of substance—"the effectiveness of the stockpile stewardship program, the capabilities of monitoring and challenge inspections," and the future of deterrence—that in some minds were uncertain factors.[22]

The Clinton administration sought to ease domestic concerns with CTBT "safeguards": a Science Based Stockpile Stewardship Program that would ensure the reliability of America's nuclear weapons; nuclear laboratory facilities to continue progress in nuclear technology; the right to resume nuclear tests should the United States withdraw from the CTBT; and comprehensive efforts to improve monitoring systems. Despite Arizona Republican senator Jon Kyl's insistence in 1992 that "as long as we have a nuclear deterrent, we have got to test it in order that it is safe and it is reliable," all of the United States' nuclear warheads have been examined since then and found to meet these standards. Three years after the Senate's action, the National Academy of Sciences reviewed the arguments offered by critics of the treaty, particularly those that questioned the adequacy of international monitoring and long-term effectiveness of the U.S. nuclear stockpile without new tests. The panel of experts concluded: "The U.S. nuclear stockpile can be safely and reliably maintained without explosive testing." Although surveillance of weapons components and retention of high-quality scientists is imperative for the upkeep of U.S. nuclear weapons, "no need was ever identified for a program that would periodically subject stockpile weapons to nuclear tests." A separate 2009 study by JASON, an independent technical review panel, reported that the "lifetimes of today's nuclear warheads could be extended for decades, with no anticipated loss in confidence."[23]

When Russia ratified the CTBT in 2000, international attention (and blame) became focused on the United States as the nation primarily responsible for the failure of the treaty to enter into force. Thus, the CTBT has languished in the U.S. Senate, as neither President George W. Bush, an opponent of arms control measures, nor President Barack Obama, who has been sympathetic to the CTBT, have been able to revive it. While the Bush administration found that the International Monitoring System (IMS), with its stations in Russia, China, and other sensitive regions, provided useful information, it reduced America's annual dues assessment, thus making it difficult for the CTBT Preparatory Commission to collect dues from other nations. Nonetheless, in 2011, more than 80 percent of the IMS facilities had been completed. Meanwhile, the U.S. Air Force Technical Applications Center, part of the Intelligence, Surveillance, and Reconnaissance Agency, continues to unilaterally conduct the unique, but significant, task of detecting nuclear explosions. The center, as Philip Coyle explains, is able to detect nuclear tests "whether conducted underground, under water, in the air or in space." The center was responsible for detecting the initial Indian nuclear test in May 1974 and the first Pakistani test in May 1998 and measuring the output of the two North Korean tests in 2006 and 2009. This poorly funded unit, however, has been struggling to maintain its Constant Phoenix aircraft, which plays a vital role in the monitoring process. Despite the failure of the CTBT to enter into force, a general moratorium on nuclear testing in effect since 1993 has been more or less honored.

During 1945–2011, a total of 2,052 nuclear tests have taken place worldwide: the United States 1,030; USSR/Russia 715; United Kingdom 45; France 210—all prior to 1993; China 45 with 6 since 1993; India 3 with 2 since 1993; Pakistan 2 since 1993; and North Korea 5 since 1993.[24] As of August 2016, 183 states have signed the CTBT, and 164, including Russia, have ratified it. India, North Korea, and Pakistan have not signed the treaty. Nine conferences have been held to facilitate entry into force, every other year, most recently on September 29, 2015. In years between these conferences, varying foreign ministers meet to encourage entry into force of the CTBT. A ministerial meeting was held on June 13, 2016, to observe the twentieth anniversary of the signing of the CTBT.[25]

THE NUCLEAR NON-PROLIFERATION TREATY

Although several nations recognized early the need for a formal arrangement to restrict the spread of atomic and later nuclear weapons, progress has been slow. The United Nations, despite an initial lack of success, eventually played a major role in the negotiations leading to the Non-Proliferation Treaty (NPT). Beginning with its first session in January 1946, at London, the General Assembly unanimously decided to establish the United Nations Atomic Energy Commission (UNAEC). Specifically, the commission was charged with defining proposals for the control of atomic energy to ensure its use for peaceful purposes, for the elimination of atomic weapons from national arsenals, and for effective safeguards against violations. There were fundamental differences in the approach of nuclear and non-nuclear states to formulas for limiting or halting the spread of nuclear weaponry; many of these differences would persist well beyond the signing of the NPT in 1968. Yet, as Thomas Graham indicated early in the twenty-first century: "When the NPT was signed in 1968, it had clearly become a centerpiece of United States and world security, and is even more so today." President Lyndon Johnson, who deserves substantial credit for finalizing the NPT, considered the treaty to be "the most important international agreement since the beginning of the nuclear age." Shortcomings aside, he was not far from correct as the non-proliferation regime expanded.[26]

After failing to gain the needed approval of the U.S.-sponsored Baruch Plan for international control of atomic energy or rallying support for a comprehensive nuclear test ban, the UNAEC gave way to the Disarmament Commission (DC) during the barren 1950s. Replacing the DC in 1962, the Eighteen Nation Disarmament Committee (ENDC) achieved greater success. Initially, the ENDC was given the task of seeking agreement on a treaty for general and complete disarmament, but when that evidently proved impossible the committee turned to seeking steps to halt the spread of nuclear weapons. Earlier, in 1958, Ireland offered the first proposal specifically aimed at preventing the spread of nuclear weapons. In 1961, the UN unanimously adopted Ireland's resolution and called on all states, particularly the nuclear weapons states, to conclude an international agreement to prevent the dissemination or acquisition of nuclear weapons. It was not until 1965, however, that the General Assembly asked the ENDC to negotiate a treaty preventing the proliferation of nuclear weapons. It listed the principles on which a treaty should be based, specifying that the agreement should "embody an acceptable balance of mutual responsibilities and obligations of the nuclear and non-nuclear powers" and should be a step toward nuclear disarmament.[27]

With the Soviet Union (1949), the United Kingdom (1952), and France (1960) testing atomic devices, international concerns mounted, especially among non-nuclear states, about where such proliferation—the "Nth country problem"—would lead. Gradually, the superpowers began to convey their own issues with nuclear weapons proliferation. After failing to dissuade France from building a bomb, Presidents Dwight Eisenhower and John F. Kennedy worried that an envious West Germany (and perhaps Italy) would also seek an independent nuclear deterrent. In response to NATO concerns on the extent to which America's nuclear umbrella covered Western Europe, Washington proposed a nuclear sharing MLF under NATO command but with the United States maintaining an operational veto. Under this scheme, as historian Hal Brands describes, "mixed-nationality crews from NATO states would man nuclear-armed naval vessels, giving each participant a claim to nuclear status." France's President de Gaulle responded contemptuously, Britain showed only moderate interest, and the Soviet Union—

alarmed at the prospect of West Germany's participation—objected vocifer-ously. Only West Germany retained measureable enthusiasm.

Additionally, the United States and the Soviet Union were uneasy with Chinese nuclear weapons activities. Fearing for the strategic balance in Asia, both President Kennedy and Lyndon Johnson's administrations gave consid-eration to preventive strikes on Chinese nuclear facilities, preferably jointly with the Soviets; Johnson even authorized consultation with Moscow to "cooperate in preventive military action." In November 1964, Secretary of State Dean Rusk suggested that the U.S. interests might be better served by encouraging Indian and Japanese efforts to develop nuclear weapons as a counterweight to communist China. "If you were Prime Minister of Japan [or India]," Rusk posited, "how much reliance would you put on U.S. protection if a threat from China or the Soviet Union developed?" At the same time, Nikita Khrushchev had earlier reneged on a Soviet promise to share nuclear weapons secrets with communist China. On June 20, 1959, Moscow unilater-ally annulled the pact that would have provided China with Soviet nuclear technology, though it did know that the Chinese would eventually be in a position to build their own bomb. In Khrushchev's words, "The later they master the mysteries of the atom, the better." China tested a low-yield device in October 1964 and a higher-yield bomb in May 1965.[28]

The initial nuclear test on October 15, 1964, prompted President Johnson to seek a comprehensive review of nuclear proliferation, as Brands writes, which involved "a higher-level, harder look at the problem of nuclear spread." Several days later, the president created the Committee on Nuclear Proliferation—known as the Gilpatric Committee, after chairman Roswell Gilpatric—that studied possible options between November 1964 and Janu-ary 1965. While the state department wanted to continue pursuing the MLF to prevent European proliferation, Gilpatric preferred the Arms Control and Disarmament Agency's effort to develop a worldwide strategy. The United States and the Soviet Union each exchanged draft treaties on non-prolifera-tion in 1965. By October 1966, as Anatoly Dobrynin, Moscow's ambassador to Washington, recalled in his memoirs, "The Soviet leadership decided to focus on the non-proliferation of nuclear weapons" because of their fears about MLF. "It frightened us to think of Europeans and especially Germans anywhere near a nuclear trigger," he continued. "So on behalf of my govern-ment I told [Secretary of State Dean] Rusk this idea was the main obstacle in the way of a non-proliferation agreement: the Soviet Union was ready for negotiations to limit the spread of nuclear weapons, but the U.S. government must make its choice between a non-proliferation agreement or a NATO nuclear force." By 1967, the two powers had resolved their differences. The United States agreed to abandon the multilateral nuclear force, while in the context of the USSR, it withdrew its opposition to setting up a nuclear planning committee in NATO. Such developments enabled the superpowers to submit separate but identical drafts of a treaty to the ENDC. [29]

With respect to negotiations, the Eighteen Nation Disarmament Committee's non-aligned members argued that a non-proliferation treaty must not simply divide the world into nuclear "haves" and "have nots," but must balance mutual obligations. They argued that in exchange for the non-nuclear states ending the "horizontal" proliferation of nuclear weapons, the nuclear powers should end their "vertical" proliferation. They listed the specific steps in the following order: (a) a comprehensive nuclear test ban; (b) a complete cessation of the production of fissionable material for weapons purposes; (c) a freeze on, and gradual reduction of, nuclear weapons stocks and their means of delivery; (d) a ban on the declared use of nuclear weapons; and (e) security assurances to the non-nuclear states by the nuclear powers. These non-aligned states' demands garnered the endorsement of some non-nuclear American and Soviet allies. While the two nuclear superpowers would not agree to listing these specific measures in the operative part of the treaty, they eventually accepted a compromise formula. After extensive negotiation and pressure, the United States and the USSR agreed to a provision relating to halting and reversing the nuclear arms race—Article VI. The agreed text of Article VI read: "Each of the Parties to the Treaty undertakes to pursue negotiations in good faith on effective measures relating to cessation of the nuclear arms race at an early date and to nuclear disarmament, and on a treaty on general and complete disarmament under strict and effective international control." Additionally, the superpowers also agreed to clarify this article by stating their intentions in paragraphs 8, 10, and 11 of the Preamble:

> Declaring their intention to achieve at the earliest possible date the cessation of the nuclear arms race and to undertake effective measures in the direction of nuclear disarmament,
> Recalling the determination expressed by the Parties to the 1963 Treaty banning nuclear weapons tests in the atmosphere, in outer space and under water in its Preamble to seek to achieve the discontinuance of all test explosions of nuclear weapons for all time and to continue negotiations to this end,
> Desiring to further the easing of international tension and the strengthening of trust between States in order to facilitate the cessation of the manufacture of nuclear weapons, the liquidation of all their existing stockpiles, and the elimination from national arsenals of nuclear weapons and the means of their delivery pursuant to a Treaty on general and complete disarmament under strict and effective international control. [30]

Although several individuals and states still considered the draft NPT to be inherently discriminatory, they also believed that it was significant as a first step that could lead to the elimination of all nuclear weapons. The Non-Proliferation Treaty was signed on July 1, 1968, but the arguments over

Article VI were far from over. The United States and Soviet Union's reluctant agreement "to pursue negotiations in good faith" to halt the nuclear arms race "at the earliest possible date," and to seek "a treaty on general and complete disarmament under strict and effective international control" became a serious point of contention at each of the subsequent five-year review conferences.

NPT REVIEW CONFERENCES

The NPT provided for conferences to be held every five years to review the operation of the treaty, "with a view to assuring that the purposes of the Preamble and the provisions of the Treaty are being realized." The first four review conferences were held in 1975, 1980, 1985, and 1990. In accordance with Article X, a conference had to be held in 1995, to determine "whether the Treaty shall continue in force indefinitely, or shall be extended for an additional fixed period or periods." Since the non-nuclear states with nuclear facilities dedicated to peaceful uses had agreed in Article III to accept full-scope IAEA safeguards to ensure their compliance with the NPT, the review procedure was provided to assure the compliance of the nuclear parties. In practice, however, the conferences have mainly served to assess the compliance of the nuclear parties. At all four early review conferences, most of the non-nuclear parties expressed dissatisfaction with the failure of the three nuclear parties to live up to the obligations regarding the implementation of the nuclear disarmament pledges contained in Article VI and the Preamble.

Differences also emerged regarding the provisions for promoting the peaceful uses of nuclear energy and the question of safeguards, which were the main interest to the nuclear powers concerned with reducing the risks of horizontal proliferation. On the whole, however, these two issues were secondary ones. The non-nuclear states did not constitute a solid bloc at any of the review conferences. Those allied to either the Eastern or Western nuclear states tended to side with the Soviet Union or the United States. On the primary disarmament issue, the non-nuclear parties most critical of the nuclear powers were the neutral and non-aligned (NNA) states. Unlike most conferences dealing with arms control issues, the three nuclear powers and their allies together resisted the demands of the NNA countries for full compliance of their commitments to nuclear disarmament. Their overriding desire to prevent the horizontal proliferation of nuclear weapons, which they feared would undermine their nuclear monopoly and dominance, prevailed during even the darkest days of the Cold War, with some lessening at the 1985 and 1990 reviews.

INDEFINITE NPT EXTENSION, 1995

Many considered the 1995 conference as a significant juncture in creating a permanent NPT regime, one that would continue working toward halting the spread of nuclear weapons and facilitating peaceful nuclear cooperation. Although there were many nations with divergent interests, some of the issues raised concerned IAEA safeguards and negotiation of a comprehensive test ban. Some states, as Thomas Graham, the U.S. chief official charged with preparing for the conference, has written, wanted "updated and legally binding negative security assurances—pledges by the nuclear weapons states not to attack non-nuclear states with nuclear weapons—and positive security assurances—pledges by the nuclear states to come to the aid of non-nuclear weapon states threatened or attacked with nuclear weapons. Some countries, primarily in the Middle East, underscored the problem of Israel not being an NPT party." Many states also desired more technical assistance for developing peaceful nuclear facilities.[31]

As Washington reviewed its position on the CTBT, some individuals were prepared—if a comprehensive test ban was the price—to have the United States abandon the NPT in 1991. *Disarmament Times*, a UN-related publication, quoted Kathleen Bailey of President Reagan's U.S. Arms Control and Disarmament Agency in December 1989 as saying: "If the U.S. is forced to choose between its own national security and its nuclear testing program versus the survival of the NPT—which we would dearly like to see—the U.S. would choose maintenance of its own national security and therefore its own nuclear testing program." The *New York Times*, which had for years opposed a comprehensive test ban, criticized the administration in a January 27, 1991, editorial for its intransigence. It charged U.S. delegate Mary Elizabeth Hoinkes with "gratuitously offending states that want a total test ban" when she told the conference that "consideration of testing limitations is a serious undertaking that should be conducted in a serious manner." The editorial concluded: "For the U.S. to insist on testing undermines nuclear arms control and sends the wrong message to potential nuclear powers: 'Do as I say and not as I do.'" It was left for Soviet foreign minister Shevardnadze to support the CTBT before the UN General Assembly, on September 25, 1990, in a forthright fashion: "As a matter of the utmost urgency, nuclear tests must be stopped. If testing is stopped, we have a chance to survive; otherwise the world will perish. I have no doubt whatever about this. We need to tell people about this frankly without taking refuge in all sorts of specious arguments."[32]

President Clinton's decision in 1993 to join negotiations on a CTBT eased the pressure on the U.S. delegation and allowed the Americans to take a leading role in preparing for the NPT's indefinite extension. In December, Graham became a leading figure in developing and pursuing America's strategy for ensuring the treaty's permanence by eventually visiting forty individual governments in North and South America, Europe, Africa, Asia, and the Pacific. He sought to take the basic issues concerning security and peaceful use related to nuclear energy directly to government officials, rather than just their permanent representative in New York. Another undertaking aimed at providing momentum for the conference took place on April 11, 1995, when the UN Security Council adopted Resolution 984, which acknowledged the unilateral pledges by the five nuclear-weapon states not to use or threaten to use nuclear weapons against non-nuclear members of the NPT. [33]

Egypt was vitally and vocally concerned that Israel possessed a nuclear arsenal, but was not a member of the NPT. Cairo would not give its support unless it received formal assurances from Tel Aviv; however, Israel was not forthcoming as it was more concerned with Iran and Iraq. At the conference, President Clinton and Vice President Albert Gore urged delegates to extend the treaty indefinitely and permanently. Meeting during the second week of the conference at Bandung, Indonesia, the non-aligned states were asked to provide consensus support for a limited NPT extension that would allow each country to engage in bilateral consultations with Washington. Ambassador Mongbe, the permanent New York representative of the African nation of Benin, became the "hero of Bandung" when he objected, declaring Benin desired an indefinite extension, and thus nullifying the non-aligned attempt for a limited extension. Graham found his most consistent international supporters to be France and Australia, although other nations did play major roles in the final decision. South Africa, for example, was a key broker. The tipping point came during the third week of the conference when Canadian ambassador Chris Wesdahl introduced a resolution on the floor of the General Assembly, backed by 105 co-sponsors (a number that quickly grew to 115), requesting an indefinite extension of the NPT. When the states aligned with South Africa were included, the number of supporters of the Canadian resolution exceeded 150.

The final agreement, adopted by consensus on May 11, 1995, consisted of three elements: the permanent extension of the NPT; the Statement of Principles and Objectives on Nuclear Non-Proliferation and Disarmament; and a strengthened review process. The agreed Statement of Principles and Objectives committed all NPT members, generally, to negotiated reductions in nuclear weapons in support of the treaty and, specifically, to a comprehensive test ban in 1996. It also called for universal treaty membership—by 1998, only India, Pakistan, Israel, and Cuba remained outside the NPT—and support of existing and future nuclear-weapon-free zones (particularly ones for the Middle East and Africa). Finally, the statement urged approval of improved NPT verification, especially ratification of the 93+2 Protocol that enhanced safeguard standards (adopted by the IAEA in June 1997). The non-aligned states, led by Indonesia and South Africa, linked the Statement of

Principles and Objectives to an enhanced review process. "All of this is part of the indefinite extension package," Graham noted, "and it is important to understand that a failure to meet the obligations of the Statement of Principles and Objectives—especially reductions of nuclear weapons—[would] endanger the permanent status of the NPT or even the NPT regime itself." Nonnuclear states were willing to remain second-class states under the treaty for only so long.[34]

THREE ENHANCED NPT REVIEWS

The 2000 Review Conference occurred following a grim period for the nonproliferation movement. The Comprehensive Test Ban Treaty, signed in 1996, was rejected by the U.S. Senate three years later, nuclear tests were held by India and Pakistan in 1998, the incoming George W. Bush administration threatened cancellation of the Antiballistic Missile (ABM) Treaty, the United States, United Kingdom, France, and Russia still adhered to declared first-use nuclear options, and no progress on negotiated nuclear reductions had taken place. Despite this state of affairs, the conference was surprisingly one of the most successful in arriving at a positive consensus on issues indicating a continued worldwide commitment to the basic principles of the NPT. This respite was in large measure managed by the New Agenda Coalition—made up of Mexico, South Africa, Brazil, Ireland, Sweden, New Zealand, and Egypt—that pressed nuclear weapons states for progress on disarmament before the enthusiasm for non-proliferation dissipated.

Discussion of Article VI of the NPT raised once again the basic question: had the nuclear weapons states done enough to meet their commitment "to nuclear disarmament"? Although Article VI did not establish a timetable for measuring results, the issue has been a major point of debate (and contention) since the treaty entered into force in 1970. To gain a consensus in 2000, as Lawrence Scheinman pointed out, the delegates "translated the 1995 principles and objectives on disarmament into an action agenda of 13 steps for systematic and progressive efforts to implement NPT Article VI." Among these "practical steps" was preserving and strengthening the ABM Treaty, continuing the test moratorium until the CTBT entered into force, an "unequivocal undertaking" by the nuclear weapons nations to proceed with eliminating their weaponry, ratifying START II and concluding START III, applying the "principle of irreversibility" to all nuclear reduction pacts, and negotiating a verifiable fissile material cutoff treaty by 2005. Additionally, the delegates called for each state to regularly report on their implementation of Article VI obligations, and for a general reaffirmation of the goals of general and complete disarmament under an effective system of international controls.[35]

As the 2005 Review Conference loomed on the horizon, the 2000 conference's thirteen steps loomed as the triumph of optimism over reality. There had been a few successes during the previous five years. Washington listed the U.S.-Russia Strategic Offensive Reductions Treaty (2002), the United States' elimination of a number of missile submarines, heavy bombers and deactivation of the Peacekeeper ICBMs, removing its nuclear triad from alert status, and a moratorium on the production of fissile material for nuclear weapons (1992) as positive steps. Other nuclear weapons states pointed to their accomplishments. These, as listed by Scheinman, were: "Russia, the United Kingdom, and France have ratified the CTBT; France and the United Kingdom have taken steps making elements of their nuclear weapons consistent with the principle of irreversibility; and the United Kingdom and France have taken some steps toward reducing the operational status of their weapons systems. China had committed to a policy of no-first-use of nuclear weapons and, along with France and the United Kingdom, Beijing has ratified an Additional Protocol to its safeguards agreement with the International Atomic Energy Agency (IAEA)." Then, unexpectedly, Libya was persuaded in 2003 to dismantle its secret, yet nascent, nuclear weapons program and agree to IAEA inspections and to its Additional Protocol. There remained, nevertheless, several of the thirteen steps that were not undertaken and, in some instances, a clear regression.

Disappointments outweighed achievements. In January 2003, North Korea announced its intent to withdraw from the NPT, and in December of the said year Iran was initially charged by the IAEA with clandestine nuclear activities. China and Russia's unsuccessful attempt during the past five years to tie negotiations for the prevention of an arms race in space with a fissile material cut-off treaty (FMCT) hindered progress on the latter. Additionally, China's modernization of its nuclear weapons and Russia's withdrawal of its pledge of no-first-use, along with its insistence on the right to use nuclear weapons in response to attack by any weapon of mass destruction (WMD), raised further doubts pertaining to these nuclear weapons states' commitment to disarmament. Further, Britain's 2000 pledge not to use nuclear weapons against non-nuclear members of the NPT was complicated by its membership in NATO which reserves the right to use nuclear weapons first in a conflict. Although NATO believes such use was "extremely remote," British officials declared that nuclear weapons would be employed only in "extreme circumstances of self-defence."[36]

Washington's actions, however, drew the most attention and frequently generated hostility. President George W. Bush withdrew from the ABM Treaty (2002) to pursue a U.S. missile defense program, prompting Russia to prevent START II from entering into force. The Bush administration further chose to ignore the thirteen steps when it announced it had no plans to reconsider ratification of the CTBT. Moreover, in 2004, the administration posited some bold pronouncements: that a final agreement on fissile material was not possible because it could not be "effectively verifiable"; that it would reconsider its "first-use" doctrine; that it rejected an irreversibility pledge in the Strategic Offensive Reductions Treaty; and it would maintain explicitly in its secret 2002 National Security Presidential Directive-17 that the United States would consider nuclear weapons among retaliation options should it be attacked by any weapons of mass destruction. "Disinclined to rely on multinational regimes and institutions that were seen as cumbersome and lacking decisiveness," as the distinguished academic commentator Lawrence Scheinman delicately phrased it, "the Bush administration chose to counter" the perceived threats of rogue states and terrorists "by unilateral means or, where necessary or appropriate, non-institutionalized multilateral arrangements." Buried in the history of American relations with foreign states there has always lingered an urge for unilateral action when tangled affairs challenged domestic desires. The same may be said of Washington's enthusiasm for international law—often applied when politically useful, ignored when it was not. The Bush administration's war to prevent Iraq from developing non-existent nuclear weapons and subsequently its deliberate evasion of the Geneva Conventions of 1949 brought to the surface both urges.[37]

NUCLEAR-WEAPONS-FREE ZONES

Although these elements contribute to the formation of the non-proliferation regime, they are not as glamorous nor do they command the public attention of the earlier described pillars. It would be a mistake, however, to ignore their contributions. Nuclear-weapons-free zones (NWFZs) are logical members of the non-proliferation regime because they commit member states to follow the regime's basic principles—forsaking production, testing, stationing, or any use of nuclear weaponry. What gives these organic agencies significance is that they are translating non-proliferation principles from documents to action.

Moreover, nuclear-weapons-free zones comprise a significant pillar supporting the non-proliferation regime since they are a means of limiting or neutralizing the activities of the nuclear weapons states in stipulated geographical areas. While there is no authoritative definition of a nuclear-weapons-free zone, there are certain accepted elements implicit in the concept. These include: (1) no manufacture or production of nuclear weapons within the zone; (2) no importation of nuclear weapons by nations within the zone; (3) no stationing or storing of nuclear weapons in nations within the zone; and, preferably when obtainable, (4) a pledge by nuclear weapons states not to use or to threaten to use nuclear weapons against non-nuclear nations within the zone. While each nation within the zone might create nuclear energy facilities for peaceful uses, they must agree to comprehensive safeguards established by the International Atomic Energy Agency (IAEA) to verify that the treaty members were not acquiring illicit nuclear weaponry. Finally, the NWFZs are to be in force indefinitely and none of the parties is to be permitted special conditions.

The frequently denigrated multilateral Antarctic Treaty (1959) defined de facto the first nuclear-weapons-free zone. In addition to assuring that the continent would be set aside for peaceful uses, Article 1 prohibited all types of military activities, and Article 5 specifically prohibited any nuclear explosions or the disposal of nuclear wastes without international assent. Signatory "compliance with the disarmament mandate throughout the Antarctic has clearly been met," Christopher Joyner has noted. "Since 1961, the Antarctic Treaty system has functioned exceedingly well as the institutional framework for preserving peace and stability, fostering scientific cooperation, and promoting standards for environmental preservation and conservation." The Antarctic Treaty has been successfully monitored because of the stipulated total prohibition rather than ceilings or ratios.[38]

Other multilateral agreements that prohibited nuclear weapons in a specific, non-populated area—outer space (1967) and the seabed (1971)—succeeded in gaining general approval and became essentially nuclear-weapons-free zones. The UN, in December 1979, sponsored an elaborate pact that sought to augment the demilitarization of "the moon and other celestial bodies" by prohibiting the placing in orbit of "objects carrying nuclear weapons or any other kinds of weapons of mass destruction or place or use such weapons on or in the moon." Also forbidden was the establishment of any military installations, fortifications, or testing of military devices on the moon. The Outer Space Treaty committed signatories "not to place in orbit around the Earth any objects carrying nuclear weapons or any other kinds of weapons of mass destruction, install such weapons on celestial bodies, or station such weapons in outer space in any other manner." In addition, the article prohibited "the establishment of military bases, installations and fortifications, the testing of any type of weapons and the conduct of military maneuvers on celestial bodies." Bolstering the pact, the nuclear test ban accords—and the abrogated ABM treaty (1972–2002)—added constraints against testing various weapons in outer space. Arms control treaties dealing with strategic weapons prohibited interference with national technical means of verification, thereby permitting the use of reconnaissance satellites; however, antisatellite weapons have not been banned and pose a serious, continuing concern. The Seabed Treaty prevents the installation of nuclear weapons on the ocean floor beyond national territorial waters and, since no nation contemplated any such deployment, the treaty met with little opposition. No reported violations of these agreements have been found.[39]

The unsuccessful Rapacki Proposals—offered by the Polish Foreign Minister in 1957 and 1962—to prevent nuclear weapons being stationed in Poland, Czechoslovakia, and West and East Germany ultimately became a model for five negotiated nuclear-weapons-free zones in populated regions. Each designated zone includes the entire territory of all of its parties, including all land holdings, internal waters, territorial seas, and archipelagic waters. The territorial clauses have caused some differences. The Treaty of Tlatelolco (1967), for example, claims to extend hundreds of kilometers from the signatories' territories into the Pacific and Atlantic Oceans. Consequently, the nuclear-weapon states, citing their freedom at sea rights, assert that these limits do not apply to their ships and aircraft that might be carrying nuclear weapons. The Raratonga Treaty (1985) posed a similar freedom of the seas issue for Washington. The inclusion of the Chagos Archipelago, which includes the U.S. military base at Diego Garcia in the Indian Ocean, as part of the African nuclear-weapon-free zone, prompted yet another dispute. Neither the United States nor the United Kingdom accepted the claim that Diego Garcia was subject to the restrictions stipulated in the Pelindaba Treaty.

Prompted by the Cuban missile crisis, thirty-three nations in Latin America and the Caribbean agreed not to test, develop, or import nuclear weapons and not to permit foreign-controlled nuclear weapon bases in the region. Compliance with the treaty obligations is overseen by the Agency for the Prohibition of Nuclear Weapons in Latin America and the Caribbean (OPANAL), based in Mexico City. The treaty initially confronted the Brazilian military's efforts to develop nuclear weapons; however, the Bilateral Agreement for the Exclusively Peaceful Uses of Nuclear Energy (1991) pledged Brazil and Argentina to adhere to the Tlatelolco pact. The Treaty of Rarotonga (1985), designed to dissuade France from testing nuclear devices in the Tuamoto Archipelago, which succeeded in 1996, includes Australia and New Zealand, along with nearby island states, and was modeled after the Tlatelolco treaty. It prohibits nuclear testing and waste disposal in the region and allows regional ports to prohibit the entry of ships carrying nuclear weapons. In addition to the Tlatelolco prohibitions, Rarotonga relies on the IAEA to verify any nuclear materials present in the treaty region. The United States signed but delayed ratifying the agreement, fearing it would restrict the movement of the navy's warships carrying nuclear weapons. The Reagan administration's talk of a winnable nuclear war prompted New Zealand, in February 1984, to ban a U.S. destroyer from its ports because the United States refused to indicate whether it carried nuclear weapons. The episode caused a rift between the two countries prompting the United States to severe diplomatic contacts with New Zealand from 1985 to 1993.[40]

The Treaty of Bangkok (1995) completed a quest for a Southeast Asia Nuclear-Weapons-Free Zone that began in November 1971, when the Association of Southeast Asian Nations issued a Declaration on a Zone of Peace,

Freedom, and Neutrality. Signatories to the treaty pledged "not to develop, manufacture or otherwise acquire, possess or have control over nuclear weapons; station nuclear weapons; or test or use nuclear weapons anywhere inside or outside the treaty zone; not to seek or receive any assistance in this; not to take any action to assist or encourage the manufacture or acquisition of any nuclear explosive device by any state; not to provide source or special fissionable materials or equipment to any non-nuclear weapon state." In addition to IAEA safeguards, verification occurs through reports and exchange of information among the member states and oversight by a Commission for the Southeast Asia Nuclear-Weapons-Free Zone. The Pelindaba Treaty (1996) arrived thirty-two years after the Organization of African Unity formally declared its aim to create a nuclear-free Africa. In 1990, South Africa's unilateral dismantlement of its nuclear bombs played a leading role in the final negotiations. As with the other NWFZs, signatories pledged not to conduct research on, develop, test, or stockpile nuclear explosive devices; to prohibit the stationing of nuclear devices on their territory; to maintain the highest standards of protection of nuclear materials, facilities, and equipment; and to prohibit the dumping of radioactive waste. The pact also created an African Commission on Nuclear Energy.

The Central Asian States of Kazakhstan, Kyrgyzstan, Tajikistan, Turkmenistan, and Uzbekistan created a nuclear-weapons-free zone in 2006—the Treaty of Semipalatinsk. In the past these states had nuclear weapons stationed on their territories and still "live in a nuclear-armed neighborhood" that consists of Russia, China, Pakistan, India, and Israel. Additionally, Russia and the United States have military facilities in the Central Asian states. [41] During the Cold War the Soviet Union generally supported NWFZ proposals, while the United States more often than not posed reservations. Washington refused to even consider the Rapacki proposals for Central Europe, though this was mainly because NATO's defense was anchored to the use of nuclear weapons. Since the Rarotonga Treaty could restrict the passage of the United States' nuclear-weapons-equipped warships, Washington refused to consider ratification of the pact. The United States joined France in objecting to the Treaty of Bangkok's unequivocal security pledges and to its definitions of area; Washington also insisted the provisions regarding the innocent passage of its warships and aircraft were "too restrictive" and has insisted on modifications. Initially, a serious obstacle to completion of the Pelindaba Treaty was the status of Diego Garcia, a large island in the Indian Ocean, administered by London and employed as a military base by Washington. Consequently, neither nuclear power recognized Diego Garcia as being within the area covered by the treaty, and thus, Russia refused ratification until the status of Diego Garcia had been resolved. While Russia and China accepted the Treaty of Semipalatinsk's final agreement's provisions, the United States, the United Kingdom, and France were critical of several provisions of the treaty and indicated that they would not sign those protocols unless their concerns were resolved.

In May 2011, President Barack Obama asked the U.S. Senate to ratify the disputed protocols of the Pelindaba and Rarotonga treaties because they would "extend the policy of the United States not to use or threaten use of nuclear weapons against regional zone parties" that are members of the Nuclear Non-Proliferation Treaty. Republican senator Jon Kyl of Arizona immediately objected to this revision of George W. Bush's secret 2002 National Security Presidential Directive-17 that explicitly stated the United States would consider nuclear weapons among retaliation options if it were the target of any weapons of mass destruction. He feared that Obama's approach, as stated in the president's 2010 revised Nuclear Posture Review Report, "would limit the instances in which the President would use nuclear weapons to defend the United States and its allies from attack." In this regard, the administration argued that advances in U.S. military capabilities actually allowed Washington to forego the nuclear response option. Washington's original objections regarding the two NWFZ treaties apparently had been resolved. The U.S. State Department review of the Pelindaba pact concluded that "Diego Garcia is not part of the 'territory' of the zone," a position also taken by Russia in ratifying the treaty, in March 2011, with a reservation that its responsibilities would not apply to Diego Garcia. As for the Rarotonga treaty, Washington pledged not to station or test nuclear weapons in the U.S. territories of American Samoa and Jarvis Island.[42]

OTHER INITIATIVES THAT SUPPORT THE GLOBAL NON-PROLIFERATION REGIME

If the global non-proliferation regime can be considered a broad church with the NPT as its central and defining pillar, there are also a myriad of other initiatives, organizations, and political instruments, both formal and informal, that work to support the regime's central goal of mitigating WMD threats. It is here that the next section looks briefly at the Cooperative Threat Reduction Program, the Global Threat Reduction Initiative, and the Nuclear Suppliers Group.

COOPERATIVE THREAT REDUCTION PROGRAM

The sudden demise of the Soviet Union and the chaos that ensued lead to the U.S. Cooperative Threat Reduction (CTR) program (otherwise referred to as the Nunn-Lugar program after its sponsors Senators Sam Nunn [D-GA] and Richard Lugar R-IN]). The Nunn-Lugar Legislative Act of November 12, 1992, provided U.S. financial assistance to the Commonwealth of Independent States, especially Russia, to consolidate the former Soviet nuclear arsenal and ensure their custodial safety. The ten-year, $4 billion program was designed to:

1. "destroy nuclear weapons, chemical weapons, and other weapons,"
2. "transport, store, disable, and safeguard weapons in connection with their destruction," and
3. "establish verifiable safeguards against the proliferation of such weapons."

The Clinton administration selected Ambassador James Goodby to refine the details of the Nunn-Lugar agreements during 1993–1994 with the states that had departed from the Soviet Union and arrange for applicable financial commitments.[43] While the program made significant progress in many areas, there were nonetheless several criticisms voiced pertaining to the management and implementation of American aid. Among the major concerns, as cited by William Potter, were: (1) "the slow pace of implementation, both at the top decision-making levels and between [the Department of Defense] and contractor on the ground"; (2) the United States' "lack of management flexibility" and the insistence of imposing American accounting systems, work plans, and schedules on Russian participants; (3) the redundant senior "level of bureaucracy" and the great "number of 'consultants' who consumed CTR resources but contributed little to specific projects"; and (4) the employment of mostly American contractors at higher cost and with greater delays than using qualified in-country personnel and suppliers. These criticisms were minor compared to the overarching security ramifications should the program's goals not be met. Indeed, if Washington were truly concerned about preventing terrorists from gaining control of these nuclear materials, the cost of the program was certainly reasonable.[44]

In two decades of CTR efforts, much has nevertheless been accomplished: 7,519 nuclear warheads have been deactivated; 768 intercontinental ballistic missiles (ICBM), 498 ICBM silos, 148 mobile ICBM launchers, 651 submarine launched ballistic missiles (SLBM), 476 SLBM launchers, 32 ballistic missile-capable submarines, 155 strategic bombers, 906 air-to-surface missiles, and 194 nuclear test tunnels have been destroyed; 24 security upgrades have been implemented at nuclear-weapon storage sites; and 469 train shipments of nuclear weapons were moved to more secure, centralized storage sites. The program purchased 500 metric tons of highly enriched uranium from dismantled warheads and helped remove all nuclear weapons from the Ukraine, Kazakhstan, and Belarus—states that once held the world's third-, fourth-, and eighth-largest nuclear arsenals. Additionally, nineteen biological-agent monitoring stations have been established.[45]

In 2009, a congressional-mandated report by the National Academy of Sciences—"Global Security Engagement: A New Model for Cooperative

Threat Reduction"—recommended expanding the Nunn-Lugar program to provide a more global engagement to counter twenty-first-century terrorist threats. The CTR program continues "to make us safer by achieving meaningful progress in the destruction and dismantlement of massive Soviet weapons systems and the facilities that developed them," Senator Lugar declared. However, "there is much more work to do in combating biological, nuclear, and chemical threats" through the global cooperative program.[46] In this regard, the program continues to play a significant role in impeding threats posed by terrorist organizations or those proliferant states seeking to attain weapons of mass destruction material, equipment, and expertise. In adapting to new and emerging twenty-first-century theaters of conflict and tension, the global threat reduction programs now focus on "front-line states such as Iraq and Yemen, critical states such as Indonesia, Philippines, and Egypt, and in regions where terrorist threats are on the rise, such as South Asia, the Middle East, and North Africa."[47]

GLOBAL THREAT REDUCTION INITIATIVE

Established in May 2004, the Global Threat Reduction Initiative (GTRI) is a collaborative program aimed at securing vast stocks of dangerous nuclear material scattered around the world. Where the CTR's focus is on nuclear weapons material in states of the former Soviet Union, the GTRI is a complementary program involved in "repatriating or otherwise securing nuclear fuel" from peaceful use facilities and converting these facilities "to use new, more proliferation-resistant technology."[48] According to Eric Hundman, "Promoting peaceful nuclear technology and selling nuclear fuel creates a logical contradiction, however, often nuclear technology is inherently dual-use." As such, in seeking to reduce and protect susceptible nuclear and radiological material situated at civilian sites globally, the GTRI undertakes a tri-pillar approach in mitigating terrorists' access to nuclear and radiological materials. Firstly, it aims to *convert* research reactors and isotope production facilities from the use of highly enriched uranium (HEU) to low enriched uranium (LEU) or authenticate their closure; secondly, it *removes* or sanctions the composition of excess nuclear and radiological materials; and thirdly, it *protects* high priority nuclear and radiological materials from theft.

Since its beginning, GTRI has made substantial progress toward decreasing the danger posed by susceptible civilian nuclear and radiological materials, which could be used by non-state actors to make an improvised nuclear device or a radiological dispersal device (RDD), or "dirty bomb." GTRI and its precursor programs have converted or verified the closure of 88 HEU research reactors and isotope production facilities; removed or ascertained the nature of more than 5,140 kilograms of HEU and plutonium—ample material for more than 205 nuclear bombs; safeguarded more than 775 bombs' worth of HEU and plutonium linked with the BN-350 reactor in Kazakhstan; secured more than 1,700 radiological sites globally containing millions of curies—a sufficient quantity to produce tens of thousands of large dirty bombs; recuperated more than 36,000 "orphan and disused radiological sources in the United States; and recovered 810 radioisotope thermoelectric generators from Russia containing millions of curies of activity."[49]

NUCLEAR SUPPLIERS GROUP

Between 1971 and 1974, delegates from fifteen nations met informally at Vienna, headed by Professor Claude Zangger of Switzerland (hence also known as the Zangger Committee), to control exports of nuclear materials. In August 1974, the committee established guidelines, adopted by consensus, that were implemented through national export control systems. The guidelines included a "trigger list"—so called because their proposed export triggered the group's concern. The list consisted of material, equipment, and facilities that if diverted from peaceful uses could contribute to a nuclear weapons program. Following the 1974 Indian nuclear test, the United States, the Soviet Union, the United Kingdom, France, West Germany, Canada, and Japan replaced the Zangger Committee with the Nuclear Suppliers Group (NSG) and began meeting in London in April 1975. In September 1977, the group adopted an expanded version of the Zangger list, *Guidelines on Nuclear Transfers,* which was sent to the IAEA in January 1978. A 1992 meeting of the group resulted in a re-examination of thousands of items on the dual-list and a tightening of export restrictions.

As an informal multinational organization with forty-eight members, the NSG is operated by consensus without any arrangement for resolving differing interpretations of its guidelines. These are quite broad and provide loopholes; for example, Russia made and conducted arrangements with India for reactors and fuel, justifying their transactions on the basis of Moscow's interpretation of NSG guidelines that other members thought overly expansive. In 2008, India was granted an exception to the guidelines, urged by the United States, allowing it to receive nuclear exports, although it is not a member of the NPT and did not have full scope safeguards. Additionally, in 2010, a question of NSG member China's planned sale of two reactors to Pakistan became a contentious issue since the said state is not a member of NPT or under IAEA safeguards. In response to these developments, the NSG has discussed the creation of more rigorous standards for exports relating to enriched uranium and spent fuel reprocessing, including adherence to the NPT, full-scope safeguards, and enhanced IAEA inspection privileges. Despite the lack of a consensus, Canada, France, Germany, Italy, Japan, Russia,

the United Kingdom, and the United States decided in June 2010 to implement these proposed standards as "national policy for a year."[50]

According to James Goodby, the NSG has become "a clearinghouse for
nuclear-related exports" and remains "one of the most effective international
anti-proliferation tools." Of course, not everyone agrees with this enthusiastic endorsement. "NPT parties have good reason to complain," former state
department official Fred McGoldrick writes, "because the actions of NSG
members have made a mockery of Article IV of the NPT by giving non-NPT
parties India and Pakistan the same benefits as NPT parties without the
accompanying obligations." He charges both Moscow and Washington with
undermining "the norm that only states with comprehensive nonproliferation
commitments should benefit from international nuclear cooperation." The
NSG failed to halt "Iran, Iraq, North Korea, Pakistan, or South Africa from
acquiring a nuclear weapons capability or sensitive nuclear technology," he
points out, because of their clandestine activities in securing the requisite
materials and weak national controls. In the future, McGoldrick argues, "to
maintain the role of the NSG as an effective multilateral barrier to proliferation, its members need to press forward to reach agreement on requiring an
additional [IAEA] protocol, to strengthen their own national export control
systems, and to help non-members to implement effective export control
systems."[51]

Perhaps it was these robust sentiments that contributed to India's failure
to attain Nuclear Suppliers Group (NSG) membership in June 2016. Current
NSG members remain intensely separated on whether India—or other states
that have not signed and ratified the Nuclear Non-Proliferation Treaty (NPT),
including Pakistan—should be considered for membership. For many analysts, India's membership pursuit was unsuccessful because many NSG
members were in simple terms not convinced that India embodies their views
on nuclear non-proliferation. While the diplomatic drive from the likes of
Modi and Obama, as well as ongoing bilateral consultations with China (the
main objector), have made some progress, it will only be tangible and definitive actions by India that will enable it to secure membership. For example, it
could sign the Comprehensive Test-Ban Treaty, end the production of weapons-grade nuclear fuel, and extend comprehensive safeguards to all civilian
nuclear facilities. Some NSG members also argue that it is imperative that
India ratify the Nuclear Non-Proliferation Treaty as a non-nuclear weapon
state before even being admitted to the NSG.[52] As stated by Laura Williams,
"India faces an important choice. It can stay on its current path—focusing on
politics rather than substantive policy concerns—knowing that this approach
is unlikely to ease the current gridlock. Or it can address NSG members'
concerns . . . and increase the odds of gaining membership. Unless and until
Indian officials choose the second path, Delhi is unlikely to achieve the
consensus it seeks—in 2016 or beyond."[53]

NUCLEAR MODERNIZATION AND THE CHALLENGE TO THE NPT

Notwithstanding many of the abovementioned positives pertaining to the expansion and, in many ways, emboldening of the NPT regime, concern with nuclear weapons proliferation and fear of their possible use continue deep into the twenty-first century. Recent substantial investments by nuclear weapon possessor states in the upkeep and modernization of their nuclear postures indicate a return of the nuclear factor in international politics— where deterrence is clearly taking precedence over nuclear arms control and disarmament, and the ultimate global goal of nuclear abolition. [54] The nuclear reductions of Russia and the United States are slowing; U.S. offers to resume bilateral arms control negotiations with Russia have been ignored; France reduced its arsenal by a third after 2008 but seems determined to retain its capability for the long term; India and Pakistan continue to upgrade their delivery and weapons capabilities; and China is also adding to its arsenal and is believed to be deploying multiple warhead (MIRVed) missiles. In short, there has been a decisive shift toward modernizing and sustaining nuclear arsenals for the indefinite future. These developments are exacerbating tensions in the nuclear non-proliferation regime, as states that have chosen to forgo nuclear weapons have become increasingly frustrated by the lack of progress on disarmament by the nuclear-possessor states. In 2008, expectations were raised by the Obama administration's revival of U.S. disarmament leadership, making the subsequent decline in disarmament momentum all the more concerning. The result has been a polarization among NPT members, with a growing number of non-nuclear weapon states (NNWS) demanding new legal instruments that ban the use and possession of nuclear weapons, while others continue to look to the existing but faltering international disarmament machinery to try to stem the tide of discontent.

At present, it is unclear whether the global nuclear non-proliferation regime will survive the fractures that are opening up as a result of these developments. If nuclear force modernization programs continue apace without a renewed focus on arms control and disarmament, the future prospects of the NPT—which is almost universally acknowledged to be the cornerstone of the nuclear non-proliferation regime and one of the most important pillars of international security—look increasingly bleak. The failure of the 2015 Review Conference on the NPT to adopt a final outcome underscores these concerns. While understanding that nuclear modernization is occurring among a group of nuclear states, the United States' strategic weight and its leadership on disarmament remain of global importance. Since the end of the Cold War, the United States has played a circuit breaker role in the global non-proliferation regime: its leadership has been critical to the success or failure of virtually every non-proliferation and disarmament initiative that has been launched, including within the NPT review process. We are still in a window where what U.S. experts and practitioners think and do significantly matters to the future of the non-proliferation regime. Global power shifts mean that that window is starting to close, but for now it remains open and opportunities for U.S. non-proliferation and disarmament leadership remain strong. It also retains the potential to make changes to its nuclear policy that would be reassuring to adversaries and stabilize strategic relationships, while also engendering a renewed momentum on cooperative disarmament and improving legal, normative, and strategic dynamics to this end.

The election of Barack Obama as the forty-fourth president of the United States promised significant changes in U.S. nuclear policy and priorities. During the 2008 presidential campaign, Obama pledged to set a new direction in U.S. nuclear weapons policy and show the world that America believed in its existing commitment under the NPT and would therefore work toward the goal of eliminating all nuclear weapons.[55] In the president's pledge, he vowed to "take concrete steps towards a world without nuclear weapons" and to "put an end to Cold War thinking" by reducing "the role of nuclear weapons in our national security strategy, and urg[ing] others to do the same."[56] This was also echoed in the 2010 NPT Review Conference (RevCon) final document that reaffirmed that "the nuclear-weapon states commit to accelerate concrete progress on the steps leading to nuclear disarmament . . . in a way that promotes international stability, peace and undiminished and increased security."[57]

Over the last two to three years, however, it is evident that the United States has been moving away from these pronouncements. Aside from slowing down its nuclear stockpile reductions during its second term in office, the Obama administration embarked on an overhaul of its entire nuclear weapons enterprise, encompassing the development of new weapons delivery systems and modernizing its enduring nuclear warhead types and nuclear weapons production facilities in a program that scholars estimate could cost more than a trillion dollars.[58] The modernized B61-12 warhead, for example, will be able to strike targets more accurately with a smaller explosive yield and reduce the radioactive fallout from a nuclear attack, and could thus become more militarily attractive and increase the likelihood of use. Other modifications under consideration, such as interoperable warheads that could be used on land- and sea-based ballistic missiles, "could significantly alter the structure of the nuclear warheads" and require nuclear test explosions, thus potentially introducing new uncertainties into the global nuclear order.[59] Simply put, work is under way to design new weapons to replace the current ones that will—of most concern—introduce new military capabilities to the weapons system.

These developments are likely to have serious implications for global disarmament efforts and are of particular concern. Given the disarmament commitments articulated in the 2000 Final Document and the 2010 NPT Action Plan, the U.S. modernization program directly undermines these commitments and runs counter to Obama's 2009 promises laid out at Prague. Not surprisingly, U.S. backtracking and the overall failure of Nuclear Weapons States (NWS) to live up to their commitments has spurred tensions from those in civil society—and has in many instances inspired the humanitarian impacts movement (which held major conferences hosted by Norway, Mexico, and Austria) and seen an expanding number of NNWS drive their own initiatives that could lead to faster pathways to disarmament such as a ban treaty. Yet, with the deterioration of bilateral relations between Moscow and Washington impeding any new arms control agreements, no multilateral disarmament negotiations in sight, and a clear preference toward nuclear modernization, there are good reasons to question the long-term prospects of the non-proliferation regime.

In recent years a number of writers have developed sophisticated analyses of the development and purposes of the non-proliferation regime and the NPT,[60] analysis that is also reflected in important reports from a series of international commissions.[61] While diverse, these works exhibit important common themes: they assert the significance of the treaty for international security; examine a number of weaknesses and contradictions in the regime, notably a division between the nuclear weapons states (NWS) and non-nuclear weapon states (NNWS) over disarmament; and the importance of disarmament as an underpinning structure for non-proliferation. They all make this latter argument as a strategic one, even though it is also a widely held normative interpretation of the NPT regime. O'Neil notably contests this interpretation of the regime and recommends efforts at managing a multipolar system of deterrence, which is an important reference point for understanding the pro-modernization viewpoint.[62]

However, these studies and reports all predate the emergence of the nuclear modernization agenda after the New START treaty was signed, and do not engage in detail with nuclear strategic postures and weapon systems. Bukovansky et al. in particular discuss the non-proliferation regime in relation to the "special responsibilities" of the P5 (Permanent 5 Members of the UN Security Council) and especially the United States for international security. They identify the clashing interpretations of Article VI (in which the NNWS expected the NWS to rapidly disarm but the United States believed that the NPT "would do little to constrain U.S. actions in the nuclear field") as a major problem in the regime. Despite citing the 1980 demand by the Non-Aligned Movement for a "cessation of the qualitative improvement and development of nuclear weapons systems" and President Obama's renewed declaration of support for disarmament after 2008, they do not connect the issue to U.S. strategic policy or postures, or cite the commitment to nuclear modernization that resulted from negotiations with the Senate to pass the

New START treaty. In echoing the 2003 WMD Commission's call to "diminish the role of nuclear weapons . . . by not developing nuclear weapons for *new* tasks," the 2010 NPT Review Conference final outcome called for nuclear states to "further diminish the role and significance of nuclear weapons in all military and security concepts, doctrines and policies."[63] Given the nuclear trajectory of the United States and all weapons states, it is evident that the literature and associated debates remain somewhat disconnected from questions of nuclear strategy and the modernization problem.

While some analysts and writers from the think tank and media domains have expressed their concerns about modernization, there is a lack of substantive analyses. Most have correctly argued that without some form of defined limitations on the pace and scope of nuclear modernization, the goals of deep cuts in, and eventual elimination of nuclear weapons, will remain elusive as the continued reaffirmation of the value of nuclear weapons threatens to extend the nuclear era indefinitely.[64] Others also contend more vigorously that what we are seeing today lies somewhere between parallel efforts to refurbish Cold War arsenals and the emergence of a new arms competition fueled by enhancements to existing weapons or production of new or significantly modified types.[65] Much of the writing has focused on Washington's upgrading of the B61-4 bomb, a version that would equip the device with a tail assembly, turning it into a precision-guided stand-off weapon.[66] Moreover, it will merge four old B61 models into a single version (B61 Model 12) that greatly reduces the range of destructive power. It would have a "dial-a-yield" feature where the lowest setting would only be 2 percent as powerful as the bomb dropped on Hiroshima in 1945. Initially, the plan seemed plausible, until attention fell on the bomb's new tail section and steerable fins. The Federation of American Scientists (FAS) have argued that the high accuracy and low destructive settings mean that military commanders could press to use the bomb in an attack, knowing the radioactive fallout and collateral damage would be limited.[67]

Proponents of modernization (and many within the U.S. nuclear establishment) have argued that such changes are *merely* refurbishments/improvements rather than wholesale redesigns and thereby fulfill the president's pledge of not producing a new nuclear weapon.[68] However, much of the recent literature has focused on the newer "agile" applications with concern. These analysts argue that while the explosive innards of the revitalized weapons may not be entirely new, given the smaller yields and better targeting the bombs might be seen as *more* conceivably usable in a limited or tactical conflict—even to use first, rather than in retaliation.[69] While official statements continue to justify nuclear modernization as simply extending the service life of existing capabilities, the "Pentagon now explicitly paints the nuclear modernization as a direct response to Russia."[70] As such, the U.S. amplified modernization strategy scrambles the calculus of nuclear disarmament and non-proliferation efforts, challenging the aging underpinnings of the NPT itself.[71] As stated by Hans Kristensen, "Despite significant reductions in the overall number of nuclear weapons compared with the Cold War era, all of the world's nine nuclear-armed states are busy modernizing their remaining nuclear forces for the long haul. None of the nuclear-armed states appears to be planning to eliminate its nuclear weapons anytime soon. Instead, all speak of the continued importance of nuclear weapons. . . . Perpetual nuclear modernization appears to undercut the promises made by the five NPT nuclear-weapon states."[72] Taken into consideration with the U.S. election of Donald Trump and his own apparent penchant for military expansion and nuclear modernization, challenges to the NPT regime will become even more acute.

NOTES

1. Susanna Schrafstetter and Stephen Twigge, *Avoiding Armageddon: Europe, the United States, and the Struggle for Nuclear Nonproliferation, 1945–1970* (Westport, CT: Praeger, 2004), 13; Special Message to Congress on Atomic Energy, October 3, 1945, *Public Papers: Truman: 1945*; Baruch's Address to the United Nations, June 14, 1946, reproduced at *Nuclear Age Peace Foundation*, NuclearFiles.org. Elements of this chapter have been adapted from Professor Siracusa's study (with Richard Dean Burns) *A Global History of the Nuclear Arms Race: Weapons, Strategy, and Politics*, 2 vols. (Santa Barbara, CA: Praeger, 2013).

2. See Richard Dean Burns, *The Evolution of Arms Control: From Antiquity to the Nuclear Age* (Santa Barbara, CA: Praeger, 2009).

3. Margaret Gowing, *Independence and Deterrence: Britain and Atomic Energy, 1945–1952*, vol. 1: *Policy Making* (London: Macmillan, 1974), 92–123; Trachtenberg, *A Constructed Peace*, 146ff; John Newhouse, *War and Peace in the Nuclear Age* (New York: Knopf, 1989), 190.

4. Burns, *The Evolution of Arms Control*, 78–79; Annette Messemer, "Konrad Adenauer: Defence Diplomat on the Backstage," in *Cold War Statesmen Confront the Bomb: Nuclear Diplomacy Since 1945*, ed. John Lewis Gaddis et al. (New York: Oxford University Press, 1999), 236–59.

5. John Clearwater, *Canadian Nuclear Weapons: The Untold Story of Canada's Cold War Arsenal* (Toronto: Dundum Press, 1968); "Nuclear Weapon Nations and Arsenals," August 9, 2001, Nuclear Weapons Archive, http://nuclearweaponarchive.org/Nwfaq/Nfaq7.html; "Egypt's Secret Nuclear Weapons Program," Defense Technology & Military Forum, http://www.defencetalk.com/forums/; William Burr, "U.S. Opposed Taiwanese Bomb during 1970s," National Security Archive *Electronic Briefing Book* No. 221, posted June 15, 2007.

6. Ibid.

7. Waldo Stumpt, "South Africa's Nuclear Weapons Program: From Deterrence to Dismantlement," *Arms Control Today* (December 1995/January 1996): 3–8; Jose Goldemberg, "Lessons from the Denuclearization of Brazil and Argentina," *Arms Control Association*, April 2006, https://www.armscontrol.org/act/2006_04/LookingBack, 41–43; "Chronology of Libya's Disarmament and Relations with the United States," *Arms Control Association*, http://www.armscontrol.org/factsheets/LibyaChronology.

8. A useful synthesis of the debate may be found in Scott D. Sagan and Kenneth N. Waltz, *The Spread of Nuclear Weapons: A Debate Renewed* (New York: W.W. Norton, 2003); Lawrence Freedman, *Evolution of Nuclear Strategy* (New York: St. Martin's, 1981), 412; Aspin address at the National Academy of Sciences, December 7, 1993, http://www.chinfo.navy.mil/navpalib/policy/aspi1207.txt.

9. Devin T. Hagerty, *The Consequences of Nuclear Proliferation: Lessons from South Asia* (Cambridge, MA: MIT Press, 1998), 184; Michael Mandelbaum, *The Nuclear Revolution: International Politics Before and After Hiroshima* (Cambridge, UK: Cambridge University Press, 1981), 115; Sagan and Waltz, *Spread of Nuclear Weapons*, 109; Pierre Gallois, "NATO's New Teeth," *Foreign Affairs* 39, no. 1 (October 1960): 73.

10. Sagan, *The Limits of Safety*; Sagan and Waltz, *Spread of Nuclear Weapons*, 46–87; John Newhouse, *War and Peace in the Nuclear Age* (New York: Knopf, 1989), 269.

11. For Rusk, see Newhouse, *War and Peace in the Nuclear Age*, 197; Francis J. Gavin, "Blasts from the Past: Proliferation Lessons from the 1960s," *International Security* 29, no. 3 (Winter 2004/2005): 100–35; Trachtenberg, *History and Strategy*, 100; Sagan and Waltz, *Spread of Nuclear Weapons*, 93.

12. Thatcher, quoted by Bruce Ackerman, "Let's Keep It Legal," *Los Angeles Times*, March 5, 2012; Victor Ostrovsky and Claire Hoy, *By Way of Deception* (New York: St. Martin's Press, 1990); Khidhir Hamza with Jeff Stein, *Saddam's Bombmaker: The Terrifying Inside Story of the Iraqi Nuclear and Biological Weapons Agenda* (New York: Scribner, 2000); Dan Raviv and Yossi Melman, *Every Spy a Prince* (Boston: Houghton-Mifflin, 1990); quotes in Russ Wellen, "Israel's 1981 Osirak Attack Poor Precedent for Attacking Iran," Institute for Policy Studies [IPS Blog], June 15, 2011, www.ips-dc.org/.../israels_1981_osirak_attack_poor_precedent_for_attacking_iran.

13. Uzi Mahnaimi, Sarah Baxter, Glenn Kessler, Robin Wright, and Michael Sheridan, "Israelis 'Blew Apart' Syrian Nuclear Cache," [London] *The Sunday Times*, September 16, 2007; "Israel, U.S. Shared Data on Suspected Nuclear Site," *Washington Post*, September 21, 2007.

14. Johan Molander, "The United Nations and the Elimination of Iraq's Weapons of Mass Destruction: The Implementation of a Cease-Fire Condition," in *From Versailles to Baghdad*, ed. Fred Tanner (New York: United Nations, 1992), 137–58; David Cortright and George A. Lopez, "Disarming Iraq: Nonmilitary Strategies and Options," *Arms Control Today* (September 2002): 3; "A Chronology of UN Inspections in Iraq," *Arms Control Today* (October 2002): 14–23.

15. Letter by U.S. secretary of state Daniel Webster addressed to the British Minister in Washington: Henry Fox, quoted in *International Law and the Use of Force: A Documentary and Reference Guide*, ed. Shirley Scott et al. (Santa Barbara, CA: Praeger, 2010), 125–27. See Derek W. Bowett, *Self-Defense in International Law* (Manchester: Manchester University Press, 1958); Yoram Dinstein, *War, Aggression and Self-Defense*, 4th ed. (Cambridge: Cambridge University Press, 2005); and Oscar Schachter, "Self-Defense and the Rule of Law," *American Journal of International Law* 83, no. 2 (1989): 259–77. Philip Zelikow has confirmed that Secretary of State Condoleeza Rice believed that the difference between *preventive* and *preemptive* was merely "a semantic difference" among lawyers. Philip Zelikow, "In Uncertain Times: American Foreign Policy after the Berlin Wall and 9/11," Seminar, Woodrow Wilson International Center for Scholars, October 13, 2011.

16. Raymond L. Garthoff, *Détente and Confrontation: American-Soviet Relations from Nixon to Reagan*, rev. ed. (Washington, DC: Brookings Institution, 1994), 606.

17. Zbigniew Brzezinski, *Power and Principle: Memoirs of the National Security Adviser, 1977–1981* (New York: Farrar, Straus, Giroux, 1983), 172, note; Garthoff, *Détente and Confrontation*, 832–35.

18. Raymond L. Garthoff, *The Great Transition: American-Soviet Relations and the End of the Cold War* (Washington, DC: Brookings Institution, 1994), 171, 214, 217, 222, 253, 307, 329, 514.

19. Ibid., 525; James B. Goodby, *At the Borderline of Armageddon: How American Presidents Managed the Atom Bomb* (Lanham, MD: Rowman & Littlefield, 2006), 171; Thomas Graham Jr., *Disarmament Sketches: Three Decades of Arms Control and International Law* (Seattle: University of Washington Press, 2002), 238.

20. U.S. Department of State, Bureau of Arms Control, Verification and Compliance, *Fact Sheet*, March 29, 2011.

21. Graham, *Disarmament Sketches*, xviii, 237–56; Joseph M. Siracusa and David G. Coleman, *Australia Looks to America: Australian-American Relations since Pearl Harbor* (Clare-

mont, CA: Regina Books, 2006), 94–95; Clinton, quoted in Terry L. Deibel, "The Death of a Treaty," *Foreign Affairs* (September/October 2002): 142.

22. Deibel, "The Death of a Treaty," 143.

23. NAS Executive Summary, "Technical Issues Related to the Comprehensive Nuclear Test Ban Treaty," *Arms Control Today* (September 2002): 25–30; Daryl G. Kimball, "Reconsider the Nuclear Test Ban," *Arms Control Today* (April 2011): 4.

24. Philip E. Coyle, "CTBT or Not, Nuclear Test Detection and Monitoring Remains Critical," *World Politics Review*, April 16, 2012.

25. Mary Beth D. Nikitin, "Comprehensive Nuclear-Test-Ban Treaty: Background and Current Developments," *CRS Report for Congress*, RL33548, Washington, DC: Congressional Research Service, September 1, 2016, https://www.fas.org/sgp/crs/nuke/RL33548.pdf.

26. Graham, *Disarmament Sketches*, xvii–xviii; Hal Brands, "Progress Unseen: U.S. Arms Control Policy and the Origins of Détente, 1963–1968," *Diplomatic History* 30, no. 2 (April 2006): 254.

27. William Epstein, "The Non-Proliferation Treaty and the Review Conferences, 1965–1991," in *Encyclopedia of Arms Control and Disarmament*, ed. Richard Dean Burns, 3 vols. (New York: Scribner's Sons, 1993), II: 855–60.

28. Paul H. Nitze, *From Hiroshima to Glasnost: At the Center of Decision, a Memoir* (New York: Grove Weidenfeld, 1989), 210–12; Brands, "Progress Unseen," 261, 262, 264; Rusk quote in John Newhouse, *War and Peace in the Nuclear Age* (New York: Knopf, 1989), 270; Sergei N. Khrushchev, *Nikita Khrushchev and the Creation of a Superpower*, trans. by Shirley Benson (University Park: Pennsylvania State University Press, 2000), 271.

29. Brands, "Progress Unseen," 266–70; Anatoly Dobrynin, *In Confidence: Moscow's Ambassador to America's Six Cold War Presidents* (Seattle: University of Washington Press, 1995), 147–48.

30. The text of the NPT may be found in *Arms Control and Disarmament Agreements: Texts and Histories of the Negotiations* (Washington, DC: U.S. Arms Control and Disarmament Agency, 1990), 98–102.

31. Graham, *Disarmament Sketches*, 262.

32. Epstein, "The Non-Proliferation Treaty and the Review Conferences," II: 869–71.

33. "The Nuclear Nonproliferation Treaty: The Past 40 Years," *Arms Control Today* (June 2008): 21.

34. Graham, *Disarmament Sketches*, 263–91; "The Nuclear Nonproliferation Treaty: The Past 40 Years," 17–23.

35. Graham, *Disarmament Sketches*, 292; Lawrence Scheinman, "Disarmament: Have the Five Nuclear Powers Done Enough?" *Arms Control Today* 35 (January/February 2005): 6–8.

36. Scheinman, "Disarmament," 10–11, 17.

37. Ibid., 8, 9, 11.

38. Christopher Joyner, "The Antarctic Treaty: 1959 to Present," in *Encyclopedia of Arms Control and Disarmament*, ed. Richard Dean Burns, 3 vols. (New York: Scribner's Sons, 1993), II: 817–26.

39. Jozef Goldblat, *Arms Control Agreements: A Handbook* (New York: Praeger, 1983), 231–36; Raymond L. Garthoff, "The Outer Space Treaty: 1967 to Present," in *Encyclopedia of Arms Control and Disarmament*, ed. Richard Dean Burns, 3 vols. (New York: Scribner's Sons, 1993), II: 877–86; United Nations, *The United Nations and Disarmament: 1945–1985* (New York: UN, 1985), 119–22. See Raymond L. Garthoff, "Banning the Bomb in Outer Space," *International Security* 5 (Winter 1980/1981): 25–40; Bennett Ramsberg, "The Seabed Treaty: 1971 to Present," in *Encyclopedia of Arms Control and Disarmament*, ed. Richard Dean Burns, 3 vols. (New York: Scribner's Sons, 1993), II: 887–94.

40. John R. Redick, "Nuclear Weapon-Free Zones," in *Encyclopedia of Arms Control and Disarmament*, ed. Richard Dean Burns, 3 vols. (New York: Scribner's Sons, 1993), II: 1081–85; Jose Goldemberg, "Lessons from the Denuclearization of Brazil and Argentina," *Arms Control Today* (April 2006): 41–43; Siracusa and Coleman, *Australia Looks to America*, 90–92.

41. "Appendix 10B: The Nuclear Weapon-Free Zones in South-East Asia and Africa," *SIPRI Yearbook 1998: Armaments, Disarmament and International Security* (Oxford: Oxford

University Press, 1998), 443–55, 590; Scott Parrish and William Potter, "Central Asian Nuclear Weapons-Free Zone, 2006," James Martin Center for Non-Proliferation Studies, Monterey Institute of International Studies, September 5, 2006, http://cns.miss.edu/pubs/.

42. Alfred Nurja, "Obama Submits NWFZ Protocols to Senate," *Arms Control Today* 41 (June 2011): 37.

43. Goodby, *At the Borderline of Armageddon*, 165–67; Senator Richard C. Lugar, "The Next Steps in U.S. Non-Proliferation Policy," *Arms Control Today* (December 2002): 3–7, 21.

44. See John M. Shields and William C. Potter, eds., *Dismantling the Cold War: U.S. and NIS Perspectives on the Nunn-Lugar Cooperative Threat Reduction Program* (Cambridge, MA: MIT Press, 1997); Sonia Ben Ouaghram-Gormley, "An Unrealized Nexus: WMD-Related Trafficking, Terrorism, and Organized Crime in the Former Soviet Union," *Arms Control Today* (July/August 2007): 6–13.

45. Paul F. Walker, "Nunn-Lugar at 15: No Time to Relax Global Threat Reduction Efforts," *Arms Control Today* (May 200): 6–11. See Cristina Hansell Chuen, "Russian Nuclear-Powered Submarine Dismantlement and Related Activities: A Critique," *Center for Nonproliferation Studies*, May 24, 2007; CTR, "Cooperative Threat Reduction Annual Report to Congress, Fiscal Year 2008," 3.

46. National Nuclear Security Administration Fact Sheet, "GTRI: Reducing Nuclear Threats," February 1, 2011, http://nnsa.energy.gov.

47. Office of Cooperative Threat Reduction (CTR), Bureau of International Security and Nonproliferation (ISN), U.S. Department of State, Washington, DC, http://www.state.gov/t/isn/offices/c55411.htm.

48. Eric Hundman, "The Global Threat Reduction Initiative's First Two Years," *Center for Defense Information*, September 6, 2006.

49. "Global Threat Reduction Initiative (GTRI): Reducing Nuclear Threats," Office of Defense Nuclear Nonproliferation, National Nuclear Security Administration, U.S. Department of Energy, Washington, DC, May 29, 2014, https://nnsa.energy.gov/mediaroom/factsheets/reducingthreats.

50. Jack Mendelson, ed., *Arms Control Chronology* (Washington, DC: Center for Defense Information, 2002) 63–64; Daniel Horner, "NSG Makes Little Headway at Meeting," *Arms Control Today* 40 (July/August 2010): 46.

51. Goodby, *At the Borderline of Armageddon*, 126; Fred McGoldrick, "The Road Ahead for Export Controls: Challenges for the Nuclear Suppliers Group," *Arms Control Today* 41 (January/February 2011): 30–36.

52. Lauryn Williams, "Politics or Policy? What's Thwarting India's Nuclear Suppliers Group Ambitions," *Bulletin of the Atomic Scientists*, October 14, 2016, http://thebulletin.org/politics-or-policy-what%E2%80%99s-thwarting-india%E2%80%99s-nuclear-suppliers-group-ambitions10040.

53. Ibid.

54. Kingston Reif, "U.S. Nuclear Modernization Programs," *Arms Control Association*, October 2016, https://www.armscontrol.org/factsheets/USNuclearModernization.

55. See Aiden Warren, *The Obama Administration's Nuclear Weapon Strategy: The Promises of Prague* (New York: Routledge, 2014); Joseph M. Siracusa, *Nuclear Weapons: A Very Short Introduction*, 2nd ed. (Oxford: Oxford University Press, 2015).

56. Barack Obama, "Remarks by President Barack Obama," Hradčany Square, Prague, Czech Republic, Washington, DC: The White House, Office of the Press Secretary, April 5, 2009.

57. United Nations, Final Documents of the 2010 NPT Review Conference, "The 2010 Review Conference of the Parties to the Treaty on the Non-Proliferation of Nuclear Weapons (NPT)," United Nations, New York, 2010.

58. Jon B. Wolfsthal, Jeffrey Lewis, and Marc Quint, "The Trillion Dollar Nuclear Triad," James Martin Center for Non-Proliferation Studies, January 2014; Reif, "U.S. Nuclear Modernization Programs"; William J. Broad and David E. Sanger, "U.S. Ramping Up Major Renewal in Nuclear Arms," *New York Times*, September 22, 2014.

59. Hans M. Kristensen, "Nuclear Weapons Modernization: A Threat to the NPT?" *Arms Control Association*, https://www.armscontrol.org/act/2014_05/Nuclear-Weapons-Modernization-A-Threat-to-the-NPT.

60. William Walker, "Nuclear Enlightenment and Counter-Enlightenment," *International Affairs* 83, no. 3 (2007): 431–53; William Walker, "Nuclear Order and Disorder," *International Affairs* 76, no. 4 (2000): 703–24; William Walker, *A Perpetual Menace: Nuclear Weapons and International Order* (New York: Routledge, 2011); Shampa Biswas, *Nuclear Desire: Power and The Postcolonial Nuclear Order* (Minneapolis: The University of Minnesota Press, 2014); William Potter and Guakhar Mukhatatzanova, *Nuclear Politics and the Non-Aligned Movement* (London: Routledge and IISS, 2012); Ramesh Thakur, ed., *Nuclear Weapons and International Security: Collected Essays* (London and New York: Routledge, 2015); Jane Boulden, Ramesh Thakur, and Thomas G. Weiss, eds., *The United Nations and Nuclear Orders* (Tokyo, New York, and Paris: United Nations University Press, 2009).

61. Gareth Evans and Yoriko Kawaguchi, *Eliminating Nuclear Threats: A Practical Agenda for Global Policymakers, International Commission on Nuclear Non-Proliferation and Disarmament* (Canberra/Tokyo, 2009).

62. See Andrew O'Neil, "Nuclear Weapons and Non-Proliferation: Is Restraint Sustainable?" *Security Challenges* 5 (2009).

63. United Nations, Final Documents of the 2010 NPT Review Conference, 2010.

64. Kristensen, "Nuclear Weapons Modernization: A Threat to the NPT?"; Tanya Ogilvie-White, "Great Power Responsibility and Nuclear Order," *The Non-Proliferation Review* 20, no. 1 (2013); Wolfsthal, Lewis, and Quint, "The Trillion Dollar Nuclear Triad"; Reif, "U.S. Nuclear Modernization Programs."

65. Hans M. Kristensen, "Video Shows Earth-Penetrating Capability of B61-12 Nuclear Bomb," *FAS Blog*, Federation of American Scientists, 2016; Warren, *The Obama Administration's Nuclear Weapon Strategy*; Siracusa, *Nuclear Weapons: A Very Short Introduction*.

66. John Mecklin, "Disarm and Modernize," *Foreign Policy*, no. 211 (March/April 2015); Kristensen, "Video Shows Earth-Penetrating Capability of B61-12 Nuclear Bomb."

67. William J. Broad and David E. Sanger, "As U.S. Modernizes Nuclear Weapons, 'Smaller' Leaves Some Uneasy," *New York Times*, January 11, 2016; Kevin Robinson-Avila, "Overhauling the Nation's Nuclear Arsenal: Sandia National Labs Achieves B61 Milestone," *Albuquerque Journal*, May 18.

68. Marina Malenic, "U.S. Completes first B-61 LEP Flight Test," *Janes Defense Weekly*, July 8, 2015. See Matthew Kroenig, "How to Approach Nuclear Modernization? A U.S. Response," *Bulletin of the Atomic Scientists* 71, no. 3 (2015); Matthew Kroenig, "Why U.S. Nuclear Modernization Is Necessary," *Bulletin of the Atomic Scientists* online, January 8, 2015.

69. Mecklin, "Disarm and Modernize"; Broad and Sanger, "As U.S. Modernizes Nuclear Weapons, 'Smaller' Leaves Some Uneasy."

70. "Pentagon Portrays Nuclear Modernization as a Response to Russia," Federation of American Scientists (FAS), February 11, 2016.

71. Mecklin, "Disarm and Modernize."

72. Kristensen, "Nuclear Weapons Modernization: A Threat to the NPT?"

Chapter Six

The Modern Era

The Post–Cold War and Beyond

For senior civilian and military leaders in Washington and Moscow—as well as in Washington and Beijing—the trappings of the Cold War's strategic nuclear environment never quite seemed to disappear as the political tides of good feelings ebbed and flowed. In spite of officials' otherwise positive rhetoric, such unreconciled attitudes became evident in statements during negotiations (and ratifications) of the post–Cold War agreements—START I and II, SORT, and New START—dealing with strategic nuclear weaponry from Presidents George H. W. Bush to Barack Obama, and from Mikhail Gorbachev to Dmitry Medvedev. These symptoms were even more apparent in the undergirding of Washington's continuing insistence on deploying missile defense systems, and Moscow and even Beijing's reactions to them. Yet, there were discernible signs of a political thaw or perhaps the recognition of certain specific mutual interests. These examples, touched on in the previous chapter, included: reciprocal unilateral pledges seeking to recall deployed tactical nuclear weapons, and programs such as the Cooperative Threat Reduction program and Global Threat Reduction Initiative that aimed at securing stocks of dangerous nuclear material from the former Soviet Union and elsewhere in the world. Former Cold War adversaries have also cooperated in the functioning of unofficial international agencies such as the Nuclear Suppliers Group that seek to control the export of material, equipment, and facilities, that if diverted from peaceful uses could contribute to a nuclear weapons program or create other weapons of mass destruction (WMD).

The Soviet Union's collapse in 1991, and the accompanying turmoil, created havoc among its once proud strategic forces. Even if often deemed inefficient by U.S. standards, Steven Zaloga points out that the Russians considered "the creation of the Soviet nuclear deterrent force" to be "a re-markable technological achievement. In spite of the technological weakness of the Soviet Union in 1945 and the impoverished state of the economy well into the 1960s, Soviet engineers had managed to create a force rivaling that of its far richer nemesis, the United States." In the aftermath of the events in 1991, the Soviet strategic missile force had lost nearly a fourth of its ICBMs, including some of its newest systems, and some one-half of its bomber fleet to the newly independent republics; only the submarine missile force was retained. Additionally, Zaloga noted, the new Russian strategic missile force "suffered major setbacks in terms of its industrial base, its command-and-control facilities, and its testing facilities." But perhaps the greatest blow came as the depleted Russian defense budget, a result of the state's faltering economy, led to a severe shortage of replacements. By 1998, for example, some 60 percent of Russia's deployed ICBMs had been operational for twice their certified life. [1]

Washington and Moscow continued their cooperation during the First Gulf War, a conflict that ended with the UN and the International Atomic Energy Agency (IAEA) embarking on the supervised demilitarization of Iraq to deprive Saddam Hussein of weapons of mass destruction. Reminiscent of Allied efforts to disarm Germany after World War I, this episode was an example of imposed non-proliferation. President George W. Bush's administration alleged that the IAEA's supervision of the destruction of Saddam Hussein's nuclear weapons infrastructure after the First Gulf War was a failure and, thus, became a major pretext for the U.S. invasion of Iraq in the Second Gulf War.

START I AND II TREATIES

When George H. W. Bush assumed the presidency in January 1989, it was generally expected that he would expedite the arms limitation process begun by Reagan and Gorbachev. Clearly, that did not happen. Because Bush believed Reagan had casually granted too many concessions to Gorbachev, he and his National Security Adviser Brent Scowcroft slowed down the momentum of U.S.-Soviet negotiations, emphasizing the continued need for vigilance and strength in dealing with the Kremlin. Neither the new president nor many of his senior advisers truly believed in the Cold War's demise. During the previous June, for example, when Reagan on a visit at Moscow retracted his characterization of the Soviet Union as an "evil empire," then-vice president Bush downplayed the president's remark in speaking to reporters: "The Cold War isn't over." The following month he warned against a "euphoric, naively optimistic view about what comes next" and privately was concerned by Reagan's "sentimentality" toward Gorbachev. Not surprisingly then, senior members of Bush's administration were unprepared to move forward. His assistant secretary of defense for international security, Stephen J. Hadley, later noted that he himself was quite "skeptical about the role of arms control in national security policy. . . . I think their general assessment was that arms control could make a fairly modest contribution, but that the security of the United States ultimately rested on what it did militarily and diplomatically in conjunction with its allies." Washington did not contact Moscow regarding arms control matters until nearly five months after Bush's inauguration— much to Gorbachev's annoyance.[2]

Bush and his secretary of state, James Baker, subscribed to the view that new presidents had often found themselves in precarious political waters by moving in haste; thus, a better approach would be to attain a substantive gauge of the status of Soviet-American relations before opening formal discussions. Scowcroft even went as far as stating that the West should keep up its guard because Gorbachev could well be a new version of the "clever bear syndrome," seeking to lull the West into a false sense of safety while pressing expansionist objectives. Such suspicions of the Kremlin's motives also characterized the outlook of his deputy, Robert M. Gates, as well as Defense Secretary Richard Cheney and Soviet experts in the Central Intelligence Agency (CIA). At his first news conference on January 27, the president was quizzed about Scowcroft's pessimistic disposition. Bush responded that he did not even want to use the phrase *Cold War* because it failed to "properly give credit to the advances that have taken place in this relationship. . . . Do we still have problems, are there still uncertainties, are we still unsure of our predictions on Soviet intentions? I'd have to say, yeah, we should be cautious."[3]

If the new administration entered office intending to move cautiously in U.S.-Soviet relations, events would soon bring Bush and Gorbachev together. During the last months of 1989, the Soviet Eastern European empire began to unravel, forcing key Washington officials to reconsider their attitude toward Moscow. After weeks of temporizing, Bush, in early December 1989, journeyed to the Malta summit with Gorbachev realizing that any success in achieving Western goals depended on Gorbachev. Amid howling winds and crashing waves in a wild Mediterranean storm, the two leaders met aboard the Soviet cruise ship *Maxim Gorky* that had been recently refurbished to provide quarters for the Soviet delegation. During their sessions, Bush and Gorbachev defined an ambitious program for cooperation and speedy progress on pending major arms control measures, enhanced trade relations, and a Washington summit in late spring 1990. The discussions were congenial and frank. Bush felt that the meeting's most "positive effect" was "upon my personal relationship with Gorbachev." Yet the president and his advisers resisted reporters' invitations to declare that the Cold War was indeed over. At a final press conference, Gorbachev declared, "The world is

leaving an era of Cold War and entering another. This is just the beginning . . . of a long peaceful period." Bush cautiously responded, "Now, with
reform under way in the Soviet Union, we stand at the threshold of a brand
new era in U.S.-Soviet relations."[4]

In a further meeting on May 30, 1990, Gorbachev arrived in Washington
beleaguered and profoundly unpopular at home but determined to sustain his
image of confidence, enthusiasm, and authority. He and Bush signed protocols on verification of nuclear testing that had been agreed to nearly two
decades earlier—the Threshold Test Ban Treaty (1974) and Peaceful Nuclear
Explosions Treaty (1976)—that finally permitted their ratification. However,
in reaffirming a policy statement in January where his administration stated
that it had "not identified any further limitations on nuclear testing . . . that
would be in the United States' national security interest," Bush balked at
considering a comprehensive nuclear test ban. While the "type" of adversary
the United States now faced was not defined, the capacity to enhance its
nuclear arsenal via testing was to remain an option. The two leaders, nevertheless, did proceed to negotiate other issues, establishing a framework that
would lead to future arms reductions—the Treaty on Conventional Forces in
Europe (CFE) in November 1990 and the Strategic Arms Reductions Treaty
(START I) in August 1991.

The asymmetrical imbalance between the larger Soviet and Warsaw Pact
forces and U.S. and NATO forces meant that Moscow held the upper hand in
the discussions. While Soviet leaders initially resisted offering substantial
concessions, discussions between 1989 and 1990 finally resolved most of the
major areas of disagreement and pointed toward a CFE agreement that a few
years earlier would have been unthinkable. The treaty vividly demonstrated
that events had overtaken the efforts of diplomacy: France joined the talks;
Gorbachev unilaterally withdrew troops and equipment from forward areas;
the Warsaw Pact disintegrated; and the reunited Germany agreed to troop
limitations. Bush signed the CFE pact in Paris on November 19, 1990, placing limits on tanks, artillery, armored combat vehicles, aircraft, helicopters,
and military personnel stationed in Europe from the Atlantic Ocean to the
Ural Mountains. In the history of arms control, Michael Beschloss and
Strobe Talbot defined the agreement as the "most impressive accomplishment." Before the signatures were dry on the CFE treaty, they noted, "Soviet
units were already committed to a complete pullout from Hungary and
Czechoslovakia in 1991 and from the eastern parts of Germany in 1994 . . .
of the original twenty three states involved in the [CFE] negotiations, one—
the German Democratic Republic—had ceased to exist, and five others had
changed their names," a clear indication of their independence from Moscow. With the Warsaw Pact dissipating, a U.S. delegate to the CFE negotiations later claimed that the treaty had "ended the Cold War."[5]

BUSH-GORBACHEV: START I

In January 1989, the new Bush White House found the basic framework of START for the main extent already constructed by the previous administration. However, due to the unresolved differences over technicalities between Reagan administration agencies, the proposed treaty remained dormant. A major impediment centered on the issue of "de-MIRVing"—that is, reducing the number of warheads placed on top of a single intercontinental missile. With new generations of ICBMs this could be achieved via monitoring of the testing and deployment of each other's new ICBMs, so as to determine the number of counted MIRVs verified on each missile. A cheaper, faster method of de-MIRVing, initially proposed by Washington in 1987, would be to "download" or remove warheads from existing ICBMs. This would allow the United States to meet START limits by removing two of three warheads from the Minuteman III. When Moscow began to download, however, U.S. intelligence agencies became uneasy because they knew the Soviets deployed two versions of their missiles—one land-based, the other submarine-launched—and that each could carry more warheads than those with which they were normally deployed. When Reagan and Gorbachev met at Washington in 1987, the United States chose to accept the Kremlin's version of the number of warheads remaining on their missiles, a decision that Scowcroft at the time disliked. He feared that the Soviets could easily reload their missiles and "breakout" of the treaty. While Scowcroft continued to object to the Soviets' proposal for downloading their missiles, it was the chairman of the Joint Chiefs of Staff, General Colin Powell, in the spring of 1991, who for all intents and purposes overrode Bush's adviser. "I'm not as exercised about it as Brent. That's not for technical or military reasons, but for political reasons. The situation is changing so fast and so profoundly that someday we'll wonder why we ever argued over this. With everything that's going on over there, I have a hard time convincing myself I should stay awake at night worrying about the Soviet's future breakout capability."[6]

Another major hurdle pertained to verifying the presence of sea-launched cruise missiles (SLCMs) on warships. American naval officers had significant concerns with the notion of Soviet officials inspecting their newest nuclear submarines. Putting aside Reagan's often repeated Russian proverb, "trust but verify," the United States finally proposed that each side "declare" the number of SLCMs it planned to deploy. Dissatisfied with this solution, Moscow pressed for thorough verification procedures. Looking back at Washington's decades-long insistence on intrusive on-site inspection systems, Reagan's secretary of defense, Frank Carlucci, reluctantly acknowledged, "Verification has proven to be more complex than we thought it would be. The flip side of the coin is its application *to us*. The more we think about it, the more difficult it becomes." It began to appear that disputes between Washington bureaucrats would derail efforts to reduce nuclear weaponry. "Even if the Soviets did not exist," a senior member of the National Security Council reluctantly acknowledged, "we might not get a START treaty because of disagreements on our side." Another high-ranking U.S. official complained that if the Soviets "came to us and said, 'You write it, we'll sign it,' we still couldn't do it."[7] To stir up the moribund START talks, President Bush urged his arms control team to look for new ideas to present at his forthcoming Malta meeting with Gorbachev. Secretary Baker and National Security Adviser Scowcroft suggested that Bush could put his stamp on the process, while at the same time win bipartisan congressional approval by proposing a ban on mobile missiles equipped with nuclear-tipped multiple independently targeted reentry vehicles (MIRVs). Surprising his advisers, the normally cautious president posited the bold notion of offering the Soviets a ban on all the threatening, vulnerable land-based MIRVed intercontinental missiles. When Secretary of Defense Richard Cheney and Pentagon officials learned of the proposed ban, an intramural struggle took place and the idea of a total MIRV ban was quickly ousted from the equation. With modest progress at the Malta summit moving START I slowly forward, perhaps the most significant accomplishment was that Bush considered the meeting a great success.[8]

After eight and a half frustrating years, on July 31, 1991, in Moscow, Presidents Bush and Gorbachev signed a detailed 750-page START I treaty. The Americans finally conceded on the downloading issue, provided that the total number of Soviet warheads was limited to 1,250, and at the last minute insisted that the Soviets test their three-stage SS-25 at 11,000 kilometers to ensure that it did not carry three warheads. As it emerged, the treaty would limit each side to the deployment of 1,600 ballistic missiles and long-range bombers, carrying 6,000 "accountable" warheads by December 5, 2001, and established further sub-limits—4,900 warheads on deployed ballistic missiles, including no more than 1,100 warheads on deployed mobile ICBM systems, and 1,100 "accountable" bomber weapons. This was the first agreement that called for each side to reduce its strategic arsenal significantly, where some 25–35 percent of the nuclear warheads carried on ballistic missiles were to be eliminated. In addition, START I incorporated the earlier INF Treaty's verification system that provided access to telemetry data and permitted on-site inspections. The agreement's complex verification system would satisfactorily serve such future accords on strategic weaponry. The United States and Russia completed their START I reductions by December 4, 2001, and awaited Belarus, Kazakhstan, and Ukraine to turn over to Russia the former Soviet strategic nuclear weapons based in their territories.[9]

BUSH-YELTSIN: START II

In his State of the Union speech, on January 28, 1992, Bush announced that the United States would unilaterally eliminate further work on the single warhead Midgetman missile, and assign a significant number of its bomber fleet to conventional roles. Additionally, he called for a START II agreement that could further reduce the number of American and new Russian warheads, especially if his de-MIRVing initiative was accepted. Concurrently, the new Russian president, Boris Yeltsin, proposed even deeper cuts that would reduce the number of warheads to 2,000–2,500 and, in a letter to Bush, denounced all MIRVs as "the root of evil—from the point of view of threats to stability." Washington perceived his proposal as radically affecting its traditional strategic triad. A major problem standing in the way of proceeding rested with the return of the former Soviet Union's strategic nuclear weapons from Belarus, Kazakhstan, and Ukraine; although this was resolved with the Lisbon Protocol, signed on May 23, 1992. The protocol created a five-state START I regime that called for all former Soviet strategic nuclear weapons be returned to Russia. With this hurdle out of the way, serious negotiations began on START II.

While Moscow pressed for substantial reductions, the Defense Department in Washington refused to accept the 2,500-warhead limit. As a concession, the Russians proposed a phased reduction with both sides beginning at 4,500 to 4,700 as the initial step, and later dropping to 2,500 by the year 2005. When the Pentagon again objected, Secretary Baker was quick with a sharp rebuttal: "They have offered us what we want, and what no one else has ever come close to—zero MIRVed ICBMs, and without eliminating MIRVed SLBMs. We can't let this slip through our fingers because we think we need a *higher* total number. That is not sustainable with the public or the Congress." Similarly, Yeltsin was also having difficulty in placating his hard-line security advisers. Finally, two critical issues were resolved: rules for counting bombers, and limitations on downloading warheads from deployed missiles. As Baker lamented in his memoirs, "Our Department of Defense seemed to be a bigger problem than Moscow," because "the arms control theologians at the Pentagon seemed to prefer no agreement than one that got us 'only' ninety percent of what we wanted."[10]

At a two-day June 1992 meeting in Washington, Yeltsin provided the approach needed to complete the START II pact. Rather than trying to apply a numerical ceiling, he suggested using a range: in phase one, each side would have 4,250 to 3,800 warheads; in phase two, the range would decrease to 3,000 to 3,500. This satisfied the Russians for economic reasons and the Pentagon for its force structure. Yeltsin recognized, according to Secretary Baker, "that in the realm of nuclear weapons, a few-hundred-warhead advantage, when both sides had over three thousand warheads, was not all that important." Bush agreed. The first phase would last until the year 2000; the second phase would limit warheads to 3,000–3,500 three years later. As final details of the treaty were being worked out, discussion arose as to whether Bush should continue with the process and the signing of the new START II, since Bill Clinton already had been elected to succeed him. A senior adviser later reported: "It was feared that the Russians would simply take whatever concessions we offered, delay until after 20 January, and pick up with a new team. President Bush made the decision to go for an agreement before he left office. He talked to President Yeltsin, who was of the same view. He also talked with President-elect Clinton." On January 3, 1993, Presidents Bush and Yeltsin signed START II. Since it relied heavily on START I for definitions, procedures, and verification, it could not enter into force until the START I ratification process was completed by 1994. Subsequently, the United States ratified START II on January 26, 1996, and Russia on April 14, 2000. At the Helsinki Summit of March 1997, Presidents Bill Clinton and Boris Yeltsin agreed to extend the time for final reductions to 2007. Nevertheless, START II did not enter into force; the United States failed to ratify the "Agreed Statements" that Presidents Bill Clinton and Boris Yeltsin signed in September 1997, a condition laid down by the new Russian president, Vladimir Putin, when endorsing Russian ratification in May 2000. Subsequently, Russia repudiated START II on June 14, 2002, the day following President George W. Bush's unilateral abrogation of the antiballistic missile treaty.[11]

RECALL OF TACTICAL NUCLEAR WEAPONS

During the Cold War, the United States and Soviet Union both deployed non-strategic nuclear weapons for use in the field during a conflict. While there are varying definitional means to differentiate between strategic and non-strategic nuclear weapons, most commentaors view non-strategic weapons as encompassing shorter-range delivery systems with lower yield warheads that could be used to strike troops or facilities on the battlefield. They have included nuclear mines; artillery; short-, medium-, and long-range ballistic missiles; cruise missiles; and gravity bombs. In distinction with the longer-range "strategic" nuclear weapons, such weapons had a lower profile in policy debates and arms control negotiations, perhaps because they did not present an overwhelming threat to the mainland United States. As stated by Amy Woolf, "At the end of the 1980s, each nation still had thousands of these weapons deployed with their troops in the field, aboard naval vessels, and on aircraft."[12] However, as the Cold War concluded, leaders in the United States and Soviet Union/Russia began the process of "retrieval."

Indeed, reciprocal unilateral pledges initiated by President George H. W. Bush in September 1991, known collectively as Presidential Nuclear Initiatives (PNIs), succeeded in removing "battlefield" nuclear weapons from foreign deployment. Concerned whether Moscow would be able to maintain control over its tactical nuclear weapons as the Warsaw Pact collapsed, Washington hoped Kremlin leaders would follow suit. In his September 27 announcement, Bush specifically committed to withdraw "all ground-launched short-range weapons deployed overseas and destroy them along with existing U.S. stockpiles of the same weapons and cease deployment of tactical nuclear weapons on surface ships, attack submarines, and land-based naval aircraft during normal circumstances." Implicitly, the United States reserved the right to redeploy these arms in a crisis. A month later, Soviet president Mikhail Gorbachev responded with his own unilateral reciprocal measures. On October 5, he pledged to: eliminate all nuclear artillery munitions, nuclear warheads for tactical missiles, and nuclear mines; remove all tactical nuclear weapons from surface ships and multipurpose submarines (these weapons would be stored in central storage sites along with all nuclear arms assigned to land-based naval aircraft); and separate nuclear warheads from air defense missiles and put the warheads in central storage. A "portion" would be destroyed. Subsequently, on January 29, 1992, Russia's President-elect Boris Yeltsin agreed to uphold Gorbachev's commitments and declared Russia would further eliminate a third of its sea-based tactical nuclear weapons and half of its ground-to-air nuclear missile warheads, while halving its airborne tactical nuclear weapons stockpile. Pending reciprocal U.S. action, the other half of this stockpile would be taken out of service and placed in central storage depots. [13]

As discussed briefly in the above, the Lisbon Protocol of July 31, 1991, promptly extended recognition to four republics of the former Soviet Union as designated successor states committed to various earlier arms control treaties such as START I. The reason for the urgency was that these republics held portions of the Soviet Union's strategic nuclear weapons and the area was threatened with the possibility of civil war(s). Many observers were concerned by the security threat that such smaller weapons posed, particularly if seized by extremist groups, used in a local conflict or stolen for resale abroad. The republics quickly understood they could not keep these weapons in their own arsenals, for, as Zaloga has pointed out, such "attempts to take over control of nuclear weapons would provide Russia with a pretext to invade." Washington believed that it wanted control of the nuclear weapons to remain in Moscow's hands and used its influence to encourage the new states to allow Russia to withdraw the tactical nuclear weapons. As such, Moscow launched "a speedy and largely secret" program that extracted all of them by May 1992; some 3,000 tactical nuclear weapons were removed from Ukraine alone. The prospect for elimination of tactical nuclear weapons has remained dormant since the early 1990s, primarily because of considerable discrepancy between the smaller American inventory and the much larger imputed Russian stockpile.[14]

During the Cold War, the United States sent some 5,000 tactical nuclear weapons overseas, most of which were assigned to NATO. By the end of 1992, it completed its pledged reductions and withdrawals; a year later it had destroyed nearly 3,000 tactical nuclear weapons. The Soviet/Russian stockpile was thought to range from 12,000 to nearly 21,700 weapons. Determining U.S. and Soviet/Russian fulfillment of their PNI obligations, however, is difficult—then and now—because of the ambiguity related to the composition, size, and location of these weapons. After confirming that all Soviet tactical nuclear weapons had been returned from the four republics of the former Soviet Union, Moscow announced in May 2005 that these arms "are now deployed only within the national territory and are concentrated at central storage facilities of the Ministry of Defense." Moreover, the Kremlin declared that its tactical nuclear arsenal "has been reduced by four times as compared to what the Soviet Union possessed in 1991." This statement did not completely satisfy the U.S. Department of State, which in June 2005 insisted that "Russia has failed to state publicly the status of the elimination of its nuclear artillery munitions, nuclear warheads for air defense missiles, nuclear mines, or nuclear weapons on land-based naval aviation."[15]

A precise assessment of U.S. and Russian tactical nuclear stockpiles, therefore, is difficult to determine since recent statements vary so much. Indeed, one account reports that U.S.-NATO forces retain hundreds of tactical nuclear weapons in Europe and the Russian arsenal contains a much higher number. Amy Woolf suggested in a report for the Congressional Research Service that "the United States now has approximately 760 non-strategic nuclear weapons, with around 200 deployed with aircraft in Europe and the remaining stored in the United States."[16] While approximations diverge, analysts believe Russia still has between 1,000 and 6,000 warheads for non-strategic nuclear weapons in its arsenal. "The Bush Administration quietly redeployed and removed some of the nuclear weapons deployed in Europe. Russia, however, seems to have increased its reliance on nuclear weapons in its national security concept." Additionally, some commentators have argued that "Russia has backed away from its commitments from 1991 and may develop and deploy new types of non-strategic nuclear weapons."[17]

Indeed, while many in the U.S. military have indicated a fundamental dislike of tactical nuclear weapons—agreeing with those who suggest that they have minimal, if any military value and possess little deterrent value—their Russian counterparts appear to differ. During 2009, statements emanating from Russian defense sources suggested that the role of tactical nuclear weapons could increase, including placing such devices on strategic submarines. With modernization funding expanding, so too were internal policy battles among the Russian services for budgetary considerations. For example, Vice Admiral Oleg Burtev declared that: "The future may belong to tactical nuclear weapons. Their range and accuracy are increasing. There is no need to carry a powerful warhead, and we can go over to low-yield nuclear charges that can be installed on existing models of cruise missiles." Thus a robust debate has continued as to whether tactical nuclear weapons serve any useful function. [18]

A defining issue is that many tactical nuclear weapons are, in fact, dual-use weapon systems that can be fitted with different types of warheads, including nuclear, high explosive conventional, biological, or chemical warheads. The wide proliferation of these delivery vehicles—without special warheads—during the Cold War has left a complicated legacy of a wide dispersal of dual-use delivery vehicles around the world. Short-range, dual-use rockets and missiles were dispersed by the Soviets precisely to the areas of greatest proliferation threat in more recent years: Iran, North Korea, Iraq, Egypt, Yemen, Afghanistan, Pakistan, Kazakhstan, Turkmenistan, Vietnam, and Belarus, among other countries. Many of those same countries, including Cuba, have also had Free Range Over Ground (FROG) rockets. Various American-developed dual-use systems were widely dispersed through Western Europe and Israel, in particular. Several of these countries have taken the original designs and improved on them to build new generations of missiles. Consequently, possession and possible use of tactical or short-range nuclear weapons in regional conflicts remain an issue in the twenty-first century. [19]

A CONTINUING NATO CONTROVERSY

In 2010, as NATO defense and foreign ministers met to review the alliance's draft "Strategic Concept," several analysts called for a comprehensive review of what they saw as an outdated nuclear policy. In the October issue of *Arms Control Today*, Oliver Meier and Paul Ingram reported that the twenty-eight members of NATO were divided toward the future role of nuclear weapons in the alliance's defense policy and urged reconsideration of the Strategic Concept. Later, at a conference addressing the "Next Steps in Arms Control," Meier noted that NATO's review of the concept should take place in the context of President Obama's global zero nuclear policy, since it had the support of a broad majority of European parliaments and publics. Regretfully, he observed, NATO's current policy "still is based on the Cold War theory that short-range nuclear weapons could be used to defeat conventional superior Soviet forces." But Meier declared, "It's important to keep in mind that U.S. nuclear weapons [currently] deployed in Europe do not have any military value"—a position not disputed by the Pentagon. If several European governments, including at least three of the five nations stockpiling the

U.S. tactical nuclear weapons, desired their withdrawal, several Central European nations and Turkey had reservations related not nearly as much to the military value of these weapons as to the credibility of U.S. and NATO's security assurances. These latter nations, according to Marek Szcygiel of the Polish Foreign Office, wanted assurances that "possible reductions in tactical nuclear weapons will not weaken NATO deterrence capability and not weaken trans-Atlantic link. . . . The presence of U.S. nuclear weapons combined with NATO's unique nuclear sharing arrangements continue to [provide] alliance cohesion and . . . reassurance to allies and partners who feel exposed to regional threats." Their concern centered on Russia's stationing of tactical nuclear weapons near its borders with NATO states, and its emphasis on nuclear readiness, not to mention Moscow's renunciation of its long-held "no-first-use" of nuclear weapons—an admission of Russia's weakened conventional arsenal.[20]

When NATO officials revealed their new "Strategic Concept" on November 19, 2010, it was immediately criticized as being "a conservative, backward-looking policy, a missed opportunity to reduce the number and role of the 200 forward-deployed U.S. tactical nuclear bombs, and [to] engage Russia in a dialogue on removing all tactical nuclear weapons from Europe." In excluding the mentioning of tactical nuclear weapons, the NATO document declared that "the supreme guarantee of the security of the Allies is provided by the strategic nuclear forces of the Alliance," which consisted of the United States, Great Britain, and France. Regretfully, Daryl G. Kimball, director of the Arms Control Association in Washington, noted: "The Strategic Concept fails to acknowledge that tactical nuclear bombs are not 'credible' weapons and are irrelevant for the defense of the alliances." While this statement reflected the difficulties in achieving withdrawal of U.S. tactical nuclear bombs at the time, it is evident that this issue and the accompanying debates have not dissipated.[21] As conveyed by Amy Woolf:

> Some argue that these weapons do not create any problems and the United States should not alter its policy. Others argue that NATO should consider expanding its deployments in response to Russia's aggression in Ukraine. Some believe the United States should reduce its reliance on these weapons and encourage Russia to do the same. Many have suggested that the United States and Russia expand efforts to cooperate on ensuring the safe and secure storage and elimination of these weapons; others have suggested that they negotiate an arms control treaty that would limit these weapons and allow for increased transparency in monitoring their deployment and elimination.[22]

THE SORT TREATY

American president George W. Bush's administration frequently demonstrated a dislike for traditional arms control agreements. This was clearly evident in its withdrawal from the antiballistic missile (ABM) treaty, an apparent disinterest in the comprehensive test ban treaty, retention of the nuclear first use policy, and a re-emphasis on the reliance on nuclear weapons. Also, it appeared to be a significant shift from candidate Bush's view conveyed to Jim Hoagland of the *Washington Post.* Taking a "highly pragmatic approach," Bush queried, "why do we need so many nuclear weapons now that the Soviet Union has disappeared?" Aside from expressing the desire for better relations with Russia, the candidate's view of missile defense was "far more tentative and far less ideological than was Reagan's Star Wars notion."

Following the terrorist events of 9/11, the role of nuclear strategists in Defense Secretary Donald Rumsfeld's Pentagon came to prominence. According to William Arkin, the administration's early 2002 secret Nuclear Posture Review instructed the Pentagon "to draft contingency plans for the use of nuclear weapons against at least seven countries, naming not only Russia and the 'axis of evil'—Iraq, Iran, and North Korea—but also China, Libya and Syria." Similar to preceding nuclear policy documents, it embodied the fundamental "inconsistency between America's diplomatic objectives of reducing nuclear arsenals and preventing the proliferation of weapons of mass destruction, on the one hand, and the military imperative to prepare for the unthinkable, on the other." Yet, as Arkin wrote, "the Bush administration's plan reverses an almost two-decade-long trend of relegating nuclear weapons to the category of weapons of last resort" as it "redefines nuclear requirements in hurried post-Sept. 11 terms." Under the new plan, nuclear weapons could be used in several instances, including "in the event of surprising military developments." Such a vaguely stated contingency indicated that officials were grasping to find a way nuclear weapons could help defeat such terrorists groups as Al-Qaeda. In approving the document, Rumsfeld declared the administration sought "a new approach to strategic deterrence" that also included missile defenses. Notwithstanding the controversy caused by the plan, some strategists defended the review for "its candor" and for focusing on "the new post-Cold War strategic environment."[23]

BUSH AND PUTIN: SORT

George W. Bush entered the White House vowing to reduce America's nuclear weapons to "the lowest possible number consistent with our national security." Initially, he sought to implement strategic offensive weapons reductions with unilateral declarations and informal agreements; however,

Russian president Vladimir Putin insisted upon a more official arrangement. Putin desired stipulated reductions that would provide a sense of parity, predictability, and reduced expenditures that could be accomplished by reducing each side to 1,500 warheads. The new administration's aversion to formal arms control agreements, coupled with its enthusiasm for unilateral actions, resulted in the Strategic Offensive Reductions Treaty (SORT) signed by Presidents Bush and Putin at Moscow on May 24, 2002, and entering into force on June 1, 2003. In reality, the treaty focused more on limits in the tradition of the early Cold War treaties than reductions that had been the hallmark of START I and II. Moreover, SORT ignored the agreement in principle reached by Presidents Clinton and Yeltsin—as an outline for START III that stipulated cuts to their strategic arsenals to 2,000–2,500 warheads each, while requiring significant reductions in delivery vehicles. [24]

While SORT, also known as the Moscow Treaty, saw the United States and Russia each agreeing to deploy no more than 1,700–2,200 strategic warheads by the end of 2012—when the treaty expired—the pact did not restrict the number of permitted delivery vehicles that could be retained as long as neither party exceeded the START I limits. Nor did the treaty require the destruction of delivery vehicles or agree on specific counting rules; hence, a MIRVed nose cone might contain a single warhead and be counted as a single warhead, although it could quickly be loaded with nine additional warheads. Warheads in excess of the stipulated limits did not have to be dismantled or destroyed, they could simply be stored. Thus, the Bush administration stated that it planned to maintain at least 2,400 warheads in a ready-reserve status. Secretary of State Colin Powell told the Senate Foreign Relations Committee on July 9, 2002: "The treaty will allow you to have as many warheads as you want." SORT also failed to provide for its own verification, thus adding to its unpredictability. START I's extensive verification regime was expected to monitor SORT; yet, it was unclear what would happen after START I's expiration at the end of 2009. To provide more transparency, the treaty created a Bilateral Implementation Commission that was expected to meet at least twice a year to discuss questions regarding compliance. According to a pessimistic assessment by arms control specialists, the treaty "totals less than 500 words, repudiates key arms control principles and achievements, eschewing predictability and compounding the proliferation dangers from Russia's unsecured nuclear weapons complex." SORT, in essence, regarded each nation's nuclear program to be its own business, much to the satisfaction of the Bush administration. For Putin, Russia received a written agreement that granted the appearance of parity, and gained economically since it would be able to keep some delivery vehicles that would have been eliminated under START II. [25]

There were, however, at least two broad areas of concern that aroused some serious consideration. The first concern was pragmatic in nature as it focused on the extent to which the two states chose to maintain large numbers of extra nuclear warheads and bombs. Could these dangerous items, especially the Russian ones, be kept from falling into terrorist's hands? The second concern was largely political. "The international community will have a hard time figuring out why the United States pressed to keep so many weapons on the shelf," John Holum, director of Clinton's Arms Control and Disarmament Agency, wrote in evaluating SORT. After all, "Washington says that Russia is not an adversary; and China, the country with the next highest number of nuclear weapons, has less than two dozen nuclear weapons that can reach the United States." Holum also noted that non-nuclear-weapon states would have difficulty in accepting an agreement that defined itself as an arms reduction treaty, but under which most of their weapons would be retained. When this episode was linked with the administration's nuclear posture that undercut earlier assurances—that nuclear weapons would not be used against non-nuclear-weapon nations unless they attacked a nuclear weapons state—signatories to the Non-Proliferation Treaty were likely to be uneasy. Therefore, Holum concluded, "perhaps the biggest question about this new agreement must be, will it help address the dominant security challenge of proliferation, or could it hurt non-proliferation issues."[26]

THE NEW START TREATY

The Bush administration was unable to devise a successor agreement before START I expired. A central element of the Strategic Arms Reduction Treaty (START I), signed by the United States and the Soviet Union in July 1991 and set to expire on December 5, 2009, was what both parties had used in its verification system to monitor the SORT pact. Knowing how long treaty negotiations may take, Bush officials could have made reaching a form agreement to extend the verification system a priority, but they did not. As the deadline had passed, it was the Obama administration that was faced with the daunting challenge of negotiating a completely new treaty that could win the votes of sixty-seven U.S. senators, while also dealing with Russian objections to proposed U.S. missile defenses in Europe that had not been a consideration when START I was first contemplated. The Obama administration was well aware of Russia's concerns, repeated regularly during the Bush years by President Putin and by Russian defense ministers and generals. But, in 2009 and 2010, the stakes were higher. Bush had only desired Russian acquiescence to his plan to deploy U.S. missile defense systems in Poland and the Czech Republic; Obama desired that too, but his administration also needed Russian cooperation on a new START treaty.

This history was reflected anew in the negotiations for a replacement to START I. Despite early setbacks in the ongoing talks, Presidents Barack Obama and Dmitry Medvedev, following a December 18, 2009, meeting at Copenhagen, were optimistic that a new pact could be concluded in the near term. "I'm confident that [a new agreement] will be completed in a timely fashion," Obama declared. For his part, Medvedev replied: "I hope that we will be able to do it in a quite brief period of time." Stalling the agreement was Washington's demand for unencrypted telemetry data from U.S. and Russian offensive missile tests to be shared; as required under the original 1991 START I agreement. Moscow, in turn, was now coupling the U.S. desire for unencrypted telemetry data to more data about U.S. missile defenses. The Americans sought, as agreed in START I, telemetric data after each flight test, together with the key to interpreting the data, and a pledge not to jam or encrypt such data. The stumbling block occurred because the United States was not building new ICBMs but was upgrading current models, such as the Trident D-5. Meanwhile, the Russians planned to test and deploy new missiles, such as the RS-24 mobile missile, as replacements for aged Soviet-era ones. Thus, the United States would have no offensive missile tests to report, but the Russians would; however, the United States would be testing antimissile interceptors but did not want to be required to share this data with Moscow.

On December 29, 2009, Prime Minister Vladimir Putin declared that Russia needed more detailed information about U.S. missile defenses. Concerned that missile defense would give the United States an advantage, Putin explained, "The problem is that our American partners are developing missile defenses, and we are not." He went on to explain that "the issues of missile defense and offensive weapons are closely interconnected. . . . There could be a danger that having created an umbrella against offensive strike systems, our partners may come to feel completely safe. After the balance is broken, they will do whatever they want and grow more aggressive." The State Department, reported the *New York Times* on December 29, responded negatively: "While the U.S. has long agreed that there is a relationship between missile offense and defense, we believe the START follow-on agreement is not the appropriate vehicle for addressing it."[27]

Disagreement over strategic delivery systems also posed a challenge. Moscow repeatedly sought lower numbers than Washington preferred. In July 2009, Obama and Medvedev had suggested that limits would range between 500 and 1,100; later the Americans focused on a middle ground of around 800. This was near the number of currently deployed U.S. delivery systems. Russia, which currently deployed only some 620 systems, pressed for a lower figure of about 550. At whatever level delivery systems were set at, it was expected that the number of warheads would be limited to around 1,600. Meanwhile, all forty Republican senators, plus Independent Joseph

Lieberman, warned President Obama on December 15 that "we don't believe further reductions can be in the national security interest of the U.S. in the absence of a significant program to modernize our nuclear deterrent." The administration was placed on notice that ratification of any new treaty was going to come at a price since a new pact required approval by two-thirds of the Senate.[28]

OBAMA AND MEDVEDEV: NEW START

On April 8, 2010, at Prague, Obama and Medvedev signed the "New START" treaty that would replace the expired 1991 START I agreement. The legally binding, verifiable pact limited each nation's deployed strategic nuclear warheads to 1,550 and strategic delivery systems to 800 deployed and non-deployed—both significant reductions. This meant, according to the Brookings Institution's Steven Pifer's detailed discussion: "The treaty-accountable warhead limit is 30 percent lower than the 2,200 limit of SORT, and the delivery vehicle limit is 50 percent lower than the 1,600 allowed in START I." The new 1,550 limit applied to deployed nuclear warheads on intercontinental ballistic missiles (ICBMs), submarine-launch ballistic missiles (SLBMs), and heavy bombers carrying a single nuclear warhead. Additionally, the new agreement provided each side with the "freedom to mix," in order to develop its own force structure, since with the end of the Cold War neither side felt it necessary to focus on the structure of the other's strategic forces.

Although each nation was limited to 800 strategic delivery systems, only 700 were allowed to be deployed, with the others used for training and testing. Launchers without missiles were counted as non-deployed. Reductions required by the pact were to be carried out within seven years after the treaty entered into force. Additionally, the agreement tailored elements of the verification regime from START I, often streamlining monitoring provisions to meet the requirements of the New START era. Such measures included on-site inspections and exhibitions, data exchanges and notifications related to strategic weaponry contained in the treaty, together with enhancing verification monitoring via national technical means. The provisions for inspections provided for two types: "Type One" would take place at ICBM, submarines, and air bases, while "Type Two" targeted other facilities such as ICBM loading areas, test ranges, and training sites. A major reason for easing the on-site inspections was the significant advances over the past two decades in the ability to verify compliance with national technical means. These enhancements made it possible to gain much more relevant information than was the case in 1991.[29]

Of course, ratification of the New START Treaty came much easier in Moscow than in Washington. The lower house of Russia's parliament gave overwhelming preliminary approval of the treaty in a 350–58 vote in late December 2010, and the next month approved the second and third reading. A day after, the upper house concurred in late January 2011and when signed by Medvedev, the ratification procedure was complete. In Washington, various Republican senators raised several questions: Would the president allocate sufficient funds for modernization of the U.S. nuclear forces? Did the treaty interfere with the United States' planned deployment of missile defenses? And why did the treaty not reduce tactical nuclear weapons? This posturing prompted a stinging editorial in the *Los Angeles Times*: "Partisan rancor is not a good reason to block a pact that, for national security reasons, is backed by the entire U.S. military leadership and such GOP [Republican] heavyweights as former President George H.W. Bush and former secretaries of State Henry A. Kissinger, George P. Shultz, Colin L. Powell and Condoleezza Rice." Following an eight-month delay and eight days of debate, the Senate on December 22 voted 71–26 to ratify the treaty that entered into force on February 5, 2011.

Approval was accomplished at a price, however, as the administration pledged $10 billion over ten years to increase an already enlarged budget for the nuclear weapons complex. Given budget constraints, some argued that the United States would reconsider the promise of additional modernization funding and perhaps even its forty-year-old-plus "triad" system of ICBMs, SLBM, and bombers. Shortly after ratification doubts began to surface as to whether the U.S. economy could actually sustain the three separate strategic systems of the triad, particularly given a bipartisan decision to cut defense spending. The outgoing vice chairman of the Joint Chiefs of Staff, General James Cartwright, declared: "The challenge here is that we have to recapitalize all three legs [of the triad], and we don't have the money to do it." General Robert Kehler, head of the Strategic Command that manages U.S. nuclear forces, pessimistically reviewed the proposed costs of a new generation of twelve nuclear-armed submarines and 100 new long-range bombers, and doubted that the capital would be available. Looking at the budget situation, Kehler noted, "affordability" will be an issue. "The amount of money we're spending on maintaining nuclear weapons is not in keeping with the modern world," commented chairman of the Senate Armed Services Committee Carl Levin on November 11, 2011. "It's much more a Cold War remnant."[30]

THE PLAUSIBILITY OF ZERO NUCLEAR WEAPONS

At Prague on April 5, 2009, President Barack Obama outlined a path toward "a world without nuclear weapons." The hope of enhancing the world's safety by abolition of nuclear weapons certainly was not a new idea. India's prime minister, Rajiv Gandhi, addressed the UN General Assembly on June 9, 1988, warning that nuclear war "will mean the extinction of four thousand million: the end of life as we know it on our planet earth. We come to the United Nations to seek your support. We seek your support to put a stop to this madness." And, of course, many others wrote or spoke for abolishing the nuclear threat. If Obama was not the first to promote the idea of zero nuclear weapons, as president of the remaining superpower, he bestowed upon the notion of eliminating nuclear weaponry a particularly significant endorsement that drew worldwide attention and approval. And in doing so, he directed attention to elements of the non-proliferation regime "to cut off the building blocks needed for a bomb." Working together, he said, "we will strengthen the nuclear Non-Proliferation Treaty as a basis for cooperation." To this end, he pledged to aggressively pursue ratification of the Comprehensive Test Ban Treaty, to seek a new treaty that would verifiably halt the production of fissile materials, and to find "a new framework for civil nuclear cooperation, including a new international fuel bank, so that countries can access peaceful power without increasing the risks of proliferation."

After due consideration in December 2010, the IAEA's board approved a fuel bank plan. Here, eligible states would agree to comprehensive safeguards to all its peaceful nuclear activities. The United States, the European Union, Kuwait, the United Arab Emirates, and Norway pledged $100 million to purchase and deliver some 60–80 metric tons of low-enriched uranium for the bank. Of course, the president's message did acknowledge that not all nations would follow the rules. "We go forward with no illusion. Some will break the rules, but that is why we need a structure in place that ensures that when any nation does, they will face consequences." Indeed, the seven decades since Hiroshima had confirmed that building the bomb was easy compared to finding the means of harnessing it. As such, Obama explained, we need to "strengthen international inspections" and implement "real and immediate consequences."[31]

Two years earlier, on January 4, 2007, four prominent American figures, two former secretaries of state, a former secretary of defense, and a former senator published their plea for "A World Free of Nuclear Weapons" in the *Wall Street Journal*. "Nuclear weapons were essential to maintaining international security during the Cold War because they were a means of deterrence," George P. Shultz, William J. Perry, Henry A. Kissinger, and Sam Nunn claimed. With the end of the Cold War, however, the doctrine of mutual Soviet-American deterrence became obsolete. "Deterrence continues to be a relevant consideration for many states with regard to threats from other states," they conceded, "but reliance on nuclear weapons for this purpose is becoming increasingly hazardous and decreasingly effective." They called for a worldwide approach to a series of practical steps that could lead to a major reduction of the nuclear danger. These included: reducing the danger of unintended or unauthorized nuclear use; reducing substantially all nuclear armed forces; eliminating short-range, forward-deployed nuclear weapons; securing all nuclear arsenals and weapons grade ingredients; and halting all production of fissile material for weapons. They also acknowledged in their op-ed that several viable non-proliferation activities were under way, including the Non-Proliferation Treaty (NPT), the Co-operative Threat Reduction program, the Global Threat Reduction Initiative, and additional protocols to enhance the operation of the International Atomic Energy Agency (IAEA). Finally, the four American advocates of seeking zero nuclear weapons noted that during the Cold War, by accident or design, no nuclear weapon was used. As a result, "the notion of a nuclear taboo developed as senior leaders came to understand the consequences of employing nuclear weapons at any level."[32]

Responding to rising fears of nuclear proliferation and terrorism, some 100 individuals from all over the world met in December 2008, at Paris, to launch "Global Zero." The new organization was focused on "the phased, verified elimination of nuclear weapons, starting with deep reductions in the U.S. and Russian arsenals, to be followed by multilateral negotiations among all nuclear powers for an agreement to eliminate all nuclear weapons." Participating in this group were former high-ranking officials from various nations, including senior military leaders, focused on expanding diplomatic contacts between major governments and building worldwide grassroots support for reducing and eliminating nuclear weapons. In London, Global Zero presented a letter to Presidents Obama and Medvedev urging them to support its goals, to which both leaders responded that their respective states would work toward "achieving a nuclear free world." Through connections with other like-minded groups, Global Zero officials hoped to organize public opinion worldwide to persuade governmental officials to join the movement toward elimination of nuclear weapons, and indeed, all weapons of mass destruction.[33]

Several critics have argued this concept of zero nuclear weapons as being illusory. Late in 2007, two prominent Americans, a former secretary of defense and a former director of the Central Intelligence Agency, responded to the sentiments of Shultz, Perry, Kissinger, and Nunn with their own critique in the *Wall Street Journal*, suggesting there was "no realistic path to a world free of nuclear weapons." While agreeing that "that the strongest possible measures must be taken to inhibit the acquisition of and roll back the possession of nuclear weapons," Harold Brown and John Deutch argued that "the goal, even the aspirational goal, of eliminating all nuclear weapons is counterproductive." Since a nation seeking nuclear weapons obviously believed this weaponry would improve its security, any U.S. or multinational initiative aimed at eventually abolishing nuclear weapons "will have no direct effect on changing this calculus." Although they found considerable merit in the various actions proposed by Shultz and his co-authors, Brown and Deutch insisted that nothing the United States did to its nuclear forces would directly influence those nations or terrorist groups determined to obtain similar weaponry. Moreover, they found it "difficult" to believe "that a comprehensive test ban treaty, a 'no first use' declaration by the U.S., a dramatic reduction in the number of deployed or total nuclear weapons in our stockpile, an end to the production of fissionable material will convince North Korea, Iran, India, Pakistan or Israel to give up their nuclear weapons programs." After listing the various nations that were persuaded to give up their nuclear weapons programs—South Korea, Taiwan, Brazil, Argentina, South Africa, Libya, and the former Soviet republics—Brown and Deutch suggested that "these successes came about by the combined application of the carrots and sticks of [a non-]proliferation policy, and a change in the way a proliferating state perceived its security circumstances."

If they objected to espousing "any unattainable vision of a nuclear-weapons-free world," Brown and Deutch did urge the pursuit of several important non-proliferation goals. "Supplier states, for one, should seek to control the transfer of fissile material and relevant technology, using the inspections of the International Atomic Energy Agency. Second: Building on the Nunn-Lugar-Domenici program, greater emphasis needs to be given to security of weapons and weapons-usable material, and not just in Russia. Third: Given the potential expansion of nuclear power around the world, it is urgent to put into place new means for controlling the aspects of the fuel cycle—enrichment and fuel reprocessing—that present the greatest proliferation risk." Finally, they emphasized that nuclear weapons play an important role as a deterrent that "cannot be eliminated." That being the case, policy "must be based on this reality." The United States and other nations should focus on "those achievable objectives that lower the risks of the spread of nuclear weapons capability and the possibility of nuclear weapons use."[34]

From Australia came another critical evaluation of Obama's vision and policies. Hugh White, professor of Strategic Studies at the Australian National University, writing for the Lowy Institute for International Policy, posited that the president's desire to eliminate nuclear weapons clashed with his Nuclear Posture Review of April 2010. In "Nuclear Weapons and American Strategy in the Age of Obama," White argued that the U.S. nuclear weapons policy, "like its broader strategic and foreign policy, is torn between the enduring vision that America can deepen and strengthen its uncontested global leadership in a new American Century, and the growing realization that the balance of global power is shifting towards other states which do not share this vision." This often moves American nuclear policy in incongruous directions, on the one hand promoting abolition of nuclear weapons in a world under benevolent American primacy, and on the other relying more on its nuclear arsenal to sustain primacy as its advantage in other elements of national power declines. In this regard, Obama's Nuclear Posture Review maintains this "hedging" approach by shying away from making a full and definitive commitment to "no-first-use" of nuclear weapons. As stated, "There remains a narrow range of contingencies in which U.S. nuclear weapons may still play a role in deterring a conventional or CBW attack against the United States or its allies and partners." If elimination of nuclear weapons is ever to truly extend beyond rhetoric, Washington must address at least four important questions. First, how can the U.S. nuclear posture be shaped to promote the eventual abolition of nuclear weapons? Second, how will America's nuclear posture deal with threats of nuclear proliferation and terrorism? Third, how in the future will Washington define America's extended deterrence? And, fourth, what role does the United States foresee nuclear weapons playing in the shifting strategic relationships between major powers? As White articulates, "These questions connect with deeper underlying issues about the future of America's place in the world."[35]

Perhaps in this regard, a rethinking of leadership is again needed to steer things back in the right direction. Notwithstanding White's sentiments—and as touched on at various intervals during this book—Barack Obama *did* come to the White House with a strong commitment to arms control and nuclear disarmament. In one of his first significant public pronouncements on foreign policy at Prague in 2009, he posited his vision of a world without nuclear weapons and ending "Cold War thinking." These seminal promises were followed up with the New START agreement with Russia, four Nuclear Security Summits, 2015's Iran deal, and a momentous visit to Hiroshima in May 2016.[36] As he rightly conveyed in an op-ed, "As the only nation ever to use nuclear weapons, the United States has a moral obligation to continue to lead the way in eliminating them."[37] Outside of these developments, Obama also pushed "to review options for executive actions on nuclear policy,"[38] including a no-first-use declaration; however, these encountered substantial demurrals from both political adversaries and allies. If Washington was to truly shift its direction, it would not only make its own arsenal safer (reduced alert levels, downgraded launch-on-warning deployments, etc.) but would potentially decrease strains in some of the most volatile parts of the world. Moreover, it could also work toward limiting the nuclear modernization drive in the United States and beyond, as well as creating a global environment conducive to arms-control efforts.[39]

On the positive, the amount of nuclear weapons on a global scale has decreased markedly since the end of the Cold War, down from a peak of approximately 70,300 in 1986 to an estimated 15,350 in 2016. While many state representatives frequently define such reductions as being the result of current arms control agreements, the major portion of this process occurred in the 1990s. In more recent times, the pace of reduction has decelerated significantly. In lieu of preparing for nuclear disarmament, the nuclear-armed states of today are seemingly planning to preserve and modernize their arsenals for the indeterminate future.[40] It goes without saying that such open-ended nuclear modernization is clearly at odds with the declarations made by the five NPT nuclear-weapon states five decades ago, in pursuing negotiations in good faith on active measures to end the "nuclear arms race at an early date and to nuclear disarmament promises that have been reaffirmed every five years at the NPT review conferences."[41]

As the subtitle of this book suggests, the "search for global security," if at all attainable or legitimately pursued, is precariously dependent on delicate conditions that require the presence of cogent decision makers behind each nuclear arsenal, as well as the "absence of any rogue launches, human-error incidents, or system malfunctions."[42] For nuclear stability to be assured, deterrence and fail-safe mechanisms must work every single time; for a nuclear devastation to take place, they only have to fail once. Clearly this is not a reassuring calculation, particularly as states evidently continue to attain nuclear weapons, and even more so, continue to busily modernize their stockpiles.[43] Indeed, despite moving away from the vast arsenals of the 1960s and 1970s, the second nuclear age encompasses a multiplicity of nuclear powers with interlinking connections of cooperation and conflict, delicate command-and-control systems, precarious cyber susceptibilities, threat perceptions occurring among three or more nuclear-armed states concurrently, asymmetric perceptions of the military and political utility of nuclear weapons, and, as a result, "a greater complexity of deterrence relations." Given this global reality it is hardly surprising that former defense secretary William Perry has argued that "The danger of nuclear catastrophe today is greater than during the Cold War."[44]

NOTES

1. Steven J. Zaloga, *The Kremlin's Nuclear Sword: The Rise and Fall of Russia's Strategic Nuclear Forces, 1945–2000* (Washington, DC: Smithsonian Institution Press, 2002), 214–15, 221. Elements of this chapter have been adapted from Professor Siracusa's study (with Richard Dean Burns) *A Global History of the Nuclear Arms Race: Weapons, Strategy, and Politics*, 2 vols. (Santa Barbara, CA: Praeger, 2013).

2. Michael R. Beschloss and Strobe Talbott, *At the Highest Levels: The Inside Story of the End of the Cold War* (Boston: Little, Brown, 1993), 9; Stephen J. Hadley, "Arms Control in the Bush Administration," in *Presidents and Arms Control: Process, Procedures, and Problems*, ed. Kenneth W. Thompson (Lanham, MD: University Press of America, 1997), IV: 58.

3. *Newsweek*, May 15, 1989, 22; Department of State Bulletin 89, April 1989: 2, 4–5; Beschloss and Talbott, *At the Highest Levels*, 12–13, 17–19; Robert M. Gates, *From the*

Shadows: The Ultimate Insider's Story of Five Presidents and How They Won the Cold War (New York: Simon & Schuster, 1996).

4. *Newsweek*, December 11, 1989, 28–32, 39; editorial, *New York Times*, December 1, 1989, Y30; *New York Times*, December 4, 1989; Elizabeth Drew, "Letter From Washington," *New Yorker*, January 1, 1990, 80–83; George H. W. Bush and Brent Scowcroft, *A World Transformed* (New York: Vintage, 1998), 164, 173; Beschloss and Talbott, *At the Highest Levels*, 155.

5. Thomas Graham Jr., *Disarmament Sketches: Three Decades of Arms Control and International Law* (Seattle: University of Washington Press, 2002), 190–205, 209; Beschloss and Talbott, *At the Highest Levels*, 288–89.

6. Beschloss and Talbott, *At the Highest Levels*, 370–73.

7. Quotes in Frances Fitzgerald, *Way Out There in the Blue: Reagan, Star Wars and the End of the Cold War* (New York: Simon & Schuster, 2000), 444–45; Raymond L. Garthoff, *The Great Transition: American-Soviet Relations and the End of the Cold War* (Washington, DC: The Brookings Institution, 1994), 252–37, 553–57; Graham, *Disarmament Sketches*, 102–42.

8. Beschloss and Talbott, *At the Highest Levels*, 166–67; Gates, *From the Shadows*, 482–83; James A. Baker III, *The Politics of Diplomacy: Revolution, War & Peace, 1989–1992* (New York: Putnam's, 1995), 236–37.

9. Beschloss and Talbott, *At the Highest Levels*, 402–6, 414–15; April Carter, *Success and Failure in Arms Control Negotiations* (Oxford: Oxford University Press/SIPRI, 1989), 172–229; Jack Mendelson and David Grahame, *Arms Control Chronology* (Washington, DC: Center for Defense Information, 2002), 36ff, 44; Jeffrey A. Larsen and James M. Smith, *Historical Dictionary of Arms Control and Disarmament* (Lanham, MD: Scarecrow Press, 2005), 204–5.

10. Baker, *The Politics of Diplomacy*, 658–65, 668–70.

11. Ibid., 671; Hadley, "Arms Control and the Bush Administration," 66–67; Larsen and Smith, *Historical Dictionary of Arms Control and Disarmament*, 206–7; Cirincione et al., *Deadly Arsenals*, 83–118. For more on START II, see SIPRI Annual Yearbook's sections on "Nuclear Arms Control."

12. Amy F. Woolf, "Non-Strategic Nuclear Weapons," *CRS Report for Congress*, RL32572 (Washington, DC: Congressional Research Service), March 23, 2016, https://www.fas.org/sgp/crs/nuke/RL32572.pdf.

13. See "The Presidential Nuclear Initiatives (PNIs) on Tactical Nuclear Weapons at a Glance," Fact Sheet, *Arms Control Association*, November 1, 2010.

14. Zaloga, *The Kremlin's Nuclear Sword*, 216.

15. Quoted in "The Presidential Nuclear Initiatives (PNIs) on Tactical Nuclear Weapons at a Glance," Arms Control Association, August 2012.

16. Woolf, "Non-Strategic Nuclear Weapons."

17. Ibid.

18. Catherine M. Kelleher and Scott L. Warren, "Getting to Zero Starts Here: Tactical Nuclear Weapons," *Arms Control Today* (December 2009): 10–11.

19. Ibid.

20. Oliver Meier and Paul Ingram, "A Nuclear Posture Review for NATO," *Arms Control Today* (October 2010): 8–16; "Next Steps in Arms Control" [a Panel moderated by Professor Catherine Kelleher] (Washington, DC: Arms Control Association), November 8, 2010, a twenty-page transcript provided by Federal News Service, available online.

21. See "Experts Call NATO Strategic Concept 'Missed Opportunity to Reduce Role of Obsolete Tactical Nukes from Europe,'" *Arms Control Association*, November 19, 2010, online; and the less strident Oliver Meier, "NATO Revises Nuclear Policy," *Arms Control Today* (December 2010): 28–31.

22. Woolf, "Non-Strategic Nuclear Weapons."

23. Graham, *Disarmament Sketches*, 334; Jim Hoagland, "Nuclear Preemption," *Washington Post National Weekly*, March 25–31, 2002, 5; William M. Arkin, "Secret Plan Outlines the Unthinkable," *Los Angeles Times*, March 10, 2002, M1, M6; Richard D. Sokolsky and Eugene B. Rumer, "Nuclear Alarmists," *The Washington Post National Weekly*, March 25–31, 2002,

27. See Aiden Warren, *Prevention, Pre-Emption, and the Nuclear Option: From Bush to Obama* (New York: Routledge, 2012).

24. "The Strategic Offensive Reductions Treaty (SORT) At a Glance," *Arms Control Association*, www.armscontrol.org; "U.S.-Russian Nuclear Arms Control Agreements at a Glance," *Arms Control Today* (May 2010): 39–41.

25. Wade Boese and J. Peter Scoblic, "The Jury Is Still Out," *Arms Control Today* (June 2002): 4–6; Wade Boese, "Senate Reviews U.S.-Russian Nuclear Reductions Treaty," *Arms Control Today* (September 2002): 13. SORT text and additional commentary appeared in the *Arms Control Today* July/August 2002 issue.

26. John Holum, "Assessing the New U.S.-Russian Pact," *Arms Control Today* (June 2002): 7–8.

27. Tom Z. Collina, "START Stalls, Talks Continue," *Arms Control Today* (January/February 2010): 40–41; Vladimir Isachenkov, "Putin Urges US to Share Missile Defense Data," *Associated Press*, December 29, 2009.

28. Ibid.

29. Steven Pifer, "New START: Good News for U.S. Security," *Arms Control Today* (May 2010): 8–14.

30. Sergei L. Loiko, "Arms Pact Passes a Russian Hurdle," *Los Angeles Times*, December 25, 2010, A-3; "Russia's Upper House Oks Nuclear Arms Treaty," *Los Angeles Times*, January 27, 2011, A-4; Paul Richter, "GOP Deal Is Sought to Ratify Nuclear Treaty," *Los Angeles Times*, November 4, 2010, A-2; "Stopping New START," *Los Angeles Times*, December 21, 2010, A-24; Tom Z. Collina, "Senate Approves New START," *Arms Control Today* (January/February 2011): 38–43; Tom Z. Collina, "Nuclear Triad Budgets Questioned," *Arms Control Today* (September 2011): 36–37.

31. Cole Harvey, "Obama Calls for Nuclear Weapons-Free World," *Arms Control Today* 39 (May 2009): 28–30; Daniel Horner, "IAEA Board Approves Fuel Bank Plan," *Arms Control Today* 40 (January/February 2011): 46–48.

32. George P. Shultz, William J. Perry, Henry A. Kissinger, and Sam Nunn, "A World Free of Nuclear Weapons," *Wall Street Journal*, January 4, 2007, A-15.

33. "International Leaders Urge Obama to Back Nuke Ban," *New York Times*, March 26, 2009; "Scrapping Nuclear Arms Is Now Realpolitik," *The Times* (London), April 1, 2009.

34. Harold Brown and John Deutch, "The Nuclear Disarmament Fantasy," *Wall Street Journal*, November 19, 2007, A-19.

35. Hugh White, *Nuclear Weapons and American Strategy in the Age of Obama* (Sydney: Lowy Institute for International Policy, September 2010), 3; U.S., "Nuclear Posture Review" (Washington, DC: White House, April 2010), 16.

36. Ramesh Thakur, "Why Obama Should Declare a No-First-Use Policy for Nuclear Weapons," *Bulletin of Atomic Scientists*, August 19, 2016, http://thebulletin.org/why-obama-should-declare-no-first-use-policy-nuclear-weapons9789.

37. Barack Obama, "How We Can Make Our Vision of a World without Nuclear Weapons a Reality," *Washington Post*, March 30, 2016, https://www.washingtonpost.com/opinions/.

38. Josh Rogin, "Obama Plans Major Nuclear Policy Changes in His Final Months," *Washington Post*, July 10, 2016, https://www.washingtonpost.com/opinions/global-opinions/.

39. Thakur, "Why Obama Should Declare a No-First-Use Policy for Nuclear Weapons."

40. Hans M. Kristensen and Robert S. Norris, "Status of World Nuclear Forces," Federation of American Scientists (FAS), October 2016, http://fas.org/issues/nuclear-weapons/status-world-nuclear-forces/.

41. Hans M. Kristensen and Robert S. Norris, "Slowing Nuclear Weapon Reductions and Endless Nuclear Weapon Modernizations: A Challenge To The NPT," *Bulletin of the Atomic Scientists* 70, no. 4 (July/August, 2014), http://bos.sagepub.com/content/70/4/94.full.pdf+html; Kristensen and Norris, "Status of World Nuclear Forces."

42. Thakur, "Why Obama Should Declare a No-First-Use Policy for Nuclear Weapons."

43. Quoted in ibid.

44. Ibid.

Chapter Seven

Biological and Chemical Weapons and Nuclear Terrorism

Aside from the nuclear arm of the WMD suite on which this book is significantly focused, biological and chemical weapons also present a security threat to our increasingly interconnected world. The advent of new diseases and the natural progression of pathogens are continuously altering the landscape of biological risks; while concurrently, there are emerging actors—both state and non-state—who are willing to use chemical weapons. Over the past twenty-five years, the dissemination of technical know-how combined with the biotechnology revolution have also significantly increased the danger posed by bioterrorism. Additionally, many previously complex and labor-intensive processes have been abridged or automated, lessening the resource and pecuniary requirements needed for illicit biological and chemical weapons activities.[1]

In relation to biological weapons, they can be considered as some of the most deadly devices ever produced. They use microorganisms or natural toxins to yield disease in humans, animals, or plants. Insofar as acting as a weapon, while pathogens require delivery via bombs or missiles, they are not necessarily imperative as a state or a terrorist group can also contaminate food and water resources, use insects, expose individuals, or use aerosols, so as to traffic and "shift" a pathogen. In a globalized world of porous borders, states are limited in their capacity to mitigate biological threats—manmade and naturally—from taking place. While there are only several states that are suspected of possessing biological weapons and/or producing and weaponizing biological agents, the security risk remains prominent. A further challenge is that it is difficult to ascertain the difference between legitimate forms of research and types of biological research gauged toward subversive and harmful activities. Indeed, knowledge and equipment pertaining to the treat-

ment and curing of diseases can be applied so as to engender terminal pathogens. Significant progress in biotechnology has meant that most states with
pharmaceutical and medical complexes possess the intellectual property and
capacities to develop biological weapons. Moreover, as technology and
know-how spread, the challenge in detecting and preventing subversive lab
activities decreases—presenting potential catastrophic ramifications in the
form of hazardous lab accidents and/or the development of "superbugs" that
are outside the control of state health systems.[2]

In the context of chemical weapons, they can be defined as toxic agents
intentionally utilized to cause death or unadorned harm. Notwithstanding the
sheer fact that most of the global community's attention has been on nuclear
weapons, chemical weapons remain the most widely used and proliferated
weapon of mass destruction. Such weapons utilize several different assets to
enervate or destroy people, animals, and plants, including blister agents that
cause skin, eye, and lung irritation; choking agents that cause extreme and
excruciating respiratory issues and, ultimately, asphyxiation; blood agents
that prevent blood from dispensing the needed oxygen throughout the body;
and lastly, nerve agents that incapacitate the nervous system, triggering mus-
cle contraction, loss of control over human functions, and death.[3]

HISTORICAL ATTEMPTS AT REGULATING WEAPONRY

Given the extreme and lethal ramifications that can emanate from the chemical and biological weapon domains, it is not surprising that over the course of
history there have been varying attempts to limit or prohibit the military use,
manufacture, and/or possession of such specific weaponry, relating to poison, chemical agents, fire, and so forth. As weapons became much more
destructive in modern times, their potential to inflict extensive casualties
among combatants and noncombatants sparked new attempts at formal restrictions and prohibitions. The rationale for these limitations or prohibitions
was that the parties involved considered the unrestricted use—or often any
use—of a designated weapon to exceed the recognized "just use of force."
Moreover, such attempts, extending back to ancient times, sought to prohibit
poison, biochemical, and combustible weapons not just on legal grounds, but
because they were seen as inhumane devices.[4]

Even before 3000 B.C., precedents had emerged leading to generally
accepted customs defining certain forbidden "military" usages, including the
prohibition of practices pertaining to the poisoning of weapons, wells, and
food. Such prohibitions were acknowledged in different civilizations, although they were not always followed. In India, the *Atharva Veda* (c.
1500–500 B.C.) and the Hindu *Laws of Manu* (c. 200 B.C.–200 A.D.) condemned the use of poisoned arrows or fire; but the *Laws* allowed the Brah-

man rulers to "continually spoil the grass and water" of a foe under siege. Customs or taboos of some non-literate societies also placed prohibitions on "poisoned" weapons. The Tangale, an ethnic group in Northeastern Nigeria, for example, poisoned their weapons for hunting elephants, but did not use poison in their warfare. The Nagas, inhabitants of the highland region near the Indian-Burma border, seldom employed poisoned arrows in combat because they thought that it failed to show respect for the opposing warriors. [5] The ancient Greeks and Romans, who engaged in savage warfare, held that the use of poison was a violation of *jus gentium*, the law of nations. (An obscure passage of the *Odyssey* apparently condemned the use of poisoned weapons.) However, this prohibition did not cover the use of smoke and incendiaries, as evidenced by the Spartan siege of Platea (429 B.C.) and the Boetian siege of Delium (424/423 B.C.). Nor did it prohibit the use of the mysterious "Greek fire," a burning-liquid weapon—the secret of which is still a matter of speculation.

Marcus Tullius Cicero (106–43 B.C.) explained the Roman view of the prohibition of poison in his account *De Officiis* ("On Duty"). He notes that Fabius Fabricus and the Roman Senate ordered a deserter, who offered to poison their foe Pyrrhus, returned to their enemy's camp. "Thus they stamped with their disapproval the treacherous murder even of an enemy who was at once powerful, unprovoked, aggressive and successful." The Koran also restricted the Muslim use of poison in warfare. As Islamic scholar Yuset suggests, based on the gathering together of Muhammad's actions and sayings in the seventh century, it is evident that the Islamic tradition "clearly prohibited . . . poisoning wells."[6] Formal decisions to prohibit the use of poisoned weapons began with the Treaty of Strassburg (1675) between the French and Germans.

An interesting example of eighteenth-century humanists exerting "moral" pressure against "inhumane" weaponry may be found during the Seven Years War and later during the early years of the French Revolution. In 1759, during the Seven Years War, a Parisian jeweler claimed to have rediscovered the secret of Greek fire—a burning-liquid weapon used by the Byzantine Greeks, Arabs, Chinese, and Mongols. Despite its potential military advantage, Louis XV expressed his desire that the secret be allowed to remain "forgotten." Thirty years later in 1790, the French Academy of Science was asked to investigate the claims of a man who insisted that he had invented an incendiary bullet. The investigating commission reported that the device might achieve even greater destruction than was claimed. However, harkening back to Louis XV's decision regarding Greek fire, the commission concluded that "faithful to its principles and to those of humanity" it could not even make experiments on the cartridge without an expressed order of the government.

The government of the Terror later sanctioned the development of an incendiary bullet. There is no evidence, however, of it becoming an accepted or decisive weapon at the time. Yet the decision to proceed might be construed as the "beginning of the dichotomy" between science and morality as justified by the German philosopher Immanuel Kant. One may also infer that the revolutionary government was less "humane" than Louis XV or that in 1793, France was in greater peril than it was during the Seven Years War. It was incorporated into the Lieber Code (1863), which governed the U.S. Army during the Civil War, and was repeated in the Declaration of Brussels (1874), and the Hague declaration on "Laws and Customs of War on Land" (1899). Article LXX of the Lieber Code put it quite succinctly: "The use of poison in any manner, be it to poison wells, or food, or arms, is wholly excluded from modern warfare."[7] Despite occasional violations, the prohibition on the use of poison has remained during the evolution of the Law of War through custom, definition, and codification.

More likely, however, is that it simply might be considered as an inevitable concomitant aspect of the first "total" war in modern history. Attempts to outlaw "war" grew slowly in the Western world, perhaps reaching their peak during the interwar years (1919–1930s). Early efforts to curtail "private" hostilities between various European nobles and principalities were instigated by the clergy in the Middle Ages with the Peace of God in the tenth century, and culminated in the secular Peace of Lands of the fifteenth century. The rise of national monarchies ended the right of local nobles to wage their own wars. It was the Peace of Lands that Professor Kunz referred to when he wrote: "Private war could be successfully forbidden in the Holy Roman Empire in 1492, when compulsory courts with sheriffs and a legislature had been firmly established."[8]

REGULATING POISONOUS "WEAPONS" IN THE TWENTIETH CENTURY AND BEYOND

As signified in the above, the customs and traditions of early peoples saw the periodical ban or restriction on the use of poisons, and by the end of the medieval period, the prohibition against poison had become a principle of customary international law. In recent times, this principle has been extended to prohibit the use of "poison" gases and bacteriological/biological agents in warfare. Indeed, concern that nineteenth-century developments in synthetic chemistry could lead to new weapons in the twentieth century prompted the delegates to the Hague Conference of 1899 to ban the use of asphyxiating or "poison" gases, formalized in the *The Hague "Poison" Gases Conventions, 1899/1907*. The special Declaration concerning Asphyxiating Gases (July 29, 1899) stated: "The contracting Powers agree to abstain from the use of projectiles the sole object of which is the diffusion of asphyxiating or deleterious gases." A similar pledge was signed at the 1907 Hague Conference. The United States and Britain did not sign the special declaration; however, the British later agreed to abide by its terms.

All of the World War I European belligerents became signatories, including Germany, who employed a toxic gas in April 1915. Initially, the Germans did not technically violate The Hague ban for they released chlorine from thousands of 100-kilogram containers deployed near the enemy's trenches. The British and French immediately retaliated, with the latter apparently the first to employ shells and cartridges to deliver toxic gas. Various toxic gases delivered by "projectiles" became a regular element of battlefield tactics in World War I, but neither side gained any significant military advantage from their usage, despite there being approximately a million gas casualties. Nonetheless, the use of toxic agents maintained its reputation as a dangerous weapon that in the future might be used against civilians as well as combatants. [9]

One of the first post–World War I initiatives came in the form of the Versailles Treaty "Poison Gas" Ban, 1919. Article 171 of the imposed Treaty of Versailles prohibited the defeated Germans from having "asphyxiating, poisonous or other gases, and all analogous liquids, materials or devices." Moreover, "their manufacture and importation" was also strictly banned, as well as any "materials specially intended for the manufacture, storage and use of said products or devices." While there were many confirmed evasions of the Versailles Treaty, it appears that there were few clandestine efforts to experiment or produce chemical weapons prior to the mid-1930s—except perhaps some experiments in the Soviet Union. Further security concerns emanating from such poisons, particularly in the context of conflict, was evident in the Washington Treaty on the Use of Gases, 1922. In this regard, an advisory committee to the U.S. delegation warned that future use of toxic gases against cities could result in "the depopulation of large sections of the country" and could threaten the basic elements of civilized society. As such, the five major naval powers at the Washington Conference in 1922 signed the separate pact—reinforcing The Hague 1899 and 1907 pledges—banning all deleterious gases. Unfortunately, this agreement was combined with the restrictions on submarine warfare that the French rejected, and thus quashed both endeavors. [10]

A significant step toward universalizing the prohibition against chemical and bacteriological weapons was undertaken on June 17 in the form of the *Geneva Protocol of 1925*. Signatories to the "Protocol for the Prohibition of the Use in War of Asphyxiating, Poisonous, or Other Gases, and of Bacteriological Methods of Warfare" acknowledged that "the use in war of asphyxiating, poisonous or other gases, and of all analogous liquids, materials or devices, has been justly condemned by the general opinion of the civilized world; and . . . this prohibition shall be universally accepted as a part of International Law, binding alike the conscience and the practice of nations." The prohibition of bacteriological weapons was added at the urging of the Polish representative, who persuasively argued that the horrors of bacteriological warfare could surpass those of chemical warfare. Literally speaking, the term "bacteriological" covered only bacterial agents, since microbiological organisms, such as viruses, were unknown in 1925. The 1972 Biological and Toxin Weapons Convention would later expand this prohibition.

If the protocol provided a more comprehensive definition of chemical warfare, it suffered from attached reservations that usually insisted on the right of retaliation; thus, the Geneva Protocol was essentially a "no-first-use" pledge. The protocol allowed a state to douse its own citizens with non-lethal riot control agents, but disagreement arose over whether these could be used in international hostilities. For example, in limited circumstances, some states reserved the right to use riot-control agents on a battlefield, arguing that their use would save lives. Notwithstanding these points of difference, before the outbreak of World War II, forty-three nations ratified the protocol establishing it as "part of customary international law." Among the signatories that initially refused to ratify the protocol were Japan and the United States, although Japan ratified the protocol in 1970 and the United States in 1975. During World War II, even though the European warring parties possessed chemical weapons including deadly nerve gases, they were not employed. In all probability, this was due more to the fear of retaliation and prevailing winds than the legal document. A party to the Hague Declaration and the 1925 protocol, Japan employed chemical agents, anthrax, typhoid, and plague in several attacks after 1937 upon Manchurian towns and cities. Doctors in the infamous Japanese Army Unit 731 used Chinese and other prisoners of war, including Americans, in experiments to see how biological agents were spread. After the war, nine Japanese doctors and nurses were convicted of having vivisected eight captured U.S. airmen; however, no senior Japanese official was charged. In fact, the United States granted immunity to the head of Unit 731 and several members, in exchange for the extensive records of their germ warfare experiments.[11]

There have been other violations of the protocol. Italy signed in 1928, but used poison gas against Ethiopia (a party) in 1936. Egypt also signed in 1928, but used poison gas against Yemen (a party) in 1967; and Iraq, a signatory since 1931, used chemical agents in its war with Iran (a party) in the 1980s, and Iran, of course, responded in kind. The communist Chinese and the Soviets charged the United States with employing bacteriological and chemical agents during the Korean War, which American officials vigorously denied. Likewise, Cuba accused the United States of spreading crop and animal diseases, which was also denied by Washington.

Further attempts to mitigate and/or regulate came in the form of the "No First Use" Gas Policies (1939, 1943, 1969). At the outbreak of World War II in 1939, Berlin acknowledged Britain's request to abide by the Geneva Protocol. As stated, "The German government will observe during the War the prohibitions which form the subject of the Geneva protocol of June 17, 1925. . . . She reserves complete freedom of action in the event that the provisions of the protocol are violated on the part of the enemy." Adolph Hitler's personal aversion to gas warfare after his own experience in the trench during World War I, combined with a lack of readiness and a fear of retaliation, prevented Germany from employing this weapon. During the last days of the Third Reich, Hitler apparently ordered its use against the Allies, but "saner minds prevented implementation." [12] In the Pacific theater, President Franklin D. Roosevelt, in response to reports that the Japanese had used gas against the Chinese, declared on June 5, 1942, that, "if Japan persists in this inhuman form of warfare against China or against any other of the United Nations, such action will be regarded by this Government as though taken against the United States, and retaliation in kind and in full measure will be meted out." In expanding on these sentiments on June 8, 1943, Roosevelt posited a no-first-use policy that restricted the United States' freedom of action: "I state categorically that we shall under no circumstances resort to the use of such weapons unless they are first used by our enemies [duplicative]." [13]

During the Cold War, the focus on nuclear weaponry and broader nuclear security meant that multilateral efforts in dealing with chemical/biological (C/B) weapons were somewhat limited, or, at least, put to the side. On November 25, 1969, President Richard Nixon did, however, restate the chemical warfare no-first-use policy, declaring that in relation to "our chemical warfare programs, the United States reaffirms its oft-repeated renunciation of the first use of lethal chemical weapons [and] extends this renunciation to the first use of incapacitating chemicals." [14] It was evident that Western nations believed the elimination of chemical weapons was a much more difficult problem than abolishing biological weapons (BW); and therefore, a less complex BW regime was plausible. Indeed, the United States' unilateral declaration of November 1969 that it was renouncing bacteriological or biological methods of warfare, was closing all facilities engaged in the production of these agents for offensive purposes, and was destroying its stockpiles of biological weapons and agents was a significant development toward this end. Other states followed suit, with Canada, Sweden, and the United Kingdom announcing that they had neither biological weapons nor plans to produce them. Because there was now considerable doubt as to the effectiveness of BWs on the battlefield, actions mitigating their use were able to be pursued. This was particularly evident when the Soviet Union in March 1971 sent a draft to the United Nations calling for biological and toxin weapons to be put on the table for discussion. The General Assembly endorsed the revised draft, agreed to by Moscow and Washington, in December 1971. President Nixon called it "the first international agreement since World War II to provide for the actual elimination of an entire class of weapons from the arsenals of nations."[15]

The Convention on the Prohibition of the Development, Production and Stockpiling of Bacteriological (Biological) and Toxin Weapons and on Their Destruction (BWC) committed its signatories never to develop, produce, stockpile, acquire, or retain microbial, or other biological agents or toxins in quantities that have no justification for peaceful purposes. They were not to possess for hostile purposes weapons, equipment, or delivery systems for these agents or toxins. Additionally, the parties were to destroy or convert those weapons to peaceful purposes, not to transfer any prohibited items in their possession, and to take necessary measures to ensure that these provisions were observed. The initial handling of complaints about compliance would take place through consultations among the parties with the ultimate recourse being the UN Security Council. There were also provisions for providing assistance to parties that may be endangered by violations of the convention, and for exchanges of scientific and technical information relating to biological agents.

Later it was learned that the Soviet Union had systematically violated the pact with an elaborate BW research program. A suspected Soviet violation involving the release of anthrax pathogens at Sverdlovsk in 1979 would prompt the convention's Second Review Conference in 1986. This required nations to formally submit "information on high-safety research facilities," provide data on "unusual outbreaks of infectious diseases," publish research related to BW agents, and include information on activities "which might be of relevance to the Convention." Of course, the threat of Iraq's biological arsenal during the Gulf War prompted the Third Review Conference's (1991) expanded reporting requirements in an effort to build confidence in the convention. States were to report information on national biological defense research and development programs, on domestic legislation relevant to the convention, declare past research on offensive and defensive BW, and identify their human vaccine production facilities. While the United States took the position that the convention was not verifiable, other nations created a "Group of Verification Experts" that began a protracted, scientific, and technical examination of potential measures, and a review of possible verification techniques.

In other interesting yet concerning developments during this time, South Africa, also a signatory to the BW Convention, had established a secret chemical and germ warfare program gauged toward its apartheid adversaries. The arsenal consisted of anthrax, botulinum toxin, Ebola, Marburg, and a human immunodeficiency virus. Varying other devices were also developed, including: poison-tipped umbrellas, walking sticks capable of firing toxic pellets, and chocolates, beer, and sugar laced with lethal agents. "This paramilitary application of official apartheid policy aimed, quite clearly, at the selective injury or death of native blacks," according to Jacques Richardson, "while leaving the white part of the population untouched: governmental terrorism in a failing state." The program ended in 1994 when Nelson Mandela became president.

In looking back to 1975, U.S. congressional investigators turned up a Central Intelligence Agency cache of "pathogens, germ toxins, and biological poisons that were strong enough to sicken or kill millions of people." In violation of President Richard Nixon's orders and the terms of the 1972 pact, the small stockpile containing a wide variety of agents was housed at Fort Detrick, Maryland. During the 1980s, the Reagan administration viewed research on biodefense projects as significant, and funding was substantially expanded. "We are doing research in genetic engineering and related disciplines to understand what's possible," Richard L. Wagoner, an assistant secretary of defense stated. "But it's for the purpose of understanding how to design a defense, not to design an offense." Yet, a narrow line separates biological agents for defense and offense. According to a review of Pentagon research activities between 1980 and 1986, "fifty-one projects aimed at making novel pathogens, thirty-two at boosting toxin production, twenty-three at defeating vaccines, fourteen at inhibiting diagnosis, and three at outwitting protective drugs."[16]

In reconnecting with previous discussion on chemical weapons, a 1984 UN investigation of Iraq's use of chemical weapons (CWs) during its war with Iran found that the Iraqi CW program used chemicals and materials purchased through legitimate trade channels. Subsequently, a number of nations placed export controls on specific chemicals that could be used in manufacturing CWs. The Australia Group, as they became known, first met in June 1985 and have done so annually ever since then to address new and emerging threats. Suspected diversion of dual-use materials to biological weapons programs in the early 1990s led to export controls on specific biological agents. The group developed control lists that included technologies and equipment used in the manufacturing or disposal of chemical and biological weapons.

CHEMICAL WEAPONS CONVENTION (CWC) AND OTHER DEVELOPMENTS

Of course, the most significant development pertaining to mitigating chemical weapons came in 1993. Following inconclusive bilateral negotiations from 1977 to 1980, a ban on chemical weapons was finally signed in January of the said year. By 2016, there were 192 signatories for the convention that entered into force April 29, 1997. According to Allan Krass, reaching agreement on the "details of the managed access regime was one of the most difficult challenges" of completing the pact. The Convention on Chemical Weapons (CWC) eliminated an entire class of weapons, and established the most elaborate verification regime in history. The Organization for the Prohibition of Chemical Weapons was created to collect declarations as to a nation's stockpiles and to oversee their destruction. The organization also maintains records, makes reports to the parties, conducts inspections, and serves as the point of receipt for complaints lodged by one party against another. In April 1997 the U.S. Senate finally granted ratification.

A most complicated arms control measure, the CWC impinges on one of the world's basic industries as well as on sensitive national security interests. Yet, the chemical industry for the most part has accepted the terms. The current version of the text contains some two hundred pages of detailed provisions for destroying chemical weapons and production facilities, the order of destruction and disposition of discovered war munitions, the criteria for determining toxicity, definitions of precursors, reports on the production of certain chemicals, and many other details. It also incorporates provisions for assistance and protection against a chemical weapons attack, sanctions against violators, and economic and technological development for signatories. The task of destroying the world's chemical weapons has been both complex and revealing. For example, in 2005, the Albanian government discovered a hidden bunker containing hundreds of canisters of lethal military chemicals that were purchased from China in the 1970s. In terms of scouring the depths of physical history, China revealed it discovered 700,000 chemical munitions left behind by retreating Japanese forces, while France encountered its own challenges in unearthing chemical weapons left over from World War I. [17]

As far as maintaining a robust verification regime, the Chemical Weapons Convention (1993) introduced a controversial concept of an "anywhere, anytime" inspection that permitted—as in the additional protocol for the IAEA—a signatory's unimpeded access to suspect locations. Initiated by the United States, it provided that whenever a state or group of states detected an activity that might be a violation of the convention, the state on whose territory the activity was taking place would be obliged to permit a prompt, internationally conducted on-site inspection to determine whether a violation had indeed occurred. This agreement permitted chemical experts to visit each nation's chemical production facilities on forty-eight hours' notice to determine whether chemical weapons were being manufactured.

Additionally, the Organization for the Prevention of Chemical Weapons, likely to be the largest arms control agency ever designed, would oversee the destruction of existing chemical weapon stocks, and consider questions raised regarding treaty compliance. Following the U.S.-led coalition's victory over Iraqi forces, the UN Security Council adopted Resolution 687 on April 3, 1991. The resolution mandated the complete elimination of Iraq's biological, chemical, and nuclear weapons projects, as well as its ballistic missiles with a range beyond 150 kilometers. To supervise compliance, the resolution created the UN Special Commission (UNSCOM) to oversee the removal of Iraq's biological, chemical, and restricted missile programs, and stipulated that the International Atomic Energy Agency (IAEA) would ensure Iraq's nuclear weapons program was dismantled.

The on-site teams headed by Hans Bix, director-general of the IAEA, and Rolf Ekeus, chairman of the UNSCOM, launched inspections in May and June 1991. They met with Iraqi obstructionism entailing the removal of prohibited items from inspection sites and the denial of access to facilities and records. This scenario persisted with varying intensities over the next decade. In 1992, the Iraqi government admitted to having had more of the proscribed missiles and chemical weapons than it initially acknowledged, but insisted that they unilaterally had destroyed them. Not only did this violate the requirement that the inspectors were to supervise such destruction, it left no formal record of the unilateral destruction. In 1999, a UN review of the inspectors' activities concluded that the bulk of the prohibited weaponry, indeed, had been destroyed. Two problems arose during the inspections. First, in 1999 the United States acknowledged it had placed intelligence agents on the inspection teams, prompting the Iraqi government to expel the inspectors. Second, President George W. Bush refused to believe reports of a successor UN commission—the UN Monitoring, Verification, and Inspection Commission—that no dire or substantive threat from Iraqi weapons of mass destruction actually existed. Despite Washington's refusal to acknowledge the inroads made, the UN on-site inspections nevertheless did meet many of their stipulated objectives. [18]

A significant development, albeit more focused toward nuclear-related material, came in the form of UN Security Council Resolution 1540 (2004). Following on from a previous resolution (UNSCR 1373 of 2001) adopted in response to the events surrounding 9/11 and relating to information-sharing in the context of acts of terrorism, "1540" was intended to mitigate WMD and related material from entering subversive market complexes and into the hands of non-state actors. UNSCR 1540, as well as other updates in the form of resolutions 1673 (2006) and 1810 (2008), stipulated that all states: thwart non-state actors from procuring access to nuclear, chemical, or biological weapons and their delivery systems; implement laws prohibiting such access; and implement other related state mechanisms to this end. Additionally, it required diligent reporting, as well as technical assistance via not just individual countries but also regional and subregional organizations. In essence,

UNSCR 1540 was (and is) about the consolidation and promotion of the physical protection of nuclear facilities around the world.[19]

SYRIA AND CHEMICAL WEAPONS

One of the most alarming developments to have brought the issue of chemical weapons to the fore in international security has been the actions of Assad's regime in Syria. Even before the world became aware of its use of chemical weapons on its own people in 2013, it was known—or at least speculated—that Syria had produced, stored, and weaponized chemical agents, stocks of nerve (sarin, VX) and blister (mustard gas) agents, possibly weaponized into bombs, shells, and missiles. As indicated earlier, most states that have had chemical weapons stockpiles in the past have had them destroyed, or are in the process of destroying such weapons under the Chemical Weapons Convention. A major policy concern of the international community has been the use or loss of control of chemical weapons stocks in Syria, which could have destabilizing ramifications for the Syrian people and adjoining states, as well as U.S. allies and forces in the region.

This was no more evident than in 2013 when it was discovered that the Syrian government had used chemical weapons against opposition forces and non-combatants. A U.N. inspection team began working in Syria on August 19, 2013, and completed their mission on August 31. The UN team's report confirmed the extensive use of sarin nerve agent against civilians in the Ghouta area of Damascus on August 21. U.S. president Barack Obama stated that the use of chemical weapons against the civilians would be met with consequences, including the potential use of military force. Despite initially leaning toward a force option, Obama eventually asked congressional leaders to postpone a vote to authorize the use of military force on September 10, so as to provide the administration with the requisite time to explore a new diplomatic alternative. Indeed, in a diplomatic piece of maneuvering, it was revealed that Syrian foreign minister Walid Mouallem had accepted a proposal by the Russians in which Syria would relinquish its chemical weapons for international control and the administered destruction of such weapons. Secretary of State John Kerry and Russian foreign minister Sergey Lavrov agreed on the Framework for Elimination of Syrian Chemical Weapons, which specified the terms pertaining to the implementation of chemical weapons destruction in Syria—including verification, inspectors' access, destruction method and location, and the security of international personnel. Not surprising, one of the main concerns pertaining to securing such weapons was their potential—amid a civil war—to be diverted to a non-state actor should stability completely deteriorate. Moreover, there was also apprehension that Syria could shift some of its chemical weapons to Hezbollah in Lebanon.[20]

Notwithstanding the fact that Syria remains in a state of chaos amid sectarian/intra-state conflict—and that 400,000-plus people have perished in the conflict—the regime did manage to meet many of the final stipulations associated with the September 2013 chemical disarmament agreement endorsed by the UN Security Council in Resolution 2118. The international community has overseen the abstraction and destruction of chemical weapons agents from Syria, and, as of September 24, 2015, 98.8 percent of all Category 1 and 2 declared chemicals had been dismantled.[21] Further removal and destruction of chemical weapons facilities is still taking place,[22] although the United States has at varying intervals queried the legitimacy of Syria's declarations pertaining to *all* of its chemical weapons stocks. According to Amy Smithson of the James Martin Center for Nonproliferation Studies (CNS), "Syria could keep inspectors away from certain areas of production facilities if it declares to the OPCW that those sites have nothing to do with chemical weapons."[23] Additionally, Zachary Kallenborn and Raymond Zilinskas argue, "lessons from the Iraq and Libyan cases suggest that while verifying the correctness of a state's declarations is feasible, it is only possible for inspectors to have a limited degree of certainty in assessing the completeness of state declarations. As such, there is some risk, as occurred in the Libyan case, that the regime could successfully retain a secret CW capability."[24]

Further concerns became particularly noticeable with the revelation of a video posted online by opposition activists, showing what appeared to be airborne chlorine gas in the Hama province village of Kfar Zeita.[25] In response to this incident and other claims of chlorine usage, the Organisation for the Prohibition of Chemical Weapons (OPCW) investigation revealed that chlorine gas was indeed used in a "systematic manner" throughout the year.[26] While chlorine is not a restricted chemical under the CWC and was therefore not removed from Syria following the agreement between the United States and Russia, the CWC nonetheless bans the use of *any* chemical in warfare.[27] In a positive development, the Assad regime did proceed to reveal previously undisclosed chemical-weapons-related facilities and, as of September 2015, ten of twelve facilities were destroyed, with plans already drafted for the termination of the others when security conditions permitted admission. Not surprisingly, opposition actors and the Syrian government have continued to exchange arguments about new chemical attacks in 2015. As such, the OPCW continues to appraise and apportion responsibility for reported chemical attacks.[28]

NUCLEAR TERRORISM

The peaceful demise of the Cold War did not mean the end of nuclear threats to global security. To quote former British prime minister Tony Blair's defense of his government's plan to update and replace the United Kingdom's Trident nuclear weapons system: "There is also a new and potentially hazardous threat from states such as North Korea which claims already to have developed nuclear weapons or Iran which is in breach of its non-proliferation duties," not to mention the "possible connection between some of those states and international terrorism." Add to this, stateless terrorist organizations bent on acquiring the means of mass murder and black-market networks of renegade suppliers only too willing to deal in the materials and technical expertise that lead to nuclear weapons, and the picture becomes disturbingly clearer. The ensuing nightmare of responding to the humanitarian, law and order, and logistical challenges of a nuclear detonation could materialize quite unexpectedly and spectacularly, in any large city, paling the experience of 9/11.

As such, there is an expanding and persistent global apprehension pertaining to nuclear terrorism. The anxiety is vindicated. There are clandestine actors who would, if they could, wield immense and undiscriminating destruction in almost any one of the world's major centers. And if their preparedness was supported by the resources and the capacity to undertake an extreme and violent act, the scenario(s) would be disastrous. In specific terms, it is not far-fetched that a terrorist actor could produce a "dirty bomb," merging conventional explosives with radioactive material, so as to engender overwhelming physical and psychological consequence. Of course, while their ability to produce a far more materially destructive nuclear explosion is significantly reduced, particularly in relation to overcoming the practical and logistical difficulties, it is not impossible. Additionally, the prospect of cyber attacks on nuclear command and control centers is a consideration that all states have had to factor in to their security calculi. In the context of nuclear weapons, this scenario would necessitate a sophisticated, systematized, and "capitalized" group to construct and/or buy such a weapon, while maintaining security at all stages, from transportation through to the proposed site for detonation. It is now known that Al-Qaeda some years ago endeavored to acquire enriched uranium, and that senior members of the group had at least one meeting with two Pakistani nuclear experts. While this group has significantly deteriorated—after being under siege for most of the last decade and a half—there have been other imitators and adaptations who, if they could attain such weapons, would use them without any threshold of restraint.[29]

The threat presented by any such group could be significantly heightened by state backing, whether for nuclear materials or know-how, or merely for the required capital. That said, the amount of states likely to provide the measured provision of this type would be minimal. Even those regimes with an extensive record of recalcitrant behavior would be unlikely to advance such support without making a calculation of the likely ramifications should they be identified—including the likelihood of a nuclear reprisal (the chances of which would be likely if those states were already nuclear-armed themselves). An additional concern is that states with frail or delicate institutions, numerous power centers, and defective provisions for fortifying weapons and hazardous materials might end up providing such backing even in the absence of any obvious government intent or direction to do so. Despite the fact that many states have made extensive adjustments to the counterterrorism approaches, the evolving nature of terrorism some ten to twenty years down the track may well be significantly different than today—the ISIS example being a case point. As stated by Evan and Kawaguchi, in offering another scenario, "The politics of war and peace, and of security, may well shift from religion-based terrorism to eco-terrorism. In this scenario, there may be an even greater prospect that scientific and technical personnel from the richest countries will aid eco-terrorist use of nuclear weapons or materials."[30]

NEW YORK CITY SCENARIO

Notwithstanding the evolution of terrorism, any attack of the nuclear kind would be catastrophic. For example, a relatively small nuclear weapon—say, in the order of a 150-kiloton bomb—constructed or stolen by terrorists, detonated in the heart of Manhattan, at the foot of the Empire State Building, at noon on a clear spring day, would have calamitous consequences. At the end of the first second, the shock wave, with an overpressure of 20psi at a distance of four-tenths of a mile from ground zero, would have destroyed the great landmarks of Manhattan, including the Empire State Building, Madison Square Gardens, Penn Central Railroad Station, and the incomparable New York Public Library. Most of the material that comprises these buildings would remain and pile up to the depth of hundreds of feet in places, but nothing inside this ring would be recognizable. Those caught outside the circle would be exposed to the full effects of the blast, including severe lung and ear drum damage, as well as exposure to flying debris. Those in the direct line of sight of the blast would be exposed to the thermal pulse and killed instantly while those shielded from some of the blast and thermal effects would be killed as buildings collapse. Roughly 75,000 New Yorkers would be killed. During the next fifteen seconds, the blast and firestorm would extend out for almost four miles, resulting in 750,000 additional fatalities and nearly 900,000 injuries. And this would just be the beginning of New York's problems.

The task of caring for the injured would literally be beyond the ability and perhaps even the imagination of the medical system to respond. All but one of Manhattan's large hospitals lie inside the blast area and would be completely destroyed. There aren't enough available hospital beds in all of New York and New Jersey for even the most critically wounded. The entire country only has a total of three thousand beds in burn centers; thousands would die from lack of medical attention. Meanwhile, most of New York would be without electricity, gas, water, or sewage. Transportation of the injured and the ability to bring in necessary supplies, people, and equipment would be problematic. Tens of thousands of New Yorkers would be homeless. The tasks of the emergency responders, in areas that remain dangerously radioactive, would pose almost insuperable problems.

The terrorists' explosion would have produced much more early radioactive fallout than a similar sized air burst where the fireball never touches the ground. This is because a surface explosion produces radioactive particles from the ground as well as from the weapon. The early fallout would drift back to earth on the prevailing wind, creating an elliptical pattern stretching from ground zero out into Long Island. Because the wind would be relatively light, the fallout would be concentrated in the area of Manhattan, just to the east of the blast. Thousands of New Yorkers would suffer serious radiation sickness effects, including chromosomal damage, marrow and intestine destruction, and hemorrhaging. Many would die in days and the weeks ahead. Each survivor of the blast would have on average about a 20 percent chance of dying of cancer of one form or another and another 80 percent probability of dying instead from other causes such as heart disease and infection.

OBAMA AND NON-STATE ACTORS

Recognizing the grave security impact of a nuclear terrorist attack—such as the New York scenario—a central tenet of Obama's Prague vision focused on non-state actors and the necessity of impeding their ability to attain a nuclear weapon, and more specifically, their associated materials. Defined as one of the most immediate and extreme threats to global security, Obama argued, a subnational actor with just one nuclear weapon could wield a massive wave of destruction on "New York or Moscow, Islamabad or Mumbai, Tokyo or Tel Aviv, Paris or Prague—could kill hundreds of thousands of people." As a means to maintain "our security, our society, our economy . . . our ultimate survival," Obama put forward his blueprint for securing all vulnerable nuclear materials, including establishing new standards for cooperating with Russia, while undertaking new partnerships as a means to "lock down these sensitive materials." Additionally, he pointed to expanding efforts in breaking up black markets, detecting and intercepting materials while in transit, and utilizing financial technology to dislocate and undermine link-ages in capital.[31] In adding detail to this plan, the president called for the existing processes of the Proliferation Security Initiative (PSI) and the Global Initiative to Combat Nuclear Terrorism to be reinvigorated into "durable international institutions." He also put forward his administration's commit-ment to orchestrating a global summit on nuclear security that would come in the form of four Nuclear Security Summits held in Washington, DC, Seoul, The Hague, and again in DC in April 2016.

If strengthening the U.S. commitment to the NPT regime was a signifi-cant component of Obama's Prague agenda, nuclear terrorism was defined by the president as "the most immediate and extreme threat to global secur-ity."[32] Indeed, the Obama administration made a sustained effort to remove and eliminate vulnerable nuclear material through other initiatives. It played an assertive role in upgrading security at nuclear facilities throughout the world and converting research reactors from HEU to Low-Enriched Uranium (LEU), with a "special emphasis on capacity-building."[33] Obama also en-couraged the development of national Counter Nuclear Smuggling teams and, via initiatives such as the Nuclear Smuggling Outreach Initiative, at-tempted to strengthen and facilitate national government capacities in pre-venting, detecting, and responding to trafficking. Additionally, there was an emphasis on continuing to work closely with other governments and interna-tional organizations—such as the IAEA—to strengthen nuclear security and the Financial Action Task Force (FATF) as a means to produce a framework for international cooperation on illicit financing networks that support nucle-ar smuggling or other proliferation activity.[34]

Obama was also consistent in encouraging states to implement their bind-ing non-proliferation obligations in UNSCR 1540, including prevention of nuclear smuggling. Through the G8 Global Partnership Against the Spread of Weapons of Mass Destruction in 2012, the administration sought ways it could assist the 1540 Committee in helping willing states strengthen their capacity to prevent the proliferation of WMDs, including a contribution of an additional $1.5 million to the UN's voluntary Trust Fund for Global and Regional Disarmament to support UNSCR 1540 implementation activities. Outside the of the Nuclear Security Summit framework, the Obama adminis-tration continued to press for the provisions of the International Convention for the Suppression of Acts of Nuclear Terrorism (ICSANT) and the Amend-ment to the Convention on the Physical Protection of Nuclear Materials (CPPNM), urging other states to sign and ratify these treaties as soon as possible. Further developments were also evident in its efforts to strengthen the Global Initiative to Combat Nuclear Terrorism (GICNT) and build its capacity to prevent, detect, and respond to a nuclear terrorism threat or exe-cuted attack via eighty-five partner nations involved in the initiative. Finally, through initiatives such as the Export Control and Related Border Security program, the Second Line of Defense and the Megaports Initiative, the administration worked to secure international land borders, seaports, and airports and enhance global capacity to detect and respond to smuggling activities.[35]

PROLIFERATION SECURITY INITIATIVE (PSI)

Other attempts to secure nuclear material were evident in the Proliferation Security Initiative (PSI). Launched on May 31, 2003, the PSI is a multilateral grouping aimed at mitigating the trafficking of WMDs, their delivery systems, and related materials to and from states and non-state actors of proliferation concern. U.S. involvement in the PSI derives from the Bush administration's National Strategy to Combat Weapons of Mass Destruction (NSCWMD) issued in December 2002, a strategy that pressed for more vigorous tools to thwart the proliferation of WMDs on a global scale and specified interdiction as a key area of focus. While considered by many as an artery of the "Bush Doctrine," the PSI secured a strong proponent in the Obama administration. In his April 2009 Prague speech, Obama called for the PSI to continue as an enduring international counterproliferation effort. As such, in supporting the PSI, a state must also endorse the PSI Statement of Interdiction Principles and thereby commit itself to establishing a coordinated and effective basis through which to stymie WMDs, their delivery systems, and related items. As signified by the U.S. State Department, these principles encompass the interdiction of transfers to and from states and non-state actors of proliferation concern and require: an improvement of the broader capabilities and legal authorities within that state; the development of procedures to facilitate exchange of information with other states; the strengthening of national legal authorities to facilitate interdiction; and the implementation of specific actions in support of interdiction efforts.[36]

The Obama administration argued that the PSI's impact could be improved by eradicating double standards, increasing transparency, and establishing an impartial organization to evaluate intelligence, coordinate and fund activities, and make recommendations or decisions regarding specific or generic interdictions, perhaps even based on the committee set up to oversee implementation of UN Security Council Resolution 1540.[37] Indeed, in emboldening the initiative's effectiveness, guaranteeing even participation, or sustaining the effort over time, a formal multilateral framework is imperative. In this regard, Obama said the PSI should be turned into an "international institution" that facilitates a criteria-based approach to cooperation agreements with states outside the NPT, compliance to end unsafeguarded fissile material production, securing nuclear facilities and materials, and controlling nuclear related exports.[38]

Interdicting shipments of dangerous materials, disrupting proliferation networks, closing down the masking companies that support them, and, ultimately, creating a web of counter-proliferation partnerships through which proliferators will have difficulty undertaking trade in WMD and missile-related technology, have all been critical components of the PSI.[39] Here, states are required to work together in a concerted fashion so as to strengthen their respective national capacities to interdict WMD shipment using a "broad range of legal, diplomatic, economic, military and other tools."[40] Moreover, in driving interdiction efforts the PSI requires participating states to agree to: review their own national legal authorities so as to ensure that they can take action; resolve "to seriously consider providing consent under the appropriate circumstances to the boarding and searching of its own flag vessels by other states, and to the seizure of such WMD-related cargoes in such vessels that may be identified by such states";[41] seek to implement agreements, such as ship-boarding agreements, with other states in advance, so that no time is lost should interdiction be required; and participate in joint interdiction exercises.[42]

Some analysts, such as Matthew Bunn, argued that that Obama administration's progress in driving the PSI produced mixed results, although there have been some related "wins" outside of the PSI specifically. For example, the Financial Action Task Force—an international body established in 1989 that includes thirty-six nations—has, according to Bunn, "expanded from dealing with laundering of drug money to dealing with terrorism financing and now to proliferation financing."[43] Notwithstanding the apparent limitations and criticisms, the administration remained firm in emphasizing its mission to strengthen and expand the PSI and "ensuring that it remains an effective tool to stop WMD proliferation." As with many of the agreements and initiatives, the key to success comes down to implementation. In this regard, the administration, particularly since 2010, has pushed "counter-proliferation efforts across the U.S. Government, by contributing military, customs, law enforcement, and other security experts and assets to interdiction exercises, by hosting PSI meetings, workshops, and exercises with other PSI-endorsing states, and by working with specific partner states to improve their capacity for combating the proliferation of WMD."[44] Indeed, while there is no doubt that Obama "institutionalized" the PSI in terms of publicizing its significance, signing applicable agreements with other states, and, overall, shifting it toward a stronger multilateral initiative that will be "enduring," improving the capacity to evaluate, monitor, and assess the PSI's effectiveness will be crucial in attaining further political capital, legitimacy, and greater global traction.

NUCLEAR SECURITY SUMMITS 2010, 2012, 2014

Should such terrorist actors strive for some form of nuclear device, the ability to acquire the requisite fissile material and the engineering expertise needed to make the device work remain critical barriers.[45] But as already indicated, this task is not impossible. In referring again to the significant landmark editorial published in the *Wall Street Journal* in 2007, George Shultz, William Perry, Henry Kissinger, and Sam Nunn argued that there must be an acceleration of "the highest possible standards of security for nuclear weapons [and] nuclear materials everywhere in the world, to prevent terrorists from acquiring a nuclear bomb."[46] In July 2009, building on this blueprint, President Obama proposed a summit to challenge world leaders by discussing "steps . . . to secure loose nuclear materials; combat smuggling; and deter, detect, and disrupt attempts at nuclear terrorism."[47] On April 12 and 13, 2010, the United States hosted the first Nuclear Security Summit in Washington, DC, bringing together forty-nine world leaders in an effort to foster cooperation and consensus on one further step toward nuclear zero. According to David Sanger, the summit was the largest gathering of heads of states called by a U.S. president since the 1945 United Nations Conference on International Organization.[48] Aside from the United States, delegations from forty-six governments attended and, of these, thirty-eight were represented by heads of state or government.[49] Additionally, representatives from the European Union, the IAEA, and the United Nations were also in attendance.

The Obama administration specifically excluded three states from the "guest list" who were deemed as noncompliant with their international obligations: Iran, North Korea, and Syria. In the lead-up to the conference, the United States and other members of the UN Security Council held discussions on whether to proceed with additional sanctions against Iran for its purported failure to comply with earlier UN resolutions and IAEA investigations.[50] In response, Iranian officials argued that any state not included in the Washington nuclear summit would not be locked in to the final result and that Iran would hold its own two-day conference called Nuclear Energy for Everyone, Nuclear Arms for No One on April 17–18, 2010.[51] Iran announced that sixty states had been invited, and China—a key holdout on new sanctions against Iran—had already agreed to attend. Despite the myriad of peripheral issues, the primary focus of the Obama-led two-day conference was the threat of the attainment of unsecured nuclear material. In his opening message at the conference, Obama emphasized that the security concerns posed by such nuclear materials should they be attained "sold or stolen and fashioned into a nuclear weapon exist in dozens of nations." Only the smallest amount of plutonium, he argued, "about the size of an apple," could kill and injure hundreds of thousands of innocent people. Subnational terrorist networks such as Al-Qaeda have attempted to obtain "the material for a nuclear weapon, and if they ever succeeded, they would surely use it. Were they to do so, it would be a catastrophe for the world—causing extraordinary loss of life, and striking a major blow to global peace and stability."[52] This dire warning captured the attention of most of the press coverage during the summit and underscored the urgency felt by the administration on matters of nuclear terrorism.

The Nuclear Security Summit (NSS) process was orchestrated by Barack Obama in 2009 and concluded in April 2016. It brought together more than fifty world leaders at four heads-of-state-level summits—Washington, DC (2010), Seoul (2012), The Hague (2014), and Washington, DC, again (2016)—in the quest to decrease the risk of nuclear and radiological terrorism via state initiatives and international collaboration. Over the journey of the first three summits, nuclear security pledges expanded in scope, where state assurances put forward at the first summit in April 2010 translated into more substantive multinational commitments during the 2012 and 2014 summits. Referred to as "house gifts" and "gift baskets," such commitments have engendered the most defining outcomes from the NSS process and have emboldened the security of nuclear and radiological materials and facilities on a global scale. Despite not being legally binding, the commitments conveyed at each summit were politically binding—declared by the states' head of state or senior officials—and at the following summit, there was an implicit expectancy that leaders would return and articulate how their respective actions in supporting NSS goals had fared.[53]

The objective of emboldening nuclear security processes through "responsible national actions and sustained and effective international cooperation" was stipulated at the 2010 NSS consensus communiqué, including the aim to "secure all vulnerable nuclear material in four years."[54] While fissile material elimination and fortification efforts subjugated the initial emphasis of the summit process, the agenda progressively expanded to encompass radiological sources, the nuclear safety and security interface, as well as varying international governance issues. Longstanding fissile material repatriation goals were augmented during the summits and became superlative announcements for leaders attending Washington (2010), Seoul (2012), and The Hague (2014). While the "four year goal" to lock down weapons-usable materials in civil programs was defined as an accomplishment by governments at the 2014 summit, a fourth summit was planned for March 31–April 1, 2016, to formulate action plans for existing international organizations after the summit process concluded.[55]

As touched on in the above, a key feature of the summit process was the emergence of "gift basket diplomacy" at the 2012 Seoul summit. In what can be considered an extension of the national commitment tradition established at the Washington summit, "gift baskets" involved multinational commitments by clusters of states that delivered joint statements articulating their common priorities, shared goals, and the actions they would undertake in meeting them. As a seemingly new form of commitment, the "baskets" spurred extensive interest around the summit outcomes in 2012 and 2014. This was evident in 2012, where thirteen gift baskets were offered, encompassing a wide spectrum of points, including: nuclear information security, counter nuclear smuggling, and educational outreach. Some groups of states used the gift basket approach to collaborate and impart knowledge on efforts they were undertaking in meeting NSS goals. These included the joint statements posited by the Global Initiative to Combat Nuclear Terrorism; Global Partnership against the Spread of Materials and Weapons of Mass Destruction; and a trilateral initiative by Russia, Kazakhstan, and the United States on the safeguarding of the Semipalatinsk test site. Other announcements articulated support and leadership on improving efforts around specific nuclear security issues, such as training and support centers, national legislation implementation, and radioactive source security. Several declarations were quite specific in terms of setting the types of efforts that its signatories would complete—specifically technical projects pertaining to low-enriched uranium (LEU) fuel production and transitioning medical isotope production from using HEU to LEU. At the 2014 summit, fourteen gift baskets were presented, many of which were apprises to the multilateral commitments from the preceding summit, as well as further actions to be completed by the DC return summit of 2016. New gift basket areas announced in 2014 included the security of the maritime supply chain, nuclear forensics, and supporting implementation of United Nations Security Council Resolution (UNSCR) 1540 (2004).[56]

NUCLEAR SECURITY SUMMIT OF 2016

The Focus

President Obama referred to the 2016 return summit at Washington, DC, as the "Transition Summit." It was envisaged that summit participants would again discuss ways to embolden international efforts, assess new national commitments, and, overall, review the degree to which past commitments had actually been met. Reported efforts of terrorist actors such as the Islamic State attempting to secure radiological materials was also on the agenda. In terms of tangible outcomes for the summit, action plans for the five international organizations and arrangements that make up the "global nuclear security architecture"—the United Nations, the IAEA, Interpol, the Global Initiative to Combat Nuclear Terrorism, and the Global Partnership against the Spread of Weapons and Materials of Mass Destruction—were posited. Once the summit process ended, future nuclear security activities would take place through these mechanisms, but mainly through the IAEA, the first of which was held in December 2016. The summit process would continue to reaffirm its commitment to emboldening nuclear security measures, specifically, actions to prevent theft or diversion of nuclear material or sabotage at an installation or in transit. On a broader nuclear security level, measures to mitigate and detect illicit trafficking—cargo inspections, border security, and interdiction measures—would also be discussed. "Nuclear security culture" was also emphasized, whereby the improvement in nuclear security practices could stymie insider threat of theft or diversion. Other nuclear and radiological source security measures pertained to training for those handling the materials, detection of smuggled material, nuclear forensics, emergency response, and cyber-security at nuclear facilities. [57]

The Outcomes

While the fourth and final Nuclear Security Summit saw some significant progress, there were also some shortcomings. On the positive side, the 2005 Amendment to the Physical Protection Convention was finally brought into force, providing a stronger legal foundation for nuclear security efforts, as well as a review conference that could ultimately contribute to a more robust nuclear security architecture. In terms of state specifics, China and India joined the strengthening Nuclear Security Implementation Initiative, where they would work toward meeting the objectives of International Atomic Energy Agency (IAEA) nuclear security recommendations and accept peer appraisals of its nuclear security provisions. Japan and the United States revealed that it had removed hundreds of kilograms of weapon-grade plutonium and highly enriched uranium (HEU) from the Fast Critical Assembly in Japan. Additionally, Japan also committed to eliminating the HEU at the critical assembly at Kyoto University. States agreed to eighteen new gift baskets on matters extending across mitigating insider threats to exchanging radiological sources with less dangerous technologies. Possibly the furthermost significant of these was the pledge to create a Nuclear Security Contact Group, involving a cohort of senior states people who would liaise in the wings of the IAEA General Conference so as to maintain momentum on nuclear security. [58]

In terms of what could be considered as shortcomings of the Nuclear Security Summit of 2016, there was still no progress in regard to creating a global obligation that *all* nuclear weapons and weapons-usable nuclear materials, regardless of geography, need to be secured against the full range of credible adversarial threats. While the communiqué did resolutely emphasize the goal of incessant improvement in nuclear security, there were no new commitments. Regarding the "action plans" for the five abovementioned international institutions, the steps posited in many ways reaffirmed what they are already doing and were significantly uninspiring given the vacuum left with the summit process' conclusion.

Additionally, many of the gift baskets were vague in their specifics or deadlines, nor detailed enough on the actions they would undertake in driving progress toward their objectives. Disappointingly, key nuclear states such as Pakistan and Russia continued to remain outside the initiative on strengthening nuclear security implementation.[59] The Russian status, not to mention non-attendance at the summit, was most concerning; particularly given the significance and necessity in having *both* Russia and the United States attending such meetings and engaging in ongoing critical fora. As stated by Matthew Bunn: "In a world grappling with threats from the Islamic State and other terrorist groups, it is essential that the two countries with the world's largest nuclear stockpiles and the world's greatest stores of experience in nuclear security find ways to work together to keep nuclear weapons and materials out of terrorist hands."[60]

NOTES

1. "Biosecurity: Balancing the Promise of Biotechnology with Preventing the Biological Weapons Threat," *Nuclear Threat Initiative (NTI)*, October 2016, http://www.nti.org/about/biosecurity/.

2. "The Biological Threat: Germs Don't Respect Borders, so Biological Threats—Manmade and Naturally Occurring—Can Quickly Have Global Impacts," *Nuclear Threat Initiative (NTI)*, October 2016, http://www.nti.org/learn/biological/.

3. "The Chemical Threat: Why These Banned Weapons Just Won't Go Away," *Nuclear Threat Initiative (NTI)*, October 2016, http://www.nti.org/learn/chemical/.

4. Richard Dean Burns, *The Evolution of Arms Control: From Antiquity to the Nuclear Age* (Santa Barbara, CA: Praeger Security International, 2009). The authors are especially indebted to Professor Burns for sharing his expert knowledge on this subject matter.

5. Adrienne Mayor, *Greek Fire, Poison Arrows & Scorpion Bombs* (New York: Overlook Books, 2003), 33; Maurice R. Davie, *Evolution of War: A Study of Its Role in Early Societies* (New Haven: Yale University Press, 1929), 182.

6. *Odyssey* 1, lines 260–63. See F. Keller, *Homeric Society* (New York: Longman, 1915), 298; Mayor, *Greek Fire, Poison Arrows & Scorpion Bombs*, 35.

7. John Ellis van Courtland Moon, "Controlling Chemical and Biological Weapons through World War II," in *Encyclopedia of Arms Control and Disarmament*, ed. Richard Dean Burns, 3 vols. (New York: Scribner's Sons, 1993), II: 657–74. See W. Hays Parks, "The Law of War," in *Encyclopedia of Arms Control and Disarmament*, ed. Richard Dean Burns, 3 vols. (New York: Scribner's Sons, 1993), II: 1053–68.

8. Paris, Archive de l'Academy, Registre, 1790, fols. 238–39; J. L. Kunz, "The Chaotic Status of the Laws of War and the Urgent Necessity for Their Revision," *American Journal of International Law* (January 1931): 44.

9. Moon, "Controlling Chemical and Biological Weapons Through World War II," II: 659; Jacques G. Richardson, "The Bane of 'Inhumane' Weapons and Overkill: An Overview of Increasingly Lethal Arms and the Inadequacy of Regulatory Controls," *Science and Engineering Ethics* 10, no. 4 (December 2004): 672–73.

10. Frederic J. Brown, *Chemical Warfare: A Study in Restraints* (Princeton, NJ: Princeton University Press, 1968), 233; Thomas H. Buckley, *The United States and the Washington Conference, 1921–1922* (Knoxville: University of Tennessee Press, 1970), 124–25.

11. Moon, "Controlling Chemical and Biological Weapons Through World War II," II: 664; Brown, *Chemical Warfare*, 3–49; Judith Miller, Stephen Engelberg, and William Broad, *Germs: Biological Weapons and America's Secret War* (New York: Simon & Schuster, 2001), 40–41, 166–67, 180; Sheldon H. Harris, *Factories of Death: Japanese Biological Warfare, 1932–45, and the American Cover-Up* (New York: Routledge, 1994).

12. Brown, *Chemical Warfare*, 237.

13. Ibid., 200–1, 230–38, 263–66.

14. Charles C. Flowerree, "Chemical and Biological Weapons and Arms Control," in *Encyclopedia of Arms Control and Disarmament*, ed. Richard Dean Burns, 3 vols. (New York: Scribner's Sons, 1993), II: 1005. See Thomas Graham Jr., *Disarmament Sketches: Three Decades of Arms Control and International Law* (Seattle: University of Washington Press, 2002), chapter 2.

15. U.S. Arms Control & Disarmament Agency, *Arms Control and Disarmament Agreements* (Washington, DC: GPO, 1982), 131.

16. Flowerree, "Chemical and Biological Weapons and Arms Control," II: 1004–6; Richardson, "The Bane of 'Inhumane' Weapons and Overkill," 677; Miller, Engelberg, and Broad, *Germs*, 73, 83–84, 150.

17. Allan S. Krass, *The United States and Arms Control: The Challenge of Leadership* (Westport, CT: Praeger, 1997), 57; Miller, Engelberg, and Broad, *Germs*, 63; Jonathan B. Tucker, "The Chemical Weapons Convention: Has It Enhanced U.S. Security?" *Arms Control Today* (April 2001): 8–12; Joby Warrick, "Albania's Farewell to Arms," *Washington Post National Weekly*, January 17–23, 2005, 6–7; "Abandoned Chemical Weapons in China," *SIPRI Yearbook, 2000*, 520; "Old Chemical Weapons," *SIPRI Yearbook, 1999*, 575.

18. "A Chronology of UN Inspections in Iraq," *Arms Control Today* (October 2002): 14–23. See chapter 3 in Lester Brune, *United States and Two Gulf Wars: Prelude and Aftermath* (Claremont, CA: Regina Books, 2007).

19. See Gareth Evans and Yoriko Kawaguchi, *Eliminating Nuclear Threats: A Practical Agenda for Global Policymakers, International Commission on Nuclear Non-Proliferation and Disarmament* (Canberra/Tokyo, 2009).

20. Mary Beth D. Nikitin, Paul K. Kerr, and Andrew Feickert, "Syria's Chemical Weapons: Issues for Congress," *CRS Report for Congress*, R42848 (Washington, DC: Congressional Research Service), September 30, 2013, https://www.fas.org/sgp/crs/nuke/R42848.pdf.

21. Progress in the elimination of the Syrian chemical weapons programme, September 23, 2015 in letter dated September 24, 2015, from the United Nations Secretary-General to the President of the Security Council, S/2015/737.

22. As of September 24, 2015, the OPCW reported that with respect to the twelve chemical weapons production facilities (CWPFs) [seven aircraft hangars and five underground structures], five of seven hangars had been destroyed along with all five underground structures; security conditions precluded safe access to two hangars. See Mary Beth D. Nikitin, Carla E. Humud, and Christopher M. Blanchard, "Armed Conflict in Syria: Overview and U.S." *CRS Report for Congress*, R L33487 (Washington, DC: Congressional Research Service), September 28, 2016, https://www.fas.org/sgp/crs/mideast/RL33487.pdf.

23. Amy Smithson, "A Phony Farewell to Arms," *Foreign Affairs*, October 1, 2013, www.foreignaffairs.com.

24. Zachary Kallenborn and Raymond Zilinskas, "Disarming Syria of its Chemical Weapons: Lessons Learned from Iraq and Libya," *Nuclear Threat Initiative (NTI)*, October 31, 2013, www.nti.org.

25. Oliver Holmes, "Syria Video Shows Chlorine Gas Floating in Streets: Activists," *Reuters* (Beirut), May 23, 2014, www.reuters.com.

26. Anne Gearan, "Syria Probably Used Chlorine Gas in Attacks This Year, Weapons Inspectors Say," *Washington Post*, June 18, 2014, www.washingtonpost.com.

27. Rick Gladstone, "Claims of Chlorine-Filled Bombs Overshadow Progress by Syria on Chemical Weapons," *New York Times*, April 22, 2014.

28. Nikitin, Humud, and Blanchard, "Armed Conflict in Syria: Overview and U.S."

29. Evans and Kawaguchi, *Eliminating Nuclear Threats*, 39.

30. Ibid.

31. Barack Obama, "Remarks By President Barack Obama," Hradčany Square, Prague, Czech Republic, The White House, Washington, DC, Office of the Press Secretary, April 5, 2009, http://www.whitehouse.gov/the_press_office/Remarks-By-President-Barack-Obama-In-Prague-As-Delivered/.

32. Ibid.

33. William J. Burns, "State's Burns at UN Meeting on Countering Nuclear Terrorism," UN Secretary-General's High-Level Meeting on Countering Nuclear Terrorism, New York, NY, September 28, 2012, http://iipdigital.usembassy.gov/st/english/texttrans/2012/09/20120929136851.html#axzz2Cuq7NE28.

34. Ibid.

35. Ibid.

36. U.S. Department of State, "Proliferation Security Initiative," Washington, DC, November 2012, http://www.state.gov/t/isn/c10390.htm.

37. Ibid.

38. Mary Beth Nikitin, "Proliferation Security Initiative (PSI)," *CRS Report for Congress*, RL34327 (Washington, DC: Congressional Research Service), June 15, 2012, 4, http://www.fas.org/sgp/crs/nuke/RL34327.pdf.

39. Ibid.

40. U.S. State Department, "Proliferation Security Initiative Frequently Asked Questions," Bureau of Non-Proliferation, Washington, DC, May 26, 2005, http://2001-2009.state.gov/t/isn/rls/fs/46839.htm.

41. U.S. Office of the Press Secretary, "Proliferation Security Initiative: Statement of Interdiction Principles," The White House, Washington, DC, September 4, 2003, http://www.state.gov/t/isn/c27726.htm.

42. Nikitin, "Proliferation Security Initiative (PSI)," 4–5.

43. Matthew Bunn, quoted in Louis Jacobson, "Rhetorical Support For WMD-Prevention Program, But Progress Hard To Document," *Tampa Bay Times*, November 15, 2012, http://www.politifact.com/truth-o-eter/promises/obameter/promise/192/strengthen-the-proliferation-security-initiative/.

44. U.S. Department of State, "Proliferation Security Initiative."

45. For example, the amount of fissile material required for one 15-kiloton atomic bomb built to a gun-type design (like that used on Hiroshima) would be around fifty kilograms of weapons-grade HEU (90 percent U-235); an implosion-type weapon of the same yield would require far less fissile material—around five kilograms of plutonium or fifteen kilograms.

46. George P. Schultz, William J. Perry, Henry A. Kissinger, and Sam Nunn, "A World Free of Nuclear Weapons," *The Wall Street Journal*, January 4, 2007, http://online.wsj.com/article/SB116787515251566636.html.

47. Barack Obama, "Press conference by President Obama in L'Aquila, Italy," Office of the Press Secretary, The White House, Washington, DC, July 10, 2009, http://www.whitehouse.gov/the_press_office/Press-Conference-by-the-President-in-LAquila-Italy-7-10-09/.

48. David Sanger and William J. Broad, "Leaders Gather for Nuclear Talks as New Threat is Seen," *New York Times*, April 11, 2010, http://www.nytimes.com/2010/04/12/world/12nuke.html.

49. Josh Rogin, "White House Announces Nuclear Summit Attendees," *Foreign Policy*, April 10, 2010, http://thecable.foreignpolicy.com/posts/2010/04/10/white_house_announces_nuclear_summit_attendees.

50. Sarah Diehl and Paula Humphrey, "The April 2010 Nuclear Security Summit: One More Step toward the Mountaintop," *Nuclear Threat Initiative (NTI)*, April 20, 2010, http://www.nti.org/analysis/articles/april-2010-nuclear-security-summit/.

51. Scott Peterson, "Iran Denounces Washington Nuclear Summit, Prepares Its Own," *The Christian Science Monitor*, April 12, 2010, http://www.csmonitor.com/World/Middle-East/2010/0412/Iran-denounces-Washington-nuclear-summit-prepares-its-own.

52. Barack Obama, "Remarks by the President at the Opening Plenary Session of the Nuclear Security Summit," Office of the Press Secretary, The White House, Washington, DC, April 13, 2010, http://www.whitehouse.gov/the-press-office/remarks-president-opening-plenary-session-nuclear-security-summit.

53. Michelle Cann, Kelsey Davenport, and Jenna Parker, "The Nuclear Security Summit: Accomplishments of the Process," an Arms Control Association and Partnership for Global Security Report, March 2016, 2, https://pgstest.files.wordpress.com/2016/03/nss-report-final.pdf.

54. Quoted in Cann, Davenport, and Parker, "The Nuclear Security Summit."

55. Ibid.

56. Ibid.

57. Mary Beth D. Nikitin, "The March 2016 Nuclear Security Summit," *CRS Insight Report for Congress*, IN10463 (Washington, DC: Congressional Research Service), March 14, 2016, https://www.fas.org/sgp/crs/nuke/IN10463.pdf.

58. Matthew Bunn, "The Nuclear Security Summit: Wins, Losses, and Draws," *Bulletin of the Atomic Scientists*, April 8, 2016, http://thebulletin.org/nuclear-security-summit-wins-losses-and-draws9310.

59. Ibid.

60. Ibid.

Conclusion

Although coming precariously close to nuclear conflict, the "clarity" of the Cold War era gave way to the ambiguities and uncertainties of a world where global security is now threatened by regime collapse, nuclear terrorism, new nuclear weapons states, regional conflict, and preexisting nuclear arsenals. The dangers inherent in such a mix are in themselves greatly magnified by easier access to nuclear technology, inadequately protected stockpiles of plutonium and highly enriched uranium, the growing availability of missiles worldwide, black market nuclear supply networks, and a trend toward acquisition of "latent" nuclear weapons capabilities through the possession of the entire nuclear fuel cycle. The results are clear: of all the potential threats to the global community today (including global warming), nuclear weapons—the most deadly weapon ever invented, and really the only true weapon of mass destruction—continue to pose the greatest risk.

Whatever else one has to say—and not much has been left unsaid about the nuclear security of the past seventy-plus years—nuclear status still imparts extraordinary prestige, power, and the security dilemma. The threat of terrorists with a WMD-type capability has given rise to a new global concern, where the risk of nuclear weapons or their associated materials falling into the hands of subversive actors cannot, and should not, be considered far-fetched. The smuggling or incremental theft of highly enriched uranium that could be used for a nuclear instrument of destruction has subsequently prompted great concern. In the years since the end of the Cold War, there have been numerous cases of theft of nuclear materials in which the thieves were captured, sometimes in Russia, on other occasions in the Czech Republic, Germany, and elsewhere.[1] As Mattew Bunn conveyed, "The biggest concern of major production, to my mind, is theft from the places where the material is being handled in bulk—the plants that produce it, convert it to metal, fabricate it into bomb parts, and so on." More alarmingly, "all but one of the real thefts" of HEU and plutonium "were insider thefts from bulk-handling facilities—that's where you can squirrel a little bit away without the loss being detected."[2] Not surprisingly, this scenario presents many questions: How effective are the methods employed to limit terrorist access to nuclear materials? How effective have the Cooperative Threat Reduction Program, Global Threat Reduction Initiative, and the Nuclear Suppliers Group been to this end? To what extent have the Nuclear Security Summits improved physical security and transparency?

As apprehensions pertaining to nuclear proliferation, nuclear terrorism, and the broader WMD "triad" continue to mount in the twenty-first century, there is of course the prospect of "nuclear alarmism" becoming perhaps "too extreme" in a state's security calculi—and as evident during the Bush administration's tenure, even misused for both political and securitization purposes. That said, according to William Potter and Gaukhar Mukhatzhanova, it is "hard to find an analyst or commentator on nuclear proliferation who is actually not pessimistic about the future." What apparently concerns these experts is that they find little in the current decades that offer means of containing nuclear proliferation. As stated by Francis Gavin, "During the Cold War, the world's security was built on a handful of interlocking truths that were dreadful to contemplate, but blessedly stable . . . every brick of that deterrent edifice is now crumbling."[3]

For Gareth Evans, the stark contrast of security threats emanating from nuclear proliferation on one hand, and limited—even insipid—responses by the global community on the other, illustrate the deterioration. In looking back to the early part of the millennium he argues that the period surrounding the breaking down of "the 2005 NPT Review Conference . . . without reaching substantive agreement on anything" and the failure of the UN World Summit "to say anything at all about nuclear non-proliferation or disarmament" during the same year, shifted the "first decade of the 21st century"— insofar as non-proliferation efforts—into a "slow-motion sleepwalk."[4] According to Robert Farley, this moribund status represented a *real* security threat, where for instance, "a genuine risk of accidents, especially for states that had not yet developed appropriately robust security precautions," could take place. "Instability and collapse in nuclear states" had been "harrowing in the past" and would undoubtedly be "harrowing in the future." In this regard, "all of these threats should" be treated with greater urgency "by policymakers" in the twenty-first century.[5]

Of course, outside of the state domain, but very much concerning to *all* states, are those materials associated with nuclear weapons and/or weapons that are chemical and biological in nature. Clearly the world has entered a new epoch of terrorism where certain actors are pursuing the capability to wreak maximum devastation in achieving their ends. While producing an unsophisticated nuclear bomb would not be a straightforward task, it is potentially within the proficiencies of a technically organized clandestine group. The main obstruction is securing the requisite nuclear material—although there have been many instances in which kilogram amounts of plutonium or highly enriched uranium (HEU) have been appropriated. The nuclear material for such a device is small and challenging to identify, making it a significant task to effectively mitigate its trafficking, or to convalesce such nuclear material after it has been stolen. The ramifications of an explosion of even a makeshift terrorist nuclear bomb would be extreme, turning a modern city into a fuming "radioactive ruin and sending reverberating economic and political aftershocks around the world."[6] As non-state actors continue to morph, regenerate, and redefine themselves in different forms, the challenge will only become more abstract. In the context of the most recent and emerging threat, ISIS, while there is no definitive evidence that the group is pursuing a nuclear weapon, inquiries into nuclear, chemical, and biological materials by the group have been made. Additionally, its apocalyptic orotundity, envisaging a war between itself and the "crusader" forces, signifies a real desire for devastating weapons and their associated materials. While the "terrorist use of nuclear weapons may not be a high probability—the global economic, political, and social consequences would be so severe that even a low probability should be enough to motivate an intense focus on steps such as nuclear security to reduce the risk."[7]

The associated threats of the biological, chemical, and other non-nuclear forms, such as cyber and drone attacks, also represent a group of weapons that, while not being able to wield as much physical devastation as nuclear weapons, could have a massive impact on a targeted populace. Indeed, certain forms of biological weapons, such as weaponized smallpox or anthrax, could cause extensive harm to millions of people depending on the city and, of course, density of the population. Chemical weapons, such as those used in Syria, and possession of blistering agents (mustard sulfur) and nerve agents—specifically sarin and VX (the latter is the most toxic chemical agent)—enable them to also have a massive physical and psychological impact.[8] Chemical weapons are often referred to as the "poor man's nuclear weapons," and the core legal instruments against chemical and biological warfare (CBW) are the 1993 Chemical Weapons Convention (CWC) and the 1972 Biological and Toxin Weapons Convention (BTWC). They inform the consideration of CBW threats and responses and efforts to ensure that science and technology are not misused for intimidating purposes or as a device of asymmetrical warfare.[9] Most concerning is that because such devices can be manufactured utilizing civilian technology and materials, stymying such threats as they develop remains a complex proposition, particularly as their production does not require substantive operations and thus makes it difficult to locate and detect their covert activity.[10]

In reconsidering what lies ahead for the most significant arm of the WMD group—nuclear weapons—there is much to be concerned about. It is almost fifty years since the five affirmed nuclear-weapon states in 1968 covenanted under the Nuclear Non-Proliferation Treaty (NPT) to "pursue negotiations in good faith on effective measures relating to cessation of the nuclear arms race at an early date and to nuclear disarmament."[11] Yet, it is very evident that all of the nuclear-weapon states are diligently modernizing their stockpiles and continue to reiterate the prominence of such weapons in their security repertoires. In fact, none of them is prepared to jettison its nuclear weapons in the conceivable future, nor even move robustly in such a direction. Despite the nuclear arms race that was an intrinsic part of the Cold War being well and truly over—with France, Russia, the United Kingdom, and the United States all reducing their stockpiles markedly—the arsenals remain significantly large, especially in Russia and the United States. Twenty-five years after the end of the Cold War there are at least 15,000 nuclear warheads still in existence, with a combined blast capacity equivalent to 100,000 Hiroshima bombs.[12]

At the same time, China, India, North Korea, Pakistan, and possibly Israel are building up their arsenal, while all nuclear-armed states continue to use rhetoric that if not overt or boldly pronounced, has been "hedged" enough to at least indicate that nuclear weapons will remain "an enduring and indefinite aspect of national and international security."[13] Equally concerning is that non-nuclear-weapon states that openly demand for movements toward nuclear disarmament also continue to call on nuclear-armed partners to defend them with nuclear weapons. Additionally, five non-nuclear-weapon states in NATO continue to work as "harborers" of nuclear-weapon states by providing their military forces with the requisite capabilities to deliver U.S. nuclear weapons in times of conflict—an arrangement accepted during the Cold War but completely incongruous in the post–Cold War era. Not to mention that such arrangements are completely at odds with NATO/U.S. proclamations that endorse the firm observance to non-proliferation norms as being a central pillar for international security.

The modernization reality only reemphasizes the fact that nuclear weapons remain a threat to global security, despite being some twenty-five-plus years on from the end of the Cold War. As signified in the earlier stages of this book, there are certainly substantially fewer nuclear weapons today than during the Cold War era, but the overall dangers of nuclear security have in many ways expanded: where non-state actors continue to pursue them, more states in more volatile parts of the world have attained such weapons, and the command and control systems in even the most erudite nuclear-armed states remain vulnerable to not only system and human error but, increasingly, to cyberattack.[14] However, it is the failure of *existing* nuclear-armed states to disarm (while busily modernizing) and the inability to inhibit *new* states from obtaining nuclear weapons that pose immense challenges to meeting NPT obligations and attaining some semblance of global security. Indeed, without a definitive set of restrictions on the pace and scope of nuclear modernization, the goals of deep cuts in, and eventual elimination of, nuclear weapons remain intangible and increasingly improbable. In this regard, the unremitting reassertion of the significance of nuclear weapons, sustained by an amplified global nuclear rivalry, threatens to extend the nuclear era indefinitely into the twenty-first century.[15]

NOTES

1. Graham Allison, *Nuclear Terrorism: The Ultimate Preventable Catastrophe* (New York: Times Books, 2004), 1.

2. David E. Sanger and Eric Schmitt, "Pakistani Nuclear Arms Pose Challenge to US Policy," *New York Times*, January 31, 2011, http://www.nytimes.com/2011/02/01/world/asia/01policy.html?pagewanted=all.

3. Francis Gavin, "Same as It Ever Was," *International Security* 34, no. 3 (Winter 2009/10): 7–9.

4. Gareth Evans and Yoriko Kawaguchi, *Eliminating Nuclear Threats: A Practical Agenda for Global Policymakers, International Commission on Nuclear Non-Proliferation and Disarmament* (Canberra/Tokyo, 2009), 6.

5. Robert Farley, "Iran and the Nuclear Paradox," *World Politics Review*, Special Report, January 3, 2012: 10.

6. Matthew Bunn, Martin B. Malin, Nickolas Roth, and William H. Tobey, *Preventing Nuclear Terrorism Continuous Improvement or Dangerous Decline?* Project on Managing the Atom, Belfer Center for Science and International Affairs Harvard Kennedy School, March 2016, http://www.belfercenter.ksg.harvard.edu/files/PreventingNuclearTerrorism-Web.pdf.

7. Ibid.

8. "Biological, Chemical, & Other Non-Nuclear Threats," Federation of American Scientists (FAS), October 2016, https://fas.org/issues/biological-chemical-and-other-non-nuclear-threats/.

9. "Reducing Security Threats from Chemical and Biological Materials," Stockholm International Peace Research Institute, https://www.sipri.org/yearbook/2014/08.

10. "Biological, Chemical, & Other Non-Nuclear Threats," Federation of American Scientists (FAS).

11. UN Office for Disarmament Affairs, "Treaty on the Non-Proliferation of Nuclear Weapons (NPT)," n.d., http://www.un.org/disarmament/WMD/Nuclear/NPTtext.shtml.

12. Evans and Kawaguchi, *Eliminating Nuclear Threats*, xviii.

13. Hans M. Kristensen, "Nuclear Weapons Modernization: A Threat to the NPT?" *Arms Control Association*, https://www.armscontrol.org/act/2014_05/Nuclear-Weapons-Modernization-A-Threat-to-the-NPT.

14. Evans and Kawaguchi, *Eliminating Nuclear Threats*; Brian Martin, "Nuclear Winter: Science and Politics," *Science and Public Policy* 15, no. 5 (1988); Peter King, "Undermining Proliferation: Nuclear Winter and Nuclear Renunciation," The Centre for Peace and Conflict Studies, Working Paper No. 09/1, October 2009.

15. Kristensen, "Nuclear Weapons Modernization: A Threat to the NPT?"

Bibliography

Ackerman, Bruce. "Let's Keep It Legal." *Los Angeles Times*, March 5, 2012.

Albright, Madeleine, with Bill Woodward. *Madame Secretary: A Memoir*. New York: Miramax Books, 2003.

Allison, Graham. *Nuclear Terrorism: The Ultimate Preventable Catastrophe*. New York: Times Books, 2004.

Arkin, William M. "Secret Plan Outlines the Unthinkable." *Los Angeles Times*, March 10, 2002.

"Arms Control and Proliferation Profile: Israel." *Arms Control Today* (July 2012). http://www.armscontrol.org/factsheets/israelprofile.

Aronson, Shlomo. *The Politics and Strategy of Nuclear Weapons in the Middle East: Opacity, Theory, and Reality, 1960–1991*. Albany, NY: Albany State University of New York Press, 1992.

Asada, Sadao. "The Shock of the Atomic Bomb and Japan's Decision to Surrender: A Reconsideration." *Pacific Historical Review* 67 (November 1998): 475–512.

Auner, Eric. "Obama Easing Export Controls on India." *Arms Control Today* (December 2010). http://armscontrol.org/act/2010_12/Obama_India.

Baker, James A. III. *The Politics of Diplomacy: Revolution, War & Peace, 1989–1992*. New York: G.P. Putnam's Sons, 1995.

Barnett, Thomas P.M. "How To Stop Worrying and Live with the Iranian Bomb." *World Politics Review*, Special Issue: Iran, Playing With Fire (January 3, 2012): 11–12.

Baruch's Address to the United Nations, June 14, 1946, reproduced at *Nuclear Age Peace Foundation*. NuclearFiles.org.

Bennett, Bruce W. *Uncertainties in the North Korean Nuclear Threat*. Santa Monica, CA: RAND, National Defense Research Institute, 2010.

Beschloss, Michael. *Presidential Courage: Brave Leaders and How They Changed America, 1789–1989*. New York: Simon & Schuster, 2007.

Beschloss, Michael R., and Strobe Talbott. *At the Highest Levels: The Inside Story of the End of the Cold War*. Boston: Little, Brown, 1993.

Betts, Richard. "The Osirak Fallacy." *The National Interest* (Spring 2006).

Bhutto, Zulfiqar Ali. *The Myth of Independence*. Oxford: Oxford University Press, 1969.

Binder, David. "CIA Says Israel has 10-20 A-Bombs." *New York Times*, March 16, 1976, A1.

"Biological, Chemical, & Other Non-Nuclear Threats." Federation of American Scientists (FAS), October 2016. https://fas.org/issues/biological-chemical-and-other-non-nuclear-threats/.

"Biosecurity: Balancing the Promise of Biotechnology with Preventing the Biological Weapons Threat." *Nuclear Threat Initiative (NTI)*, October 2016. http://www.nti.org/about/biosecurity/.

Biswas, Shampa. *Nuclear Desire: Power and the Postcolonial Nuclear Order*. Minneapolis: University of Minnesota Press, 2014.

Blanton, Thomas, and Sveltana Savranskaya. "The Reykjavik File: Previously Secret Documents from U.S. and Soviet Archives on the 1986 Reagan-Gorbachev Summit." National Security Archive, *Electronic Briefing Book* No. 203, October 13, 2006.

Boese, Wade. "Senate Reviews U.S.-Russian Nuclear Reductions Treaty." *Arms Control Today* (September 2002). http://legacy.armscontrol.org/print/1109.

Boese, Wade, and J. Peter Scoblic. "The Jury Is Still Out." *Arms Control Today* (June 2002). https://www.armscontrol.org/act/2002_06/sortanaljune02.

Borger, Julian. "Kim Jong-Un's Growing Nuclear Arsenal Could Force U.S. Back to Negotiating Table." *The Guardian*, September 9, 2016. https://www.theguardian.com/world/2016/sep/09/north-koreas-growing-ambition-nuclear-arsenal-force-us-negotiating-table.

Boulden, Jane, Ramesh Thakur, and Thomas G. Weiss, eds. *The United Nations and Nuclear Orders*. Tokyo, New York, and Paris: United Nations University Press, 2009.

Bower, Kenneth S. "A Propensity for Conflict: Potential Scenarios and Outcomes of War in the Middle East." *Jane's Intelligence Review*, Special Report Number 14 (February 1997): 14–15.

Bowett, Derek W. *Self-Defense in International Law*. Manchester: Manchester University Press, 1958.

Boyer, Paul. *By the Bomb's Early Light: American Thought and Culture at the Dawn of the Atomic Age*. New York: Pantheon, 1985.

Brands, Hal. "Progress Unseen: U.S. Arms Control Policy and the Origins of Détente, 1963–1968." *Diplomatic History* 30, no. 2 (April 2006): 253–85.

Brands, William J. *India, Pakistan and the Great Powers*. London: Pall Mall Press, 1972.

"Britain's Nuclear Weapons: Accounting and the Bomb." *The Economist*, July 30, 2010, 1. www.economist.com/blogs/blighty/2010/07/britains_nuclear_weapons.

Britain's Nuclear Weapons: The Current British Arsenal. April 30, 2001. nuclearweaponarchive.org/Uk/UKArsenalRecent.html.

"British Jobs Secured Through Upgrade to Nuclear Deterrent Submarine." Royal Navy, December 7, 2015. www.royalnavy.mod.uk.

Broad, William J., and David E. Sanger. "U.S. Ramping Up Major Renewal in Nuclear Arms." *New York Times*, September 22, 2014.

Broad, William J., and David E. Sanger. "As U.S. Modernizes Nuclear Weapons, 'Smaller' Leaves Some Uneasy." *New York Times*, January 11, 2016.

Brodie, Bernard. *War and Peace*. New York: Macmillan, 1973.

Brodie, Janet Farrell. "Learning Secrecy in the Early Cold War: The RAND Corporation." *Diplomatic History* 35, no. 4 (September 2011): 643–70.

Brown, Frederic J. *Chemical Warfare: A Study in Restraints*. Princeton, NJ: Princeton University Press, 1968.

Brown, Harold, and John Deutch. "The Nuclear Disarmament Fantasy." *Wall Street Journal*, November 19, 2007, A-19.

Brune, Lester. *United States and Two Gulf Wars: Prelude and Aftermath*. Claremont, CA: Regina Books, 2007.

Brzezinski, Zbigniew. *Power and Principle: Memoirs of the National Security Adviser, 1977–1981*. New York: Farrar Straus & Giroux, 1983.

Buckley, Thomas H. *The United States and the Washington Conference, 1921–1922*. Knoxville: University of Tennessee Press, 1970.

Bulletin of the Atomic Scientists. "It Is Two and a Half Minutes to Midnight, 2017 Doomsday Clock Statement." January 2017. http://thebulletin.org/timeline.

Bundy, McGeorge. *Danger and Survival: Choices about the Bomb in the First Fifty Years*. New York: Random House, 1988.

Bunn, Matthew. "The Nuclear Security Summit: Wins, Losses, and Draws." *Bulletin of the Atomic Scientists*, April 8, 2016. http://thebulletin.org/nuclear-security-summit-wins-losses-and-draws9310.

Bunn, Matthew, Martin B. Malin, Nickolas Roth, and William H. Tobey. *Preventing Nuclear Terrorism Continuous Improvement or Dangerous Decline?* Project on Managing the Atom, Belfer Center for Science and International Affairs Harvard Kennedy School, March 2016. http://belfercenter.ksg.harvard.edu/files/PreventingNuclearTerrorism-Web.pdf.

Burns, Richard Dean, ed. *Encyclopedia of Arms Control and Disarmament*, 3 vols. New York: Scribner's Sons, 1993.

Burns, Richard Dean. *The Evolution of Arms Control: From Antiquity to the Nuclear Age.* Santa Barbara, CA: Praeger, 2009.

Burns, Richard Dean. *The Missile Defense Systems of George W. Bush: A Critical Assessment.* Santa Barbara, CA: Praeger, 2010.

Burns, Richard Dean, and Joseph M. Siracusa. *A Global History of the Nuclear Arms Race: Weapons, Strategy, and Politics*, 2 vols. Santa Barbara, CA: Praeger, 2013.

Burns, William J. "State's Burns at UN Meeting on Countering Nuclear Terrorism." UN Secretary-General's High-Level Meeting on Countering Nuclear Terrorism, New York, NY, September 28, 2012. http://iipdigital.usembassy.gov/st/english/texttrans/2012/09/20120929136851.html#axzz4OeCKbvh8.

Burr, William. "A Brief History of U.S.-Iranian Nuclear Negotiations." *Bulletin of the Atomic Scientists*, January/February 2009.

Burr, William. "New Evidence on the Origins of Overkill." National Security Archive, *Electronic Briefing Book* No. 236, October 1, 2009.

Burr, William. "Reagan Administration Supported Sale of F-16." National Security Archive, *Electronic Briefing Book* No. 377, April 27, 2012.

Burr, William. "U.S. Opposed Taiwanese Bomb during 1970s." National Security Archive, *Electronic Briefing Book* No. 221, posted June 15, 2007.

Burr, William, ed. "Launch on Warning: The Development of U.S. Capabilities, 1959–1979." National Security Archive, *Electronic Briefing Book*, April 2001. www.gwu.edu/~nsarchiv/NSAEBB/NSAEBB43/.

Burr, William, ed. "The French Bomb, with Secret U.S. Help: Documents from Nixon and Ford Administrations." National Security Archive, *Electronic Briefing Book* No. 346, posted May 26, 2011.

Burr, William, and Jeffrey T. Richelson. "Whether to 'Strangle the Baby in the Cradle': The United States and the Chinese Nuclear Program, 1960–64." *International Security* 25, no. 3 (2000/2001): 54–99.

Bush, George H. W., and Brent Scowcroft. *A World Transformed.* New York: Vintage, 1999.

Butler, Declan, and Elizabeth Gibney. "What Kind of Bomb Did North Korea Test?" *Nature*, January 8, 2016.

Cann, Michelle, Kelsey Davenport, and Jenna Parker. "The Nuclear Security Summit: Accomplishments of the Process." An Arms Control Association and Partnership for Global Security Report, March 2016, 2. https://pgstest.files.wordpress.com/2016/03/nss-report-final.pdf.

Cannon, Lou. "Dealings with the Soviets Raise Uncomfortable Questions." *Washington Post*, July 2, 1984, A13.

Cannon, Lou. *President Reagan: The Role of a Lifetime*, 2nd ed. New York: Public Affairs, 2000.

Cantelon, Philip L., Richard C. Hewlett, and Robert C. Williams, eds. *The American Atom: A Documentary History of Nuclear Policies from the Discovery of Fission to the Present*, 2nd ed. Philadelphia: University of Pennsylvania Press, 1991.

Carter, April. *Success and Failure in Arms Control Negotiations.* Oxford: Oxford University Press/SIPRI, 1989.

Cassidy, David C. "Germany and the Atomic Bomb: New Evidence." *Scientific American*, February 1993.

Cha, Victor. "Badges, Shields or Swords? North Korea's WMD Threat." *Political Science Quarterly* 117, no. 2 (2002): 209–30.

Cha, Victor, and David C. Kang. *Nuclear North Korea: A Debate on Engagement Strategies.* New York: Columbia University Press, 2003.

Charnysh, Volha. *Pakistan's Nuclear Program.* Santa Barbara, CA: Nuclear Age Peace Foundation, September 3, 2009. www.wagingpeace.org/articles/pdfs/Proliferation_History.pdf.

Chase, Michael S., Andrew S. Erickson, and Christopher Yeaw. "Chinese Theater and Strategic Missile Force Modernization and Its Implications for the United States." *Journal of Strategic Studies* 32, no. 1 (February 2009): 67–114.

"Chronology of Libya's Disarmament and Relations with the United States." *Arms Control Association.* www.armscontrol.org/factsheets/LibyaChronology.

Chuen, Cristina Hansell. "Russian Nuclear-Powered Submarine Dismantlement and Related Activities: A Critique." *Center for Non-Proliferation Studies,* May 24, 2007.

Cirincione, Joseph, Jon B. Wolfsthal, and Miriam Rajkumar. *Deadly Arsenals: Nuclear, Biological, and Chemical Threats,* 2nd ed. Washington, DC: Carnegie Endowment for International Peace, 2005.

Clearwater, John. *Canadian Nuclear Weapons: The Untold Story of Canada's Cold War Arsenal.* Toronto: Dundum Press, 1968.

Cohen, Avner. National Security Archive, *Electronic Briefing Book* No. 189, April 28, 2006.

Cohen, Avner. *Israel and the Bomb.* New York: Columbia University Press, 1998.

Cohen, Avner, and William Burr. "Israel Crosses the Threshold." *Bulletin of the Atomic Scientists,* May/June 2006.

Cohen, Michael. "What Happens If Iran Gets the Bomb? *Global Policy Journal* (May 8, 2012). Online.

Coleman, David G., and Joseph M Siracusa. *Real-World Nuclear Deterrence: The Making of International Strategy.* Westport, CT: Praeger Security International, 2006.

Coleman, David. "Camelot's Nuclear Conscience." *Bulletin of the Atomic Scientists* 62, no. 3 (May/June 2006): 40–45.

Collina, Tom Z. "Israel Has Nuclear-Armed Sub, Report Says." *Arms Control Today* (July/ August 2012). http://www.armscontrol.org/2012_07-08/Israel_Has_Nuclear-Armed_Sub_Report_Says.

Collina, Tom Z. "Nuclear Triad Budgets Questioned." *Arms Control Today* (September 2011): 36–37.

Collina, Tom Z. "Senate Approves New START." *Arms Control Today* (January/February 2011): 38–43.

Collina, Tom Z. "START Stalls, Talks Continue." *Arms Control Today* (January/February 2010): 40–41.

Communication from the Resident Representative of India to the International Atomic Energy Agency regarding India's Nuclear Export Policies and Practices. International Atomic Energy Agency, INFCIRC/647, June 25 2005. www.iaea.org.

Conant, James B. *My Several Lives.* New York: Harper & Row, 1970.

Cordesman, Anthony H., and Adam C. Seitz. *Iranian Weapons of Mass Destruction: The Birth of a Regional Nuclear Arms Race?* New York: Praeger, 2009.

Cortright, David, and George A. Lopez. "Disarming Iraq: Non-military Strategies and Options." *Arms Control Today* (September 2002).

Coyle, Philip E. "CTBT or Not, Nuclear Test Detection and Monitoring Remains Critical." *World Politics Review,* April 16, 2012.

CTR. "Cooperative Threat Reduction Annual Report to Congress, Fiscal Year 2008."

Cumings, Bruce. *The Origins of the Korean War, vol. 2, The Roaring of the Cataract, 1947–1950.* Princeton: Princeton University Press, 1990.

Datta, Rekha. "U.S. Security Policy in India and Pakistan and the Question of Nuclear Proliferation." *Journal of South Asian and Middle Eastern Studies* 21, no. 2 (1998): 21–40.

Davenport, Kelsey. "WMD-Free Middle East Proposal at a Glance." *Arms Control Association,* June 2015. https://www.armscontrol.org/factsheets/mewmdfz.

Davie, Maurice R. *Evolution of War: A Study of Its Role in Early Societies.* New Haven, CT: Yale University Press, 1929.

Deibel, Terry L. "The Death of a Treaty." *Foreign Affairs* (September/October 2002): 142–61.

Department of Defense. *Nuclear Posture Review Report.* Washington, DC: DoD, April 2010.

Diamond, Howard. "India Conducts Nuclear Tests; Pakistan Follows Suit." Arms Control Today (May 1998). www.armscontrol.org.

Diehl, Sarah, and Paula Humphrey. "The April 2010 Nuclear Security Summit: One More Step toward the Mountaintop." *Nuclear Threat Initiative (NTI)*, April 20, 2010. http://www.nti.org/analysis/articles/april-2010-nuclear-security-summit/.

Dinstein, Yoram. *War, Aggression and Self-Defense*, 4th ed. Cambridge: Cambridge University Press, 2005.

Director of Central Intelligence. "Soviet Policy toward the West: The Gorbachev Challenge." NIE 11-4-89, in National Security Archive, *Electronic Briefing Book* No. 261, December 8, 2008.

Director General. "Implementation of the NPT Safeguards Agreement and Relevant Provisions of Security Council Resolutions in the Islamic Republic of Iran." IAEA Report, GOV/2011/65, November 8, 2011.

Dixit, J. N. *Across Borders: Fifty Years of Indian Foreign Policy*. New Delhi: Picus Books, 1998.

Dobrynin, Anatoly. *In Confidence: Moscow's Ambassador to America's Six Cold War Presidents*. Seattle: University of Washington Press, 1995.

Document 180. "Editorial Note." In *Foreign Relations of the United States*, 500. http://www.stategov/r/pa/ho/frus/nixon/xi/index.htm.

Editorial Board. "An Iran Nuclear Deal That Reduces the Chance of War." *New York Times*, July 14, 2015. http://www.nytimes.com/2015/07/15/opinion/an-iran-nuclear-deal-that-reduces-the-chance-of-war.html.

"Egypt's Secret Nuclear Weapons Program." Defense Technology & Military Forum. http://www.defencetalk.com/forums/.

Eliot, Theodore L. (to Henry Kissinger). "Briefing Book—Visit of Mrs. Gold Meir." September 19, 1969, enclosing "Background—Israel's Nuclear Weapons and Missile Programs." In Record Group 59, General Records of the Department of State, Top Secret Subject-Numeric Files, 1967-69, Pol lsr, National Archives, College Park, Maryland.

English, Robert D. *Russia and the Idea of the West: Gorbachev, Intellectuals & the End of the Cold War*. New York: Columbia University Press, 2000.

Evans, Gareth, and Yoriko Kawaguchi. *Eliminating Nuclear Threats: A Practical Agenda for Global Policymakers, International Commission on Nuclear Non-Proliferation and Disarmament*. Canberra/Tokyo, 2009.

"Experts Call NATO Strategic Concept 'Missed Opportunity to Reduce Role of Obsolete Tactical Nukes from Europe.'" *Arms Control Association*, November 19, 2010, online.

Farley, Robert. "Iran and the Nuclear Paradox." *World Politics Review*, Special Report, January 3, 2012.

Fifield, Anna. "North Korea Conducts Fifth Nuclear Test, Claims It Has Made Warheads with 'Higher Strike Power.'" *Washington Post*, September 9, 2016. www.washingtonpost.com.

Fitzgerald, France. *Way Out There in the Blue: Reagan and Star Wars and the End of the Cold War*. New York: Simon & Schuster, 2000.

Forden, Geoffrey. "Reducing a Common Danger: Improving Russia's Early Warning System." *Policy Analysis*, No. 399, May 3, 2001.

Fouquet, David. *Christian Science Monitor*, December, 13, 1984.

"France." *Nuclear Threat Initiative*, October 2016. http://www.nti.org/learn/countries/france/nuclear/.

Frank, Richard B. *Downfall: The End of the Imperial Japanese Empire*. New York: Random House, 1999.

Freedman, Lawrence. *Evolution of Nuclear Strategy*. New York: St. Martin's, 1981.

Freedman, Lawrence. *The Evolution of Nuclear Strategy*, 2nd ed. London: Macmillan, 1989.

Furlong, Ray. "Hitler 'Tested Small Atom Bomb,'" *BBC News*, Berlin, 2005. http://news.bbc.co.uk/go/pr/fr/-/2/hi/europe/4348497.stm.

Gaddis, John Lewis. *George F. Kennan: An American Life*. New York: Penguin Press, 2011.

Gaddis, John Lewis. *The Long Peace: Inquiries into the History of the Cold War*. New York: Oxford University Press, 1989.

Gaddis, John Lewis. *We Now Know: Rethinking Cold War History*. New York: Clarendon Press, 1997.

Gaddis, John Lewis, Philip Gordon, Ernest May, and Jonathan Rosenberg. *Cold War Statesmen Confront the Bomb: Nuclear Diplomacy Since 1945*. New York: Oxford University Press, 1999.

Gallois, Pierre. "NATO's New Teeth." *Foreign Affairs* 39, no. 1 (October 1960).

Ganguly, Sumit. *Conflict Unending: India-Pakistan Tensions since 1947*. New York: Columbia University Press, 2001.

Garthoff, Raymond L. "Banning the Bomb in Outer Space." *International Security* 5 (Winter 1980/1981): 25–40.

Garthoff, Raymond L. *Détente and Confrontation: American-Soviet Relations from Nixon to Reagan*, rev. ed. Washington, DC: Brookings Institution, 1994.

Garthoff, Raymond L. *The Great Transition: American-Soviet Relations and the End of the Cold War*. Washington, DC: Brookings Institution, 1994.

Gates, Robert M. *From the Shadows: The Ultimate Insider's Story of Five Presidents and How They Won the Cold War*. New York: Simon & Schuster, 1996.

Gavin, Francis J. "Blasts from the Past: Proliferation Lessons from the 1960s." *International Security* 29, no. 3 (Winter 2004/5): 100–35.

Gavin, Francis J. "Same as It Ever Was." *International Security* 34, no. 3 (Winter 2009/10): 7–37.

Gearan, Anne. "Syria Probably Used Chlorine Gas in Attacks This Year, Weapons Inspectors Say." *Washington Post*, June 18, 2014. www.washingtonpost.com.

Gelb, Leslie. "The Mind of the President." *New York Times Magazine*, October 6, 1985, 21ff.

Gillis, Melissa. *Disarmament: A Basic Guide*. United Nations Office for Disarmament Affairs, 3rd ed., 2012. https://www.un.org/disarmament/publications/basic-guide/edition-3/.

Gladstone, Rick. "Claims of Chlorine-Filled Bombs Overshadow Progress by Syria on Chemical Weapons." *New York Times*, April 22, 2014.

Glanz, James. "Of Physics, Friendship and Nazi Germany's Atomic Bomb Efforts." *New York Times*, March 21, 2000.

Global Fissile Material Report 2011: Nuclear Weapon and Fissile Material Stockpiles and Production. The International Panel on Fissile Materials, Princeton, NJ, January 2012. http://fissilematerials.org/library/gfmr11.pdf.

Global Governance Monitor: Nuclear Proliferation. *Council for Foreign Relations*, 2016. http://www.cfr.org/global-governance/global-governance-monitor/p18985#!/nuclear-proliferation?cid=soc-facebook-in-ggm_nuclear_prolif-082916.

"Global Threat Reduction Initiative (GTRI): Reducing Nuclear Threats." Office of Defense Nuclear Non-Proliferation, National Nuclear Security Administration, U.S. Department of Energy, Washington DC, May 29, 2014. https://nnsa.energy.gov/mediaroom/factsheets/reducingthreats.

Goldblat, Jozef. *Arms Control Agreements: A Handbook*. New York: Praeger, 1983.

Goldemberg, Jose. "Lessons from the Denuclearization of Brazil and Argentina." *Arms Control Association*, April 2006. https://www.armscontrol.org/act/2006_04/LookingBack.

Goldschmidt, Bertrand. *Atomic Complex: A Worldwide Political History of Nuclear Energy*. Translated by Bruce M. Adkins. La Grange Park, IL: American Nuclear Society, 1982.

Goodby, James B. *At the Borderline of Armageddon: How American Presidents Managed the Atom Bomb*. Lanham, MD: Rowman & Littlefield, 2006.

Gorbachev, Mikhail. *Memoirs*. New York: Doubleday, 1995.

Gorbachev, Mikhail. *Perestroika: New Thinking for Our Country and the World*. New York: Harper & Row, 1987.

Gowing, Margaret. *Britain and Atomic Energy, 1939–1945*. London: Macmillan, 1964.

Gowing, Margaret. *Independence and Deterrence: Britain and Atomic Energy, 1945–1952, Vol. 1: Policy Making*. London: Macmillan, 1974.

Graham, Thomas Jr. *Disarmament Sketches: Three Decades of Arms Control and International Law*. Seattle: University of Washington Press, 2002.

Gupta, Vipin, and Frank Pabian. "Investigating the Allegations of Indian Nuclear Test Preparations in the Rajasthan Desert." *Science & Global Security* 6 (1997): 101–88. www.princeton.edu.

Hagerty, Devin T. *The Consequences of Nuclear Proliferation: Lessons from South Asia.* Cambridge, MA: MIT Press, 1998.

Haksar, P. N. *India's Foreign Policy.* New Delhi: Patriot Publishers, 1989.

Hamza, Khidhir, with Jeff Stein. *Saddam's Bombmaker: The Terrifying Inside Story of the Iraqi Nuclear and Biological Weapons Agenda.* New York: Scribner, 2000.

Harrell, Eben. "Britain Takes Another Look at Its Nuclear Subs." *Time World*, July 30, 2010. www.time.com/time/world/article/0,8599,2007441,00.html.

Harvey, Cole. "Obama Calls for Nuclear Weapons-Free World." *Arms Control Today* 39 (May 2009): 28–30.

Harris, Sheldon H. *Factories of Death: Japanese Biological Warfare, 1932–45, and the American Cover-Up.* New York: Routledge, 1994.

Haslam, Jonathan. "Russian Archival Revelations and Our Understanding of the Cold War." *Diplomatic History* 21 (Spring 1997): 217–28.

Herken, Greg. *The Winning Weapon: The Atomic Bomb in the Cold War, 1945–1950.* New York: Knopf, 1980.

Hess, Gary R. *The United States at War, 1941–1945,* 2nd ed. Wheeling, Illinois: Harlan Davidson, 2000.

Hewlett, Richard G., and Oscar E. Anderson Jr. *The New World, 1939–1946, Vol. I: A History of the United States Atomic Energy Commission.* University Park: Pennsylvania State University Press, 1962.

Hiroshima and Nagasaki: The Physical, Medical, and Social Effects of the Atomic Bombings. Translated by Eisei Ishikawa and David L. Swain. New York: Basic Books, 1981.

Historical Documents Regarding India's Misuse of Civilian Nuclear Technology Assistance. *Arms Control Association.* www.nci.org.

"History of the NSG." *Nuclear Suppliers Group.* www.nuclearsuppliersgroup.org.

Hoagland, Jim. "Nuclear Pre-emption." *Washington Post National Weekly*, March 25–31, 2002, 5.

Hoffman, David E. *The Dead Hand: The Untold Story of the Cold War Arms Race and Its Dangerous Legacy.* New York: Doubleday, 2009.

Holloway, David. *Stalin and the Bomb: The Soviet Union and Atomic Energy, 1939–1956.* New Haven, CT: Yale University Press, 1994.

Holmes, Oliver. "Syria Video Shows Chlorine Gas Floating in Streets: Activists." *Reuters* (Beirut), May 23, 2014. www.reuters.com.

Holum, John. "Assessing the New U.S.-Russian Pact." *Arms Control Today* (June 2002): 7–8.

Horner, Daniel. "IAEA Board Approves Fuel Bank Plan." *Arms Control Today* 40 (January/ February 2011): 46–48.

Horner, Daniel. "NSG Makes Little Headway at Meeting." *Arms Control Today* 40 (July/ August 2010): 46.

House of Commons. Defence Committee, *The Future of the UK's Strategic Deterrent: The White Paper, Vol. 1.* London: The Stationery Office Limited, March 7, 2007, online.

Hundman, Eric. "The Global Threat Reduction Initiative's First Two Years." *Center for Defense Information*, September 6, 2006.

Huntington, Samuel. *Common Defense: Strategic Program in National Politics.* New York: Columbia University Press, 1961.

Hymans, Jacques E. C. *The Psychology of Nuclear Proliferation: Identity, Emotions, and Foreign Policy.* Cambridge: Cambridge University Press, 2006.

"India." *Nuclear Threat Initiative (NTI).* http://www.nti.org/learn/countries/india/nuclear/.

India's Draft Nuclear Doctrine. Arms Control Today (July/August 1999). http://www.armscontrol.org.

"International Leaders Urge Obama to Back Nuke Ban." *New York Times*, March 26, 2009.

"Iran's Rial Hits an All-Time-Low against the U.S. Dollar." *BBC News*, October 1 2012. http://www.bbc.co.uk/news/business-19786662.

"Iraq: A Chronology of UN Inspections." *Arms Control Today* (October 2002): 14–23.

Irving, David. *The German Atomic Bomb: The History of Nuclear Research in Nazi Germany.* New York: Simon & Schuster, 1968.

Isachenkov, Vladimir. "Putin Urges U.S. to Share Missile Defense Data." *Associated Press,* December 29, 2009.

"Israel, U.S. Shared Data on Suspected Nuclear Site" *Washington Post,* September 21, 2007.

"Israelis Criticize Article in the Times." *New York Times,* July 19, 1970.

Jacobson, Louis. "Rhetorical Support for WMD-Prevention Program, But Progress Hard To Document." *Tampa Bay Times,* November 15, 2012.

Jervis, Robert. "The Political Effects of Nuclear Weapons." *International Security* 13, no. 2 (Fall 1988): 80–90.

Joby, Warrick. "A North Korean H-bomb? Not Likely, Experts Say." *Washington Post,* January 6, 2016. www.washingtonpost.com.

Johnson, Alastair Iain. "China's New 'Old Thinking': The Concept of Limited Deterrence." *International Security* 20, no. 3 (1995–1996): 5–42.

Johnson, Rebecca, Nicola Butler, and Stephen Pullinger. *Worse than Irrelevant? British Nuclear Weapons in the 21st Century.* London: Acronym Institute for Disarmament Diplomacy, 2006.

Jungk, Robert. *Brighter than a Thousand Suns: A Personal History of the Atomic Scientists.* Translated by James Cleugh. New York: Harcourt, Brace and World, 1958.

Kallenborn, Zachary, and Raymond Zilinskas. "Disarming Syria of its Chemical Weapons: Lessons Learned from Iraq and Libya." *Nuclear Threat Initiative (NTI),* October 31, 2013. www.nti.org.

Karlsch, Rainer. *Hitler's Bombe: die geheime Geschichte der deutschen Kernwaffenversuche.* Munchen: Deutsche Verlags-Anstalt, 2005.

Karnad, Bharat. *India's Nuclear Policy.* Westport, CT: Praeger Security International, 2008.

Karpin, Michael. *The Bomb in the Basement: How Israel Went Nuclear and What That Means for the World.* New York: Simon & Schuster, 2006.

Katzman, Kenneth. "Iran Sanctions." *CRS Report for Congress,* RS20871. Washington, DC: Congressional Research Service, June 23, 2010, 1–10.

Katzman, Kenneth. "Iran: US Concerns and Policy Responses." *CRS Report for Congress,* RS34544. Washington, DC: Congressional Research Service, October 17, 2012, 60–61.

Kearns, Ian. *Beyond the United Kingdom: Trends in the Other Nuclear Armed States.* Discussion Paper 1 of the Trident Commission. London: British American Security Information Council [BASIC], November 2011, 20.

Kegley, Charles W. Jr. *The Long Postwar Peace.* New York: Harper Collins, 1990.

Kelleher, Catherine M., and Scott L. Warren. "Getting to Zero Starts Here: Tactical Nuclear Weapons." *Arms Control Today* (December 2009): 10–11.

Kerr, Paul K. "Iran's Nuclear Programs: Status." *CRS Report for Congress,* RL34544. Washington, DC: Congressional Research Service, September 18, 2009.

Kerr, Paul K., and Mary Beth Nikitin. "Pakistan's Nuclear Weapons." *CRS Report for Congress,* RL34248. Washington, DC: Congressional Research Service, August 1, 2016, https://www.fas.org/sgp/crs/nuke/RL34248.pdf.

Khrushchev, Sergei N. *Nikita Khrushchev and the Creation of a Superpower.* Translated by Shirley Benson. University Park: Pennsylvania State University Press, 2000.

"Kim Jong Un Visits Reconstructed Pyongchon Revolutionary Site." *Rodong Sinmun,* December 10, 2015. http://rodong.rep.kp.

Kimball, Daryl G. "Arms Control Association Praises Obama's Commitment to a Nuclear Weapons Free World." *Arms Control Association,* April 5 2009. http://www.armscontrol.org/print/3616.

Kimball, Daryl G. "India's Choice, Congress' Responsibility." *Arms Control Today* 36 (January/February 2006): 3.

Kimball, Daryl G. "Pursue the Diplomatic Track on Iran." *Arms Control Today* (July/August 2012). http://www.armscontrol.org/act/2012_0708/Focus.

Kimball, Daryl G. "Reconsider the Nuclear Test Ban." *Arms Control Today* (April 2011): 4.

Kimball, Daryl G., and Peter Crail. "Chronology of U.S.-North Korean Nuclear and Missile Diplomacy." *Arms Control Association*, April 2012. http://www.armscontrol.org/factsheets/dprkchron.

King, Peter. "Undermining Proliferation: Nuclear Winter and Nuclear Renunciation." The Centre for Peace and Conflict Studies, Working Paper No. 09/1, October 2009.

Kissinger, Henry A. Memorandum for the President, Subject, Rabin's Proposed Assurances on Israeli Nuclear Policy, October, 8, 1969. DF 18—Arms Control and Disarmament, Record Group 59, General Records of the Department of State, NSC Files, Country Files, Middle East; Folder 4—Israeli Nuclear Program; Box 612, 1, National Archives.

Kissinger, Henry A. "National Security Study Memorandum 156, Subject Indian Nuclear Developments." July 5, 1972. http://nixon archives.gov/virtuallibrary/documents/national securitystudymemoranda.php.

Kohl, Wilfrid. *French Nuclear Diplomacy*. Princeton, NJ: Princeton University Press, 1971.

Kort, Michael. *The Columbia Guide to Hiroshima and the Bomb*. New York: Columbia University Press, 2007.

Krass, Allan S. *The United States and Arms Control: The Challenge of Leadership*. Westport, CT: Praeger, 1997.

Kristensen, Hans M. "Nuclear Weapons Modernization: A Threat to the NPT?" *Arms Control Association*, 2014. https://www.armscontrol.org/act/2014_05/Nuclear-Weapons-Modernization-A-Threat-to-the-NPT.

Kristensen, Hans M. "Pentagon Portrays Nuclear Modernization as a Response to Russia." Federation of American Scientists (FAS), February 11, 2016. https://fas.org/blogs/security/2016/02/russiajustification/.

Kristensen, Hans M. "Video Shows Earth-Penetrating Capability of B61-12 Nuclear Bomb." *FAS Blog*, Federation of American Scientists, 2016.

Kristensen, Hans M., and Robert S. Norris. "Slowing Nuclear Weapon Reductions and Endless Nuclear Weapon Modernizations: A Challenge to The NPT." *Bulletin of the Atomic Scientists* 70, no. 4 (July/August 2014). http://bos.sagepub.com/content/70/4/94.full.pdf+html.

Kristensen, Hans M., and Robert S. Norris. "Status of World Nuclear Forces." Federation of American Scientists (FAS), October 2016. http://fas.org/issues/nuclear-weapons/status-world-nuclear-forces/.

Kristensen, Hans M., and Robert S. Norris. "Worldwide Deployments of Nuclear Weapons." *Bulletin of the Atomic Scientists*, September 2014. http://thebulletin.org/2014/september/worldwide-deployments-nuclear-weapons-20147595.

Kroenig, Matthew. "How to Approach Nuclear Modernization? A U.S. Response." *Bulletin of the Atomic Scientists* 71, no. 3 (2015).

Kroenig, Matthew. *A Time to Attack: The Looming Iranian Nuclear Threat*. New York: St. Martin's Press, 2014.

Kroenig, Matthew. "Time to Attack Iran: Why a Strike Is the Least Bad Option." *Foreign Affairs* 91, no. 1 (2012): 76–86.

Kroenig, Matthew. "Why Is Obama Abandoning 70 Years of U.S. Non-Proliferation Policy?" *Tablet*, June 15, 2015.

Kroenig, Matthew. "Why U.S. Nuclear Modernization Is Necessary." *Bulletin of the Atomic Scientists*, online, January 8, 2015.

Kulacki, Gregory. "Chickens Talking With Ducks: The U.S.-Chinese Nuclear Dialogue." *Arms Control Today* (October 2011): 15–16.

Kunz, J. L. "The Chaotic Status of the Laws of War and the Urgent Necessity for Their Revision." *American Journal of International Law* (January 1931): 37–61.

LaMongagne, Steve. "India-Pakistan Sanctions Legislation Fact Sheet." The Center for Arms Control and Non-Proliferation, 2011. http://armscontrolcenter.org.

Lapp, Ralph E. *Arms beyond Doubt: The Tyranny of Weapons Technology*. New York: Cowles, 1970.

Larsen, Jeffrey A., and James M. Smith. *Historical Dictionary of Arms Control and Disarmament*. Lanham, MD: Scarecrow Press, 2005.

Lawrence, Robert M., and Joel Laurus, eds. *Nuclear Proliferation: Phase II*. Lawrence: University of Kansas Press, 1973.

Levy, Adrian, and Catherine Scott-Clark. *Deception: Pakistan, the United States, and the Secret Trade in Nuclear Weapons*. New York: Walker, 2007.

Lewis, Jeffrey. "North Korea's Nuclear-Program Is Way More Sophisticated and Dangerous than You Think." *Foreign Policy*, September 9, 2016. http://foreignpolicy.com/2016/09/09/north-koreas-nuclear-program-is-way-more-sophisticated-and-dangerous-than-you-think/.

Lewis, John Wilson, and Hua Di. "China's Ballistic Missile Program: Technologies, Strategies, Goals." *International Security* 17, no. 2 (Fall 1992): 5–40.

Lewis, John Wilson, and Xue Litai. *China Builds the Bomb*. Stanford, CA: Stanford University Press, 1988.

Linenthal, Edward Tabor. *Symbolic Defense: The Cultural Significance of the Strategic Defense Initiative*. Urbana, IL: University of Illinois Press, 1989.

Loiko, Sergei L. "Arms Pact Passes a Russian Hurtle." *Los Angeles Times*, December 25, 2010, A-3.

Lugar, Richard C. "The Next Steps in U.S. Non-Proliferation Policy." *Arms Control Today* (December 2002).

Mahnaimi, Uzi, Sarah Baxter, Glenn Kessler, Robin Wright, and Michael Sheridan. "Israelis 'Blew Apart' Syrian Nuclear Cache." [London] *The Sunday Times*, September 16, 2007.

Malenic, Marina. "U.S. Completes First B-61 LEP Flight Test." *Janes Defense Weekly*, July 8, 2015.

Mandelbaum, Michael. *The Nuclear Revolution: International Politics before and after Hiroshima*. Cambridge: Cambridge University Press, 1981.

Martin, Brian. "Nuclear Winter: Science and Politics." *Science and Public Policy* 15, no. 5 (1988).

Masterson, Kathleen E. "China Cited by Foes of Nuclear Budget Cuts." *Arms Control Today* (December 2011): 48.

Matlock, Jack R. Jr. *Reagan and Gorbachev: How the Cold War Ended*. New York: Random House, 2004.

Mayor, Adrienne. *Greek Fire, Poison Arrows & Scorpion Bombs*. New York: Overlook Books, 2003.

Mazarr, Michael J. *North Korea and the Bomb: A Case Study in Non-Proliferation*. London: Macmillan, 1995.

McGoldrick, Fred. "The Road Ahead for Export Controls: Challenges for the Nuclear Suppliers Group." *Arms Control Today* 41 (January/February 2011): 30–36.

Mecklin, John. "Disarm and Modernize." *Foreign Policy*, no. 211 (March/April 2015).

Medvedev, Zhores A. "Stalin and the Atomic Bomb." Translated by Tony Simpson, 1999. www.spokesmanbooks.com/Spokesman/PDF/medvedev.pdf.

Meier, Oliver. "NATO Revises Nuclear Policy." *Arms Control Today* (December 2010): 28–31.

Meier, Oliver, and Paul Ingram. "A Nuclear Posture Review for NATO." *Arms Control Today* (October 2010): 8–16.

MemCon. January 26, 1956, *Foreign Relations of the United States, 1955–1957*. Washington DC: GPO, 1980, vol. 20, 297.

Memorandum by the Director of the Policy Planning Staff (Nitze) to the Secretary of State. January 17, 1950, *FRUS: 1950*, I: 13–17.

Mendelson, Jack, ed. *Arms Control Chronology*. Washington, DC: Center for Defense Information, 2002.

Mendelson, Jack, and David Grahame. *Arms Control Chronology*. Washington, DC: Center for Defense Information, 2002: 36ff.

Meyer, Paul. "Prague One Year Later: From Words to Deed." *Arms Control Today* (May 2010). http://www.armscontrol.org/act/2010_05/LookingBack.

Miller, Judith, Stephen Engelberg, and William Broad. *Germs: Biological Weapons and America's Secret War*. New York: Simon & Schuster, 2001.

Ministry of External Affairs of India. "The Cabinet Committee on Security Reviews Operationalization of India's Nuclear Doctrine." Press Release, January 4, 2003. www.mea.gov.in.

Miscamble, Wilson D. *From Roosevelt to Truman: Potsdam, Hiroshima, and the Cold War*. New York: Cambridge University Press, 2007.

Mueller, John. "The Essential Irrelevance of Nuclear Weapons: Stability in the Post-War World." *International Security* 13, no. 2 (Fall 1998): 55–79.

Mukherjee, Pranab. "Statement by External Affairs Minister of India Mr Pranab Mukherjee on the Civil Nuclear Initiative." Embassy of India in Washington, DC, September 5, 2008. www.indianembassy.org.

Müller, Harald, ed. *A Non-Proliferation Policy: Prospects and Problems*. Oxford: Clarendon Press, 1987.

Müller, Harald. *The 2005 NPT Review Conference: Reasons and Consequences of Failure and Options for Repair*. Weapons of Mass Destruction Commission (WMDC), UN Secretariat, Stockholm, Sweden, 2005. http://www.blixassociates.com/wp-content/uploads/2011/03/No31.pdf.

Myers, Steven Lee, and Choe Sang-Hun. "North Korea Agrees to Curb Nuclear Work; US Offers Aid." *New York Times*, February 29, 2012. http://www.nytimes.com/2012/03/01/world/asia/us-says-north-korea-agrees-to-curb-nuclear-work.html?_r=1&hp.

Narang, Vipin. "India's Nuclear Weapons Policy." In *Engaging the World: India's Foreign Policy since 1947*, ed. Sumit Ganguly. Oxford: Oxford University Press, 2015.

Narang, Vipin. *Nuclear Strategy in the Modern Era: Regional Powers and International Conflict*. Princeton, NJ: Princeton University Press, 2014.

Narang, Vipin. "Posturing for Peace? Pakistan's Nuclear Postures and South Asian Stability." *International Security* 34, no. 3 (2009/2010): 46. http://belfercenter.ksg.harvard.edu/files/Narang.pdf.

NAS Executive Summary. "Technical Issues Related to the Comprehensive Nuclear Test Ban Treaty." *Arms Control Today* (September 2002).

National Nuclear Security Administration Fact Sheet. "GTRI: Reducing Nuclear Threats." February 1, 2011. http://nnsa.energy.gov.

Newhouse, John. "Annals of Diplomacy: The Abolitionist—I." *The New Yorker*, January 2, 1989, 48–49.

Newhouse, John. *War and Peace in the Nuclear Age*. New York: Knopf, 1989.

"Next Steps in Arms Control" [a Panel moderated by Professor Catherine Kelleher]. Washington, DC: Arms Control Association, November 8, 2010, a twenty-page transcript provided by Federal News Service, available online.

Nikitin, Mary Beth D. "Comprehensive Nuclear-Test-Ban Treaty: Background and Current Developments." *CRS Report for Congress*, RL33548. Washington, DC: Congressional Research Service, September 1, 2016. https://www.fas.org/sgp/crs/nuke/RL33548.pdf.

Nikitin, Mary Beth D. "The March 2016 Nuclear Security Summit." *CRS Insight Report for Congress*, IN10463. Washington, DC: Congressional Research Service, March 14, 2016. https://www.fas.org/sgp/crs/nuke/IN10463.pdf.

Nikitin, Mary Beth D. "Proliferation Security Initiative (PSI)." *CRS Report for Congress*, RL34327. Washington, DC: Congressional Research Service, June 15 2012, 4. http://www.fas.org/sgp/crs/nuke/RL34327.pdf.

Nikitin, Mary Beth D., Carla E. Humud, and Christopher M. Blanchard. "Armed Conflict in Syria: Overview and U.S." *CRS Report for Congress*, RL33487. Washington, DC: Congressional Research Service, September 28, 2016. https://www.fas.org/sgp/crs/mideast/RL33487.pdf.

Nikitin, Mary Beth D., Paul K. Kerr, and Andrew Feickert. "Syria's Chemical Weapons: Issues for Congress." *CRS Report for Congress*, R42848. Washington, DC: Congressional Research Service, September 30, 2013. https://www.fas.org/sgp/crs/nuke/R42848.pdf.

Nimark, Agnieszka. "The Nuclear Deal with Iran, the NPT Review Deadlock and the Ukrainian Crisis." CIDOB Barcelona Centre for International Affairs, November 2015. http://www.cidob.org/en/.

Nitze, Paul H. *From Hiroshima to Glasnost: At the Center of Decision, a Memoir*. New York: Grove Weidenfeld, 1989.

Nizamani, Haider K. *The Roots of Rhetoric: Politics of Nuclear Weapons in India and Pakistan*. Westport, CT: Praeger, 2000.

Norris, Robert S., William M. Arkin, and Hans M. Kristensen. "Israeli Nuclear Forces, 2002." *Bulletin of the Atomic Scientists*, September/October 2002.

Norris, Robert, Andrew Burrows, and Richard Fieldhouse. *British, French, and Chinese Nuclear Weapons*, vol. 5. Boulder, CO: Westview Press, 1994.

"North Korea." *Nuclear Threat Initiative (NTI)*. http://www.nti.org/learn/countries/north-korea/.

NSC 68. A Report to the National Security Council, "United States Objectives and Programs for National Security." April 14, 1950, 3, President's Secretary's File (PSF), Papers of Harry S. Truman, Harry S. Truman Library, Independence, Missouri (hereafter cited as NSC 68).

NSC 68/1. Minutes of the 55th Meeting of the National Security Council, PSF, Papers of Harry S. Truman, Truman Library.

NSC 68/4. (Various programs were described in) NSC 68/3. A Report to the National Security Council, "United States Objectives and Programs for National Security." December 8, 1950, NSCF, Modern Military Records Division, National Archives.

NSC 8/1. A Report to the National Security Council. "The Position of the United States with Regard to Korea." March 16, 1949, NSCF, Modern Military Records Division, National Archives.

"Nuclear Non-Proliferation Chronology of Key Events." IAEA.org, https://www.iaea.org/newscenter/focus/npt/chronology-of-key-events#2000.

"Nuclear Posture Review." Washington, DC: White House, April 2010.

Nuclear Weapon Free Zones and the Middle East: A [draft] Report of the Monterey Non-Proliferation Strategy Group. James Martin Center for Non-Proliferation Studies, August 2009.

Nuclear Weapon Nations and Arsenals. August 9, 2001, Nuclear Weapons Archive. http://nuclearweaponarchive.org/Nwfaq/Nfaq7.html.

Nurja, Alfred. "Obama Submits NWFZ Protocols to Senate." *Arms Control Today* 41 (June 2011): 37.

Obama, Barack. "How We Can Make Our Vision of a World without Nuclear Weapons a Reality." *Washington Post*, March 30, 2016. https://www.washingtonpost.com/opinions/.

Obama, Barack. "Remarks by President Barack Obama." Hradcany Square, Prague, Czech Republic, The White House, Washington, DC, Office of the Press Secretary, April 5 2009. http://www.whitehouse.gov/the_press_office/Remarks-By-President-Barack-Obama-In-Prague-As-Delivered/.

Obama, Barack. "Remarks by the President in Celebration of Nowruz." The White House, Office of the Press Secretary, Washington, DC, March 20, 2009. http://www.whitehouse.gov/video/The-Presidents-Message-to-the-Iranian-People#transcript.

Obama, Barack. "Remarks by the President on the Iran Nuclear Deal." American University, Washington, DC: The White House, Office of the Press Secretary, August 5, 2015. https://www.whitehouse.gov/the-press-office/2015/08/05/remarks-president-iran-nuclear-deal.

Obama, Barack. "Press Conference by President Obama in L'Aquila, Italy." Office of the Press Secretary, The White House, Washington, DC, July 10, 2009. http://www.whitehouse.gov/the_press_office/Press-Conference-by-the-President-in-LAquila-Italy-7-10-09/.

Obama, Barack. "Remarks by the President at the Opening Plenary Session of the Nuclear Security Summit." Office of the Press Secretary, The White House, Washington, DC, April 13, 2010. http://www.whitehouse.gov/the-press-office/remarks-president-opening-plenary-session-nuclear-security-summit.

Obama Pledges Diplomatic Push on Iran. *Nuclear Threat Initiative*, November 15, 2012. http://www.nti.org/gsn/article/obama-pledges-diplomatic-push-iran.

O'Donnell, Svenja. "U.K. to Sign Contract to Refit Royal Navy Nuclear Submarine." Bloomberg, March 25, 2012. www.bloomberg.com.

Office of Cooperative Threat Reduction (CTR). Bureau of International Security and Non-Proliferation (ISN), U.S. Department of State, Washington DC. http://www.state.gov/t/isn/offices/c55411.htm.

Office of the Secretary of Defense. *Proliferation: Threat and Response*. Washington, DC, January 2001. http://www.defenselink.mil.

Office of the Secretary of Defense. U.S. Department of Defense. "Annual Report to Congress: Military and Security Developments Involving the People's Republic of China 2013." May 2013.

Ogilvie-White, Tanya. "Great Power Responsibility and Nuclear Order." *The Non-Proliferation Review* 20 (2013): 173–77.

O'Neil, Andrew. "Nuclear Weapons and Non-Proliferation: Is Restraint Sustainable?" *Security Challenges* 5 (2009).

Ostrovsky, Victor, and Claire Hoy. *By Way of Deception*. New York: St. Martin's Press, 1990.

Ouaghram-Gormley, Sonia Ben. "An Unrealized Nexus: WMD-related Trafficking, Terrorism, and Organized Crime in the Former Soviet Union." *Arms Control Today* (July/August 2007): 6–13.

Pakistan Nuclear Weapons: A Brief History of Pakistan's Nuclear Program. Federation of American Scientists (FAS). www.fas.org/nuke/guide/pakistan/nuke/.

"Pakistan Profile." *Nuclear Threat Initiative*, 2011.

Parameters for a Joint Comprehensive Plan of Action regarding the Islamic Republic of Iran's Nuclear Program. P5+1 (UN Security Council's five permanent members: namely China, France, Russia, the United Kingdom, and the United States, plus Germany), April 2, 2015. https://www.armscontrol.org/files/Parameters-for-a-Joint-Comprehensive-Plan-of-Action-regarding-the-Islamic-Republic-of-Irans-Nuclear-Program-2015-04-02.pdf.

Parks, W. Hays. "The Law of War." In *Encyclopedia of Arms Control and Disarmament*, ed. Richard Dean Burns, 3 vols. New York: Scribner's Sons, 1993, volume II: 1053–68.

Parrish, Scott, and William Potter. "Central Asian Nuclear Weapons-Free Zone, 2006." James Martin Center for Non-Proliferation Studies, Monterey Institute of International Studies, September 5, 2006. http://cns.miss.edu/pubs/.

Peres, Shimon. *Battling for Peace: Memoirs*. London: Weidenfeld and Nicolson, 1995.

Perkovich, George. *India's Nuclear Bomb: The Impact on Global Proliferation*. Berkeley: University of California Press, 1999.

Peterson, Scott. "Iran Denounces Washington Nuclear Summit, Prepares Its Own." *The Christian Science Monitor*, April 12, 2010. http://www.csmonitor.com/World/Middle-East/2010/0412/Iran-denounces-Washington-nuclear-summit-prepares-its-own.

Pfaff, William. *Barbarian Sentiments: How the American Century Ends*. New York: Hill & Wang, 1989.

Pifer, Steven. "New START: Good News for U.S. Security." *Arms Control Today* (May 2010): 8–14.

Pipes, Richard. "Misinterpreting the Cold War: The Hardliners Had It Right." *Foreign Affairs* 74, no. 1 (1995): 154–60.

Pollack, Joshua. "The Secret Treachery of A.Q. Khan." *Playboy Magazine*, January/February 2012.

Potter, William, and Guakhar Mukhatatzanova. *Nuclear Politics and the Non-Aligned Movement*. London: Routledge and IISS, 2012.

Princeton Seminar. 11 Oct. 1953; Note by the Executive Secretary, James S. Lay, Jr., to the National Security Council, Apr. 14, 1950 (attached to NSC 68).

Pritchard, Charles L. *Failed Diplomacy: The Tragic Story of How North Korea Got the Bomb*. Washington, DC: Brookings Institution Press, 2007.

Rabin, Yitzhak. *The Rabin Memoirs*. Berkeley, CA: University of California Press, 1996.

Ramberg, Bennet. "Redemption Paradox." *Bulletin of Atomic Scientists*, July/August 2006, 50–56.

Rao, Hamid Ali. "Remarks by Ambassador Hamid Ali Rao of India." February 3, 2011, Reaching Critical Will, Women's International League for Peace and Freedom (WILPF). www.reachingcriticalwill.org.

Raviv, Dan, and Yossi Melman. *Every Spy a Prince*. Boston: Houghton-Mifflin, 1990.

"Record of the Meeting of the State-Defense Policy Review Group." *FRUS: 1950*, 1: 162–82.

Reif, Kingston. "U.S. Nuclear Modernization Programs." *Arms Control Association*, October 2016, https://www.armscontrol.org/factsheets/USNuclearModernization.

Reiss, Edward. *The Strategic Defense Initiative*. Cambridge: Cambridge University Press, 1992.

Rep. Ed Royce Holds a Hearing on U.S.-Pakistan Relations. House Committee on Foreign Affairs, December 16, 2015.

Report by the Special Committee of the National Security Council to the President. January 31, 1950, U.S. Department of State, *Foreign Relations of the United States: 1950*, Washington, DC: GPO, 1977, 513-23, hereafter cited as *FRUS*.

Reston, James, and Flora Lewis. *The New York Times*, November 15, 1981.

Rhodes, Richard. *The Making of the Atomic Bomb*. New York: Random House, 1986.

Richardson, Jacques G. "The Bane of 'Inhumane' Weapons and Overkill: An Overview of Increasingly Lethal Arms and the Inadequacy of Regulatory Controls." *Science and Engineering Ethics* 10, no. 4 (December 2004): 667–92.

Richelson, Jeffrey T. *Spying on the Bomb: American Nuclear Intelligence from Nazi Germany to Iran and North Korea*. New York: W. W. Norton, 2006.

Richter, Paul. "GOP Deal Is Sought to Ratify Nuclear Treaty." *Los Angeles Times*, November 4, 2010, A-2.

Robinson-Avila, Kevin. "Overhauling the Nation's Nuclear Arsenal: Sandia National Labs Achieves B61 Milestone." *Albuquerque Journal*, May 18.

Rogin, Josh. "Obama Plans Major Nuclear Policy Changes in His Final Months." *Washington Post*, July 10, 2016. https://www.washingtonpost.com/opinions/global-opinions/.

Rogin, Josh. "White House Announces Nuclear Summit Attendees." *Foreign Policy*, April 10, 2010. http://thecable.foreignpolicy.com/posts/2010/04/10/white_house_announces_nuclear_summit_attendees.

Rotter, Andrew J. *Hiroshima: The World's Bomb*. New York: Oxford University Press, 2008.

"Russia's Upper House Oks Nuclear Arms Treaty." *Los Angeles Times*, January 27, 2011, A-4.

Sagan, Scott D., ed. *Inside Nuclear South Asia*. Stanford: Stanford University Press, 2009.

Sagan, Scott D., and Kenneth N. Waltz. *The Spread of Nuclear Weapons: A Debate Renewed*. New York: W.W. Norton, 2003.

Sanger, David E., and Eric Schmitt. "Pakistani Nuclear Arms Pose Challenge to US Policy." *New York Times*, January 31, 2011. http://www.nytimes.com/2011/02/01/world/asia/01policy.html?pagewanted=all.

Sanger, David, and William J. Broad. "Leaders Gather for Nuclear Talks as New Threat Is Seen." *New York Times*, April 11, 2010. http://www.nytimes.com/2010/04/12/world/12nuke.html.

Savranskaya, Svetlana, and Thomas Blanton, eds. "The INF Treaty and the Washington Summit: 20 Years Later." National Security Archive, *Electronic Briefing Book* No. 238, December 10, 2007.

Savranskaya, Svetlana, and Tom Blanton, eds. "To the Geneva Summit: Perestroika and the Transformationof U.S.-Soviet Relations." National Security Archive, *Electronic Briefing Book* No. 172, November 22, 2005.

Schachter, Oscar. "Self-Defense and the Rule of Law." *American Journal of International Law* 83, no. 2 (1989): 259–77.

Scheinman, Lawrence. *Atomic Energy in France under the Fourth Republic*. Princeton, NJ: Princeton University Press, 1965.

Scheinman, Lawrence. "Disarmament: Have the Five Nuclear Powers Done Enough?" *Arms Control Today* 35 (January/February 2005): 6–8.

Schrafstetter, Susanna, and Stephen Twigge. *Avoiding Armageddon: Europe, the United States, and the Struggle for Nuclear Non-Proliferation, 1945–1970*. Westport, CT: Praeger, 2004.

Schultz, George P., William J. Perry, Henry A. Kissinger, and Sam Nunn. "A World Free of Nuclear Weapons." *The Wall Street Journal*, January 4, 2007. http://online.wsj.com/article/SB116787515251566636.html.

Schultz, Tammy S. "The U.S. Defense Budget and Strategic Overmatch." *World Politics Review*, November 7, 2011.

Schwartz, Stephen I., ed. *Atomic Audit: The Costs and Consequences of U.S. Nuclear Weapons since 1940*. Washington, DC: Brookings Institution Press, 1998.

Scott, Shirley V., Anthony John Billingsley, and Christopher Michaelsen, eds. *International Law and the Use of Force: A Documentary and Reference Guide*. Santa Barbara, CA: Praeger, 2010.

"Scrapping Nuclear Arms is Now Realpolitik." *The Times* (London), April 1, 2009.

Sehgal, Rashme. "Panel: Keep N-Arms Option Open." *The Asian Age*, October 21, 2007. www.lexis-nexis.com.

Shields, John M., and William C. Potter, eds. *Dismantling the Cold War: U.S. and NIS Perspectives on the Nunn-Lugar Cooperative Threat Reduction Program*. Cambridge, MA: MIT Press, 1997.

Shultz, George. "U.S.-Soviet Agreement on the Structure of New Arms Control Negotiations." *American Foreign Policy, Current Documents, 1985*. Washington, DC: U.S. State Department, 1986.

Shultz, George P., William J. Perry, Henry A. Kissinger, and Sam Nunn. "A World Free of Nuclear Weapons." *Wall Street Journal*, January 4, 2007, A-15.

Siler, Michael J. "U.S. Nuclear Non-Proliferation Policy Towards India During and After the Cold War: A Conflict Bargaining Analysis." *Journal of the Third World Spectrum* 5, no. 2 (Fall 1998).

SIPRI Yearbook 1998. Armaments, Disarmament and International Security. Oxford: Oxford University Press, 1998.

Siracusa, Joseph M. *Nuclear Weapons: A Very Short Introduction*, 2nd ed. Oxford: Oxford University Press, 2015.

Siracusa, Joseph M., and David G. Coleman. *Australia Looks to America: Australian-American Relations since Pearl Harbor*. Claremont, CA: Regina Books, 2006.

Skinner, Kiron K., Annelise Anderson, and Martin Anderson, eds. *Reagan: A Life in Letters*. New York: Free Press, 2003.

Smith, Gerald C. *Disarming Diplomat: The Memoirs of Gerald C. Smith, Arms Control Negotiator*. Lanham, MD: Madison Books, 1996.

Smith, Hedrick. "U.S. Assumes the Israelis Have the A-Bomb or Its Parts." *New York Times*, July 18, 1970.

Smith, P. D. *Doomsday Men: The Real Dr. Strangelove and the Dream of the Superweapon*. New York: St. Martin's Press.

Smithson, Amy. "A Phony Farewell to Arms." *Foreign Affairs*, October 1, 2013. www.foreignaffairs.com.

Sokolsky, Richard D., and Eugene B. Rumer. "Nuclear Alarmists." *The Washington Post National Weekly*, March 25–31, 2002.

Sonnenfeldt, Helmut. "Memorandum for Mr. Kissinger, Subject: Implications of the Sino-Soviet Treaty." August 18, 1971. NSC Files, Country Files—Middle East, India Vol. IV 01/06-30/11/71 to India Vol. IV 1/07-30/11/7;

Special Message to Congress on Atomic Energy. October 3, 1945, *Public Papers: Truman: 1945*.

Spector, Leonard S., Chen Kane, Bryan L. Lee, Miles A. Pomper, Amy E. Smithson, Nikolai Sokov, Jessica C. Varnum, and Jon B. Wolfsthal. "Critical Questions: Urgent Decisions for the Second Obama Administration." *Nuclear Threat Initiative*, November 27, 2012. http://www.nti.org/analysis/articles/issues-obama-administration-its-second-term/.

Speer, Albert. *Inside the Third Reich: Memoirs by Albert Speer*. Translated by Richard and Clara Winston. New York: Macmillan, 1970.

Statement by India in the CD Plenary after the Adoption of Decision on Programme of Work Contained in CD/1863. Permanent Representative of India to the Conference on Disarmament, May 29, 2009. http://www.unog.ch/80256EDD006B8954/(httpAssets)/70F44FC9546F2038C12575C50044C565/$file/1139_India.pdf.

"Stopping New START." *Los Angeles Times*, December 21, 2010, A-24.

Strategic Arms Reduction Treaty (START I). Federation of Atomic Scientist (FAS). http://www.fas.org/nuke/control/start1/index.html.

Strobel, Warren P. "Absence of A-Bomb: Were the Nazis Duped—or Simply Dumb?" *U.S. News and World Report*, July 24, 2000, U.S. News Online. www.usnews.com/usnews/doubleissue/mysteries/nazi.htm.

Stumpt, Walto. "South Africa's Nuclear Weapons Program: From Deterrence to Dismantlement." *Arms Control Today* (December 1995/January 1996): 3–8.

Swaine, Michael. "Avoiding U.S.-China Military Rivalry." *The Diplomat*, February 27, 2011. http://thediplomat.com/whats-next-china/avoiding-us-china-military-rivalry.

Szalontai, Balazs. "The Elephant in the Room: The Soviet Union and India's Nuclear Program, 1967–1989." Washington, DC: Nuclear Proliferation International History Project, the Woodrow Wilson International Center, NPIHP Working Paper #1, November 2011: 1.

Tan, Huileng. "North Korea Prepares for Next Nuclear Test as UN, U.S. Weigh Sanction." *CNBC*, September 12, 2016. http://www.cnbc.com/2016/09/11/north-korea-prepares-for-next-nuclear-test-as-un-us-weigh-sanctions.html.

Tanner, Fred, ed. *From Versailles to Baghdad*. New York: United Nations, 1992.

Tannenwald, Nina. "Stigmatizing the Bomb: Origins of the Nuclear Taboo." *International Security* 29, no. 4 (Spring 2005): 5–49.

Taubman, William. *Khrushchev: The Man and His Era*. New York: Norton, 2003.

Televised Strategic Defense Initiative speech. March 23, 1983, *Public Papers: Reagan, 1983*, I.

Thakur, Ramesh, ed. *Nuclear Weapons and International Security: Collected Essays*. London and New York: Routledge, 2015.

Thakur, Ramesh. "Why Obama Should Declare a No-First-Use Policy for Nuclear Weapons." *Bulletin of the Atomic Scientists*, August 19, 2016. http://thebulletin.org/why-obama-should-declare-no-first-use-policy-nuclear-weapons9789.

"The Biological Threat: Germs Don't Respect Borders, So Biological Threats—Manmade And Naturally Occurring—Can Quickly Have Global Impacts." *Nuclear Threat Initiative (NTI)*, October 2016. http://www.nti.org/learn/biological/.

"The Chemical Threat: Why These Banned Weapons Just Won't Go Away." *Nuclear Threat Initiative (NTI)*, October 2016. http://www.nti.org/learn/chemical/.

"The Nixon Administration and the Indian Nuclear Program, 1972–1974. U.S. Post-Mortem on 1974 Indian Test Criticized Intelligence Community Performance for 'Waffling Judgments' and Not Following Up Leads." National Security Archive, *Electronic Briefing Book* No. 367, December 5, 2011.

"The Nixon Administration and the Indian Nuclear Program, 1972–1974." National Security Archive, *Electronic Briefing Book* No. 367.

The President to the Executive Secretary of the National Security Council. *FRUS: 1950*, vol. 1: 235.

"The Strategic Offensive Reductions Treaty (SORT) at a Glance." *Arms Control Association.* www.armscontrol.org.

Thompson, Kenneth W. *Leadership in the Reagan Presidency: Seven Intimate Perspectives*. Lanham, MD: Madison Books, 1992.

Thompson, Kenneth W., ed. *Presidents and Arms Control: Process, Procedures, and Problems*. Lanham, MD: University Press of America, 1997.

Tirman, John, ed. *The Empty Promise: The Growing Case against Star Wars*. Boston: Beacon Press 1986.

Trachtenberg, Marc. *History and Strategy*. Princeton, NJ: Princeton University Press, 1991.

"Trident Costs Must Come from MoD Budget, Osborne Says." BBC News, July 20, 2010. www.bbc.co.uk/news/uk-10812825.

Truman, Harry S. *The Memoirs of Harry S. Truman: Years of Trial and Hope 1946–1953*, 2 vols. New York: Doubleday, 1956, volume II.

Tucker, Jonathan B. "The Chemical Weapons Convention: Has It Enhanced U.S. Security?" *Arms Control Today* (April 2001): 8–12.

U.S. Arms Control & Disarmament Agency. *Arms Control and Disarmament Agreements*. Washington, DC: GPO, 1982.

U.S. Department of State. "Proliferation Security Initiative." Washington, DC, November 2012. http://www.state.gov/t/isn/c10390.htm.

U.S. Department of State. Bureau of Arms Control, Verification and Compliance. *Fact Sheet*, March 29, 2011. http://www.state.gov/t/avc/rls/c29712.htm.

U.S. Office of the Press Secretary. "Proliferation Security Initiative: Statement of Interdiction Principles." The White House, Washington, DC, September 4, 2003. http://www.state.gov/t/isn/c27726.htm.

U.S. State Department. "Proliferation Security Initiative Frequently Asked Questions." Bureau of Non-Proliferation, Washington, DC, May 26, 2005. http://2001-2009.state.gov/t/isn/rls/fs/46839.htm.

"U.S., Russia, India Driving China's Nuclear Modernisation: Pentagon." *The Economic Times*, May 14, 2016. http://economictimes.indiatimes.com.

"U.S.-Russian Nuclear Arms Control Agreements at a Glance." *Arms Control Today* (May 2010): 39–41.

UN Office for Disarmament Affairs. "Treaty on the Non-Proliferation of Nuclear Weapons (NPT)." N.d. http://www.un.org/disarmament/WMD/Nuclear/NPTtext.shtml.

United Nations. Final Documents of the 2010 NPT Review Conference, "The 2010 Review Conference of the Parties to the Treaty on the Non-Proliferation of Nuclear Weapons (NPT)." United Nations: New York, 2010.

United Nations. New York, NY, 2009. http://www.un.org/disarmament/HomePage/ODAPublications/AdhocPublications/PDF/guide.pdf.

United Nations. *The United Nations and Disarmament: 1945–1985*. New York: UN, 1985.

Walker, John R. *British Nuclear Weapons and the Test Ban, 1954–1973: Britain, the United States, Weapons Policy and Nuclear Testing, Tensions and Contradictions*. Surrey UK: Ashgate, 2010.

Walker, Martin. *The Cold War: A History*. New York: Henry Holt, 1993.

Walker, Paul F. "Nunn-Lugar at 15: No Time to Relax Global Threat Reduction Efforts." *Arms Control Today* (May 2006): 6–11.

Walker, William. "Nuclear Enlightenment and Counter-Enlightenment." *International Affairs* 83, no. 3 (2007): 431–53.

Walker, William. "Nuclear Order and Disorder." *International Affairs* 76, no. 4 (2000): 703–24.

Walker, William. *A Perpetual Menace: Nuclear Weapons and International Order*. New York: Routledge, 2011.

Warren, Aiden. *The Obama Administration's Nuclear Weapon Strategy: The Promises of Prague*. New York: Routledge, 2014.

Warren, Aiden. *Prevention, Pre-Emption and the Nuclear Option: From Bush to Obama*. New York: Routledge, 2012.

Warrick, Joby. "Albania's Farewell to Arms." *Washington Post National Weekly*, January 17–23, 2005.

Weart, Spencer, and Gertrude Weiss Szilard, eds. *Leo Szilard: His Version of the Facts: Selected Recollections and Correspondence*. Cambridge, MA: MIT Press, 1978.

Wellen, Russ. "Israel's 1981 Osirak Attack Poor Precedent for Attacking Iran." Institute for Policy Studies [IPS Blog], June 15, 2011.

"What Are the Risks of Nuclear Weapons?" Global Security Institute, September 2012. http://www.gsinstitute.org/dpe/docs/FactSheetRisks.pdf.

White, Hugh. *Nuclear Weapons and American Strategy in the Age of Obama*. Sydney: Lowy Institute for International Policy, September 2010.

Williams, Lauryn. "Politics or Policy? What's Thwarting India's Nuclear Suppliers Group Ambitions." *Bulletin of the Atomic Scientists*, October 14, 2016. http://thebulletin.org/politics-or-policy-what%E2%80%99s-thwarting-india%E2%80%99s-nuclear-suppliers-group-ambitions10040.

Wills, Garry. *Bomb Power: The Modern Presidency and the National Security State*. New York: Penguin, 2010.

Wohlstetter, Albert. "Nuclear Sharing: NATO and the N + 1 Country." *Foreign Affairs* 39 (April 1961): 355–87.

Wohlsetter, Roberta. *The Buddha Smiles: Absent-Minded Peaceful Aid and the Indian Bomb*. Los Angeles: Pan Heuristics, 1977.

Wolfsthal, Jon B., Jeffrey Lewis, and Marc Quint. "The Trillion Dollar Nuclear Triad." James Martin Center for Non-Proliferation Studies, January 2014.

Woolf, Amy F. "Non-Strategic Nuclear Weapons." *CRS Report for Congress*, RL32572. Washington, DC: Congressional Research Service, March 23, 2016. https://www.fas.org/sgp/crs/nuke/RL32572.pdf.

Yergin, Daniel. *Shattered Peace: The Origins of the Cold War and the National Security States*. Boston: Houghton Mifflin, 1977.

Young, Ken. *The American Bomb in Britain: US Air Forces' Strategic Presence, 1946–64.* Manchester: Manchester University Press, 2016.

Younger, Stephen M. *The Bomb: A New History.* New York: Harper-Collins, 2009.

Zaloga, Steven J. *The Kremlin's Nuclear Sword: The Rise and Fall of Russia's Strategic Nuclear Forces, 1945–2000.* Washington, DC: Smithsonian Institution Press, 2002.

Zuberi, Martin. "Stalin and the Bomb." *Strategic Analysis* 23, no. 7 (October 1999). Online.

Zubok, Vladislav M. *A Failed Empire: The Soviet Union in the Cold War from Stalin to Gorbachev.* Chapel Hill: University of North Carolina Press, 2007.

Index

ABM treaty, 179; for NWFZs, 42, 43, 146, 147, 149
Abraham, Itty, 106
Acheson, Dean, 27, 29–30, 61
Adenauer, Konrad, 62, 127
Agency for the Prohibition of Nuclear Weapons in Latin America, 150
Ahmadinejad, Mahmoud, 95–96
Akhromeyev, Sergei, 38–39, 44–45
Albright, Madeleine, 115
Allison, Graham, 53
Anderson, John, 7–8
Andropov, Yuri, 42, 135
Antarctic Treaty (1959), 149
Antiballistic Missile treaty. *See* ABM treaty
AQ Khan Ring, xii, xiv
Arkin, William, 179
arms race, 27–35, 39–40
Aspin, Les, 129–130
Atomic Audit, 35, 50, 50–51, 51
atomic bombs. *See* nuclear weapons
atomic diplomacy, 15
"Atoms for Peace", 90, 104, 126
Attlee, Clement, 63

Bailey, Kathleen, 144
Bainbridge, Kenneth, 14
Baker, James, 169, 172, 173–174
Ballistic Missile Early Warning System, 51
Barnett, Thomas, 97

Baruch, Bernard, 125–126
Baruch Plan, 125–126, 140
Begin, Menachem, 94
Begin Doctrine, 94
Ben-Gurion, David, 90–91
Bennett, Bruce W., 112, 116
Beria, Lavrenti, 19, 21
Beschloss, Michael, 37–38, 170
Bethe, Hans, 12
Betts, Richard, 132
Bevin, Ernest, 59
Bhutto, Zulfiqar Ali, 109, 109–110
biological weapons. *See* poisonous weapons
Bix, Hans, 203
Blackett, P. M. S., 8, 19, 63
Blair, Bruce, 50
Blair, Tony, 133, 206
Bloch, Felix, 12
Bohr, Neils, 4
Bosworth, Stephen, 117
Bradley, Omar N., 31
Brands, Hal, 140–141, 141
Brands, William, 109
Brandt, Willy, 127–128
Brazil, xiii, 129
Brezhnev, Leonid, 35, 38–39, 49, 134, 135
Briggs, Lyman J., 9–10
Brighter than a Thousand Suns (Jungk), 4
Brodie, Bernard, 53
Brodie, Janet Farrell, 35

Brown, Harold, 49, 186–187
Brzezinski, Zbigniew, 48–49, 135
Bulletin of Atomic Scientists, 53
Bundy, McGeorge, 1–2, 5, 62, 71
Bunn, Matthew, 211, 216, 221–222, 223
Burr, William, 32, 51, 72–73, 80, 91–92
Burtev, Oleg, 176–177
Bush, George H. W., 113–114, 184; Cold War for, 168–170; disarmament by, 175; Gorbachev and, 169–172; NPT and, 136–137; Yeltsin and, 173–174
Bush, George W., xiv, 49, 50, 115–116, 133, 174; ABM treaty for, 179; CTBT and, 139, 146, 147–148; Iraq and, 203; nuclear weapons for, 152; Putin and, 179–181
Bush, Vannevar, 9–10, 12
Butler, Nicola, 68

Cairncross, John, 19
Cameron, David, 68
Canada, 8, 11, 69, 128, 199
Cannon, Lou, 37
Carlucci, Frank, 47, 171
Carter, Jimmy, 48–49, 114–115, 117, 135
Cartwright, James, 184
Cha, Victor, 113
chemical weapons. *See* poisonous weapons
Cheney, Richard, 169, 172
Chernenko, Konstantin, 135
Chernobyl disaster, 38–39
Cherwell (Lord), 6, 8
Chiang Ching-kuo, 128
China, xii, xvii; in Cold War, 27; delivery systems in, 84–85; deterrence for, 82–84; fission for, 78–79; in global security, 141; ICBMs for, 79–80, 81–85; India and, 103, 108; Korean War and, 76–77; North Korea and, 114, 116–117; NPT and, 83–84; nuclear modernization in, 147, 157; nuclear programs in, 76–77; nuclear security summits for, 212; nuclear weapons in, 59–60, 78–79; Pakistan and, 110; poisonous weapons and, 202; Russia and, 83; *The Science of Operations of the Second Artillery*, 81, 82; United States and, 76–77, 79–85; USSR and, 60, 78–79, 141

Chirac, Jacques, 74
Churchill, Winston, 6, 7–8, 11, 63
Clinton, Bill, 49, 113–115, 137–138, 144, 145, 174
Cohen, Avner, 91–92
Cohen, Michael, 97
Cold War, 179; arms race in, 27–35, 39–40; for Bush, George H. W., 168–170; China in, 27; Cuban missile crisis in, 38–39, 66, 130, 150; delivery systems in, 33–34, 50–51; Doomsday Machine in, 50–51; for France, 73–76; Geneva Summit for, 41–43; global security and, xi, 221; Gorbachev and, 31, 35, 35–36, 52–53; Helsinki Accords in, 40; ICBMs in, 33, 40–41, 46; INF treaty for, 46–47; NATO in, xii, 40–41, 43, 46, 61–63; North Korea in, 30–31; NSC 68 and, 27–35, 55n9; nuclear modernization after, 167–168; nuclear weapons in, 18–19; *One Minute to Midnight: Kennedy, Khrushchev, and Castro on the Brink of Nuclear War* (Dobbs), 48; peace and, 35–36; poisonous weapons in, 199–201; politics of, 31–35, 37–38, 113, 125–126; Reagan and, 35–36, 52–53; Reykjavik Summit for, 43–45; SALT II in, 40, 44; SALT I in, 40, 44; South Korea in, 30–31, 113–115, 117–118; START and, xiii, 41, 42, 171–172; Strategic Defense Initiative in, 37, 41–42, 42–43, 43–45, 46; for United Kingdom, 67–69; *War and Peace* (Brodie), 53; warning systems in, 48–51; Washington summits for, 40–41, 171
comprehensive nuclear test ban (CTBT), 134; Russia and, 138–139; United Nations and, 137–139; United States and, xiv, xvi, 134–136, 136–139, 146–148, 185; for USSR, 134
Conant, James B., 10, 28
Convention on Chemical Weapons, 201–202, 205, 223
Convention on the Prohibition of the Development, Production and Stockpiling of Bateriological (Biological) and Toxin Weapons,

200–201
cooperative threat reduction (CTR), 152–154
Coyle, Philip, 139
CTBT. *See* comprehensive nuclear test ban
CTR. *See* cooperative threat reduction
Cuban missile crisis, 38–39, 66, 130, 150
cyberattacks, xi, xviii, 97
Czechoslovakia, 22

Davenport, Kelsey, 118
Defense Support Program, 50–51
DeKlerk, F. W., 129
delivery systems, 171; in China, 84–85; in Cold War, 33–34, 50–51; CTR for, 153; in France, 75, 75–76; ICBMs for, 33, 50; for India, 107–108; for Israel, 94–95; in North Korea, 117–118; for Pakistan, 112; Polaris for, 65–67; Skybolt for, 65–67; submarine-launched ballistic missiles in, 33, 50, 67, 108, 153; for United Kingdom, 66–67. *See also* intercontinental ballistic missiles
deterrence, 82–84
Deutch, John, 186–187
dirty bombs, xii, 154–155, 206, 212
disarmament, 140; CTR for, 153; Eighteen Nation Disarmament Committee for, 142; Geneva Conference on Disarmament, xiv; for global security, xvi, xvii; of ICBMs, 147; of nuclear weapons, 174–177; by Russia, 172, 174–177; in United Kingdom, 68–69; by United States, xv–xvii, 172, 174–177. *See also* Non-Proliferation Treaty; SORT treaty
Dobbs, Michael, 48
Dobrynin, Anatoly, 52, 53, 141
Doomsday Machine, 50–51
Douglas-Home, Alec, 64
Duckett, Carl, 93
Duefler, Charles, 133
Dulles, John Foster, 77

Egypt, 90, 101–102, 128, 145
Eighteen Nation Disarmament Committee, 142
Einstein, Albert, 9

Eisenhower, Dwight D., 34, 53, 62, 65, 77; "Atoms for Peace" by, 90, 104, 126; France and, 70–72
English, Robert, 36
Europe, 170, 196–199
Evans, Gareth, 222

Farley, Robert, 222
Fermi, Enrico, 3, 7
Financial Action Task Force, 209, 211
Fisher, Richard, 83
fission: for China, 78–79; for Germany, 7; for India, 104, 108; for Iran, 95–96, 98–99; for Israel, 90–91, 94; in Manhattan Project, 11, 11–14, 17, 125; for North Korea, 113–116; for nuclear weapons, 1–2, 2–4, 5, 5–6, 12–14; for Pakistan, 110–111; for terrorism, 218n45; for United Kingdom, 63–64; for USSR, 19–22
Fitzgerald, Frances, 36
Flerov, Georgi, 19
Ford, Gerald, 72–73, 135
Forden, Geoffrey, 49
Fox, Liam, 68
France, xii, xiii, xvii; Cold War for, 73–76; delivery systems in, 75, 75–76; funding in, 74; Israel and, 90–91; NATO and, 71–72; nuclear programs in, 60–61, 69–70; nuclear weapons in, 59–60, 70–73; Pakistan and, 110; poisonous weapons in, 202; Treaty of Strassburg for, 195; in Tripartite Agreement, 90; United Kingdom and, 71; United States and, 60–61; USSR and, 72
Freedman, Lawrence, 61, 66
Frisch, Otto, 6, 7
Fuchs, Klaus, 7, 19, 22, 63
funding: for arms race, 29–31, 34–35; Financial Action Task Force and, 209, 211; in France, 74; for terrorism, 209; in United Kingdom, 67–68; for United Nations, 209; in United States, 29–31, 34–35, 37; in USSR, 35, 38–39

Gaddafi, Moammar, 129
Gaddis, John Lewis, 32–33
Galamas, Francisco, 102–103
Galley, Robert, 73

Gallois, Pierre, 131
Gallucci, Robert, 115
Gandhi, Indira, 104–106, 109, 121n49
Gandhi, Rajiv, 185
Garchev, Pavel, 49
Garthoff, Raymond, 37, 135
Gates, Robert M., 36, 47, 169
de Gaulle, Charles, 59, 61, 66, 69–72, 127
Gavin, Frances, 97, 222
Geneva Conference on Disarmament, xiv
Geneva Protocol of 1925, 197–199
Geneva Summit, 41–43
Germany, 1, 2–5, 7, 195
Gilpatric, Roswell, 141
Glass, Andrew J., 44
Global Initiative to Combat Nuclear
    Terrorism, 208, 209, 214
global security, 101–103, 193–194,
    221–222; China in, 141; Cold War and,
    xi, xiv–xv, 221; dirty bombs in, xii,
    154–155, 206, 212; disarmament for,
    xvi, xvii; Eighteen Nation Disarmament
    Committee for, 142; "Global Security
    Engagement: A New Model for
    Cooperative Threat Reduction",
    153–154; International Monitoring
    System for, 137, 139; Joint
    Comprehensive Plan of Action for, 100;
    North Korea in, 117–118; NPT and, xii,
    xvii, 40, 157–158; nuclear
    modernization and, 224–225; nuclear
    security summits for, 212–216;
    poisonous weapons and, 217n22,
    222–224; regulation for, 194–196;
    Taiwan in, 81, 84, 128; terrorism in, xi,
    xiii, xvi, 52–53, 111, 207–208; for
    United Kingdom, 67–69; for United
    States, 27–28, 30–31, 158–159. *See
    also* global zero; non-proliferation
    regime; peace; Strategic Arms
    Reduction Treaties
Global Threat Reduction Initiative (GTRI),
    154–155
global zero, xiv, 136, 185–189, 212
Gomberg, Henry Jacob, 91
Goodby, James, 153, 156
Gorbachev, Mikhail, 168, 175; Bush,
    George H. W., and, 169–172; Cold War
    and, 31, 35, 35–36, 52–53; at Geneva

Summit, 41–43; INF treaty and, 46–47;
    NPT and, 136; nuclear weapons and,
    37–40; Reagan and, 135–136; at
    Reykjavik Summit, 43–45; warning
    systems and, 48–51; at Washington
    summits, 40–41
Gore, Al, 145
Goudsmit, Samuel A., 4
Gowing, Margaret, 6, 63–64
Graham, Thomas, 46, 137, 140, 144,
    144–145, 146
Grechko, Andrei, 32, 35
Gromyko, Andrei, 42
Groves, Leslie R., 11, 12, 13, 14–15, 22
GTRI. *See* Global Threat Reduction
    Initiative
Gupta, Vipin, 107

Hadley, Stephen J., 169

The Hague "Poison" Gases Conventions,
    196–197
Hahn, Otto, 2–3
von Halban, Hans, 7
Hammond, Philip, 69
ul-Haq, Zia, 110–111
Hatfield-Mitchell-Exon amendment,
    136–137
Hathaway, Robert, 83
Heisenberg, Werner, 3–4
Heisenberg's War (Power), 4
Helsinki Accords, 40
Hezbollah, 204
Hirohito (Emperor), 18
Hiroshima, 14–19
Hitler, Adolf, 4, 5, 199
Hoagland, Jim, 179
Hoinkes, Mary Elizabeth, 144
Holloway, David, 19, 20, 22
Holum, John, 180–181
Hussein, Saddam, 133

IAEA. *See* International Atomic Energy
    Agency
ICBMs. *See* intercontinental ballistic
    missiles
India, xii, xiv, xvii, 52, 107; China and,
    103, 108; delivery systems for,
    107–108; fission for, 104, 108; NPT

for, 103, 104, 107–108; NSG and, 155–156; nuclear modernization in, 157; nuclear weapons and, 89, 103–108, 121n49; Pakistan and, 103, 105–106, 108, 109–110; peaceful nuclear explosions for, 105, 106; United Nations Security Council and, 107; United States and, 103–107; USSR and, 105–106

INF treaty, 46–47

Ingram, Paul, 177

intercontinental ballistic missiles (ICBMs), 50; for China, 79–80, 81–85, 84; in Cold War, 33, 40–41, 46; CTR for, 153; disarmament of, 147; in warning systems, 48

Intermediate Nuclear Forces treaty. *See* INF treaty

International Atomic Energy Agency (IAEA), xv, 187; Iran and, 96–97, 99–100; in North Korea, 113–115, 117; NPT and, 126–127, 143, 144, 147; nuclear modernization for, 185; NWFZs and, 149; poisonous weapons for, 202; United Nations and, 133

International Monitoring System, 137, 139

Iran, xii, xiv, xvi; fission for, 95–96, 98–99; IAEA and, 96–97, 99–100; Islam and, 96, 97, 98; *Middle East-South Asia: Nuclear Handbook* (CIA), 95; NPT and, 95, 96, 98–99; nuclear programs in, 95–100; nuclear security summits for, 212; nuclear weapons for, 89; P5+1 and, 98–100; United Nations and, 95–98

Iraq, 94, 132, 133, 168, 201, 202–203

ISIS, 207, 223

Islam, 96, 97, 98, 195

Israel, xii, xiv, 101; Begin Doctrine for, 94; delivery systems for, 94–95; Egypt and, 145; fission for, 90–91, 94; France and, 90–91; Middle East and, 92–93, 93–94; military action by, 132–133; NPT and, 93; nuclear programs in, 91; nuclear weapons in, 90–95

Italy, 198

Japan: North Korea and, 115, 118–119; nuclear programs in, 1, 127; nuclear

security summits for, 215; poisonous weapons and, 198, 199, 202; United States against, 14–18; USSR against, 18–19

Johnson, Louis, 27, 28–29

Johnson, Lyndon, 62–63, 79–80, 140, 141–142

Johnson, Rebecca, 68

Johnson, Robert, 79–80

Joint Comprehensive Plan of Action, 100

Joliot-Curie, Frédéric, 59

Joyner, Christopher, 149

Jungk, Robert, 4

Kallenborn, Zach, 205

Kang, David, 115

Kant, Immanuel, 196

Kapitsa, Peter, 19

Karlsch, Rainer, 4–5

Karpin, Michael, 90, 91

Kehler, Robert, 184

Kennan, George F., 53

Kennedy, John F., 62, 65–66, 72, 91, 127; China for, 141; Cuban missile crisis for, 130; Khrushchev and, 134

Kerr, Paul, 95, 111

Kerry, John, 204

Kevles, Daniel, 8

Khamene'i, Ayatollah, 96, 97

Khan, Abdul Qadeer, 110, 111, 115, 127

Khlopin, Vitalii, 20

Khrushchev, Nikita, 38–39, 60, 66, 72, 78–79; China for, 141; Kennedy and, 134

Kimball, Daryl G., xvi, 178

Kim Gye Gwan, 117

Kim Il Sung, 113

Kim Jong Un, 116, 118

Kissinger, Henry, 73, 91–92, 93, 103, 106, 184; for global zero, xiv–xv, 185–187, 212

Kistiakowsky, George B., 7, 10

Korean War, 76–77, 198

Kowarski, Lev, 7

Krass, Allan, 201

Kristensen, Hans, 161

Kroenig, Matthew, 97–98

Kulacki, Gregory, 81–82

Kurchatov, Igor, 19–20, 21–22

Kyl, Jon, 138, 152

Lamborn, Doug, 83
Landau, Lev, 19
Lapp, Ralph, 32
Laurence, William, 20
Lavrov, Sergey, 204
Lawrence, Ernest, 8, 10
Levin, Carl, 184
Lewis, Jeffrey, 118
Libya, 129, 147
Lieber Code, 196
Lieberman, Joseph, 182
Lilienthal, David, 17–18
Limited Nuclear Test Ban (1963), 40, 134
Lindemann, Frederick, 6
Lisbon Protocol, 175
Louis XV, 195–196
Lugar, Richard, 152

MacArthur, Douglas, 18
Macmillan, Harold, 64, 66
Malta summit, 169–170
Mandelbaum, Michael, 33
Manhattan Project, 11–14, 17, 125
Manley, John H., 12
Mao Zedong, 60, 76–79
Mark, Carson, 22
Markey, Edward J., 41
Marshall, George C., 10
Matlock, Jack F., Jr., 36, 47
the MAUD committee, 6–8, 10, 63
McGoldrick, Fred, 156
McGovern, George, 53
McMahon, Brien, 63
McMahon Act, 63, 64, 65
McNamara, Robert, 60, 72, 80
Medvedev, Dmitry, 182–184, 186
Meier, Oliver, 177
Meir, Golda, 91–92, 93
Meitner, Lise, 2, 6–7
Middle East: Israel and, 92–93, 93–94;
　　NPT and, 101–103; nuclear weapons
　　and, 89, 99–100, 101–103
*Middle East-South Asia: Nuclear
　　Handbook* (CIA), 95
military action: by Israel, 132–133; for
　　non-proliferation regime, 132–133; by
　　United States, 133

military-industrial complex (United
　　States), 34–35
Missile Defense Alert System, 51
Mitterrand, Francois, 136
MLF. *See* Multilateral Force
Molotov, Vyacheslav, 19
Mongbe, Rene Valery, 145
Moon Sang-gyun, 118
Mouallem, Walid, 204
Mueller, John, 32
Mukhatzhanova, Gaukhar, 222
Müller, Harald, xiv
Multilateral Force (MLF), 61–63, 127,
　　140–141
Myrdal, Alva, 53
The Myth of Independence (Bhutto), 109

Narang, Vipin, 103–104
National Defense Research Committee, 10
NATO, 61, 224; in Cold War, xii, 40–41,
　　43, 46, 61–63; France and, 71–72; MLF
　　and, 140–141; "Nuclear Sharing:
　　NATO and the N + 1 Country"
　　(Wohlstetter), 72; nuclear weapons and,
　　177–178; Russia and, 177–178; United
　　States and, 151. *See also* Multilateral
　　Force
Newhouse, John, 5, 10, 64–65, 127,
　　131–132
New START. *See* Strategic Arms
　　Reduction Treaties
New York City, 207–208
Nichols, Kenneth D., 22
Nikitin, Mary Beth, 111
Nitze, Paul H., 28–30, 31
Nixon, Richard, 72–73, 77, 80, 199–200,
　　201; Brezhnev and, 134; India for, 103,
　　106; for Israel, 91–92, 93
non-proliferation regime, 139–143, 152;
　　for CTBT, 134–139; CTR for,
　　152–154; GTRI for, 154–155; military
　　action for, 132–133; MLF for, 127;
　　NSG and, 155–156; nuclear weapons
　　and, 125–129; NWFZs and, 148–152
Non-Proliferation Treaty (NPT), 129, 188,
　　224, 225; China and, 83–84; global
　　security and, xii, xvii, 40, 157–158;
　　IAEA and, 126–127, 143, 144, 147;
　　indefinite extension of, 144–146; for

India, 103, 104, 107–108; Iran and, 95, 96, 98–99; Israel and, 93; Middle East and, 101–103; for North Korea, 147; nuclear modernization and, 157–161; Pakistan and, 103, 109–110; review conferences for, 143, 146–148, 200; for United Kingdom, 147; for United Nations, 139–143; United States and, 136–139, 209; USSR and, 103

non-state actors. *See* terrorism

Norstad, Lauris, 62

North Atlantic Treaty Organization. *See* NATO

North Korea, xii, xiv; China and, 114, 116–117; in Cold War, 30–31; delivery systems in, 117–118; fission for, 113–116; in global security, 117–118; IAEA in, 113–115, 117; Japan and, 115, 118–119; NPT for, 147; nuclear weapons and, 89, 112–118; South Korea and, 30–31, 113–115, 117–118; United Nations and, 116–117; United Nations Security Council and, 116; United States and, 113–116; USSR and, 113

NPT. *See* Non-Proliferation Treaty

NSC 68, 27–35, 55n9

NSG. *See* Nuclear Suppliers Group

nuclear modernization: in China, 147, 157; after Cold War, 167–168; global security and, 224–225; for IAEA, 185; in India, 157; NPT and, 157–161; in Pakistan, 157; in Russia, 157, 160, 167–168; SORT treaty and, 179–181, 183; START and, 167, 168–170, 173–174, 181–184; in United States, 157–161, 167–168

nuclear programs, 40; Brazil and, xiii, 129; in China, 76–77; in Egypt, 128; in France, 60–61, 69–70; in Germany, 1, 2–5; GTRI and, 154–155; in Iran, 95–100; in Iraq, 132; in Israel, 91; in Japan, 1, 127; Libya and, 129, 147; Manhattan Project for, 11–14, 17, 125; the MAUD committee, 6–8, 10; nuclear security summits and, 213–214; nuclear weapons and, 143; in Pakistan, 110–111; South Africa and, xiii, 128–129, 200–201; Switzerland and,

128; Taiwan and, 128; in United Kingdom, 5–6, 60–61; United Nations Security Council and, 59–60; in United States, 1, 1–2, 8–11; in USSR, 19–22

nuclear proliferation, 129–132, 139

nuclear security summits: for China, 212; for global security, 212–216; for Iran, 212; for Japan, 215; nuclear programs and, 213–214; Pakistan and, 216; Russia and, 216; for United Nations, 212; for United States, 212–216

"Nuclear Sharing: NATO and the N + 1 Country" (Wohlstetter), 72

Nuclear Suppliers Group (NSG), 155–156

nuclear-weapon-free zones (NWFZs), 126; ABM treaty for, 42, 43, 146, 147, 149; Antarctic Treaty (1959) as, 149; Bilateral Agreement for the Exclusively Peaceful Uses of Nuclear Energy for, 150; Cuban missile crisis and, 150; IAEA and, 149; non-proliferation regime and, 148–152; Outer Space Treaty as, 149; Pelindaba Treaty for, 151–152; Rapacki Proposals for, 150, 151; Raratonga Treaty for, 150, 152; Seabed Treaty as, 149; Treaty of Bangkok for, 150–151; Treaty of Semipalatinsk for, 151–152; United Nations for, 101, 149

nuclear weapons, 37–40; Canada and, 8, 11, 69, 128, 199; in China, 59–60, 78–79; in Cold War, 18–19; disarmament of, 174–177; fission for, 1–2, 2–4, 5, 5–6, 12–14; in France, 59–60, 70–73; Hiroshima and, 14–19; India and, 89, 103–108, 121n49; in Iran, 89; in Israel, 90–95; Manhattan Project for, 11, 11–14, 17, 125; Middle East and, 89, 99–100, 101–103; NATO and, 177–178; non-proliferation regime and, 125–129; North Korea and, 89, 112–118; nuclear programs and, 143; "Nuclear Sharing: NATO and the N + 1 Country" (Wohlstetter), 72; in Pakistan, 89, 103–104, 109–112; peace and, 32–33, 52–53, 74–75, 129–132; Russia and, xii, xiii, 53; Syria and, 89, 133; terrorism and, 206–207; in United Kingdom, 59–60, 63–65; United

Nations and, 89–90; United States and, xii, xiii, xv, xvii, 14–18, 53; "Worse than Irrelevant? British Nuclear Weapons in the 21st Century", 68. *See also* nuclear modernization; Weapons of Mass Destruction

Nunn, Sam, xiv–xv, 152, 185–187, 212

NWFZs. *See* nuclear-weapon-free zones

Obama, Barack, 186, 187–188, 204; China and, 81, 84; CTBT and, 139; global security for, xv–xvi, 158–159, 177, 185; India and, 107–108; Iran and, 98–100; Medvedev and, 182–184; North Korea and, 116–118; at nuclear security summits, 212–213, 214; NWFZs for, 152; Proliferation Security Initiative for, 210, 211; terrorism and, 208–209

Olson, Richard, 112

O'Neil, Andrew, 159

One Minute to Midnight: Kennedy, Khrushchev, and Castro on the Brink of Nuclear War (Dobbs), 48

Oppenheimer, Robert J., 12–14, 28, 29

Osborne, George, 68

Outer Space Treaty, 149

P5+1, 98–100

Pabian, Frank, 107

Pakistan, xii, xiv, xvii, 52; China and, 110; delivery systems for, 112; fission for, 110–111; France and, 110; India and, 103, 105–106, 108, 109–110; *The Myth of Independence* (Bhutto), 109; NPT and, 103, 109–110; nuclear modernization in, 157; nuclear programs in, 110–111; nuclear security summits and, 216; nuclear weapons in, 89, 103–104, 109–112; United Kingdom and, 109; United States and, 106, 109–112

peace: "Atoms for Peace", 90, 104, 126; Bilateral Agreement for the Exclusively Peaceful Uses of Nuclear Energy for, 150; Cold War and, 35–36; deterrence for, 82–84; Islam for, 195; nuclear weapons and, 32–33, 52–53, 74–75, 129–132; peaceful nuclear explosions

for, 105, 106; United Nations for, 101

Peaceful Nuclear Explosions Treaty, 170

Peierls, Rudolf, 6, 7

Pelindaba Treaty, 151–152

Peng Dehaui, 77

Perle, Richard, 37, 46

Perry, William, xiv–xv, 185–187, 189, 212

Petrazhak, Konstantin, 19

Petrov, Stanislav, 48

Pifer, Steven, 183

Pipes, Richard, 37–38

Poindexter, John, 44

poisonous weapons: China and, 202; in Cold War, 199–201; in Europe, 196–199; in France, 202; *Geneva Protocol of 1925* against, 197–199; global security and, 217n22, 222–224; *The Hague "Poison" Gases Conventions*, 196–197; for IAEA, 202; in Iraq, 201, 202–203; Italy and, 198; Japan and, 198, 199, 202; in Korean War, 198; Louis XV against, 195–196; regulation of, 196–203; South Africa and, 200–201; terrorism and, 193–194; United Nations Security Council on, 200; USSR and, 197, 200; Versailles Treaty "Poison Gas" Ban, 197; Washington Treaty on Use of Gases, 197

Polaris, 65–67

politics, 31–35, 37–38, 113, 125–126

Pollack, Jonathan, 83

Pompidou, Georges, 72–73

Pontecorvo, Bruno, 19

Potsdam Conference, 14, 18

Potter, William, 153, 222

Powell, Colin, 115–116, 171, 180, 184

Power, Thomas, 4

Proliferation Security Initiative, 208, 210–211

Pullinger, Stephen, 68

Putin, Vladimir, 179–181

Al-Qaeda, 206

Qian Xuesen, 78

Rabi, Isador, 13, 22

Rabin, Yitzhak, 91, 93

Rambert, Bennett, 132

Rapacki Proposals, 150, 151
Raratonga Treaty, 150, 152
Ray, Maud, 6–7
Reagan, Ronald, 168–169; Cold War and, 35–36, 52–53; CTBT for, 135–136; at Geneva Summit, 41–43; INF treaty and, 46–47; nuclear weapons and, 37–40; Pakistan and, 110–111; at Reykjavik Summit, 43–45; warning systems and, 48–51; at Washington summits, 40–41
regulation: for global security, 194–196; of poisonous weapons, 196–203
Republic of Korea. *See* South Korea
Reston, James, 43–44
review conferences, 143, 146–148, 200
Reykjavik Summit, 43–45
Rice, Condoleezza, 184
Richardson, Jacques, 201
Roosevelt, Franklin D., 9–11, 14, 22, 199
Rotter, Andrew, 18–19
Rouhani, Hassan, 99
Rumsfeld, Donald, 179
Rusk, Dean, 141
Russia, 52–53; China and, 83; CTBT and, 138–139; CTR for, 152–153; disarmament by, 172, 174–177; NATO and, 177–178; NSG and, 155–156; nuclear modernization in, 157, 160, 167–168; nuclear security summits and, 216; nuclear weapons and, xii, xiii, 53; SORT treaty for, 179–181, 183; Syria and, 204–205; United States and, 147, 208–209. *See also* Putin, Vladimir; USSR; Yeltsin, Boris

Sachs, Alexander, 9
Sagan, Scott, 131
SALT I, 40, 44
SALT II, 40, 44
Sanger, David, 212
Sarkozy, Nicolas, 75
Schaaf, Michael, 5
Scheinman, Lawrence, 146, 147
Schlesinger, James, 73, 135
Schultz, Tammy, 80
The Science of Operations of the Second Artillery, 81, 82
Scowcroft, Brent, 168–169, 171, 172
Seabed Treaty, 149

Seaborg, Glenn, 3, 10
Seber, Robert, 12–13
Second Artillery. *See* China
Shales, Tom, 47
Shcherbakov, Dmitrii, 20
Sherman, Forrest P., 31
Shevardnadze, Eduard, 39–40, 43, 46, 113, 136, 144
Shu Guang Zhang, 78
Shulman, Marshal, 49
Shultz, George, 42, 44, 46, 47, 111; for global zero, xiv–xv, 136, 184, 185–187, 212
Skybolt, 65–67
Smith, Gerald C., 33
Smith, Hedrick, 91–93
Smithson, Amy, 205
SORT treaty, 179–181, 183
South Africa, xiii, 128–129, 200–201
South Asia. *See* India; Pakistan
South Korea, 30–31, 113–115, 117–118
Soviet Union. *See* USSR
Speer, Albert, 5
Der Spiegel, 5
Stalin, Joseph, 8, 14, 15, 19, 38–39, 76
START. *See* Strategic Arms Reduction Treaties
Star Wars program. *See* Strategic Defense Initiative
Stimson, Henry L., 10, 14–15, 17
Strassman, Fritz, 2
Strategic Arms Reduction Treaties (START), 159–160, 188; Cold War and, xiii, 41, 42, 171–172; nuclear modernization and, 167, 168–170, 173–174, 181–184
Strategic Defense Initiative, 37, 41–42, 42–43, 43–45, 46
Strauss, Lewis L., 2, 63
Strobel, Warren, 4
Strong, Anna Louise, 76
submarine-launched ballistic missiles, 33, 50, 67, 108, 153
Switzerland, 128
Symington, Stuart, 92
Syria, 89, 133, 204–205
Szalontai, Balazs, 103
Szcygiel, Marek, 178
Szilard, Leo, 2, 7, 8–10

Taiwan, 81, 84, 128
Talbot, Strobe, 170
Teller, Edward, 12
terrorism: CTR and, 153–154; Financial
    Action Task Force against, 209, 211;
    fission for, 218n45; funding for, 209;
    Global Initiative to Combat Nuclear
    Terrorism, 208, 209, 214; in global
    security, xi, xiii, xvi, 52–53, 111,
    207–208; Hezbollah in, 204; ISIS as,
    207, 223; in New York City, 207–208;
    nuclear weapons and, 206–207; Obama
    and, 208–209; poisonous weapons and,
    193–194; Al-Qaeda in, 206; United
    States and, 179, 207–208
Thatcher, Margaret, 132
Thomson, G. P., 6
Threshold Test Ban Treaty, 170
Tizard, Henry, 6, 8
Trachtenberg, Marc, 32–33
Treaty of Bangkok, 150–151
Treaty of Semipalatinsk, 151–152
Treaty of Strassburg, 195
Treaty on Conventional Forces in Europe,
    170
Trinity test. *See* Manhattan Project
Tripartite Agreement, 90
Truman, Harry S., 14–17, 27–30, 55n9, 62,
    125
Turner, Michael, 83

United Kingdom, xiii; Cold War for,
    67–69; delivery systems for, 66–67;
    disarmament in, 68–69; fission for,
    63–64; France and, 71; funding in,
    67–68; global security for, 67–69; the
    MAUD committee in, 6–8, 10, 63; NPT
    for, 147; nuclear programs in, 5–6,
    60–61; nuclear weapons in, 59–60,
    63–65; Pakistan and, 109; in Tripartite
    Agreement, 90; United States and, 11,
    60–61, 65–67; USSR and, 72
United Nations, 203; Baruch Plan for,
    125–126, 140; CTBT and, 137–139;
    funding for, 209; IAEA and, 133; Iran
    and, 95–98; North Korea and, 116–117;
    NPT for, 139–143; nuclear security
    summits for, 212; nuclear weapons and,
    89–90; for NWFZs, 101, 149; for

peace, 101
United Nations Security Council: India
    and, 107; Iraq and, 133; MLF and,
    61–63; North Korea and, 116; nuclear
    programs and, 59–60; on poisonous
    weapons, 200. *See also* China; France;
    P5+1; Russia; United Kingdom; United
    States; USSR
United States: atomic diplomacy for, 15;
    China and, 76–77, 79–85; CTBT and,
    xiv, xvi, 134–136, 136–139, 146–148,
    185; CTR for, 152–154; Defense
    Support Program for, 50–51; deterrence
    for, 82–84; disarmament by, xv–xvii,
    172, 174–177; France and, 60–61;
    funding in, 29–31, 34–35, 37; global
    security for, 27–28, 30–31, 158–159;
    Hatfield-Mitchell-Exon amendment in,
    136–137; India and, 103–107; against
    Japan, 14–18; Manhattan Project in,
    11–14, 17, 125; military action by, 133;
    military-industrial complex for, 34–35;
    Missile Defense Alert System for, 51;
    National Defense Research Committee
    for, 10; NATO and, 151; North Korea
    and, 113–116; NPT and, 136–139, 209;
    NSG and, 155–156; nuclear
    modernization in, 157–161, 167–168;
    nuclear programs in, 1–2, 8–11; nuclear
    security summits for, 212–216; nuclear
    weapons and, xii, xiii, xv, xvii, 14–18,
    53; P5+1 and, 98–100; Pakistan and,
    106, 109–112; Polaris for, 65–67;
    Russia and, 147, 208–209; Skybolt for,
    65–67; SORT treaty for, 179–181, 183;
    Strategic Defense Initiative for, 37,
    41–42, 42–43, 43–45, 46; terrorism
    and, 179, 207–208; in Tripartite
    Agreement, 90; United Kingdom and,
    11, 60–61, 65–67. *See also* Cold War;
    Strategic Arms Reduction Treaties;
    specific presidents
uranium. *See* fission
USSR: atomic diplomacy for, 15;
    Chernobyl disaster for, 38–39; China
    and, 60, 78–79, 141; collapse of, 52–53;
    CTBT for, 134; Czechoslovakia and,
    22; Egypt and, 90; fission for, 19–22;
    France and, 72; funding in, 35, 38–39;

India and, 105–106; against Japan, 18–19; Mao and, 60; North Korea and, 113; NPT and, 103; nuclear programs in, 19–22; poisonous weapons and, 197, 200; United Kingdom and, 72. *See also* Cold War; Russia; Strategic Arms Reduction Treaties; specific leaders
Ustinov, Dmitry, 32, 35, 38

Vajpayee, Atal Bihari, 107
Vernadskii, Vladimir, 20
Versailles Treaty "Poison Gas" Ban, 197

Wagoner, Richard L., 201
Wallace, Henry, 10, 15
Walters, Vernon, 111
Waltz, Kenneth, 52, 131
War and Peace (Brodie), 53
War and Peace in the Nuclear Age (Newhouse), 10
warning systems, 48–51
Warnke, Paul C., 91
Warsaw Pact, 170
Washington summits, 40–41, 171. *See also* INF treaty
Washington Treaty on Use of Gases, 197
Watson, Edwin, 9
weapons of mass destruction (WMDs), 94, 193–194, 203, 208, 210–211, 221–225.

See also nuclear weapons; poisonous weapons
weapons of mass destruction free zones (WMDFZs), 101–103
Webster, Daniel, 133
von Weizsäcker, Carl-Friedrich, 3–4
Wesdahl, Chris, 145
White, Hugh, 187–188
Wigner, Eugene, 8–10
Williams, Laura, 156
Wills, Garry, 11–12
Wohlstetter, Albert, 72
Woolf, Amy, 174, 176, 178
"A World Free of Nuclear Weapons", 185–186
"Worse than Irrelevant? British Nuclear Weapons in the 21st Century", 68

Yeltsin, Boris, 49, 173–174, 175
Young, Ken, 66
Yuset, 195

Zaloga, Steven, 48, 167–168, 175
Zangger, Claude, 155
Zangger Committee, 155
Zhou Enlai, 77
Zilinskas, Raymond, 205
Zuberi, Martin, 19
Zubok, Vladislav, 35, 39

About the Authors

Joseph M. Siracusa is professor of human security and international diplomacy at the Royal Melbourne Institute of Technology (RMIT) University, Australia, and president of Australia's Council for Humanities, Arts and Social Sciences. American-born, he is the author and co-author of many books, including *Presidential Doctrines: U.S. National Security from George Washington to Barack Obama* (with Aiden Warren, 2016); *Nuclear Weapons: A Very Short Introduction* (2nd ed., 2015); *America and the Cold War, 1941–1991: A Realist Interpretation*, 2 vols. (with Norman A. Graebner and Richard Dean Burns, 2010); and *A Global History of the Nuclear Arms Race: Weapons, Strategy, and Politics*, 2 vols. (with Richard Dean Burns, 2013).

Dr. Aiden Warren is senior lecturer in the School of Global, Urban and Social Studies at the Royal Melbourne Institute of Technology (RMIT) University in Melbourne, Australia. His teaching and research interests are in the areas of international security, U.S. national security and foreign policy, U.S. politics (ideas, institutions, contemporary, and historical), international relations (especially great power politics), and issues associated with weapons of mass destruction proliferation, non-proliferation, and arms control. He is the sole author of *The Obama Administration's Nuclear Weapon Strategy: The Promises of Prague,* and *Prevention, Pre-Emption and the Nuclear Option: From Bush to Obama*; and co-author of *Governing the Use of Force in International Relations: The Post-9/11 US Challenge on International Law* (with Ingvild Bode), and *Presidential Doctrines* (with Joseph M. Siracusa).

Professor Joseph M. Siracusa and Dr Aiden Warren are also the editors of the WMD Series with Rowman & Littlefield.